Shelley's venomed melody

Shelley's venomed melody)

NORA CROOK
Cambridgeshire College of Arts and Technology

DEREK GUITON

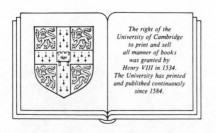

The right of the
University of Cambridge
to print and sell
all manner of books
was granted by
Henry VIII in 1534.
The University has printed
and published continuously
since 1584.

CAMBRIDGE UNIVERSITY PRESS

Cambridge
London   New York   New Rochelle
Melbourne   Sydney

Published by the Press Syndicate of the University of Cambridge
The Pitt Building, Trumpington Street, Cambridge CB2 1RP
32 East 57th Street, New York, NY 10022, USA
10 Stamford Road, Oakleigh, Melbourne 3166, Australia

First published 1986

Printed in Great Britain at
the University Press, Cambridge

British Library cataloguing in publication data

Crook, Nora
Shelley's venomed melody.
1. Shelley, Percy Bysshe − Criticism
and interpretation. 2. Venereal diseases
in literature
I. Title. II. Guiton, Derek
821'.7 PR5438

Library of Congress cataloguing in publication data

Crook, Nora.
Shelley's venomed melody.
Includes index.
1. Shelley, Percy Bysshe, 1792–1822 − Knowledge −
Medicine. 2. Shelley, Percy Bysshe, 1792–1822 −
Criticism and interpretation. 3. Medicine in
literature. I. Guiton, Derek. II. Title.
PR5442.M43C76 1986 821'.7 85–31395

ISBN 0 521 32084 4

GG

Ce qu'il a d'affreux pour toi, c'est que la nature a empoisonné dans les trois quarts de la terre les plaisirs de l'amour et les sources de la vie par une maladie épouvantable, à laquelle l'homme seul est sujet, et qui n'infecte que chez lui les organes de la génération.

Il n'en est point de cette peste comme de tant d'autres maladies qui sont la suite de nos excès. Ce n'est point la débauche qui l'a introduite dans le monde. Les Phryné, les Lais, les Flora, les Messaline n'en furent point attaquées; elle est née des îles où les hommes vivaient dans l'innocence et de là elle s'est répandue dans l'ancien monde.

Si jamais on a pu accuser la nature de mépriser son ouvrage, de contredire son plan, d'agir contre ses vues, c'est dans cette occasion. Est-ce là le meilleur des mondes possible? . . je le veux croire, mais cela est dur.

Voltaire, Dictionnaire Philosophique, 'Amour'

What in him seems the diffuseness of one idea is the conglomerate of many and this species of concision it is, which renders him obscure.

Poe on Shelley, 'Marginalia', Southern Literary Messenger, May 1849

> The other was a softer voice,
> As soft as honey-dew:
> Quoth he, 'The man hath penance done,
> And penance more will do.'

Coleridge, The Ancient Mariner

Contents

Illustrations

Between pages 116 and 117

Hogarth's *The Harlot's Progress*, Pl. V (detail)
Silhouette of Dr Lind (British Library, B.L.Add ms.22898 fol.1b)
Chalvey Well, Slough. From R. R. Tighe and J. E. Davies, *Annals of Windsor*, 2 vols. (1858)
The Windmill Inn, Salt Hill, early railway era
Charles Kirkpatrick Sharpe as a young man (National Museums of Scotland)
Self-caricature of the same in later life (Trustees of the National Library of Scotland)
The Jones Memorial by Flaxman, University College Chapel, Oxford
Abernethy delivering his anatomical lectures. From G. MacIlwain, *Memoirs of John Abernethy, F.R.S.*, 2 vols., 1853
Thomas Trotter in the uniform of a naval surgeon. From *Medical History*, VII (1963), facing p. 155
Gonsalves, an elephantiac of Madeira. From Joseph Adams, *Observations on the Morbific Poisons*, 2nd edn (1807)
Albrecht Dürer's *The Syphilitic*
Electrical Apparatus recommended by Adam Walker: i. Leyden Jar accumulator. From *Walker*, 'Electricity' Pl. IV; ii. Generator, ibid., Pl. I
Electrical experimentalist on glass-footed stool. From *Walker*, 'Electricity', Pl. III
Goblet mentioned in *Letter to Maria Gisborne* (B.M. Dept of Medieval and Later Antiquities, 85, 6–16, 1)
Light represented as whirling spokes. From *Walker*, 'On Light', Pl. II
The Grotta del Cane, late eighteenth century
The Grotto of Posilipo, Naples, c. 1798

Preface

Despite its title, this book does not seek to show that those Victorian critics were right after all who saw Shelley's poems as essentially unhealthy and dangerously enervating 'like those fine pearls which . . . are the products of disease in the parent shell. All Shelley's poetry is, as it were, a gale blown from a richly dowered but not healthy land, and the taint . . . hangs more or less over many of the finest [lyrics].'[1] In a similar vein Walter Bagehot wrote: '[Shelley] has a perverse tendency to draw out into lingering keenness the torture of agony . . . The nightshade is commoner in his poems than the daisy.'[2]

Substitute 'violet' for 'daisy' and Bagehot's illustration becomes silly and false. In our opinion Shelley's poetry is, taken as a whole, a triumph of healthy instincts over diseased ones. Nevertheless, Victorian critics were reacting to a real peculiarity, and one which merits investigation − the obsessive recurrence of images of pain and disease.[3] Bagehot's linking of the nightshade with a subtle and morbid preoccupation with suffering is of considerable interest.

Almost thirty years ago, the late G. M. Matthews wrote 'To find out all that *winter*, or *intoxication*, implies in a given context, one must reckon with the whole of Shelley − and not with his texts alone, but also with his science, his politics, his theories of literature, his medical record.'[4] It may seem a violation of both spirit and letter of Matthews' words to single out the last item of his list as a starting point for our study. However, 'medical record' is given an extended meaning, just as our self-imposed interpretative brief goes beyond the glossing of individual words. This book is attempting to assess not merely the significance of Shelley's description of himself, throughout his adulthood, as an ill man, but also of the effect on his life and work of doctors and writers on medical subjects. It regards Shelley as a 'wounded surgeon' who translated his own pursuit of health into a passionate concern for the health of society and is an attempt to relate the poetry to the context of early nineteenth-century medical enterprise, and in particular to the energy that was channelled into trying to defeat the scourge of syphilis.

That Shelley's biographers have touched on this subject incidentally but have never attempted a serious investigation of it and that, odd as it may seem, the readings that emerge from the investigation are, we believe, ones

which increase respect for and understanding of Shelley's artistry, are our ex-
cuses for writing this book. It is not a summation of our total experience of
reading Shelley. To have undertaken such a task and simultaneously preserved what claim to originality this book possesses would have made it probably
unpublishable; Shelley himself regarded each poet as making a contribution
to a great poem – the sum of all the poetry that had ever been or ever would
be made. If one may compare a lesser activity to a greater one, this book is
offered as a very small portion of the body of Shelley criticism, in the hope
that it will prove living tissue and not be totally rejected as an alien growth.
It does not pretend to be 'Shelley plain at last' (though we hope to have torn
some of the veils woven by Hogg and Peacock), and certainly does not propose that the heart of Shelley's mystery can be plucked out through a study
of venereal disease in the early nineteenth century.

Our debt to Shelleyans is incalculable; there are few among those consulted
who have not, at the very least, supplied us with some useful piece of information, opened up some profitable line of investigation, corrected an error
or stimulated a fruitful disagreement. But if we are to single out those to
whom we have an especial debt it is to Nathaniel Brown, Peter Butter, Ken-
neth Neill Cameron and G. M. Matthews. Though we do not suppose that
they would agree or would have agreed with our conclusions or the
biographical hypothesis which we put forward, we believe, as they do in
varying ways, that Shelley's poetry is grounded in his experience of the
phenomenal world and in the social realities of his day.

At several points we attempt to show how our readings can accord with
and complement others – formalist, mythopoeic, philosophical and political
ones for instance – though to do so consistently would have made for a fussy
book. For the same reason, there are many points at which we have refrained
from making overt our disagreements with other Shelleyans; it is sufficiently
obvious that the book is not so protean as to accommodate those who would
detach Shelley criticism from biography as far as is possible or those who
maintain that Shelley's concern with the literal level of his allegories and
'idealisms' was perfunctory, or that he offers us not an engagement with
external reality but 'nothing but words'.[5]

In addition to the debt referred to above, there are more particular ones
incurred to those who have helped in the production of this book. It began
life as Derek Guiton's doctoral thesis 'Shelley's Interest in Medicine'
(University of Sheffield, 1979). He intended it for publication but, owing to
pressure of work as a teacher at a large comprehensive, he had to lay it aside
for three years. At this point, Nora Crook undertook to do the necessary
rewriting and additional research which she and Derek Guiton felt to be
desirable. So the book differs from the thesis in marked ways; some documentation and much close engagement with the work of other critics has been
omitted in the interests of a tighter argument. Regretfully, a chapter

on *Julian and Maddalo*, which Derek Guiton intends to publish elsewhere, has been dropped because of its length.

The number of those to whom our thanks are due is therefore doubly great. In particular, we must mention two who died while the book was being prepared: Sir William Empson, without whose encouragement the thesis might not have been undertaken at all, and whose convictions about the relationship of biography and criticism have directed us, perhaps, more than those of any other critic; and G. M. Matthews, who, as its external examiner, was an exacting and constructive critic. It was his hope that Derek Guiton's research would be published. That we shall now never know what their reaction to this book would have been is our loss.

Others involved in the production of the thesis are Neil Roberts, its supervisor, and Dr C. Hackett who as a historian of venereology was also external examiner. Cambridgeshire College of Arts and Technology allowed some timetable remission for a year in order that Nora Crook could pursue the necessary research. Thanks are due to friends and colleagues for their support, especially Ian Gordon, for his encouraging her to take it up, Peter Fisher, who helped translate Shelley's Latin and Greek; Joan Hall, who helped with Shelley's Italian; Ted Holt, who read and criticised part of the revision, as did John Gilroy, who also lent books from his Shelley library indefinitely, and Barbara Hudson, who offered Oxford hospitality; Henry Merritt. Keith Crook read the whole of the final draft making suggestions and corrections with patient exactitude.

Our thanks are due, moreover, to the staff of many libraries: the Bodleian, especially to Dr Bruce Barker-Benfield (who also showed us Shelley's raisin dish), the British Library, Cambridge University Library, Edinburgh University Library, Sheffield Public Library, Slough Public Library, University College Library, Oxford, and the Library of the Wellcome Institute for the History of Medicine. We are also very grateful to the anonymous readers of the manuscript first submitted for publication, whose fair-minded and thoughtful advice we have taken to heart, and to our editor, Terence Moore. Among others who have generously helped us over particular matters are Nicholas Joukovsky, Dr Irvine Loudon, Dr R. S. Morton, Donald Reiman, the late Neville Rogers, Helena Shire, Patrick Strong, and Martin Swales. The views expressed in this book, and its shortcomings, are our own.

Above all, we thank our families for their patience and support for a project which involved us in reading which was often the reverse of cheerful and removed us from their company all too frequently. We dedicate this book to them.

Acknowledgements

For kind permission to quote from copyright material, our thanks are due to: Lord Abinger, for permission to quote from unpublished material in the manuscript of Mary Shelley's journal; the Curators of The Bodleian Library, Oxford; Oxford University Press, for permission to quote from *The Letters of Shelley*, edited by Frederick L. Jones; the Carl and Lily Pforzheimer Foundation, Inc., for permission to quote from items in the Carl H. Pforzheimer Library, namely *The Esdaile Notebook* and the contents of *Shelley and his Circle, I–VI*; Alfred A. Knopf Inc., for permission to quote from *The Esdaile Notebook*; Donald Reiman, for use of his 'Shelley's *The Triumph of Life*' and his 1977 text of *The Triumph of Life*; the Trustees of the British Library; John Murray of Albemarle Street; the University of Oklahoma Press, for permission to quote from *Mary Shelley's Journal*, edited by Frederick L. Jones, copyright 1947 by the University of Oklahoma Press; the Johns Hopkins University Press, for permission to quote from *The Letters of Mary Wollstonecraft Shelley*, edited by Betty T. Bennett; Yale University and William Heinemann Ltd, for permission to publish material from *Boswell's London Journal*, edited by Frederick A. Pottle.

For permission to reproduce illustrative material, we thank: the Trustees of the British Library; the Masters and Fellows of University College, Oxford; the Syndics of Cambridge University Library; the editors of *Medical History*; the Curators of the National Museum of Antiquities of Scotland; the Trustees of the National Library of Scotland; the Curators of the Department of Medieval and Later Antiquities, the British Museum.

1

The antient infirmity

An episode in Shelley's life which is seldom commented upon is the brief period in April 1811 when, just after being sent down from Oxford for publishing *The Necessity of Atheism*, he attempted to become a surgeon. He enrolled for a course of anatomical lectures and paid some visits to the wards of St Bartholomew's Hospital with his cousin, Charles Grove.[1] His commitment did not last long, though it was greater than the above account might suggest. Attending a course of lectures and touring a hospital ward with a famous surgeon were alternative means of acquiring a qualification. Shelley seems to have been attempting both, and without much encouragement from his family.[2] His intention appears to have lasted beyond the month of April, for he did not finally give up the idea until his elopement with his first wife, Harriet Westbrook, in August 1811.[3]

Shelley in April 1811 was under pressure to adopt a career of some sort, and the influence of his two Grove cousins, the elder of whom actually was a surgeon, must have been very strong. But undoubtedly his ambition owed something to the influence of an early mentor at Eton, of whom we shall have more to say in the next chapter, and to the prevailing temper of the time. For it is in the late eighteenth century and early nineteenth that the figure of the medical man as hero begins to emerge. Shelley was not the first Romantic poet to have been briefly tempted by a medical career. Coleridge as a schoolboy became 'wild to be apprenticed to a surgeon'. (This ambition was soon sublimated into 'a rage for metaphysics'.)[4] Late in life, Shelley told another cousin, Thomas Medwin, that he 'should have preferred [the profession of medicine] to all others, as offering greater opportunities of alleviating the sufferings of humanity'.[5]

Shelley did not necessarily witness the dissections. It is hard to imagine him doing so without a spirit of Frankensteinian curiosity mingled with loathing. His later remark on a sculpture of the flaying of Marsyas suggests this, though the context is actually the application of anatomical knowledge to art: 'If [the sculptor] knew as much as the moderns about anatomy, as I hope to God he did not.'[6] Yet he possessed some of the qualities of a good medical man; he was an efficient and compassionate home nurse, and kept a cool head in a crisis. Medwin wrote that during a bout of illness at Pisa in 1820 he was tended 'like a brother' by Shelley, who applied leeches and administered medicines with unremitting and affectionate care for six weeks.[7] He also on occasion attended to Claire Clairmont, the stepsister of his second wife Mary, to cottagers in the Marlow area where he lived in 1817, and to the Williams, friends who came to live with the Shelleys at their last home, the Casa Magni, Lerici. His medical knowledge saved Mary's life when she had a serious miscarriage in 1822; he used ice to stop her haemorrhaging.[8]

The possible significance of Shelley's desire to alleviate human suffering through this particular vocation and his acquisition of expertise is extended by the consideration that, for most of his adult life, he described himself as suffering from a painful illness which he called variously his 'constitutional disease', 'habitual disorder' or 'antient infirmity'. Many readers and some biographers, following certain remarks of his friend Thomas Jefferson Hogg, have concluded that the condition was largely imaginary,[9] and have seen it as part of a personality which found it difficult to separate fantasy from reality, suffered delusions of persecution, and nurtured the self-image of a sensitive plant. True, some recent biographers have been more sympathetically willing to grant that from about 1815 onwards Shelley was genuinely ill and often in pain. Richard Holmes (1974) sums up this more modern approach:

> The question of Shelley's ill-health is a problematic one, and becomes increasingly important after 1815. It seems to have three elements: hysterical and nervous attacks after periods of great strain and emotional upheaval; the spasmodic symptoms of a chronic disease associated with his kidneys and bladder, and a shadowy psychosomatic area in which the two inter-reacted . . . As a young man, he showed traces of hypochondria and undoubtedly cultivated the pose of ill-health for the benefit of such as Godwin.   (Holmes, p. 143n)

However, as long ago as 1863, a claim was advanced which purported to explain a good deal of Shelley's illness as physical rather than psychic in origin. The *Atlantic Monthly*, in its February number, published an article entitled 'Shelley, by one who knew him' which contained the surprising passage:

> Accident has made me aware of facts which give me to understand, that in passing through the usual curriculum of a college life in all its paths, Shelley did not go scatheless, − but that in the tampering with venal pleasures, his health was seriously, and not transiently injured.   (T. Hunt, p. 193)

The author was Thornton Hunt, son of Leigh Hunt, one of Shelley's closest friends and in whose house the poet had stayed during the painful early months of 1817 when awaiting the outcome of the Chancery suit which was to deprive him of his children. Thornton was then six years old. It was a highly sympathetic article, yet his revelation that Shelley's health had been permanently damaged by an early contraction of venereal disease could not have pleased those who, like the poet's son Sir Percy and his wife Lady Jane, were struggling to establish Shelley's respectability in the face of his avowed anti-Christianity and belief in free love, not to mention his desertion of his first wife, Harriet.

There are features of Thornton Hunt's claim which induce caution. There is something a little suspicious about his publishing in an American magazine, and moreover only after the death in the previous August of Hogg, the chief authority for Shelley's Oxford years and the person who would have been in the best position to challenge him. The words 'facts which give me to understand' show that he was making inferences. William Michael Rossetti, the editor of the 1870 *Collected Poems of Shelley*, mentioned Hunt's accidental discovery in his *Memoir*, and dismissed it as being without weight. Yet Hunt seems to have made no response to Rossetti nor ever to have named his sources and specified his facts.

On the other hand, *The Atlantic Monthly* had a London office. Hunt expected his article to be read 'on both sides of the Atlantic' (p. 184), and had been associated with the journal for some years. He seems to have thought that Hogg was alive when he wrote his article: 'Hogg is a gentleman of independent property' is Hunt's description (p. 202). Moreover, if he had been lying or making an irresponsible guess, he would have known that he risked being discredited by two living persons who had been intimate friends of Shelley in his youth and whose word would have carried more weight than his. These were Medwin and Thomas Love Peacock. Medwin was revising his 1847 *Life of Shelley* in the 1860s and could have inserted a correction to Hunt. There were also three others – Claire Clairmont, Jane Williams, Hogg's common-law widow, and Edward Trelawny, Shelley's friend during the last months of his life – who could also have cast considerable doubt on Hunt's testimony, the women through intermediaries. Yet as far as we have been able to discover, the only one to have attempted to do so, either in public or in private, was Trelawny; of all the five he was the one least likely to have been Shelley's confidant on this point, and his testimony is couched in such terms as to leave the matter as open as it was before.

Rossetti, who strove to meet almost everyone who had seen Shelley plain while gathering material for his memoir, evidently asked Trelawny his opinion of Hunt, and received the reply that Shelley was 'incapable of gross amours with prostitutes'[10] – something more than Shelley claimed for himself, as will be seen later. In a subsequent interview, Rossetti reported that Trelawny 'strongly believes that Shelley never had any sexual knowledge of any woman other than his two wives'.[11]

Yet despite this belief, Trelawny made only an oblique and ambivalent allusion to Hunt in the 1878 revision of his own earlier memoir. Of Shelley he wrote 'The gross and sensual passions and feelings that link men together had no hold on him', but almost immediately added 'My slight sketch is of the end of his brief life; the beginning and middle will doubtless furnish the critic with ample material for darkening the picture if it is too bright. Excessive laudation is nauseous.'[12] Evidently this was a matter on which Trelawny did not feel confident.

This almost total silence on the part of Shelley's surviving friends and relatives is matched by Rossetti's curious omission of any record of an approach to Hunt during the period when he was preparing his edition and memoir, despite the fact that the two men knew each other and had been fellow contributors to the *Atlantic Monthly*.[13] If any such contact was made, it was excised from *The Rossetti Papers*, a compilation of diary entries and letters covering this period. Reading through these one can discern a motive for holding aloof from Hunt. Rossetti, in a letter to William Allingham, through whom he hoped to approach Sir Percy and Lady Jane, declared that he was making a thorough investigation of Shelley's life, and would suppress nothing. Allingham's reply was strongly to counsel him against making conjectures about the poet's sexual life. One certain way of being able simultaneously to ensure the Shelleys' approval of his enterprise and fearless publication of all that might be revealed was not to ask questions of anyone likely to have information that might bring the two aims into conflict. Rossetti was to write a peroration to his memoir in which the sigh of relief is almost audible: 'I feel not at all ashamed of Shelley. He asks for no suppressions, he needs none and from me he gets none. After everything has been stated, we find the man Shelley worthy to be the poet Shelley, and praise cannot reach higher than that.'[14]

In Hunt's favour, too, it must be said that he was not likely to have repeated malicious gossip and that the words 'Accident has made me aware of facts' indicate that he had some sort of information that was independent of published work; the 'accident' cannot be the circumstance of having read a poem of Shelley's and stumbled upon a novel interpretation, though he did use Shelley's poetry to corroborate his statement. He was also in a position to receive genuine information owing to his father's friendship with Shelley and the family's continuing friendship with Mary. When Medwin tried to blackmail Mary in 1847 Leigh Hunt and Thornton were her chief supporters.[15] Elsewhere in his article he mentioned 'some circumstances of which I became accidentally aware', and which in his belief 'were never disclosed at all, except to Mary' (p. 188).

As might be expected, all nineteenth-century biographers followed Rossetti in briefly dismissing Hunt, if they paid any attention to him at all. Dowden's authoritative *Life* (1886) disposed of him by declaring that 'Amid the turbulent animalities of young Oxford, [Shelley] remained untouched by grossness.'[16] Even a hostile biographer, John Cordy Jeaffreson, whose *The Real Shelley* appeared the year before Dowden's book, shied away from Hunt, though with visible regret: 'Too much may have been said of the purity of the poet's personal tastes.' But he concluded that 'in respect to common kinds of dissipation, [Shelley's] habits accorded with the manners of

Victorian much more closely than with the manners of Georgian Oxford'.[17]

Twentieth-century biographers were content to follow the line laid down by their Victorian predecessors until comparatively recently. With the exception of Walter Peck, who did not get very far and whose suggestions were compromised by faulty scholarship,[18] no biographer was disposed to consider that Hunt might have been right until Cameron in *The Young Shelley* (1950) and *Shelley: The Golden Years* (1974). He was followed by Holmes, who added some perceptive observations concerning the curious stress on venereal disease in Shelley's writings. In what is the most complete treatment of the subject to date, Nathaniel Brown in *Sexuality and Feminism in Shelley* (1979) devoted eleven pages to the subject of seduction and prostitution in Shelley's work, in the course of which he again examined Hunt's testimony. Like Cameron and Holmes, however, he was not prepared to go further than saying that Hunt could not simply be dismissed. In the meantime Holmes became less guarded; in his anthology *Shelley on Love* he wrote that the figure of an evil woman in *Epipsychidion* – to be discussed later – is 'generally thought to have been a prostitute whom Shelley met at Oxford or immediately after his expulsion'.[19]

There the matter rests: there could be something in it, but not, one gets the impression, a very great deal. Cameron consulted a doctor, detailing Shelley's medical record, and concluded that Shelley might have had intercourse with a prostitute at Oxford, as a result of which he contracted gonorrhoea but that if so it had cleared up 'with no particular symptoms'.[20]

But this was not what Hunt said or meant. If he had thought that Shelley's infection had been trivial, he would have been irresponsible indeed to have revealed it. On the contrary, he published it because he felt that an injustice had been done to Shelley's memory through misplaced loyalty: 'The worst of all these biographical sketches of remarkable men is, that delicacy, discretion, or some other euphemistically named form of hesitancy, induces writers to suppress the very angles of the form they want to delineate; and it is especially so in Shelley's case' (p. 193). He believed that his disclosure was a fact of major importance in Shelley's life, affecting his self-image, determining the content of his poetry and his role as the conscience of his generation. After the passage quoted earlier, Hunt continued:

The effect was far greater on his mind than on his body; and the intellectual being greater than the physical powers, the healthy reaction was greater. But that reaction was also, especially in early youth, principally marked by horror and antagonism. Conscientious, far beyond even the ordinary maximum amongst ordinary men, he felt bound to denounce the mischief from which he saw others suffer more severely than himself, since in them there was no such reaction. I have no doubt that he himself would have spoken even plainer language, though to me his language is perfectly transparent, if he had not been restrained by a superstitious notion of his own that the true escape from the pestilent and abhorrent brutalities which he detected around him in 'real' life is found in 'the ideal' form of thought and language. Ardent and romantic, he was eager to discover beauty 'beneath' every natural object.

(pp. 193–4)

One of the passages of Shelley's poetry which Hunt found 'perfectly transparent' is from *Epipsychidion*. There Shelley wrote of having encountered 'One, whose voice was venomed melody' whose 'touch was as electric poison'. 'Flame' and 'a killing air' came out of her looks, cheeks and bosom, piercing into 'the core of my green heart', 'until, as hair grown gray / O'er a young brow, they hid its unblown prime / With ruins of unseasonable time' (lines 256–66). Hunt commented:

This is a plain and only too intelligible reference to the college experiences to which I have alluded. The youth for the moment thought he had encountered her whom he was seeking, but instead of the Florimel, he found her venal, hideous and fatal simulacrum; and he indicated even the material consequences to himself in his injured aspect and hair touched with grey.   (p. 200)

Hunt's last sentence alludes to the belief that premature grey hair was a result of sexual errors. (The belief is partly founded on the fact that some syphilitics contract a patchy alopecia. When the hair grows again it is often grey.) Shelley himself was well aware of this connection. When Byron settled down to faithful adultery with La Guiccioli, putting behind him his dissolute Venetian life, and recovering his health, Shelley wrote 'Fletcher [Byron's valet] also has recovered his good looks & from amidst the unseasonable grey hairs a fresh harvest of flaxen locks put forth.'[21] Hunt seems to be offering a hint that Shelley's ardent flight into Platonism, the search for the 'ideal' beauty 'beneath' the material appearance of nature, had been an escape from the 'pestilent and abhorrent brutalities' of 'real' life. Here, in the passage just quoted, may be discovered, perhaps, the root of that distinction between Pandemos, 'the earthly and unworthy Venus', and Urania, the type of ideal beauty and spiritualised love on which is centred so much of the mythic element in Shelley's poetry. Here too, might be found the basis on which he constructed his vision of a world purged of corruption and restored to health and beauty, the basis also for his fear that such a restoration might never be permanent, but a prelude to another relapse. It is likely too, that if Hunt was right about *Epipsychidion*, there are other passages which may be similarly elucidated.

Hunt made – without explanation – a curious remark about 'circumstances of which I became accidentally aware', apparently referring to the same 'facts', to which, he said, he could trace allusions in Mary's writing and which would have been 'absolutely unintelligible' but for these references. They reminded him of passages in authors such as Ovid (p. 188). We have been unable to discover to what the last can refer, but there *are* some curious passages in Mary's novel *The Last Man*, which, dubious though they are as evidence, might be what Hunt had in mind.

The Last Man (1826), heavy with Mary's loneliness and the horror of a succession of deaths — children, friends and husband — has as its central theme the annihilation of the human race through a mysterious and terrible plague. Its chief character is a Shelleyan figure, Adrian, Earl of Windsor, who, when the pestilence strikes England, dedicates his powers, hitherto seemingly atrophied by 'disappointment and sickness', to checking its spread and alleviating suffering. When criticised for risking his life in this fashion his reply is 'As to my peculiar liability to infection, I could easily prove, both logically and physically, that in the midst of contagion I have a better chance of life than you'. No such proof is offered, but later, when the scene shifts to Marlow (the novel is largely set in areas where the Shelleys had lived) a possible explanation for Adrian's confidence emerges. An old woman fearlessly enters the cottages of the sick, relieves their wants and inspires hope, rather as Shelley did in 1817. Her source of strength is that she has had the plague and recovered. Later, however, Adrian undergoes a period of despair: 'Why am I reserved for this? Why the tainted wether of the flock am I not struck to earth among the first?'[22] Adrian would seem to owe his strength, like the old woman, to his experience of having survived and thus become immune to disease. From this he also derives his sense of fitness to undertake his heroic mission. At the same time the experience is the source of his self-doubt; he is a 'tainted wether'.

Hunt believed that Mary Shelley's portrait of Shelley was the truest. His criticism of other biographers did not spare his own father, whose recollections of the poet were among the first to be published; he thought his father's picture over-conscientious and 'doubtful'. He did not add that Leigh Hunt had in 1858 privately refused to write or review a life of Shelley because of 'truths he could not suppress without falsifying the biography nor utter without deeply injuring the living.'[23] But Thornton's chief criticisms were aimed at Shelley's friends Hogg and Thomas Love Peacock. He accused Hogg of distorting the portrait of Shelley into a fantastic caricature and Peacock of seeing him through the medium of his dry wit.

Thornton strongly implies that Hogg and Peacock knew something of Shelley's 'tampering with venal pleasures' — though not as much as Mary — and suppressed it, substituting the image of an effeminate figure. Certainly the memoirs of those two are notably insistent on the 'embarrassing' Shelley. Hogg is especially strong on Shelley's hypochondria: 'Whenever he was hard-pressed, his poetical imagination invented the touching fable of a delicate and dangerous state of health; his robust microcosm became in an instant the frame of dire disease.'[24] Peacock tends to dwell on Shelley's 'semi-delusions' and paranoia. The question must now arise as to whether the existing portrait of Shelley is not still distorted by relics of well-meaning attempts on the part of Shelley's relatives and friends to win acceptance for his poetry and creed — at least as much of it as the public would take.

It was essential to prove to this public that Shelley's creed of atheism and free love did not in his case lead to libertinage, and that his morals were not merely as good as but purer than those of ordinary mortals. (It was in particular for his sexual morality that he was attacked during his lifetime.) In order to preserve his good name various tactics were adopted – euphemising his atheism as 'hatred of bigotry', for instance, and in particular presenting a Shelley too naive, impractical, and 'boyish' to be a threat to anyone – though always 'enthusiastic', of course, and passionate for reforming the world. It was also important to present a Shelley who was truthful – or, where untruthful, innocently so because he lived in a dream world. One of the tactics used by Hogg and, to a lesser extent, by Peacock, was to colour up the portrait of the self-deluding nincompoop.

One must not regard this process as a conspiracy; Shelley's friends tended to be suspicious of one another and to undermine one another's work. They could not agree, for instance, to refrain from mentioning Claire Clairmont's liaison with Byron and the birth of her illegitimate child. Medwin broke rank there, and alluded in veiled terms to a scandal circulating in 1821 that claimed she had had a child by Shelley. Nor, as the above example shows, do suppressions and concealments necessarily centre around Shelley's illness.

There is, however, no single feature of Shelley's life over which there is a greater discrepancy in the various accounts than his health. Some of this, but not all, can be explained by the fact that the various memoirists knew him at different times of his life. But if Hunt was right there is another complicating factor; that some of his memoirists, but not others, knew of or suspected an important cause of his ill-health and suppressed it, and that Shelley himself during his lifetime would have frequently prevaricated. Mary's Shelley is the martyr to ill-health. Medwin, both in his *Shelley Papers* of 1833 and in his 1847 *Life*, said that he had a basically strong constitution weakened by opium and vegetarianism. He added the detail that madness hung over Shelley 'as by a hair'. Leigh Hunt wrote that his constitution was consumptive, but that he had prolonged his life through exercise and habits of strict diet. Thornton Hunt wrote that Shelley merely believed, on medical advice, that he was consumptive. Trelawny (1858) agreed with Medwin that his constitution was strong, but said that it had been weakened by study and fasting. (In his 1878 version, he moved nearer to Medwin, and said that Shelley had overdosed himself with medicines, including laudanum.) Hogg in his 1832 articles for the *New Monthly Magazine*, adumbrated the portrait of the whimsical hypochondriac. This was developed in his 1858 *Life*. He was followed by Peacock's *Memoirs* which appeared by instalments in *Fraser's Magazine* (1858–62). Peacock makes fun of Shelley's vegetarianism and implies that it ruined his health; his Shelley is both a sufferer from delusive illness and someone who suffered intolerable pain for much of his life.

This is an appropriate point at which to consider more closely the reliability of the two memoirists singled out by Thornton Hunt.

It has long been established that Hogg took liberties with facts in order to make a good story and that he deliberately falsified the record in order to show himself in a better light. The two notorious examples are his presentation of his own attempted seduction of Harriet Shelley as a fragment of a Wertheresque novel by Shelley and his alteration of pronouns in letters in order to disguise his infatuation with Shelley's sister Elizabeth. He has also been frequently accused of trying to boost his own image by denigrating Shelley. 'Hogg, as a matter of routine, refers to Shelley as "the divine poet", but in the same way as Antony referred to Brutus as "an honourable man". The more he exhibited the ridiculous aspects of Shelley, the more fervently he asserted his belief in his divinity.'[25] What has not been fully recognised is the extent of Hogg's deviousness or the complexity of his motives.

Hogg's *New Monthly Magazine* articles entitled 'Percy Bysshe Shelley at Oxford' were written to gratify the interest in Shelley among young intellectuals such as the Cambridge Apostles and to disarm the establishment, for whom Shelley continued to be the damned atheist. In 1832 there were still a great many old Etonians and Oxonians about with potentially damaging memories of him; Hogg's articles seem designed to nip trouble in the bud by presenting such a credible picture of an innocent that no scandal could touch him, no matter what came to light subsequently. They pleased some of Shelley's friends. Claire Clairmont wrote to Jane Williams: 'These articles will give reputation to Shelley and particularly among the sober and moral, who have imagined . . . that he must have been in his private life most profligate and disagreeable.'[26]

The lengths to which Hogg was prepared to go in order to 'give reputation' to Shelley are well illustrated by his story of Shelley's pawning of his 'beautiful solar microscope' for five pounds in order to relieve the distress of 'some old man'. Hogg learned of Shelley's charitable act when the microscope was redeemed, 'on returning to town [London] after the long vacation at the end of October', the pawning having taken place the previous summer. This story has several queer features. Every commentator has supposed that Hogg is referring to October 1810, the only October when he and Shelley were at Oxford. Hogg obviously intends that the average reader should think this. But why is he returning to *town* instead of to Oxford? Why has he not arranged to meet Shelley, whose acquaintance he had only just made, in either of their college rooms? How did Shelley just happen to have the microscope with him when he encountered the distressed old man in London?[27]

These oddities are completely explained when one realises that Hogg has transferred to Shelley's Oxford period an event of four years later when, on 24 October 1814 under threat of arrest for debt and pursued by bailiffs, Shelley did pawn his microscope for five pounds.[28] The act of charity, if the microscope was indeed redeemed on this occasion, must have been Hogg's, who had just returned to London after the long vacation for his *law* term. Hogg closes his anecdote with the words:

Such is the story of the microscope, and no rightly judging person who hears it will require the further accumulation of proofs of a benevolent heart; nor can I, perhaps, better close these sketches than with that impression of the pure and genial beauty of Shelley's nature which this simple anecdote will bequeath.

This is a cleverly worded piece of irony. The 'rightly judging' persons must be those few – Mary Shelley, Claire Clairmont and Jane Williams – who know the truth about the microscope story; the 'benevolent heart' of which no further proofs are required is Hogg's, who has played free with the facts in order to display Shelley in the best possible light, and, if anything, has effaced himself, at least as far as the unwitting reader is concerned. 'Perhaps' is a nice joke, as is 'impression'. It is indeed Hogg's intention to leave the bemused reader with an *impression* that Shelley's nature was pure and genial. And yet, has not Hogg told the essential truth? If Shelley was not generous on this occasion, he was on others. And did he not impoverish himself in order to relieve the distresses of an old man – Godwin, Mary Shelley's father, who when Hogg wrote that article was still alive? Hogg's story has a concealed sting. He is warning those few readers with inside knowledge that he has embarrassing information which he, being a pearl in a rough oyster shell, has chosen not to make public.

When Hogg wrote his 1858 *Life* he grafted onto it, without revision, the text of 'Percy Bysshe Shelley at Oxford', which results in some interesting contradictions. He also became more reckless and more malicious. The *Life* contains many hurtful portraits readily recognisable to the Shelley circle. For instance, 'Matilda', a 'coarse fat woman' who used to impose upon Shelley with stories of being tubercular and make three hundred pounds a year from her broken veins, while remaining habitually drunk, is plainly Marianne Hunt.[29]

Almost every reader of Hogg's *Life* has commented on its 'facetiousness', yet it has never been remarked how often this facetiousness involves flirting with impropriety, and how many of his stories turn upon the instance of one person puzzling others with a piece of secret information. In the first category fall such digressions as his reservations about Dr Graham's earth-baths, especially when the patient comes to be released, having been sunk naked up to his collar bone in garden soil:

It is not easy to take up a large and vigorous plant without injury – without breaking its roots; but to dig up a portly, ponderous parson, must be a process in medical horticulture requiring extreme nicety of manipulation, lest unhappily a sharp spade should cut off unawares some portion of his radical fibres.

(Wolfe, I, p. 298)

Even naughtier is his declaration at a mixed 'conversation party' that he 'would choose to be buried under the kerbstone, before the door of the most fashionable milliner in London; it would be no mean consolation to know that the prettiest feet and ankles in the world were stepping backwards and forwards into and out of carriages, all day long, over my head'. In a previous conversation he had located fashionable milliners in Cranbourne Alley, where, he declared to the company, Paradise was certainly situated, 'for there so many pretty faces may be seen flitting about the bonnet shops on a fine day, that it is impossible to believe that Paradise can be anywhere else'. The 'philosophers' present appeared disgusted by his 'impertinences', not surprisingly.[30] In the first decade of the Regency – Hogg's date for the story – Cranbourne Alley, which was indeed famous for its milliners, was also a mecca for the better class of prostitute, the 'high flyer' or 'second rater', as she was called.[31] According to the *London Guide and Strangers' Safeguard*, an anonymous publication of 1818 ostensibly designed to warn provincials of the dangers of the capital, there were three prostitutes' 'parades' across London every day, of which one extended 'across Newgate Street into Lincoln's Inn Fields across Covent Garden, in various directions, through Cranbourn Alley and into Picadilly. In these celebrated Alleys is the favourite shopping promenade of the Bon Ton and here it is the greatest number of the high-flyers are to be met with, and the handsomest women' (p. 122). Any 'man of the town' would have known this, and, obviously, respectable women did too. Mary, in a bitter letter to Maria Gisborne concerning the end of Shelley's friendship with Emilia Viviani, wrote that it reminded her of a rhyme:

> As I was going down Cranbourne lane,
> Cranbourne lane was dirty,
> And there I met a pretty maid,
> Who dropt to me a curt'sey;
> I gave her cakes, I gave her wine,
> I gave her sugar candy,
> But oh! the little naughty girl!
> She asked me for some brandy.   (MWS, *Letters*, I, 223)

Mary is saying that Emilia was no better than a modest-seeming Cranbourne Alley tart. 'Milliner's shop' was slang for the vagina, and 'Paradise' for 'sexual pleasure'.[32] By 1858 all this would have been lost; the fashionable prostitutes' beat had shifted to the Haymarket, and in any case Hogg had taken care to write 'bonnet-shops'.

The significance of the occasional sexual innuendoes in Hogg's book will become clearer in subsequent chapters. At this point, it is sufficient to establish that Hogg does sometimes intend to be misunderstood by all but a select few. He belonged to a generation and a class that had made 'smoking', 'bamming', 'humming', and 'quizzing' into a fine art. The very proliferation of terms indicates how widespread the practice was. Writing in 1883, Jeaffreson, who regarded himself with some justice as having a special insight into the *mores* of a vanished age, had to explain to the late Victorians what was entailed in a Regency 'bam'.

'To bam' was to hoax with a humorous fiction . . . when George the Fourth entertained a dinner table by describing gravely how he commanded in chief at Waterloo,
he was not mad or tipsy; he was telling a 'bam' for the fun of seeing how it would
be received by one of his guests, the Duke of Wellington . . .[33]

The 'bam' could involve treating serious things flippantly, leaving the
listener baffled as to whether a true thing was being spoken in jest. Byron
was an arch bammer; Trelawny complained that it was often quite impossible
to know whether to believe him or not. The story of his tossing off the
remark 'My father cut his throat' while washing his hands and singing a gay
Neapolitan air is a good example.[34]

Some of Hogg's most celebrated stories, such as the one of Shelley asking
the woman on Magdalen bridge if her baby would divulge the secrets of pre-
existence, are almost certainly records of undergraduate 'bams' perpetrated
by both young men. It is unfortunate for the credibility of the story as it
stands that Shelley was more likely than most undergraduates to have known
the capabilities of babies. He was the eldest of five and played a great deal
with his younger brothers and sisters; he is actually on record as having tried
to teach his brother John the latter's first words.[35] The story has, however,
gone down in the annals of Shelleyana as an example of the poet's utter lack
of common sense, as no doubt it was intended to do.

At other times, however, Hogg makes it clear that Shelley enjoyed 'bams'
and hoaxes and perpetrated a few himself. (He is extremely shifty about
anything to do with Shelley's sense of humour.) It is to Hogg that one owes
the story of Shelley introducing verses into his Latin prose compositions.
When he pointed them out to Shelley as defects, liable to be censured by his
tutors, the poet 'smiled archly, and asked in his piercing whisper − "Do you
think they will observe them? I inserted them intentionally to try their
ears."'[36] The story is paradigmatic; Hogg's *Life* is larded with tryings of
our ears; the story should alert the reader to the possibility that the same may
also be true of Shelley's poetry at times.

One finds then in Hogg a disposition both to conceal and reveal, to protect
Shelley while flirting with embarrassing material. Peacock, though of a very
different temperament, resembles Hogg in having the same sort of relationship to Victorian society. Both were survivors from the Regency who found
themselves in a bogus position vis-à-vis an age where prim children were
shocked by the manners of their elders, while at the same time relishing the
survivors as 'characters'. Robert Buchanan, author of the notorious attack on
the Pre-Raphaelite poets, 'The Fleshly School of Poetry', and who hovered
in fascination around the aged Peacock, epitomises this ambivalent attitude:
he portrays an old scholar, stranded like an antediluvian mammoth,
withdrawing from an age where 'Lord Byron was a dim memory . . . beards
were worn. Rotten boroughs were no more. The Times, like a colossal
Podsnap, dominated journalism.' Buchanan made it clear that it was especially

in matters of sexual propriety that Peacock was out of step with the official mood of the 1860s:

He would fain have had the world one vast Maypole with all humanity dancing round it . . . his mind was in itself a terrible thesaurus eroticus, and there was to be found in it many a Petronian quibble and Catullan double entendre not to be discovered in Rambach.   (Buchanan, pp. 101–2, 104, 105)

In return, one finds in Regency survivors an amused disdain for the timidity, shockability and sense of guilt possessed by the younger generation which had grown up with Dr Arnold's reformation of the public schools.[37]

Peacock has a taste for arcane humour and secret allusions. One has, for instance, to know Greek in order to appreciate the aptness of the nomenclature in *Nightmare Abbey*. His writings contain references which are as inaccessible to the common reader as medieval graffiti in cathedral towers. *Crochet Castle*, for instance, describes one character as 'in the expressive language of German romance . . . "scathed by the ineradicable traces of the thunderbolts of Heaven"'. The 'German romance' is Shelley's obscure Gothic novel *St Irvyne*, which Peacock is misquoting from memory. In *The Misfortunes of Elphin* a new-born infant arrives by river in a coracle at the court of King Elphin. The babe grows up to be the bard Taliesin, the closest to an ideal figure in the story. Peacock departed from his sources in making Taliesin arrive in July. The significance of this seemingly irrelevant change is that 8 July 1822 was the date on which Shelley died – in a boat. The incident is a serious yet comic tribute to the power of the poetic voice to be continuously reborn; it is Peacock's 'farewell and hail' to Shelley.[38]

It would not be out of character, then, for Peacock to have inserted occasional coded messages into his portrait of Shelley, either for the eyes of a few, such as Hogg, or for his private satisfaction at the expense of Victorian prudery. Unlike Hogg, however, who claims in his *Life* to be laying out all so that the reader may make a true judgement of Shelley, Peacock virtually informs the reader that he is concealing information about his subject:

No man is bound to write the life of another. No man who does so is bound to tell the public all he knows. On the contrary, he is bound to keep to himself whatever may injure the interests or hurt the feelings of the living, especially when the latter have in no way injured or calumniated the dead . . . Neither if there be in the life of the subject of the biography any event which he himself would willingly have blotted from the tablet of his own memory, can it possibly be the duty of a survivor to drag it into daylight.   (Wolfe, II, p. 306)

Peacock is not merely laying down guidelines for the ideal biography; he continues by saying that he has always refused to write a life 'for the reasons above given'. He has broken silence only because so much has already been written about Shelley; his original motives for keeping silence do not prevent him from commenting on what has been written, correcting errors 'if such should appear to me to occur', without injuring the innocent living. Peacock still has not promised to tell the whole truth, nor has he bound himself to correct all errors already perpetrated.

This passage is followed by an allusion to a 'cardinal point' in Shelley's life which poses especial problems for the memoirist, who would be better advised to say nothing at all of it if he cannot speak the whole truth. It is generally agreed that Peacock must have been referring to the break-up of the marriage of Shelley and Harriet, though there are other matters to which it could apply – a possible love affair with Claire Clairmont or unhappiness caused by his marriage to Mary.

However, the quoted passage makes it clear that Peacock is referring to all the events in Shelley's life which he would have wished expunged from the record. That he did conceal much was confirmed by Buchanan, who wrote that Peacock's private conversation about Shelley was very different from his discreet printed account. 'Two subjects he did not refer to in his articles may safely be mentioned now – Shelley's violent fits of passion and the difficulty Peacock found in keeping on friendly terms with Mary Godwin.'[39] This implies that there were other subjects discussed that it was still not safe to mention in 1883. Certainly a contraction of venereal disease on Shelley's part would have fallen into that category; such a revelation would undoubtedly have injured the innocent living – Shelley's daughter Ianthe and his son Sir Percy.

It seems clear, though, that if Peacock was privy to Thornton Hunt's information, he did not – unless he was telling the lie direct – in 1858 ascribe to it the same importance that Hunt did – which, in Peacock, would not be very surprising. He discounted the significance in Shelley's life of the broken engagement to his first love, Harriet Grove, whereas since the publication of Shelley's early poems, *The Esdaile Notebook*, this has been recognised as a formative event. Peacock writes of his expulsion from Oxford as being 'the first really important event of his life' though the broken engagement had occurred before this.[40]

It is now time to turn from the atmosphere of concealment and protectiveness surrounding the presentation of Shelley's image in Victorian times to a brief sketch of knowledge about the venereal diseases and social attitudes towards them during the Romantic period. Thornton Hunt does not specify which of the two major diseases he considered Shelley to have contracted, and the likelihood is that he had both possibilities in mind. Either gonorrhoea or syphilis could have 'not transiently' damaged Shelley's health.

In the nineteenth century badly treated or repeated gonorrhoeal infections often left blockages of the urethra or 'strictures', which resulted in partial or sometimes total retention of urine. To unblock the urethra, a thin probe or 'bougie' was used. These sometimes had to be left in all night; haemorrhages often resulted from insertion of bougies of the wrong size, which created more scar tissue and an even greater narrowing of the urethral canal. Kidney troubles were a frequent resultant complication.[41] Complete retention of urine could lead to death.

Moreover the most authoritative medical opinion of Shelley's day held that gonorrhoea could be driven up into the blood stream and become syphilis, that the two diseases were really one. It was, of course, recognised that this did not always happen; medical treatises of the period abounded in advice as to how to prevent a simple gonorrhoea from becoming a syphilitic one, the best precaution being not to stop prematurely the stage of urethral discharge or 'running'. But there were dangers in protracting the running too, for this could lay the foundation of a very stubborn *gleet* – a ropy, non-infectious discharge which could persist intermittently for years. The latter complication could occur even in apparently mild cases.

The surgeon who must be held partly responsible for this confusion is the great John Hunter who, in a famous experiment of 1767, set out to determine once and for all whether the diseases were the same. He inoculated himself with gonorrhoeal pus. Upon contracting syphilis as well, he drew what seemed to be the obvious conclusion. What had happened of course was that the pus was doubly infected. Such was his prestige that the error was perpetuated for another seventy years. Another brilliant surgeon, Benjamin Bell, discovered the truth in the 1790s, but although he had his adherents, his work could not prevail against Hunter. Among the doctors with whom Shelley had dealings, Abernethy, Lawrence, and his own cousins, the Groves, were all of the Hunterian school. Only with the work of Ricord in 1838 was Bell finally vindicated.[42]

There were misconceptions about syphilis other than that detailed above. To understand what these were it will be necessary to give a brief description of the progress of the disease as understood today. Ricord divided it into three stages. The primary stage is that of the genital chancre or sore which appears on average about three weeks after infection. About six to twelve weeks after that the secondary stage begins with a rash. The rash, untreated, may heal in weeks or months, and may be accompanied by other symptoms such as the falling hair described earlier, pain, particularly at night, in the joints and long bones, fever, hepatitis, nephrosis and lesions of the mouth and throat. Primary and secondary syphilis usually disappear within three to twelve months, though about a quarter of all sufferers have relapses for another year or so. The disease has now entered its insidious, symptomless latency period.

In up to thirty percent of cases it 'burns itself out'. In another thirty, latency is permanent and symptomless, apart from general sub-health. For the remainder, the tertiary stage begins. This may start as little as a year after infection with 'gummas', though the usual gap is considerably longer. The body literally rots away. Some gummas attack the skin, the mucous membranes, the nose bridge and palate, producing collapse of the face, a hoarse voice and foul breath. Some can be internal, appearing on the liver, lungs, stomach and kidneys. Osseous gummas can create outgrowths of diseased bone called 'exostoses' with resultant crippling. Necrosis of the cranial bones results in distortion of the skull and pressure on the brain. Blindness, deafness and deep bone pain are other complications. In twenty-five percent of all cases, the final stage takes the form of neurosyphilis, which may appear from anything between seven and thirty years after infection. *Tabes dorsalis* (paralysis) and dementia are among the manifestations. When these two are combined, the condition is known as General Paresis of the Insane (GPI). Death from heart disease often mercifully intervenes before this.

This description does not attempt to detail the variability and degrees of severity of the disease, nor its response to treatment. Penicillin can retard and arrest the progress of even late syphilis, while at the early stages a complete cure can be hoped for. The gross deformities described above are infrequently met with in Britain today, and its mental hospitals are no longer crowded with patients in the last stages of GPI.[43]

This variability was recognised in Shelley's day, and for the most part the symptoms and progress of the disease had been accurately mapped out. However the number of internal organs which could be attacked had not been appreciated; descriptions tend to focus on damage to bones, skin and mucous membranes. Nor was it realised that paralysis and madness could be the direct result of an infection contracted even decades earlier, though there was a general recognition that early 'imprudences' led to later 'infirmities'. However, that early nineteenth-century doctors had no inkling that syphilis could be latent is a misconception. 'How often does latent venereal taint produce glandular obstructions [tumours] among its multifarious protean shapes?' was the rhetorical question to which the expected answer was 'Many times'.[44] The author, George Nesse Hill, is recommending caution in operating for cancer until the possibility of syphilis has been eliminated. It seems to have been believed that 'a syphilitic virus' could lie 'dormant in the system' until activated by some irritating circumstance,[45] or that it could, even if never activated, continue to weaken the constitution, and that this weakness could be passed on to future generations. It is this habit of mind which lies behind Baudelaire's remark: 'All of us have the Republican spirit in our veins, like syphilis in our bones; we are democratised and syphilitic.'[46] Syphilitic crippling was certainly recognised (though what the early nineteenth century called *tabes dorsalis* was applied to a wasting condition, often supposed to be the result of masturbation) as was syphilitic mania. For Shelley's generation as for Spenser's, syphilis was the 'foul evil' that 'rots the marrow and consumes the brain'.[47] Concerning treatment, we shall have more to say in the next chapter, and turn now to a consideration of social attitudes.

Trelawny, *à propos* of Byron's reputation for viciousness, characterised the

Regency as a time when men of fashion 'were ashamed of being thought virtuous and bragged of their profligacy'.[48] This strain can certainly be found
in Byron's letters, and manifests itself in attempts to treat his contractions
of gonorrhoea as so many opportunities to defy middle-class morality: 'I had
a number of Greek and Turkish women, and I believe the rest of the English
were equally lucky for we were all *clapped*.' 'Elena de Mosta – a gentil
Donna was clapt – & she has clapt me – to be sure it was gratis, the first
Gonorrhea I have not paid for.' Byron's bravado is accomplished against a
background of knowledge that this was a disease that could kill: 'Pearson [a
Hunterian surgeon] wears a woeful visage as he prescribes, however I am
now *better* and I trust my hour is not yet arrived.'[49]

The fear which lay behind the joking is even better illustrated by a document of a slightly earlier date than the period under consideration – James
Boswell's journal. After running up and down the town 'like a wild colt'
'then came sorrow. Too, too plain was Signor Gonorrhoea.'

Thursday 20 January 1763
I arose very disconsolate, having rested very ill by the poisonous infection raging in my
veins, and anxiety and vexation boiling in my breast . . . I thought of applying to a quack
who would cure me quickly and cheaply. But then the horrors of being imperfectly
cured and having the distemper thrown back into my blood terrified me exceedingly.

He 'looked with a degree of horror upon death' despite recourse to a more
expensive but skilful surgeon. Then after being confined to the house for five
doleful weeks he received a breezy letter from his cousin:

Who in the performance of a manly part would not wish to get *claps*? The brave only
are wounded in the front, and heroes are not ashamed of such scars. Yours are the
offspring of fun and merriment, and would you make them the parents of doulour
and care? I intend to laugh and breakfast with you tomorrow. Pray give the necessary
orders for my admission; otherwise, *pox* take you.[50]

'The syphilitic virus combines everything that is painful, loathsome, permanent and dreadful. Yet we laugh at this murderous poison and talk of it with
pleasantry, as a fashionable complaint' wrote the author of *A Treatise on the
Art of Prolonging Life*. 'The pox joke,' wrote D. H. Lawrence, 'was invented
as an evasion, and following that, the great hush! hush! was imposed. Man
was *too* frightened.'[51]

The risk was felt to attend all classes; it was not only the common streetwalker of St Giles who was a carrier. The demi-rep, 'under the protection'
of some noble or even royal personage was not immune; witness the story
of lovely Kate North. It is especially interesting because it is told by Captain
Gronow, a contemporary of Shelley at Eton and, like Hogg, a Regency survivor. The story illustrates both the Victorian love of reading about the
wicked ways of their predecessors (Gronow's memoirs were very popular)
and the kind of euphemistic language which rendered a racy tale acceptable
to the readership of the 1860s.

Into Kate's room came the Duke of York, 'one of the finest men England could boast of. . . his brow was full and prominent, the eye greyish, beaming with benevolence; and a noble forehead, with premature grey hairs, though the Prince was hardly in the vale of years.' (Shelley called him 'mud from a muddy spring'.) 'The Duke was made happy', but the King, his father, eventually ordered him to renounce her. 'Poor Kate's heart was full . . . the sting which had been inflicted was more than she could bear and she was seized with brain fever.' She recovered, resumed her career and became 'the most admired woman in London'. But 'the canker in Kate's mind was all this while corroding her life. She visited Paris for change of air and scene, but there her senses left her; she became raving mad and died in a foreign land without a friend to close her eyes.'[52] Gronow allows the naive to suppose that she had died of a broken heart; men of the world of his generation would perceive his insinuation that she died of an occupational disease, the 'unnecessary' detail about the Duke's premature grey hair clinching the matter.

Sometimes syphilis is portrayed as a disease belonging to the aristocracy, which infects the already corrupted lower classes. Crabbe's *The Village* (1783) has the unchaste village girls repairing to the city where their fresh faces win them noble protectors:

> . . . the clown's trull receives the peer's embrace;
> From whom, should chance again convey her down,
> The peer's disease in turn attacks the clown.[53]

Blake sees the prostitute and her disease as symbolic of the rottenness of English society. His famous lines about the 'youthful harlot's curse' which 'Blasts the new-born infant's tear / And blights with plagues the marriage hearse' are echoed in his gnomic verses 'The harlot's cry from street to street / Shall weave Old England's winding sheet.'[54]

Poets, social theorists, moralists and doctors concurred in seeing prostitution and its accompaniments as one of the greatest social evils of the time. A surgical compendium of 1809 wrote of syphilis as 'a disease which tends more than any other to the destruction of the human species'.[55] Cautious optimism that the disease was growing milder was tempered by the fear that it was also growing more prevalent. It was a widely believed statistic that over a million of the populace of Great Britain was annually infected by venereal disease. Curry, Keats' lecturer, asked rhetorically: 'Without accusing the male youth of the present day of greater laxity than those of former generations . . . how many arrive at the adult age without having occasion to use mercury? . . . few escape the necessity.' Estimates of the numbers of prostitutes in London varied. The author of *The London Guide* said that, on any fine day, 'not less than twelve thousand women of the town, of all degrees except the lowest, parade the streets in search of whom they may devour'. The highest estimate of all was supplied by Thomas Holcroft, the friend of Godwin, who put the total figure at a hundred thousand, a statistic recorded by Claire Clairmont in her journal.[56]

This seems to be the source of Shelley's belief that one tenth of the population of London were prostitutes. All his remarks on prostitution are characterised by extreme revulsion, surpassing that of his sources where these are to be found. 'This subject is almost too horrible for a joke.' 'The usual intercourse endured by almost every youth of England with a diseased and insensible prostitute.' On a notebook page this jotting appears: 'Loathsome diseases the cause of modern obscenity exceeding the worst of antiquity in hideousness & horror.' Leigh Hunt wrote, in words which hint at an obsession, that Shelley was continually depressed by the subject of prostitution and its origin in the institution of marriage. 'In a moment's notice [it] would overshadow the liveliest of his moods.'[57]

Such revulsion, of course, is not evidence of actual experience. One of the most prevalent images of Shelley's writing is that of *blood*, yet one knows that he never fought in a battle. Having said that, one immediately remembers that Shelley carried duelling pistols. There is also the story of how, goaded to fury, he struck a knife, or pair of scissors, into a school-fellow's hand.[58] As Richard Holmes clearly demonstrated in *The Pursuit*, Shelley found it hard to come to terms with his own violence; his hatred of it in society is all the greater because it is something which he can recognise and abhor in himself. That the same might have been true of lust should not be very surprising.[59] Nor does anyone dispute the proposition that Shelley's poetry is in certain respects the poetry of personal experience. Recurrent features such as the figure of the Wanderer, or boat and mirror imagery, have not only literary antecedents but also counterparts in Shelley's own wanderings, boat journeys and love of gazing into pools.

It looks, therefore, as though rather more may hang on a close investigation of Hunt's claim than the exercise of idle curiosity, which, we may as well say at the outset, this book will not satisfy. We have not found evidence which will settle the matter conclusively one way or another. What we do claim to have done is to have discovered some new reasons for believing that Hunt was essentially right and to have provided explanations for some of the episodes in Shelley's life which are as good as, and in some cases better than existing ones. We also give due attention to the prevalence of pathological imagery in Shelley's work. In the course of doing so we discuss the extent to which this imagery is drawn from the symptomatology of the venereal diseases, and assess the part played in Shelley's life and work by his involvement with doctors and his reading of medical books.

It is important to note that the implications of this study are not dependent upon clinical certainty, which in this case cannot be established, quite apart from the unreliability of posthumous diagnosis.[60] Syphilis, 'the great imitator', has the potential for presenting the symptoms of many different diseases, including all those which Shelley is supposed to have suffered from. It was difficult enough to diagnose accurately in the days before Wassermann tests and in the absence of gross symptoms, even during the subjects' lifetimes. But an adjustment of Shelleyan biography and criticism would hold good even if Shelley merely thought that he had 'the venereal disease', to use his own term, that is, if he had really been suffering from something else. Nor would this belief have had to be unremitting: Shelley could have run the gamut from terror to hope at various times of his life. The early nineteenth century was a time when a condition called *Syphilis imaginaria* was first recognised. This, wrote Erasmus Darwin, in a book owned by Shelley, 'the fear that they are infected with the venereal disease when they have only deserved it, is a very common insanity amongst modest young men'. The 'insanity' was aided by doctors' own admissions of the variability of the disease. The Frenchman Astruc, whose authority was probably equal to Hunter's, wrote that after 'impure coition', appearances were sometimes so 'very slight and trifling, as not to occasion any alarm, and much less to create a suspicion of the mischief which has been frequently known to follow. Thus there have been sometimes only a slight heat and pain in making water, at other times only a slight excoriation of the parts. . . which have either got well of their own accord, or been easily healed by some desiccative ointment. And yet how trifling soever such complaints may have appeared at first, they have been known to be followed by evident symptoms of a confirmed lues.'[61]

Nathaniel Brown made the following suggestion: that Thornton Hunt might have heard of 'College experiences' and assumed that this referred to Oxford. But, Brown pointed out, Shelley's school Eton was also known as a college; he suggested that if such infection did occur, it was more likely to have happened at school than at University.[62] We therefore start our investigation with Shelley's schooldays, where the roots of his concern with disease and healing first struck.

2

From natural magic to natural science: Eton 1804–10

One of the most formative influences on Shelley's youth was Dr James Lind (1736–1812), a remarkable man who, like so many of the medical profession of his day, was a 'natural philosopher', that is, a scientist. After graduating from Edinburgh, he went to Bengal where he observed Eastern diseases at first hand; he retained an interest in them until quite late in his life.[1] He was a skilled botanist and a Fellow of the Royal Society. About 1777 he settled at Windsor and became a physician to the royal household. Despite that, he may have had subversive sentiments; Shelley claimed that they both used to indulge in demoniacal execrations against George III. From him Shelley learned how to conduct polemical arguments by correspondence. He had a passion for air-balloons, which resulted in Shelley using them to disseminate propaganda in 1812. Shelley's volcanic imagery and interest in Iceland could have originated in Lind's experiences as geologist to the Banks expedition of 1772, one of the first to conquer the volcano Hecla. Hogg, ignoring Adam Walker, the peripatetic scientist who had lectured at both Shelley's preparatory school and Eton, reported that Shelley acquired from Lind a taste for chemistry and the occult.[2]

Lind's surviving correspondence shows that he kept closely in touch with the important scientific ideas of his day and continued to practice medicine at Windsor. One half of such a correspondence has been preserved – the letters to him from Tiberius Cavallo, an expatriate Italian. An FRS like Lind and the distinguished author of several important books on electricity, Cavallo exchanged letters with the great Volta himself. The correspondence with Lind extended over twenty-five years. They shared a number of interests, including such endearing ones as collecting autographs, and making silhouettes and phantasmagoria. Names that were to surface in Shelley's biography flitted through these letters of the 1790s – Berlinghieri and Pacchiani, for example. Both Cavallo and Lind were compulsive experimentalists; Cavallo egged on Lind to try his hand at galvanism, asking 'Have you made any dead frogs jump up like live ones?'[3]

Lind guided Shelley's reading. His home lay only a few oar strokes across the Thames from Eton College, and he seems to have been sympathetic to the boys. Mrs Delany, whose botanical scissor pictures were lauded by Erasmus Darwin, recorded Lind's account of the Eton rebellion, including 'some laughable anecdotes of the boys' destroying the whipping post and then selling it to one another'. In Shelley's day collegers were not allowed into the library, so the best thing that could happen to a boy with an appetite for knowledge was to be given access to a well-stocked private collection of books. Lind almost certainly introduced Shelley to Plato, Godwin, Condorcet and the botanical poetry of Erasmus Darwin. From him, too, probably stems a life-long interest in the East. It was to Lind that Shelley went when he undertook to translate the whole of Pliny's *Natural History*; Lind would have been able to explain both the astronomy and the plant names. If it was not Lind who lent Shelley Paracelsus and Albertus Magnus, over whom he self-confessedly 'pored', then it was the combined influence of Lind and Walker that brought Shelley to a balanced appreciation of the worth of these men, and to a realisation that modern chemistry had the same capacity for firing the imagination that had once belonged to the alchemists. An idealised version of Shelley's education, where Lind and Walker appear compounded under the name of Dr Waldman, can be found in Mary Shelley's *Frankenstein*.[4]

Discussion of Lind's influence on Shelley has focussed on the above topics – philosophy, politics, the natural sciences and the occult – and tended to obscure the significance of the following suggestive paragraph in Trelawny's *Records*. For Trelawny wrote that Shelley knew Lind importantly in his capacity as a *physician*:

At Eton, after an illness, the doctor who attended him took a liking to him, and Shelley borrowed his medical books and was deeply interested in chemistry from that time, and, unlike doctors, he experimented with some of the drugs on himself.[5]

What kind of a physician was Lind? To judge by Madame D'Arblay, an unorthodox one. Many of his patients, she wrote, 'were afraid of trying experiments with their constitutions and thought him a better conjuror than a physician'. He commented approvingly to his son-in-law Captain Sherwill on the use of the thorn apple in treating asthma. Thorn apple, along with henbane and belladonna, belongs to a group of vegetable alkaloids which had been investigated by Baron Stoerck in around 1770, taken out of the enchanter's bag of simples and made semi-respectable. They were still regarded as dangerous (thorn apple is also a hallucinogen) and it sounds typical of Lind that he should have been favourably disposed towards one of them.[6] But even more interesting is Lind's involvement with pneumatic medicine, an experimental movement which caused great excitement during the decade beginning in 1793.

The discovery of the components of atmospheric air, and especially of oxygen, by Black, Scheele, Priestley and Lavoisier during the second half of the eighteenth century, was quickly seen as offering great possibilities for medicine. One of the vanguard who were applying this new knowledge was Dr Thomas Beddoes (1760–1808), father of the poet T. L. Beddoes, the early

Shelleyan. Beddoes, as well as being an Edinburgh-trained doctor, was a physicist and chemist; he was nicknamed 'Plutonian Beddoes' because he held to the volcanic theory of the origin of mountains (as opposed to the 'Neptunian' one). In 1792 his revolutionary pamphleteering lost him his readership in chemistry at Oxford – a prefiguring of Shelley's own expulsion. Beddoes retreated to Bristol where he began to practice medicine again, dedicating his life to relieving the suffering of the poor from tuberculosis and scrofula in particular. The chief weapon in his armoury was inhalation, based on the rational belief that the lungs might furnish a more direct route for remediation than the alimentary canal or the rectum. The oxygen tent is a modern application of that principle.[7]

Beddoes was not an isolated figure; he had links with some of the most distinguished radical minds of the late eighteenth century. He was a friend of the leading members of the Birmingham Lunar Society, most famous of the provincial dining clubs dedicated to the promotion of literature and science, and so called because members met at the full moon. He was thus in contact with men like Erasmus Darwin, the engineers Watt and Boulton (whose firm manufactured his pneumatic apparatus), Priestley, and Lovell Edgeworth the educationist. Many of these were Unitarians or sceptics; they tended to be republicans and supporters of the French Revolution. Darwin and Beddoes were also Brunonians.[8]

Brunonianism was an interesting cross-current in the history of the rise of scientific medicine. John Brown, an unorthodox figure at Edinburgh during the period of Beddoes' training, had evolved a vitalist theory of medicine which regarded all disease as due to either an excess or a defect of excitement, usually the latter. Consequently he recommended 'stimulating remedies'. Among his favourites was opium. Brown publicised his system at Edinburgh as a radical alternative to the mainstream medicine of William Cullen. Brunonianism, always more popular on the continent, especially at Göttingen and Florence, did not long survive the first generation of his disciples, yet it left its mark. It was essentially a holistic approach, probably deriving ultimately from Paracelsus, but claiming of course to be scientific; Brown was credited with having given the coup de grâce to humoral pathology, and was said to have introduced a 'more correct language' into medicine. He probably exercised a malign influence in his advocacy of laudanum. Brunonians in the late eighteenth century had a stronghold among army and navy doctors and 'practitioners of the East and West Indies'.[9]

Brown himself was not a pneumatic physician. Beddoes claimed that he owed the idea to the forgotten John Mayow, a seventeenth-century chemist whose work startlingly anticipated that of Priestley and Scheele, and who almost discovered oxygen. In 1799, after an experimental period, Beddoes set up the Pneumatic Institution in Clifton, Bristol, in order to treat the sick with 'factitious airs' – artificially made oxygen, carbon dioxide, nitrogen and others including the fumes of charred meat and vegetables; it was here that Humphry Davy, the Cornish youth whom Beddoes had employed as his laboratory director, discovered the intoxicating properties of nitrous oxide (laughing gas). Southey and Coleridge, both of whom were friends of Beddoes during his Bristol period, inhaled it, and Southey's *The Curse of Kehama* is said to derive some of its ecstatic imagery from this experience. It is not surprising that these poets should have been fascinated by the Pneumatic Institution, for inhalation was an analogue of poetic inspiration. To be thus inspired was not only to be possessed by divine frenzy or the 'intellectual breeze' of the Aeolian harp, but by a literally regenerative excitement.[10]

Lind knew of Beddoes' work. Cavallo discouraged him from giving up so much of his time to it, believing that Beddoes' notions were unsound. Then all of a sudden Cavallo became a semi-convert; he wrote begging for case histories from Lind and published a pamphlet cautiously welcoming the new treatment. Those of Lind which he included show that the former used ether and 'diluted hydrocarbonate' for pulmonary complaints. (This was one of Beddoes' 'airs'; one of its components can be carbon monoxide and Davy nearly killed himself with it.) It is possible that documents will one day be found which will reveal a much closer connection between Lind and Darwin, Beddoes and their circles than present knowledge allows us to conclude. One link could have been James Watt, designer of Beddoes' apparatus and co-author of one of his books, a close friend and correspondent. Another must have been James Keir, a friend of both Watt and Darwin, who was Lind's cousin and a Lunar Society member; Lind was still in touch with him in 1792.[11]

The Pneumatic Institution, despite its name, had objectives other than the testing of 'the airs' on tubercular and scrofulous patients. Beddoes saw the place as giving him a chance 'of verifying, perhaps of essentially improving, the new treatment of syphilis'.[12]

The standard cure, mercury, was not infallible, though how fallible was not fully realised at the time. It was reasonably successful in removing the external symptoms but did not effectively eradicate the treponemes from the nervous system. The effects were often as bad as the disease. The mercury cure involved salivation; Sydenham, the early eighteenth-century authority, recommended that the patient spit four pints of saliva a day. It caused a hard, dry cough, swelling of the tongue and gums, skin eruptions, loss of teeth and even necrosis of the jaw. A drastic purge, it left patients feeling debilitated and suicidal. Mercury treatment often produced results years later in the form of palsy, *tic douloureux* and mental disorder. One of Shelley's doctors (Pemberton) was rumoured to have died as a delayed result of 'quacking himself' in youth after dissipation with women. True, during the latter part of the eighteenth century the so-called 'Montpellier method' crept across the channel from Southern France, and one finds frequent references in the early nineteenth century to an 'improved treatment' and a greater refinement in suiting the dose to the individual constitution. The Montpellier method advocated a prolonged rather than a short and drastic course. The harshest form of the mineral – corrosive sublimate – fell out of favour. While this palliated, it could not remove the unpleasantness of the treatment. Mercurial ointments rotted clothes; the smell was difficult to conceal, and unless there was some salivation, doctors agreed, it was hard to know if the mercury was working. Some doctors were reckless in their prescription; Beddoes has a story of a Scottish doctor, who, wearied by the importunities of a patient with an obstinate case, would simply shout in the street upon the latter's approach: 'Go on with the marcray, Mr—!' By 1810 mercury poisoning or 'hydrargia' had been recognised as a morbid condition in its own right and the metal was believed to reside in the bones causing problems for years after treatment. Dr Thomas Trotter, in a book owned by Shelley, was disturbed that mercury was so frequently prescribed for jaundice when jaundice itself so frequently accompanied the 'mercurial treatment for lues venerea' (the eighteenth-century term which 'syphilis' was just beginning to replace).[13]

Many doctors were anxious not to prescribe mercury unnecessarily. Abernethy, the surgeon whose lectures Shelley attended, was one of the first to attempt systematically to distinguish syphilis from diseases resembling it, and advocated a wise delay until the former had declared itself as certain. A category of diseases called 'pseudosyphilis' and 'cachexia syphiloidea' was created, and its existence promptly doubted. Such a controversy seems to have increased anxiety as often as it relieved it; one doctor complained that a patient who had 'imagined the disease was lurking in his blood' deliberately infected himself with syphilis so that he could receive the only sure treatment, rather than suffer the mental agony of uncertainty.[14]

From the sixteenth century (the dangers of mercury were known even then) there had been a search for a non-mercurial cure. Exotic plants – guaiacum (lignum vitae), china root, sassafras and sarsaparilla – had been brought from the New World or the East. Each had its day and was then relegated to the status of the useful adjuvant, though new ones kept on coming in. From about 1770 onwards, the search had been accelerated by the progress of chemistry. But the same pattern was repeated. In 1780 the wonder cure was opium. In 1800 it was oxygen. In 1811 it was gold (another Montpellier 'discovery'). In 1796 it was the nitrous and nitric acids.[15]

Beddoes first learnt of the latter from the *Bombay Courier*, which published a series of letters from Dr Helenus Scott, an 'experimental practitioner' like himself, who claimed to have removed syphilitic symptoms with dilute nitric acid inside a fortnight. After two years not one patient had suffered a relapse. His final letter ended euphorically:

In some of my Dreams for the improvement of the condition of Man, I even imagine
that the poison of syphilis may in a great measure be extinguished over the face of
the Earth, not by the effort of the Magistrate, but by an agent like this, safe, simple
and efficacious.[16]

How naturally dreams for social improvement focussed on the eradication
not merely of disease, but of that particular one! One notices, too, Scott's
non-judgemental attitude. The idea that syphilis was a necessary scourge of
God and that its elimination would corrupt morals is completely absent.
Examples such as this bring home the connection that existed between
religious unorthodoxy, 'natural philosophy' and experimental medicine during this period.[17]

Beddoes publicised Scott's work and asked for case histories from those
willing to try his method; he received hundreds of letters, most of them
favourable. He and his associates were not acting by trial and error alone.
They had a theoretical explanation for why nitric acid should work, and this
fitted neatly with the pneumatic experiments. Oxygen or 'vital air' was absorbed by the blood, to the benefit of the patient. Oxygenated medicines
ought to have the same effect. In Beddoes' day it was widely believed that
all acids were oxidising agents ('oxygen' means 'the acid producer') and that
therefore acids of all kinds were likely to be good medicines. Citrus fruit, for
instance, was held to cure scurvy because of the oxygen in citric acid, despite
failure to replicate the effect with other oxygen-containing acids.[18]

Controversy over nitric acid raged in the medical press for the next few
years. In 1810 Murray's influential *A System of Materia Medica and Pharmacy* pronounced it successful in completely removing the primary symptoms (chancre and bubo) but was less certain about secondary ones. Murray
thought its operation less reliable than that of mercury, but considered it
valuable in combination with mercury and in counteracting the latter's harmful effects. In reality, of course, nitric acid could not possibly have eradicated
the disease. Reports of it as an anti-syphilitic fizzle out in the 1820s.
Presumably it was found to be thoroughly unreliable and replaced by
potassium iodide, which really was a major breakthrough in the treatment
of gummas, and continued to be used until comparatively recently.[19]

One of Beddoes' correspondents had a special interest in the simple cure.
This was Thomas Trotter, surgeon to the Fleet, and later the author of *On
Drunkenness* and *A View of the Nervous Temperament*. (Shelley used both of
them for his 'Notes on *Queen Mab*'. The second title lays particular stress
on the threat posed to society by venereal disease and the widespread use of
mercury.) The health of fighting men was an important consideration during
the Napoleonic Wars, and Trotter expected that Scott's cure would save
many a sailor from 'premature old age' or untimely death. Perhaps it was indirectly through him that Lind heard of this remedy. In a letter of 22
February 1797, Cavallo wrote to Lind:

It is likewise mentioned with great confidence that an unfailing remedy for the lues venerea has been lately discovered. The discovery came from India and upon trial was found to succeed extremely well in this country. It is nothing more than a dram of nitrous acid dissolved in a pint of water and given in the course of 24 hours. It must be repeated every day and for about a fortnight more or less according to the nature of the case.[20]

Cavallo's informant was Admiral Young, who in turn had his information from the surgeon of the Fleet in the Mediterranean.

Since Cavallo gave directions, and since the two men's exchanges seem always to have had a practical application in view, he evidently thought that Lind would be able to make use of the information. It is very unlikely that Lind, who had been a ship's surgeon, was inexperienced in treating the venereal diseases. There could, in any case, have been few doctors who were not obliged to know how to apply treatment.

The influence of Lind on Shelley in the area of medicine can perhaps be discerned in the latter's ordering of Darwin and Trotter's books in December 1812 and, earlier that year, a work called *Medical Extracts*.[21] This was the better-known name of Robert Thornton's *Progress of Philosophy*. Thornton, now chiefly remembered as the compiler of *The Temple of Flora*, was a correspondent of Beddoes and a Brunonian. As Shelley scholars have not hitherto identified *Medical Extracts*, the book is worth describing briefly. It is a collection of essays, in which a treatise on the correct prescription of opium and the methods used by the Humane Society to revive drowned persons (something which interested Shelley) jostle with an account of the habits of sensitive plants. There is an extensive description of pneumatic medicine, in which Trotter figures prominently. The first essay, 'The Progress of Chemistry', is perhaps the most interesting of all, for there Thornton attempts to show that the work of Priestley, Lavoisier and Scheele can be traced back via Stahl, Mayow and Van Helmont in an unbroken line to Paracelsus; modern chemistry is thus the product of Paracelsian vision fused with correct scientific method (initiated by Bacon), which has purged chemistry of error. The true inheritors of this fusion are Brown and Beddoes, according to Thornton, who incidentally gives a beautifully lucid account of the displacement of the erroneous phlogiston theory. It is not surprising that the book went into five editions between 1796 and 1812, for it is a model of popular scientific writing. Waldman in *Frankenstein* explains the achievements of the alchemists in very similar terms: '[They] were men to whose indefatigable zeal modern philosophers were indebted for most of the foundations of their knowledge . . . the labours of men of genius, however erroneously directed, scarcely ever fail in ultimately turning to the solid advantage of mankind.'[22]

Critics often compare Shelley's art to alchemy, yet his debt to Paracelsus and the alchemists has never been fully studied; it would repay a deeper investigation than this book can attempt. Paracelsus (1493–1541) was above all a doctor – and incidentally one of the first European venereologists. For him the object of scientific enquiry was not the transmutation of base metals into gold but the panacea or universal cure, the elixir of life. In Shelley's day he was credited – rightly or wrongly – with being both the first to apply mercury systematically to the cure of syphilis and the inventor of laudanum. Paracelsus' 'labdanum' seems to have had for him some of the properties of the Elixir. Eighteenth-century 'empirics' – originators of patent medicines – picked up the idea; and mixtures containing laudanum were often marketed under the name of so-and-so's 'Elixir'.[23]

One must distinguish wishes from hopes. Paracelsus might have wished, as Shelley certainly did, to find some formula which would bestow the secret of immortal life on man. But neither believed that such a thing was literally possible. In Paracelsus' iatro-chemical writings, notably *The Archidoxes of Magic*, it is clear that his object was the conquest of disease, 'to preserve and keep mortal men to a long, sound and perfect age' as one translation put it. He had a metaphysical axe to grind; the body was to be raised to as near perfection as possible precisely because it was the casket of the soul, and to allow it to be the receptacle of disease defiled the soul as well. However, in his expectations Paracelsus was being no more mystical than the perfectibilian natural philosophers of the Enlightenment such as Condorcet (cited approvingly by Shelley), or Benjamin Franklin. These men did not believe that science could confer immortality, but that the span of healthy life could be indefinitely though not infinitely increased, and that premature death, except in cases of accident, could be eliminated.[24]

In the later eighteenth century Paracelsus and the Renaissance medicine with which his name was associated were often held up for ridicule by mainstream doctors, who used the example of the sympathetic 'wound salve' and the doctrine of signatures as easy targets when reviewing the progress of medicine. No longer were wounds treated by anointing the offending weapon, or plants fancifully resembling a lung in appearance taken as specifics against phthisis, except by the ignorant. Yet to dwell on the shooting of these sitting ducks is to ignore the extent to which the valuable and positive spirit of Paracelsian medicine was alive and indeed even undergoing a revival during the Romantic period.[25]

Thornton's essay is a clear attempt at accommodating Paracelsus and scientific medicine, but such an accommodation had many manifestations, even at the heart of the mainstream medicine which affected to despise Paracelsus. The revived emphasis on 'sympathy' – nervous affection of the whole body by one part, a concept which is at least as old as Galen and which became the cardinal doctrine of Hunter and Abernethy his pupil; the 'semi-animism' of the Edinburgh school of medicine; the efforts of the French *idéologue* Cabanis to place the healing art within the context of a total science of man – all these are imaginative responses to the phenomenon of the human body and an effort to see 'matter' as being instinct with 'spirit', which is of the essence of Paracelsianism. This moving spirit in the medicine of the late eighteenth century is an aspect of what Herbert Piper has described as 'a current of thought which between 1750 and 1800 in England and France swept away the Newtonian mechanical "universe of death" and brought a new conception of life, development and purpose in the natural world'.[26] In this new current the doctor played an important role; he was Promethean in being not only a healer, but a bringer of light:

The volume of Nature lies open to the medical philosopher: in all regions he is excited to peruse her pages, to interpret her language, and explain her laws. In the expeditions, whether of discovery, war, or commerce, made to remote parts, and into every climate of this earth, we see with a pardonable satisfaction, that the most interesting facts in natural history and science, have been collected by medical persons; or by those educated in that profession.[27]

The promise offered by medicine generated both by the vitalistic Zeitgeist and by recent discoveries in chemistry had never seemed more realisable. That Shelley should have been excited by the prospect of the conquest of disease, especially under the inspiration of a physician father-figure, is not surprising. Yet he was obviously obsessed with it to an unusual degree according to Medwin's testimony. 'If Shelley was at that time a believer in alchymy he was even more so in the Panacea.'[28]

In a letter to Godwin of 1812, Shelley associated health concerns with his fascination with natural magic. Until his marriage, he said, his life had been 'a series of illness . . .' of a 'nervous, or spasmodic nature', which had partly incapacitated him for study. Nevertheless, 'in the intervals of comparative health' he had read romances and 'pored over the reveries of Albertus Magnus, & Paracelsus'.[29] His interest in that medical aspect of alchemy which embraced botany and chemistry can be seen in his second long poem, Alastor (1815), where, after the death of the sick idealist poet, the narrator wishes for 'Medea's wondrous alchemy' and that the 'dream of dark magician in his visioned cave / Raking the cinders of a crucible / For life and power' could be the true law of the world (681–5). Implicit here is a central Shelleyan theme: the wish to believe in the miraculous cure, whether of the individual or the sick condition of the world.

Yet if the idea of the conquest of disease and of perpetual self-renewal excited him, an immortal body in the present state of the world was always portrayed by him as a curse. Taking shape simultaneously in his imagination was an emblem of an infinitely prolonged existence of pain and infirmity, linked to an undying, tormented body. This emblem was the figure of the Wandering Jew, a Romantic topic which obsessed Shelley to a greater degree even than it did his contemporaries. In addition to The Wandering Jew (1809–10) and 'The Wandering Jew's Soliloquy' (?1812), the figure appears in an early poem entitled 'Ghasta', in Queen Mab (1813), The Assassins

(1814), *Alastor* (1815), and *Hellas* (1821). No fewer than four times Shelley quoted a fragment of a prose translation of the Jew story taken from a German original, and in each case the fragment (the wording of which varies) deals with the Jew's search for release in death. Ginotti in *St Irvyne*, Sadak the Wanderer and Prince Athanase (a-thanatos = without death) are also quasi-Jew figures. The Jew is usually a character who protests vehemently against Christianity, though not against Christ. His suffering gives him the moral authority to denounce both divine and secular tyranny. The prose fragment lays great stress on the torments which his body undergoes, and expresses horror at being 'doomed to be imprisoned for ever in the clay-formed dungeon − to be ever clogged with this worthless body, its load of diseases and infirmities'. The final appearance of the Jew in *Hellas* is of an unsubdued soul inhabiting a decrepit body, the existence of which he has managed to prolong 'by dreadful abstinence / And conquering penance of the mutinous flesh' (155–6). It was a few months after writing *Hellas* that Shelley made the remark that he could be counted among the nonagenarians.[30]

At this point it becomes necessary to consider how seriously one should take Shelley's claim to Godwin that his *life* had been a series of illness. Clearly he was exaggerating; he was later to look back on his boyhood as a time of untamed youthful energies. Yet scanty as the record is, there are indications that Shelley was not particularly healthy during the Eton period; some of the ill-health would appear to have been self-inflicted.

Most of the known facts of Shelley's boyhood derive from ten letters by Hellen Shelley to her niece by marriage, Lady Jane. On one occasion Shelley 'came home in the midst of the half-year [the Eton term] to be nursed'. When he was allowed to leave the house her younger sister Margaret kissed him through the pane of glass.[31] This detail suggests that the illness was considered to be infectious. Hellen thought Margaret was about five years old, which, as she was born in January 1801, fixes the episode somewhere between 1805 and 1807. On another occasion Shelley came home in a 'dreadful state' which would have required medical treatment. His hands and face had been 'burned and blackened by some badly managed experiment, either at Eton or Oxford'. As we do hear (from Medwin) of him blowing himself up at Eton, this event certainly took place at school, not university. According to Rossetti, Shelley also told his sister that he had swallowed arsenic by mistake.[32]

It was at Eton, too, according to Trelawny, that Shelley first started taking laudanum. This was a life-long habit, though Trelawny insisted that unlike Coleridge or De Quincey Shelley was not a daily addict. He was, however, a compulsive and immoderate user at certain times and probably far more dependent upon it than his biographers have hitherto stated.[33] It was Trelawny's opinion that Shelley's 'spasms' in later life were caused by the drug; this may seem surprising in view of the widespread use of laudanum as a sedative, but has the support of Trotter who believed that opium abuse was one of the causes of nervous illness and John Hunter who warned that opium did not agree with everyone, 'Often producing irritability, in some lassitude and debility, in others spasms.'[34] As spasms are among the withdrawal symptoms it is possible that they were noting the effects of intermittent addiction to laudanum. In our opinion a great deal of Shelley's ill-health was iatrogenic (caused by medicine), as his last doctor, Vaccà, diagnosed.

There is also a story Shelley told about illness and Dr Lind which has often been dismissed as a fantasy. Once when he was 'very ill during the holidays' recovering from 'a fever which had attacked my brain' a servant overheard his father 'consult about sending me to a private madhouse'. Horrified, he sent an express message to Dr Lind who arrived and by sheer moral authority prevented Timothy Shelley from executing his threat. Mary remembered the occasion on which Shelley told her the story as 'that night that decided my destiny, when he opened at first with the confidence of friendship, and then with the ardour of love, his whole heart to me'. She implied that this incident was crucial to her decision to enter on a 'free union' with Shelley, and awakened both pity and trust. Hogg, however, presented the story as evidence that his friend had been a little touched:

I have heard Shelley speak of his fever and this scene at Field Place more than once, in nearly the same terms as Mrs Shelley adopts. It appeared to myself and to others also that his recollections were those of a person not quite recovered from a fever (which had attacked his brain) and still disturbed by the horrors of the disease.[35]

Peacock, implying strongly that Shelley suffered paranoid fantasies about his father wishing to imprison him, and that the Dr Lind story fell into that category, commented on Hogg that Shelley was haunted throughout life by the idea 'that his father was continually on the watch for a pretext to lock him up' and that this threat was driving him out of England.

Shelley did have grounds for thinking this; in October 1817 he actually was arrested for two days, probably for defaulting on a payment, by his uncle Captain Pilfold. From their point of view Shelley's family had good reason for wishing to imprison him; it was one way of curbing his alarming habit of raising post-obits on his expectations and thus encumbering the Shelley estates.[36] Shelley's madhouse story could well have been true too. Certainly he felt an important debt of gratitude towards Lind. In *Laon and Cythna* an idealised Lind, according to Mary's identification, figures as the rescuer and nurse of the brain-fevered hero.[37]

Do any of these records of Shelley's illnesses at Eton indicate that he had contracted venereal disease? The arsenic incident will be discussed in the next chapter. The use of laudanum was so general that not much weight can be attached to the fact that Shelley took it at Eton. It is worth noting, however, that there was a strong association of opium with the venereal diseases, witness the previously mentioned 1780 attempt to cure syphilis with opium alone. Erasmus Darwin believed that 'Opium contributes much to expedite the cure both of the simple gonorrhoea and of venereal ulcers.' Hunter, most influential of all venereologists in England during the period, encouraged its use, as did Woodville, the authoritative medical botanist. Sometimes it was the only medicine which could give any relief during the burning urethritic stage of gonorrhoea called 'the running'.[38] The incident of the explosion could have been a suicide attempt rather than a scientific experiment gone wrong (the same question mark hangs over the arsenic, as we shall show).[39]

Hogg's comment on Shelley's madhouse tale has not been quoted in its entirety. Immediately after the words 'horrors of the disease' he added:

Truth and justice demand that no event of his life should be kept back, but that all the materials for the formation of a correct judgment should be freely given.

(Wolfe, I, p. 36)

The solar microscope episode illustrated how disingenuous Hogg could be, and this innocent-sounding sentence has the same potential for irony. Does Hogg mean that if you read him correctly, between the lines, you will arrive at the truth about Shelley's 'brain-fever' (the same term as is used by Gronow about Kate North)? When he says that Shelley's recollections were those of a person 'not quite recovered from a fever' and that he was 'still disturbed by the horrors of the disease' does he mean, perhaps, that Shelley believed himself to be still diseased years after this event? And does this interpretation cast a different light on Timothy Shelley's behaviour − could he, for instance, have been wanting to send Shelley away in case he literally contaminated his other children, who, Hellen Shelley records, adored their elder brother and made frequent visits to his bedroom?

Brown made the point that Eton provided opportunities as wide as Oxford for Shelley to have contracted venereal disease; it also had a sympathetic doctor who could have treated him, and, for that matter, other boys too. At some of the most illustrious 'great schools' sexual laxity among the boys was bad enough for a doctor to be in semi-official attendance. 'At Westminster a surgeon is kept, with the Privity and under the connivance of the Master, whose chief business is to attend the boys, *peste venerea contaminatos*.' It was this discovery which led Cowper to write *Tirocinium*, an impassioned attack on public schools.[40] Beddoes, writing nearly twenty years later, corroborates Cowper; among the case histories furnished by correspondents is the following:

I engaged in gallantry; and to complete the measure of necessary qualifications, I wore my leather breeches so tight as nearly to stop the circulation of my blood. It may be supposed that the indulgencies above mentioned, were interrupted by the officiousness of the Master. This did not often happen. The usher, on adding a guinea to his *new-year's gift*, was ever our firm friend − There were indeed *casual incidents*, which for a time deranged our plans. But here again the assistance of the usher, or his friend the surgeon, set all things to rights.[41]

In 1798 the *Gentleman's Magazine* published an exposé of the sexual debauchery at Eton. The school's defenders did not deny the charges, but merely countered that the boys brought their bad morals from home and that schools could not be expected to keep Argus eyes on the pupils.[42]

A document that Brown thought suggestive of an Eton encounter was a fragmentary piece of Shelleyan 'ideal biography' called by a Victorian editor *Una Favola*. Written in Italian in 1820–1, it tells the story of a youth who is awakened by Love 'at the dawn of the fifteenth spring of his life', led through a wilderness into a gloomy garden where he abides 'a whole year', during which he is 'nourished on a plant, bitter and sweet at once, the fruit of a certain tree which was in the middle of the labyrinth which being cold as ice to the lips seemed like fire to the veins'.[43] (This is the feature which Brown thought might indicate a sexual lapse.) An enchantress called Life unveils herself and seems to intend well towards him. But before very long she proves false, abandons him in the wilderness and persuades Love to desert him also. Disastrous consequences follow for the youth. Loathsome forms parade before his eyes, he longs for death and wanders through the world. His form becomes bowed with misery and his hair eventually turns grey.

It is hard to believe that Shelley at Eton would have indulged in the same practices as the coarse schoolboy tyrants whom he loathed, nor is it our supposition that he did. Yet his first published book – *Zastrozzi* (1810) – has as its theme the passion of lust. Its entire plot turns on the seduction of a modest young man.

Shelley was to deny that the book was in any way self-revealing. When Joseph Gibbons Merle tried to draw him into intimacy, apparently on the strength of having read it, he reacted suspiciously: 'If he takes me for any one whose character I have drawn in Zastrozzi he is mistaken quite.'[44] *Zastrozzi* has been regarded as virtual proof that Shelley could not have had sexual experience before writing it precisely because the sexuality in the book is so derivative of *The Monk*, *Zofloya* and other hot, horrid novels of the time. Yet to choose a stereotyped formula is an effective disguise for confessional material. Shelley's touchiness towards Merle ('I fear the man has some deep scheme')[45] cuts both ways. No one today would dismiss *Zastrozzi* as mere pastiche, devoid of any sort of personal involvement. It contains a scene which seems to derive from the 'madhouse' episode, and which reappears in *Laon and Cythna*. There are prefigurings of characteristically Shelleyan themes such as the Doppelgänger, free love and the Christian God's hatred of man. The book's epigraph is from *Paradise Lost* and hints at a serious theme which is never developed:

> – that their God
> May prove their foe, and with repenting hand

> Abolish his own works – This would surpass
> Common revenge.

The theme is taken up by Matilda, the villainess of the piece, with a conviction which seems to stem less from the character than from Shelley himself: 'Where is the boasted mercy of God . . . if he suffer his creatures to endure agony such as this? or where his wisdom, if he implant in the heart passions furious – uncontrollable – as mine, doomed to destroy their happiness?' (p. 108)

It is in *Zastrozzi*, too, that one finds the first treatment of an idea which is encountered many times in Shelley: that the loss of a divine and spiritualised love leaves the bereft lover a prey to lawless appetite, and that it is thus that the 'pure' may be 'led astray'. *Pace* Trelawny, Shelley had no illusions that he was incapable of succumbing to such an influence. In 1814 when he was dodging arrest during the period of the 'solar microscope' episode, unable to spend the night with Mary except at weekends, he wrote a series of urgent love-letters to her in which he speaks of his terror that without her presence he will quickly become a prey to 'impurity & vice. If I were absent from you long I should shudder with horror at myself.' 'Know you my best Mary that I feel myself in your absence almost degraded to the level of the vulgar & impure. I feel their vacant stiff eyeballs fixed upon me – until I seem to have been infected by the loathsome meaning – to inhale a sickness that subdues me to languor.' Even when he finds prostitutes repellent ('the impures' was a common euphemism during the years 1780–1820, and the area where Shelley was moving included Covent Garden, London's brothel centre at that period), he still doubts his self-control.[46]

In *Zastrozzi*, too, is found mystification and coded message. The victim – hero, Verezzi, in love with Julia, an ethereal being, is pursued by a voluptuous, depraved creature, called Matilda in imitation of a similar figure in *The Monk*. Verezzi resists until she plays her trump card: Julia, she tells him, is dead. Verezzi faints away in horror. Restoratives are tried. 'At last his lips unclosed – he seemed to take his breath easier – he moved – he opened his eyes.' Chapter VI ends. In some copies of *Zastrozzi* there is no Chapter VII. Chapter VIII begins apparently without a break. 'His head reposed upon Matilda's bosom; he started from her violently as if stung by a scorpion and fell upon the floor.' Burning sensations, emaciation, brain fever and a visit from the physician follow.[47]

Omitting chapters had become almost a convention of the novel of sensibility that derived from Sterne, an author whom Shelley knew well. *Tristram Shandy* omits Chapters 19 and 20 of Volume IX – the famous episode in which the Widow Wadman attempts to find out whether Uncle Toby's groin wound is incurable. Mackenzie's *The Man of Feeling* begins at Chapter 11. In these cases, as in *St Irvyne*, Shelley's second novel, absence of a chapter denotes some hiatus – the unmentionable or just the passage of time – which the reader's imagination must fill up. In *Zastrozzi* the message to the reader who notices the omission is that Verezzi has been seduced, or perhaps raped, having despaired of finding virtuous spiritual love. The significance of the scorpion will emerge later. (The rest of the book hinges on Matilda's efforts to persuade Verezzi to *love* her and thus accomplish a double degradation.)

If *Zastrozzi* is a glamorised record of a sexual initiation, it is not necessary to suppose that Shelley had an experience with the sort of person normally thought of as a prostitute. She could have been an adventuress looking for a protector among the Eton youths, who included the wealthiest and noblest heirs in Britain, or a 'ruined' girl of good family – many prostitutes were drawn from the governess class in the early nineteenth century. Shelley was exceedingly sympathetic to victims of seduction whom he saw as perched on the slippery slope to prostitution. Leigh Hunt tells the story of his selecting such a girl as a dancing partner.[48] Verezzi accomplishes his own downfall through misplaced pity for someone whom he takes to be society's victim, a 'woman of strong passions, who, having resisted them to the utmost of her power, was at last borne away in the current'. (p. 83)

Zastrozzi provides a scenario for the seduction of a modest youth like Shelley, whether or not such a thing actually happened. (In *The Monk*, by contrast, Matilda's victim is a mature man.) A guilty secret figures in *The Wandering Jew* which Medwin claimed he and Shelley wrote together in the winter of 1809–10. (Modern scholarship assigns the existing version to Shelley.) Paolo has an awful disclosure to make to Rosa – that he is the Wandering Jew himself. A disastrous sexual encounter is suggested in *St Irvyne* (1810). The book opens with Verezzi's counterpart, Wolfstein (a Shelley ancestor lived at Wolf's Hill), calling upon God to strike him with an exterminating thunderbolt: 'For what then should I longer drag on the galling chain of existence?' What has driven him to despair the reader never learns, except that it is an 'event which imposed upon him an insuperable barrier to ever again returning [to his native country]'. A glimpse of his past, however, is revealed. Having fallen in love with Megalena he chafes at his confinement to a bandit's cave: 'He longed to re-enter that world which he had never tried but once, and that indeed for a short time, sufficiently long, however, to blast his blooming hopes, and to graft on the stock, which otherwise might have produced virtue, the seeds of vice.'

Ginotti, the Wandering Jew figure in the story and Wolfstein's evil Doppelgänger, has become as he is through '*curiosity*, and a desire of unveiling the latent mysteries of nature'. The penalty for thus attempting to plumb the secrets of existence itself (a quest which involves the rejection of religion) is possession by a diabolic figure whose appearance seems to be derived as much from the incident of Shelley blowing himself up at Eton as from the final appearance of Satan in *The Monk*. 'Gigantic and deformed', the form is seemingly 'blackened by the inerasible traces of the thunderbolts of God'.[49] Ginotti has rejected love; the strong suggestion is that his insatiable desire for 'unveiling the secrets of nature' is a perverted kind of sensuality and the counterpart to enslavement of his *alter ego*, Wolfstein, by Megalena. Elsewhere in Shelley one finds an association of the ideas of sexual curiosity and scientific investigation. Perhaps the best exemplification of this is in the lines of *Prometheus Unbound* which celebrate man's conquest of nature, his control of the elements and ultimate possession of all the secrets of 'the abyss':

> The tempest is his steed, he strides the air;
> And the abyss shouts from her depth laid bare,
> Heaven, hast thou secrets? Man unveils me; I have none.
>
> (IV, 421–3)

The preoccupations that we have discussed above – concern with health, belief in a panacea, self-projection as both undying sufferer and victim of lust, rejection of Christianity, hints at a guilty secret – all these are at least compatible with Brown's conjecture, though nothing more. We now return to *Una Favola* to discover whether anything in Shelley's fable gives against it, making two assumptions: that the time scale fixed in the story (such as it is) is realistic, and that sexual intercourse with an unknown woman was less likely to have occurred during a period when Shelley's romance with his cousin Harriet Grove was prospering, than before it commenced or when he felt himself to be rejected by her.

There is circumstantial evidence that Shelley's courtship of Harriet began in August 1808 with a visit paid by the Grove family to Field Place.[50] Assuming that 'dawn of the fifteenth spring of his life' meant 'beginning of his fifteenth year' (Shelley's draft cancellation shows that this was what he first wrote),[51] this would put the 'call by love', that is, the onset of puberty, at around August 1806. The journey to the gloomy garden, the sojourn of a year and the deceit of Life could all be accommodated in the time before August 1808, as could treatment for either or both forms of the venereal disease. On the other hand 'dawn of the fifteenth spring' might mean 'at the beginning of his fifteenth spring, counting from his birth', that is, the early spring of 1808. This was when he began a correspondence with the young Denbighshire poetess Felicia Browne, and is an early occasion recorded of Shelley's taking an interest in the opposite sex. This correspondence was put a stop to when Shelley's religious scepticism became manifest. He was later to refer to Felicia as a 'tyger', by which he probably meant the reverse of the amiable and unprejudiced female who might be induced to enter into a 'free love' relationship.[52] The year's sojourn in the garden culminating in the unveiling of Life would thus be the period April 1808 – April 1809, and the nourishment with the bitter-sweet fruit adolescent fantasising which inflamed his imagination. It was in April 1809 that Shelley went up to

London and accompanied his cousin to the theatre. Hellen Shelley recorded that he was in a state of high excitement, upsetting the port wine and needing to have his wild spirits calmed by Harriet.[53] One then has to make sense of the passage in *Una Favola* which says that 'before very long' (*ben presto*) he discovered the falsity of Life.

Harriet Grove did not finally break with him until late in 1810. But there is a period in Shelley's life from which no letters survive and about which little is known. This is May 1809 to April 1810. During this time Shelley wrote *Zastrozzi* and *The Wandering Jew*.[54] There is also some evidence of a crisis in the relationship between Harriet and Shelley in September 1809. Some of the 1809 poems in the *Esdaile Notebook* (a collection of his early work which remained unpublished until 1964 and which Shelley declared had the merit of being 'faithful pictures of my feelings at the time of writing them')[55] hint at a suicide attempt. These poems, 'A Dialogue' and 'To the Moonbeam' (the latter having the date 23 September) speak of seeking refuge in 'the death of despair' where 'no longer the scorpions of perfidy goad'. There is also a curious entry in Harriet Grove's diary which suggests that for some reason Timothy Shelley had determined not to invite her family to Field Place during August 1809.[56] It is perhaps during this period that Shelley wrote 'St Irvyne's Tower', a poem in which he imagines his Harriet as lost to him forever and projects himself for the first time as a 'frail form'.[57]

As Medwin recorded walking, shooting and collaborating on *The Wandering Jew* during the winter holiday of 1809–10, Shelley must have been fairly recovered from any illness contracted earlier that year. The time scale for the treatment of gonorrhoea varied enormously even within the same individual. Byron, for instance, seems to have been confined indoors on one occasion for four weeks, on another to have suffered off and on for several months, and on a third for eighteen days at the most. Someone with a mild case – sometimes there was no more than a simple running or slight pain in passing water – would have been confined for even less time. Mercury treatment of syphilis, according to one practitioner, destroyed the virus within twenty-five to thirty days, with another fortnight's or three weeks' treatment as a safety precaution, provided that the disease had not yet attacked the skin and bones. (If it had, a three to four months' course was needed.) Nitric acid, as we said earlier, was supposed to remove the symptoms of syphilis in only two weeks. A respectable surgeon of the London Lock Dispensary, Mr Kiernan, claimed in an advertisement in an Oxford paper, that his 'superior and scientific' treatment for all venereal complaints required no confinement, that the early symptoms yielded 'in a few days' and even the most complicated forms 'seldom exceed a few weeks'. (He offered a confidential postal service.)[58]

It would seem, therefore, that 'a college life' could refer to Eton, with the 'madhouse' and perhaps the 'blowing up' incidents – if they took place about the same time – marking the results of Shelley's 'tampering with venal pleasures', including treatment by Dr Lind. Self-medication by some unorthodox method might also have been involved in the 'brain fever'.

Of course Shelley's Eton writings might be the products of something rather different: a fear of what might happen based on a knowledge of his own propensities. That Shelley's writing frequently anticipates actual events in his life has often been remarked; the most famous incidence of this is the apparent prefiguration of his death by drowning in poetry containing imagery of drowning and shipwreck. Another is the fact that he wrote poetry to an imaginary Mary and envisaged a suicide pact with her four years before he proposed a suicide pact to a real Mary. Shelley himself at times gave credence to the notion of 'pure anticipated cognition', or at any rate he played with the hypothesis in order to explain how it was that he imagined situations before they actually occurred. The example he gave was of having created the character of the Lady in *The Sensitive Plant* a year before he met Jane Williams, whom he recognised as the 'exact antitype' of his creation.[59] Perhaps what we have described was, as it were, an impure anticipated cognition. Moreover the time scale of *Una Favola* is not clear, for there is no indication of how long a time elapsed between the awakening by Love and the arrival at the garden.

After a hiatus of nearly six months, communication between Harriet and Shelley was re-established. Although puzzled by his behaviour in April 1810 when she visited Field Place, she was clearly fond of him. Charles Grove recalled forty-six years later that Shelley was then 'full of life' and 'well pleased with his successful devotion to my sister'. Shelley however seems to have been veering between manic high spirits and gloomy foreboding, if his letters at that period to his friend Edward Fergus Graham are anything to go by. By the time his *Victor and Cazire* volume came out in September, the month before he went up to Oxford, he and Harriet were obviously estranged again.[60]

3

Arsenic and aquafortis: Oxford 1810–11

Shelley was at University College, Oxford, between October 1810 and March 1811. It has often been said that he was conspicuous for his chastity there, which, in the opinion of many biographers, has been enough to weight the balance of probabilities very much against his having contracted venereal disease.[1] Of course, as Thornton Hunt and Jeaffreson in the last century, and Cameron, Holmes and Brown in this, have recognised, it could be simultaneously true that in the Oxford of 1810 he passed for a Sir Galahad and had, in Jeaffreson's words, a 'fit of rakishness'. The wording of Mary's description of him at the age of seventeen – before he went up – 'of the purest *habits* of morals' (our italics), admits of just such an interpretation.[2] However, as Shelley's reputation for purity has dogged all discussion of the subject and certainly does not support our argument, it is as well to go over the ground and see what it amounts to.

It derives almost entirely from the phrase of Mary's quoted above and from Hogg's 1832 articles. No other account of Shelley at Oxford, with one interesting exception, has anything to say about Shelley's purity. Hogg, however, amply compensates for the silence of others. He applies the word 'virgin' freely to Shelley's speech, deportment and mind; the rapid reader could easily suppose that Hogg has actually said that Shelley was a virgin. Reading legalistically though – and Hogg was a trained lawyer – one sees that he has not. What he gives the reader by way of an illustration of 'the purity and sanctity of his life' is an account of Shelley's devotion to his sisters and his strange eating habits, especially his addiction to cakes, gingerbread and stewed fruit.[3] Hogg relies on his reader's equating two kinds of carnal lusts: if Shelley has such a 'childish' sweet tooth and no taste for red meat, it must follow that his sexual appetites were equally underdeveloped.

At one point, Hogg raised the question of whether Shelley's conduct was altogether admirable:

whether he was ever misled by an ardent imagination, a glowing temperament, something of hastiness in choice, and a certain constitutional impatience; whether like less gifted mortals, he ever shared in the common portion of mortality – repentance; and to what extent? (Wolfe, I, p. 82)

Hogg is obviously referring to Shelley's disastrous first marriage in August

1811, something too well known to be overlooked, but in doing so he admits that Shelley had a 'glowing temperament' and was constitutionally impatient. This sorts oddly with his next statement:

Such inquiries, however, do not fall within the compass of a brief narrative of his career at the university. [True enough, if a sexual lapse took place during the vacation.] The unmatured mind of a boy is capable of good intentions only, and of generous and kindly feelings, and these were pre-eminent in him.   (ibid.)

Hogg is implying the Shelley, at eighteen, was so sexually immature that any tampering with venal pleasures was impossible. One notices, however, the shiftiness of 'pre-eminent' and the manner in which he directs attention away from Shelley's behaviour to his disposition.

Hogg several times repeated the statement that Shelley hated coarse jokes. Here he overstated. It seems that Shelley, like a good many people, was capable of amusing himself with risqué remarks in certain conditions and in the company of those whom he trusted. It is clear that he was acquainted with sexual slang in a way that, say, Robert Browning was not.[4] In *Peter Bell III* (1819), for instance, he used the contemporary term for a pathic homosexual − 'molly' (617). When in May 1811 Hogg moved to Coney Street, York, Shelley, upon learning the new address wrote 'I blush when I write the directions to you. − How salacious a street!' (It is characteristic of Hogg that he should have quite unnecessarily given his address twenty pages later so that the puzzled reader might work out the point of Shelley's remark.)[5] Of course Shelley did not blush, for if he had he would not have made a comment on the street name at all. If anything, he was making a feeble joke at the expense of his own reputation for purity with Hogg. A verse letter written about the same time to his friend Graham is unpleasantly ribald; he gloats over the idea of his father being 'cornuted' (cuckolded) by Graham and his mother 'dancing' like Ninon de l'Enclos, the octogenarian *fille*.[6] When the genre allowed, Shelley could be coarse enough, as evidenced in the following stanza from 'The Devil's Walk', an essay in the broadside ballad manner:

> Satan poked his red nose into crannies so small
> One would think that the innocents fair,
> Poor lambkins! were just doing nothing at all
> But settling some dress or arranging some ball,
> But the Devil saw deeper there.   (VII)

The words describing the particular vice which the Devil sees are equally applicable to female vanity and to a couple caught *in flagrante*. A surprising Shelley − a writer of double entendres − appears; though perhaps not so surprising if one remembers that he had read Sterne and was the friend of Peacock, *thesaurus eroticus* and connoisseur of quibbles. Shelley's mind can be seen working at a rather more witty level of sexual punning in a notebook remark on the nude statue of an athlete: 'Curse these fig leaves; why is a round tin thing more decent than a cylindrical marble one?',[7] which shows him juggling the usual and slang meanings of 'thing'. And yet, as with the solar microscope story, Hogg could have claimed that he was telling the essential truth, and that Shelley lived up to a far stricter standard of chastity than the average Oxford gownsman, including, almost certainly, Hogg himself.

While Hogg's testimony is equivocal, there is evidence that Shelley enjoyed a reputation for sexual wildness in at least one quarter of Oxford – the Charles Kirkpatrick Sharpe set. Sharpe, artist, antiquary and wit, is remembered today chiefly for his friendship with Walter Scott. An M.A. at Oxford during Shelley's sojourn, he had many correspondents among the titled and the rakish whom he regaled with Oxford gossip. On 15 March 1811, ten days before Shelley's expulsion, he wrote to Lady Charlotte Campbell, then a celebrated Edinburgh hostess, concerning Shelley's book of poems, *Posthumous Fragments of Margaret Nicholson*:

Talking of books, we have lately had a literary Sun shine forth upon us here, before whom our former luminaries must hide their diminished heads – a Mr Shelley, of University College, who lives upon arsenic, aquafortis, half-an-hour's sleep in the night, and is desperately in love with the memory of Margaret Nicholson . . . Shelley's style is most like that of Moore burlesqued; for Frank is a very foul-mouthed fellow, and Charlotte, one of the most impudent brides that I ever met with in a book.[8]

He wrote a similar letter about the same time to the talented, debauched E. B. Impey, son of the former Chief Justice of Bengal. This letter has been lost but Impey replied to it on 18 March:

As for the literary meteor who is now performing his perhelion [sic] in your learned hemisphere, I have nothing to do – but hide my diminished beams – and congratulate myself on being beyond the scope of his fiery tail – which he seems to whisk about with such wonderful volubility that I would have Miss Burton beware of the laws of gravitation and vigilantly guard her centre of attraction.[9]

The 'literary meteor' is obviously Shelley; the similarity of phrasing – the hiding of heads and beams – is too striking to admit of any other interpretation, and Sharpe speaks of a 'literary Sun' to Lady Charlotte. Evidently he used the phrase 'literary meteor' in the Impey letter and dropped some broader hints to his male correspondent than he did to his female. (Even so, Lady Charlotte obviously felt that Sharpe's letter to her was not altogether proper; in editing it for publication she made it appear that it was addressed to her brother, the Marquis of Lorne. The original letter has been cut about and her reply shows that it must have originally contained a far more detailed description of what Sharpe considered to be the juicy bits of Shelley's volume.)[10]

Impey, who moves straight on to Shelley from commenting on 'an Oxford

Lais', Dolly Hands, has inferred from Sharpe that Shelley's poetry is so salacious as to be diseased. 'To have one's tail on fire' was current slang for 'to be infected with either the clap or the pox', and 'to guard her centre of attraction' slang for 'to protect her virginity'.[11] Miss Burton was probably two or three times Shelley's age and a butt of the Sharpe circle, who referred to her as the *lovely* Miss Burton or *the Brown Jack*. She was evidently something of an 'Oxford belle', one of those 'venerable spinsters' described by J. G. Lockhart in his Oxford novel *Reginald Dalton* (1823) who were 'flirted with by transient hundreds, and made love to (serious love I mean) by nobody'.[12] Impey's innuendo contrives to suggest both sophisticated disdain at the naiveté of the Miss Burtons of this world, frustrated prudes who are taken in by that sort of thing – and disapproval of Shelley's morals. 'Volubility' suggests that he uses his poetry to inflame and seduce, and the implication is that by his poetry ye may know him. Impey is thankful that being out of Oxford he is not in competition with Shelley for the dubious honour of being the most dissolute Oxford poet.

Undoubtedly what had laid Shelley open to Sharpe's innuendoes was the *Margaret Nicholson* volume, published the previous November. It purported to be written by a crazed would-be assassin of George III and was anti-monarchist, but it seems that what made it a talking point in Oxford was its libertinism as much as its politics. This centred around one episode – the 'Epithalamium' of Francis Ravaillac and Charlotte Corday. The text casts an interesting light on what passed for 'foul-mouthed' and 'impudent' – which still retained its meaning of 'sexually shameless' – among sophisticates of 1810. Francis Ravaillac, the 'Frank' of Sharpe's letter, speaks:

> 'Soft, my dearest angel, stay,
> Oh! you suck my soul away;
> Suck on, suck on, I glow, I glow!
> Tides of maddening passion roll,
> And streams of rapture drown my soul.
> Now give me one more billing kiss,
> Let your lips now repeat the bliss,
> Endless kisses steal my breath,
> No life can equal such a death.'   (82–90)

Charlotte in return sings of clasping her lover's form and 'mingling' with him in 'a long, long night of bliss'.

Brown is surely right to disagree with Cameron, who claimed that the lines depict fellatio, but as surely errs himself in limiting Shelley's meaning to kissing, for otherwise why should Sharpe have called Frank 'foul-mouthed'? The lines would certainly have been considered 'rather too warm' in an undergraduate poet, though permissible in a 'luscious' Latin author. We have discovered that they are, in fact, a free borrowing from an eighteenth-century translation of 'Lydia, bella puella candida', an erotic lyric then attributed to the Renaissance poet Cornelius Gallus. It belongs to a genre where the theme of 'kisses' provides an opportunity to describe the sensations preceding sexual climax.[13] But this does not mean that Shelley contributed nothing. Significantly, he includes the *woman's* delighted response, which his source does not. And the line 'Suck on, suck on, I glow, I glow!' was his. It seems to have become notorious; at any rate, it was the one which stuck in Hogg's mind when, twenty-two years later, he disingenuously described the genesis, intention and reception of the volume. With an elaborate pretence of racking his memory he wrote that he had 'one copy, if not more, somewhere or other':

There were some verses, I remember, with a good deal about *sucking* in them;[14] to these I objected as unsuitable to the gravity of a University, but Shelley declared they would be the most impressive of all. There was a poem concerning a young woman, one Charlotte Somebody, who attempted to assassinate Robespierre, or some such person.   (Wolfe, I, p. 162)

Hogg could count on mystifying the majority of his readers; the book had, by 1832, virtually disappeared. (Even by 1883 only four copies, one of which was Hogg's, had turned up.) His remarks were aimed at the few old Oxonians who might fish out *their* copies, to Shelley's detriment; his claim that the volume was only a hoax was intended to pre-empt them. Hogg reported tongue-in-cheek that it became a 'kind of fashion to be seen reading it in public' pensively 'with a grave and sage delight' as the mark of 'a delicate and fastidious taste'. (ibid.) For 'grave and sage delight' one may safely read 'scandalised glee'. And all suspicions that Sharpe's description of the poem's intentions may stem from his own indecent mind finally disappear when one reads Shelley's letter to Graham of November 1810, in which it is made clear that the passage (which he said was the production of 'a friend's mistress') was inserted to 'make it sell like wildfire' and had been omitted from his mother's copy. The authorship being a 'profound secret, there can arise no danger from the indelicacy . . . It sells wonderfully here, & is become the fashionable subject of discussion – What particular subject do you mean, I cannot make out I confess.'[15]

    The Sharpe circle makes no distinction between Shelley the poet and Shelley the man; one can assume that readers of the 'Epithalamium' would have read it as a boast of actual sexual experience. In his misplaced confidence in his own anonymity and by ascribing it to someone's mistress, Shelley seems to have recognised as much.

    Contemporary reviews of *Zastrozzi* and *St Irvyne* contain a similar mixture of outrage and ridicule. Of the first the reviewer asked 'Does the author, whoever he may be, think his gross and wanton pages fit to meet the eye of a modest young woman? . . . such trash . . . is fit only for the inmates of a brothel . . . We know not when we have felt so much indignation as in the perusal of this execrable production.' The review of *St Irvyne* in the *Anti-*

Jacobin was even more severe upon the personal morals of the author: 'Tis not surprising that the writer, who can outrage nature and common sense in almost every page of his book, should libel a sex, of whom, we suppose, he has no knowledge, but such as may be collected in the streets or in a brothel.' Since Sharpe was a contributor to the *Anti-Jacobin* and knew that Shelley had written *St Irvyne*, it is possible that he had fed some information to the reviewer, though the anti-matrimonialism and barely disguised infidelity of the two books would have also provided an excuse for the reviewer to make inferences. The spectacular charges of incest and driving Harriet Shelley to prostitution and suicide that were later brought against him have obscured the fact that the first attacks made on Shelley's personal morals involved the ordinary kinds of debauchery.[16]

Yet, in itself, authorship of a *succès de scandale* does not account for Sharpe and Impey's hint that Shelley is not merely licentious but diseased. There is another revealing phrase in Sharpe's letter; this is the statement that Shelley 'lives upon arsenic, aquafortis, half-an-hour's sleep in the night'. Sharpe liked his *mot*, for nine years later he wrote to an unknown correspondent:

I send you the 'Cenci', written by that wicked wretch Shelley, and well written. I remember him at Oxford, mad – bad – and trying to persuade people that he lived on arsenic and *aquafortis*.[17]

The formula 'mad – bad – ' itself carried nuances of libertinage. (Compare Lady Caroline Lamb on Byron: 'Mad – bad – and dangerous to know.') It is unlikely that Sharpe was referring merely to burning holes in college carpets and writing atheistic pamphlets. Similarly, 'living on arsenic and aquafortis' is not merely his facetious way of saying 'having a passion for chemistry'. Sharpe is hinting here – and it is typical of the manners of his set that he should do so – that Shelley was treating himself for syphilis, and passing the treatment off as an eccentricity. Sharpe's reason for bringing up the matter again with reference to the *Cenci* is that in that play evil is presented in terms of syphilitic infection.

'Aquafortis' was the name which the modern 'nitric acid' was fast replacing; its place in the contemporary treatment of syphilis was seen in Chapter 2. Arsenic was yet another substance of which great things were hoped. It comes into the literature of syphilis by means of the writings of Ulrich von Hutten, an early victim, well known to historians of medicine for his advocacy of guaiacum. 'Arsnick' was one of the most effective of all the 'drinks and corrosives' which he tried – interestingly, aquafortis was another – but it occasioned 'such bitter Pains' that death seemed preferable. It was partly because it contained arsenic that Paracelsus used the 'sulphur of sapphire' to treat syphilis. Boyle mentions a balsam made of it in combination with nitre and 'spirits of wine of vinegar' as effective in the cure of venereal ulcers.

During the eighteenth century arsenic went underground. The active ingredient of 'tasteless ague drops', it had a continuous sale as a 'secret remedy' – a
'quack' or 'empiric' patent medicine. Then quite suddenly it came back into
prominence as one of the 'oxygenated medicines' – a wonder cure.[18]

William Buchan, a sceptic about these new remedies, wrote dryly in his
Observations concerning the Prevention and Cure of the Venereal Disease: 'It is
maintained that it is not the mercury itself but something mixed with it, a kind
of air (oxygene) which has done so much good and which may be found . . . in
much larger proportion as well as in much greater quantity in the purest air that
we breathe, in pure spring water and in aqua-fortis, which may be found in
white arsenic, and in fifty other substances.'[19] A figure instrumental in the
revival of arsenic was a remarkable man, whose influence on Shelley's mind
and art merits more attention – Sir William 'Oriental' Jones (1746–94).

Jones, a former alumnus of University College, judge of the supreme court of
Bengal and friend of Impey's father, had been England's foremost Orientalist
and populariser of Eastern poetry. His prestige was still very high in 1810. A
cheap edition of his works had been published in 1807 and must have been the
one that Shelley received when he ordered Jones' works in December 1812. His
elegant and inventive memorial by Flaxman, a sculptor in whom Shelley showed some interest, is on the right hand of the entrance to the college chapel, daily
attendance at which was compulsory in 1810.[20]

It is very likely that Shelley first heard of Jones through Lind. The centre of
Lind's sojourn in the East was Bengal, as it was for Jones. Both corresponded
with Sir Joseph Banks, and shared interests in Eastern medicine, botany and
astronomy. Lind lived only three miles away from Sir William Herschel's
observatory in Slough, and in the 1780s seems to have been a reporter to Banks
of Herschel's exciting discoveries concerning volcanic activity on the moon.
Jones, in Crishna Nagar, heard of them too, though there is no evidence that he
and Lind ever corresponded directly.[21] The notes to Southey's *Curse of
Kehama*, which Shelley ordered in December 1810 and probably read early in
January 1811, contain numerous citations of Jones. The most likely place for
Shelley to have first read Jones, however, was University College. Hogg
recorded his passion for Orientalism and that he 'perused with more than ordinary eagerness the relations of travellers in the East'.[22] The influence of
Jones can be seen in an *Esdaile* poem, 'Zeinab and Kathema', which was almost
certainly written before Shelley ordered Jones' works, and of which we shall
have more to say later.

Furthermore, Jones' works were available to Shelley at the college, for in
1799 Lady Jones had presented a set to the library in the more lavish six-
volume quarto edition. In the first volume of the 1799 edition, placed in an
eye-catching position at the end of the contents page, is one of Jones' *Asiatic
Researches*, an article recommending arsenic in the cure of two diseases, one
of which was the Persian fire. (The other will be encountered in Chapter

6.) This article, which was merely translated by Jones and actually written by an Indian doctor, revealed 'an old secret of Hindu physicians'. The writer claimed to have cured a man so afflicted by the Persian fire – yet another of the names for syphilis – that 'his hands and his feet were entirely ulcerated and almost corroded'. The cure was an arsenical pill, for which the doctor gave a detailed recipe. 'In a fortnight his recovery was complete.' More soberly, in his preface to the article Jones urged the trial of a remedy which seemed to have been used successfully in India for years. He appears to have regarded the article as a contribution to the search for a non-mercurial cure; it included the cautionary story of a patient who was given cinnabar (mercuric sulphide) with bad results.[23] (Hindu medicine was in part vindicated when in 1909 salvarsan, a complicated arsenical compound, became the first true substitute for mercury in treating syphilis and remained so until replaced by penicillin in 1943.)

Jones' doctor speaks of the application of arsenic in syphilitic skin conditions, but during the years 1800–10 it was also used 'in the wandering pains and anomalous ailments of those syphilitic patients who have sustained permanent injury both from the disease and its cure' – the cure being, of course, mercury. In 1809 arsenic was finally received into the London Pharmacopeia, but in a rather defensive manner: 'Its powers as a medicine are marked and useful, and the College, by its introduction, have hoped rather to obviate those abundant evils which follow its irregular use as a secret [empiric] medicine.'[24]

Now there is a record that Shelley experienced 'evils which follow its irregular use'. One cannot be sure that he was using the arsenic medicinally, but Hogg's account is so peculiar as to make one suspect that here again he is covering up something. First, he gives two disparate accounts. In his earlier 1832 version, he said that Shelley had accidentally swallowed some mineral poison – 'I think arsenic' – during a careless scientific experiment at Eton. (This was what Shelley told his sister.) In his 1858 version, Hogg wrote, without eliminating the first story, that the poison, by now *definitely* arsenic, had been taken for love of a young lady who had refused his hand shortly before he came up to Oxford. There is no way of telling which, if indeed either, version is the true one, or whether the disparity is Hogg's or Hogg's faithful rendering of two differing accounts given by Shelley at different times. Perhaps the only thing of which one might be reasonably sure is that Shelley had taken arsenic prior to the Oxford period; according to Sharpe, he took it at Oxford as well.[25]

Both arsenic and nitric acid were used in the treatment of diseases other than syphilis. But in this very period (1810) for the first, and as far as we know, only time since Paracelsus,[26] arsenic and aquafortis were used *together* as a specific for syphilis. Between 1809 and 1810 George Nesse Hill, a Chester surgeon, published in the *Edinburgh Medical and Surgical Journal* a long series of articles entitled 'On the Use of Arsenic'. Hill had read the *Asiatic Researches*, and referred to Jones as an authority on the subject. He recommended arsenic for nineteen different morbid conditions, but in only two of them did he prescribe nitric acid as an adjuvant. One was syphilis, the other was lepra, a disease which for historical reasons was associated with the former. Only in the case of syphilis were both substances to be taken *internally*. (Shelley was supposed to be 'living' on them.)

Hill believed that 'the conjoint effect of these two powerful medicines, will accomplish what either separately would not',

The improved treatment [of syphilis] now so universally established, has greatly contributed to disarm this cruel hydra of many of its heads; still there are too many left, the obstinacy of which occasionally render existence burdensome, or form the first irrevocable step towards an untimely grave. I allude to those cases, where the common remedy appears to have lost its power over the enemy, or some untoward symptom exists, which is manifestly aggravated by continuance in the use of mercury . . . Ancient syphilitic ulcers . . . cutaneous eruptions of long standing . . . the excruciating pains of the limbs, forcing the wretched sufferer from a wearisome bed, at the midnight hour . . . will all generally yield to arsenical remedies; with nitric acid in a decoction of the woods.[27]

A 'decoction of the woods' was pharmacological shorthand for a mixture of the extracts of four anti-syphilitic plants: guaiacum, sassafras, china root and sarsaparilla.

The relevant article appeared in the January 1810 number. As a graduate of Edinburgh College of Physicians, Lind very likely subscribed or had copies lent to him by richer colleagues. (Cavallo used to pass on the *Philosophical Transactions of the Royal Society* to him.) We are inclined to believe that Shelley read the article, maybe even at Eton, because of both his general interest in arsenic and the similarity between Hill's image of the 'cruel hydra' and its 'heads' and a passage in *Queen Mab* where Shelley writes of venereal disease as having 'filled / All human life with hydra-headed woes' (*Q.M.*, V, 194–6). Shelley was renowned for the quickness and retentiveness of his memory; it would have been nothing for him to have stored up this image over a period of three years. It is an apt metaphor: the hydra's heads of mythology were extirpated by cautery – burning – and 'actual cautery' had been an old and barbarous method of removing venereal ulcers. Even when replaced by lunar caustic the process was still called 'cautery'.[28] Shelley could of course have extrapolated the metaphor himself. Still, the coincidence is curious, and, in what we have managed to retrace of Shelley's voluminous reading, we have found no phrase applied to venereal disease that is quite as close to the metaphor as Hill's.

The reference in Hill's article to excruciating pains of the limbs in the context of treatment with arsenic and aquafortis suggests that when Sharpe talked of Shelley living on half-an-hour's sleep in the night he was probably not referring to the latter's known habits of assiduous study or even making a jocular allusion to the pangs of unrequited love for Margaret Nicholson. Shelley, Sharpe hints, is suffering from 'night pains'. The force of Sharpe's later remark that Shelley was trying to persuade people that he was 'living' on the minerals would then be 'Oh, yes, I remember his trying to palm off his arsenic and aquafortis as some kind of alchemist's food; we know what he was really up to, don't we?' Shelley might well have made some such defensive joke if he had been using a 'secret remedy' – in both senses of the word – and it had been discovered. Although he had already apparently had a bad experience with arsenic (Hogg's story) this would not have precluded his learning how to regulate the dose; arsenic is a poison for which one can build up a tolerance, and anything would seem better than mercury.

It is possible, of course, that Sharpe was maliciously misrepresenting Shelley's experiments with chemistry; as a contributor to the *Anti-Jacobin* and an opponent of Shelley's politics, he was quite capable of doing so. But there is some evidence from a friendly quarter – Medwin – that Shelley did have a medical purpose for fitting out his room as a laboratory, and that this was not such an absurd set-up as Hogg made it out to be. This medical purpose we interpret as being, in the first place, that of restoring himself to perfect health. If he saw himself as a frail form and subject to a series of illnesses, this was a very reasonable ambition, whatever the source of the frailty. Secondly, we hypothesise that the laboratory either was or became a convenient cover for self-medication against real or suspected syphilis, contracted or thought to be contracted at Eton or during the Oxford period. This is not to deny that Shelley simply enjoyed messing around with Leyden jars and retorts, or that the laboratory did have a social purpose. In fact Shelley's quasi-mystical belief in the panacea probably determined the nature of some of his experiments. He could have been trying out something Paracelsian when he dissolved a gold third-guinea in *aqua regia*. (Carl Grabo thought he was making 'Diana's Trees' with a silver coin, but this cannot be right.) The 'potable gold' of the alchemists had a perennial fascination, and was one of the substances which, like opium, acquired the prestige of kinship with the elixir of life.[29]

When Medwin wrote his 1847 *Life of Shelley*, he incorporated passages from Hogg's 1832 articles in order to fill out his account of Shelley's Oxford period. His transcription is careless, and he sometimes slips in a comment of his own as if it were Hogg's. But he is usually honest about acknowledging his source. However, when recalling his own visit to Shelley's rooms, for once he used Hogg's material, almost verbatim, without such acknowledgement. This passage is unusually full of Medwin's interpolated material – so full, in fact, that it looks as though Medwin simply could not be bothered on this occasion to sort out which belonged to whom. Here is the passage, with Medwin's additions and alterations italicised:

Such, with some variations, was, as they come back on me, the appearance of Shelley and his rooms during this visit to him in the November of 1810.

He had not forgotten our Walker's Lectures, and was deep in the mysteries of chemistry, and had apparently been making some experiments; but it is highly improbable that Shelley was qualified to succeed in that science where scrupulous minuteness and a mechanical accuracy are indispensable. His chemical operations seemed to an unskilful observer to premise nothing but disasters. *He had blown himself up at Eton.* He had inadvertently swallowed some mineral poison [Hogg's 'I think arsenic' omitted and this entire sentence transposed and abridged from the succeeding paragraph in Hogg], which he declared had seriously injured his health, and from the effects of which he should never recover. His hands, his clothes, his books and his furniture were stained and covered by *medical* acids.   (Medwin, pp. 69–70)

In Medwin, Hogg's 'mineral' becomes 'medical'. Although Newby, the publishers, were careless in their production, the balance of probabilities is in favour of an alteration by Medwin rather than a typesetter's misreading of the manuscript. (Medwin wrote a looped 'd', hard to mistake for an 'n'.)[30] Medwin, we think, was either pedantically putting the record straight or telling the truth via an inadvertence. (In the hypothesis we put forward, Medwin's role is uncertain, and we do not claim to know whether he was a confidant of Shelley or not.) Of all Shelley's biographers he is the one who is most informative about Shelley's illnesses and involvement with medicine, and he later shows some acquaintance with 'medical acids'. One notes here an unbroken sequence of ideas. Medwin moves from Shelley's 'blowing himself up' at Eton to the permanent damage to his health there – and he has transposed Hogg's narrative to do this – to the 'medical' acids. There were several items in Shelley's rooms, following Hogg's description, which had a medical use, some of which involved acids; of course one gets no inkling of this from Hogg.

Shelley mixed ether 'with some other fluid' thus causing a combustion which burned his carpet. Ether is made by the action of an acid – usually sulphuric – upon alcohol. Lind, as Cavallo's book showed, prescribed it for pulmonary complaints, and so did other pneumatic practitioners. (Polidori, Byron's doctor, gave it to Shelley when the latter collapsed on a memorable occasion in 1816.)[31] Robert Thornton in a letter printed in Beddoes' *Considerations on . . . factitious Airs* suggested warming the ether in a teapot and breathing it in through the spout. Pearson, another of Beddoes' correspondents, advocated inhaling what sounds like the same mixture as Dr Lind's from a teacup or wine glass. (It is mentioned as one of Shelley's eccentricities by Hogg that he used his tea equipage for experiments, but this was normal practice among pneumatic practitioners when mixing up medicines.) The 'soda water, lemons, sugar and remains of an effervescing drink' which Hogg noticed in Shelley's room also point to self-medication of a fairly basic kind. Cavallo recommended for 'putrid fevers' effervescing alkaline and acid mixtures containing a 'solution of salt of tartar' to which lemon juice or dilute mineral acid was added just before drinking. He believed that this would be effective 'on account of the carbonic acid gas which they contain'.[32]

Shelley also had an electrical machine in his room, which he had owned from his Eton days. During the eighteenth century electricity became something of a panacea. By 1810 electricity was applied chiefly in cases of ophthalmia, pain relief, and tumours. It was regarded as a very useful aid in both venereal diseases. Like opium, it was supposed to assist the action of mercury. Hunter wrote that it caused venereal warts to drop off and that he had known 'several old gleets' which had previously 'baffled all common attempts' completely cured by it. It was also hoped that it might replace the use of bougies in strictures.[33] Small currents of electricity can cause the body to release the natural pain-killers called endorphins; endorphins are also released to the brain during sexual intercourse and can be artificially introduced by opium. It is interesting to find that in Shelley there is an association between electricity, love-making and 'nepenthe', an opiate. Perhaps Shelley (and other Romantics) intuited on the basis of their own experience a common factor which science has subsequently established.

There is, of course, no hint in Hogg that the apparatus might have served as a medical aid:

> He then proceeded, with much eagerness and enthusiasm, to show me the various instruments, especially the electrical apparatus; turning round the handle very rapidly, so that the fierce, crackling sparks flew forth; and presently standing upon the stool with glass feet, he begged me to work the machine until he was filled with the fluid, so that his long, wild locks bristled and stood on end.   (Wolfe, I, p. 56)

Hogg not only succeeds in making Shelley's behaviour look wildy eccentric, but even finds a correlative for it in the curious features of the machine itself. But the equipment was the same as that used for medication and Shelley's antics were no different from those exhibited by patients. Adam Walker's *A System of Familiar Philosophy*, the book of the lectures he gave at Eton, describes the following experiment:

> *How to increase the circulation of the blood, and the pulsation of the heart*
>
> Let the person stand on a stool with glass feet, and take hold of the conductor, or a chain connected with it; he will now become a part of the conductor himself; and when the machine is put in motion, he will feel his hair begin to spread out, and stand erect; his pulse will be accelerated; and if he should be bled in that situation, the blood would be propelled to an unusual distance, diverge into small drops, and each drop be seen luminous in the dark.   (pp. 381–2)

Walker then gives hints as to how this human battery can amaze and amuse his friends, but earlier in the lecture he lists many beneficial results of increasing the circulation of the blood by electricity. 'An electric shock has given tone to a flaccid fibre, has rendered palsied limbs plump . . . Insulated, and connected with the conductor, the pulsation has increased; by this mode both male and female obstructions have been removed. Sparks administered to chilblains have in assisting the circulation of the blood generally effected a cure.'[34]

Attempting to cure his sister's chilblains with electricity is exactly what Shelley did with his apparatus.[35] Undoubtedly he got the idea from Walker's lectures. Whether Shelley was using electricity at Oxford to cure a specific ailment or as a general tonic cannot of course be determined, but it is impossible that he should have been using it without a hope of improved health. Another of Shelley's 'eccentric' practices involving hair also had its origin in what was supposed to be a health measure. According to Hogg, he used to immerse his head in cold water several times a day and dry it by running his fingers through it, making the hair wilder still. De Quincey also used to have a daily cold hair-wash; what the rationale behind the practice was we have not discovered, but De Quincey regarded it as a prophylactic against toothache. It was the opium taken for a toothache contracted, he thought, by omission of this regimen, that began his famous addiction.[36]

It might be objected that if Shelley were debilitated while at Oxford one would have heard more of this, but in fact the dominant impression conveyed by Hogg is of manic energy and rude health – Shelley striding over the Oxfordshire countryside with duelling pistols, or discoursing energetically into the night. Even the description of his complexion, said to be 'of the purest red and white', enhances this impression. Gibbons Merle, meeting him in the spring of 1810 reported that 'the blush of health was on his cheek'. Actually, just as pale persons are often assumed to be sickly, so those with florid complexions tend to look healthier than they really are. Medwin, even meeting Shelley in Pisa in 1820 when he was emaciated and visibly ill, reported that his complexion never lost 'a freshness and purity'. Taking exercise could itself have been a health measure; the 'constitutional' – a long brisk walk – was to become a craze among Oxbridge students a generation later.[37] And Hogg's 'Percy Bysshe Shelley at Oxford' is, as mentioned previously, a piece of image-making; it is in Hogg's interest to forestall any suspicion that Shelley was dissipated. Hence the emphasis on purity and health. Even so, there are hints that all was not well.

To set against the Shelley of apparently limitless stamina, there is the Shelley who shivers with the cold and curls up so close to the fire that Hogg wonders that his head is not burned. When Shelley first invited Hogg to his rooms, he 'complained of his health and said that he was very unwell'. Hogg (typically) added that 'he did not appear to be affected by any disorder more serious than a slight aguish cold', though it was on that occasion that he noticed the remains of the effervescing drink.[38] As remarked in Chapter 1, one of the side effects of latent syphilis is that the patient is perpetually under par.

When discussing Shelley's diet of bread and fruit at Oxford, Hogg implied that he was debilitated:

As Shelley's health and strength were visibly augmented, if by accident he were obliged to accept a more generous diet than ordinary, and as his mind sometimes appeared to be exhausted by never-ending toil, I often blamed his abstinence and perpetual application.   (Wolfe, I, p. 86)

Hogg describes this diet of Shelley's as 'plain and simple as that of a hermit', though he was not yet a vegetarian. He ate fruit, vegetables and especially salads, pies, puddings, and drank tea ('cup after cup') and coffee. It sounds very like the 'low diet' or 'cooling regimen' that was invariably recommended to aid recovery from any sort of illness caused by dissipation. In fact Hogg later described Shelley's Oxford diet as 'cool'.[39] The contradictions that we have outlined above were, we think, forced on Hogg because he was never sure at any point whether demonic *furor*, angelic gentleness, ill-health, or hypochondria would best serve the purpose of doing justice to Shelley's memory.

So far this discussion has confined itself to Shelley's reputation at Oxford and what of his health record can be deduced. The arsenic and aquafortis point towards a syphilitic infection, real or supposed; this could have occurred at Eton, Oxford or during the summer vacation of 1810. It is not likely, however, that Shelley really contracted syphilis during the Oxford period. Even if treated he would not have been free of the transmissible form of the disease by the time he eloped with Harriet Westbrook in August 1811 and would have thus infected both her and their children. This certainly did not happen.[40]

However he might have gone through a period of fearing that he had the diseases like Erasmus Darwin's 'modest young men'. Brown doubted that he could have contracted gonorrhoea or even had a 'disagreeable experience with a prostitute', on the grounds that there is no record of his having been 'laid up' for any length of time and no trauma consistent with such an event during the Oxford period.[41] This seems a rather sanguine judgement in view of the variability concerning confinement for the venereal diseases and Shelley's behaviour during the Christmas vacation of 1810–11.

4

The mill-wheel's sound

It is well known that Shelley recognised in Scythrop, the hero of Peacock's *Nightmare Abbey*, a comic version of himself. One of the characteristics ascribed to Scythrop is his use of numbers for myth-making purposes. When he hears that only seven copies of his subversive book have been sold, he takes comfort in the following thought: 'Seven is a mystic number, and the omen is good. Let me find the seven purchasers of my seven copies, and they shall be the seven golden candlesticks with which I will illuminate the world.'[1]

In his poetry Shelley does exploit the possibilities offered by the magical associations of numbers and he finds correspondences in the world of fact. For instance, the 'seven bloodhounds' that follow Castlereagh in *The Mask of Anarchy* are seven because they intensify the apocalyptic and incantatory quality of the poem, since devils, vials of wrath and deadly sins come in sevens. But they are seven too because there were seven nations which in 1815 agreed with Britain to defer the abolition of the universal slave trade.[2] Without claiming that every number in Shelley is significant, Peacock can be said to have exaggerated for comic effect a noticeable tendency in him. There are signs that in Shelley's life this tendency extended to dates.

The twenty-seventh of December had some meaning for him. It appears in the preface to *Adonais* in Mary's 1839 edition of the *Poetical Works*. In the first (Pisan) edition Shelley had written 'John Keats died in Rome of a consumption, in his twenty-fourth year, on the — of — 1821.' The 1839 edition changed this to 'the 27th of December 1820'. At least three major variants in the 1839 text must have had the authorisation of Shelley himself,[3] and it is not likely that Mary would have made such a change unilaterally. Shelley also got Keats' age wrong: he died in his twenty-sixth year. In his own twenty-fourth year, though, Shelley had thought himself to be dying from consumption.

This date had appeared in *The Cenci* (1819) where the evil Count gloatingly announces the deaths of his two sons.

> For Rocco
> Was kneeling at the mass, with sixteen others,
> When the church fell and crushed him to a mummy,
> The rest escaped unhurt. Cristofano

> Was stabbed in error by a jealous man,
> Whilst she he loved was sleeping with his rival;
> All in the self-same hour of the same night;
> Which shows that Heaven has special care of me.
> I beg those friends who love me, that they mark
> The day a feast upon their calendars.
> It was the twenty-seventh of December.   (I, iii, 58–68)

The date is not found in Shelley's source. An explanation has been put forward: that it is the feast day of St John in the Christian calendar and St John's gospel contains the words 'God is Love'. While this is the kind of added irony which Shelley would have appreciated *after* having made a choice of the date, it does not seem to be a specific enough reference to have determined that choice. One also notes that Shelley added the details about the 'sixteen others' and that he changed the manner in which the two sons died. This increases the sense that some private meaning is embedded here.

Holmes, the first to see this likelihood, noted that the twenty-seventh of December 1818 was the date Shelley gave as the birthday of a baby girl, Elena Adelaide, whom he registered while at Naples as the child of Mary and himself. He also wrongly gave Mary's age as twenty-seven. Holmes' first theory was that Elena was Shelley's child by the maid and that he had also impregnated Claire, who was ill on that day. Her illness, he suggested, was really a miscarriage. Holmes now believes, more plausibly, that the maid is irrelevant, and that Elena was impulsively adopted to compensate Claire for this miscarriage.[4]

There is a case for re-examining whether Dowden's suggestion about Shelley's 'Neapolitan charge' is not after all nearest to the truth. Dowden speculated that she was consigned to Shelley by a highborn lady who, Shelley told Medwin, had been converted to anti-matrimonialism by reading *Queen Mab* and offered to become his mistress. Shelley declined, but she followed him to Naples in 1818 where she died. The lady has been written off as a Shelleyan fantasy, but apparently Claire saw her and knew her name.[5] This would not mean that Shelley was the father of her child. If the lady had been abandoned by a lover and died at Naples in childbirth, or suicide following therefrom, he might have felt responsible for raising the child in his own faith, and that in a sense it *was* his child, the child of his doctrines. A small pointer suggesting that she was the daughter of an aristocrat has so far been overlooked: 'Adelaide' means 'of noble birth'.

There is no proof, apart from the registration date, that the baby was born on the twenty-seventh. Shelley could have given her the birth date – near enough perhaps to the real one – in a darkly ironic mood, since the day had already been established in his private mythology as a day of ill omen. Presumably it was in the same spirit that he foisted this dying day onto Keats, whom he considered to have been killed by 'literary prostitutes'.[6] As we shall show later, December, and in particular *late* December, was a time that Shelley especially associated with sexual disaster, and that, in turn, was associated with the opposition of Christianity to 'free love'.

Shelley associated the calendar opposite, the twenty-seventh of June, with *rebirth*. An entry in Mary's journal for 4 August 1814 reads: 'Mary told me that this was my birthday; I thought it had been the 27th June.' The twenty-sixth of June was the day on which Mary made her protestation of love to Shelley in St Pancras churchyard over the grave of Mary Wollstonecraft. Cameron believes that the next day was the one on which Mary and Shelley first made love, though a mutual pledge would also fit the case.[7]

June figures in *Rosalind and Helen* as the month of his idealised union with Mary (957–87). There is also a beautiful fragment in which *late* June figures:

> It was a bright and cheerful afternoon
> Towards the end of the sunny month of June,
> When the north wind congregates in crowds
> The floating mountains of the silver clouds
> From the horizon, and the stainless sky
> Opens beyond them like eternity.
> All things rejoiced beneath the sun – the weeds,
> The river and the cornfields, and the reeds;
> And the new mown grass smelt pleasantly & lay
> An emblem of the mower –
> The willow leaves that glanced in the light breeze,
> And the firm foliage of the larger trees.

In editing Shelley's manuscripts, Mary conflated this fragment with another from a different notebook and called the result 'Summer and Winter'. It is virtually certain that Shelley never intended them to form a pair, but the point is that Mary thought they did. They are very similar in style; both have the quality which Shelley is often said to lack: the ability to create, like Keats, memorable, painterly, single lines.

> It was a winter such as when birds die
> In the deep forests & the fishes lie
> Stiffened in the transparent ice, which makes
> Even the mud and slime of the warm lakes
> A wrinkled clod as hard as brick, – and when,
> Among their children, comfortable men
> Gather about great fires, and yet feel cold –[8]

As linked by Mary, the two fragments could well have been called 'The Twenty-seventh of June and December'. That this creation had a private meaning for her is suggested by the following episode from *The Last Man*.

At the time that the plague strikes England, Verney, the narrator, is living at Windsor, and has the task of supporting afflicted families during the hard winter. 'I extended my ride towards Salt Hill', passing through a deserted Eton, reflecting 'Were those the fertile fields I loved – was that the interchange of gentle upland and cultivated dale, once covered with waving corn, diversified by stately trees, watered by the meandering Thames? One sheet of white covered it.' One frosty day he seeks what was formerly a favourite haunt, 'a little wood not far distant from Salt Hill. A bubbling spring prattles over stones on one side.' This spot, which has been identified as the Chalvey brook, 'had been a favourite resort of Adrian; it was secluded; and he often said that in boyhood, his happiest hours were spent here'.

The resemblance to the contrasting seasons of *Summer and Winter* is clear. There is even a dying bird in this scene, a frozen robin redbreast 'dropt from the frosty branches of the trees', which Verney rescues from seizure by a hawk and revives by placing it in his bosom: 'I cannot tell why I detail this trifling incident − ' he says, 'but the scene is still before me; the snow-clad fields seen through the silvered trunks of the beeches, − the brook, in days of happiness alive with sparkling waters, now choked by ice − . . . the dusky sky, drear cold, and unbroken silence.' In a burst of emotion, not fully justified by the context and bearing an obvious reference to Mary's self-image as Shelley's support in life as in death, Verney exclaims: 'But that my firm courage and cheerful exertions might shelter the dear mate, whom I chose in the spring of my life . . . while you derive from [my heart's] fostering care, comfort and hope, my struggles shall not cease.'[9]

It seems then, that these two dates were temporal points around which Mary and Shelley constructed a mythology, and we shall argue that they are associated with a recurring dream experience which underwent various mutations as Shelley struggled to objectify it in his art.

The image in *Summer and Winter* of men retreating to their fires occurs also in another wintry Shelleyan landscape. Holmes described it as 'one of the most peculiar records of composition that he ever made'.[10]

I have beheld scenes, with the intimate and unaccountable connection of which with the obscure parts of my own nature, I have been irresistibly impressed. I have beheld a scene which has produced no unusual effect on my thoughts. After the lapse of many years I have dreamed of this scene. It has hung on my memory; it has haunted my thoughts at intervals with the pertinacity of an object connected with human affections. I have visited this scene again. Neither the dream could be dissociated from the landscape, nor the landscape from the dream, nor feelings, such as neither singly could have awakened, from both. But the most remarkable event of this nature which ever occurred to me happened five years ago at Oxford. I was walking with a friend in the neighbourhood of that city engaged in earnest and interesting conversation. We suddenly turned the corner of a lane, and the view which its high banks and hedges had concealed presented itself. The view consisted of a windmill, standing in one among many plashy meadows, inclosed with stone walls; the irregular and broken ground between the wall and the road on which we stood; a long low hill behind the windmill, and a grey covering of uniform cloud spread over the evening sky. It was that season when the last leaf had just fallen from the scant and stunted ash. The scene surely was a common scene; the season and the hour little calculated to kindle lawless thought; it was a tame uninteresting assemblage of objects, such as would drive the imagination for refuge in serious and sober talk, to the evening fireside and the dessert of winter fruits and wine. The effect which it produced on me was not such as could have been expected. I suddenly remembered to have seen that exact scene in some dream of long — [11]

Shelley stopped, leaving the note 'Here I was obliged to leave off, overcome by thrilling horror.' Mary appended a footnote: 'I remember well his coming to me from writing it, pale and agitated, to seek refuge in conversation from the fearful emotions it excited. No man, as these fragments prove, had such keen sensations as Shelley. His nervous temperament was wound up by the delicacy of his health to an intense degree of sensibility.' Holmes was nonplussed, and, perceiving a sexual reference in the phrase 'lawless thought' and that the Oxford friend was Hogg, suggested that a recollection of passionate feelings for Hogg at Oxford in 1810 prompted this horror. But this cannot be right. Shelley says that the sight of the windmill in Hogg's company sparked off an anterior, horrific memory of a dream which had occurred long before he met Hogg. It is also clear – though Shelley is trying not to reveal too much – that the 'exact scene' in the 'dream of long . . .' and the landscape which has 'hung on his memory' and which he says he has revisited are connected in some way.

Shelley wrote this in late 1815. The previous April, he and Mary had run away for a few days to the Windmill Inn, Salt Hill, Slough, three miles from Eton. The record of this visit would have been lost but for the survival of some letters which Mary wrote to Hogg from that address, for the relevant pages were torn out of her journal. One presumes that the Slough area is the one he revisited and of which he dreamt after a long interval and which continued to haunt him. It is also the setting of the *Last Man* passage.

The Windmill was the leading Slough inn on the London—Bath road. It had beautiful gardens of conifers which extended to the Chalvey brook; near these stood a windmill which gave the inn its name and was the survivor of a pair called 'The Two Sisters'. It was a 'tarred smock stage-and-fantail mill, with two floors of brickwork under the stage and three above'.[12] It is this windmill, which, we believe, figured in Shelley's dreams, and which interwove itself into the 'horror' of the Oxford mill.

Turning to Hogg's *Life* in search of a reference to the Oxford walk, one finds a story which bears the marks of Hogg's suppressions or inventiveness. He describes a long walk in the course of which the friends found themselves in an area apparently remote from all habitations and Shelley discovered a 'magic circle', a small winter garden with numerous evergreens. Suddenly he 'startled me by turning with astonishing rapidity and dashing though the bushes and the gap in the fence with the mysterious and whimsical agility of a kangaroo' and headed for home. 'I tried in vain to discover what object had scared him away.' Catching up, Hogg learned that his friend had caught a glimpse of a gentleman's house and taken alarm at his trespass in the latter's garden; Hogg put this down to Shelley's 'superior and highly sensitive delicacy' and 'modest confusion'.

That Shelley, heir to a baronetcy and broad acres, should have been terrified of trespassing on another gentleman's property makes no sense. Strangely, Hogg immediately launches into a discussion of Shelley's fastidiousness in sexual love, though he adds 'It is equally impossible to refuse to believe' (Hogg gets tangled in his double negatives) '. . . that he was never practically as blind, at the least, as men of ordinary talent. How sadly should we disparage the triumphs of Love were we to maintain that he is able to lead astray the senses of the vulgar alone!' In other words, for all his fastidiousness, Hogg is saying, Shelley has 'gone astray' in some way involving a matter of the heart. Fancifully, Shelley declares the garden to be Eden, paints in a 'glowing harangue' an imaginary portrait of its mistress, an 'ideal nymph', but says that he is incapable of finding it again. Then, changing his mind, he declares, 'the seclusion is too sweet, too holy, to be the theatre of ordinary love; the love of the sexes, however pure, still retains some taint of earthly grossness.' Accordingly he assigns the garden to the asexual care of 'two sisters'. This last detail further establishes the link with the Slough area; Shelley had seen a windmill which reminded him through an intermediary nightmare of the 'Two Sisters' mill, as the 'trim garden' of evergreens would have reminded him of the gardens belonging to the Windmill Inn.[13]

The only feature going against this identification of Shelley's account with Hogg's is that Shelley places the event in early November, at the fall of the ash leaf, whereas Hogg speaks of an intensely cold and frosty day in the 'heart of winter'. However, Hogg places the narrative before the Christmas vacation in his 1858 *Life*, nor would he have drawn the line at working up the wintriness of the day in order to enhance his story – it hinges on the astonishing admiration by Shelley of the garden amid such bleakness.[14]

Medwin, who took Shelley's views on dreams seriously and had conversations with him on the subject (he quoted the 'windmill' passage in his *Life*) was the author of *Sydney*, a fiction based on Shelley's 'Platonics' with Emilia Viviani at Pisa in 1821. The Shelleyan hero (an immoderate laudanum user) argues with the physician narrator that separation between mind and body is possible. As an example he gives this remarkable vision:

I had a sister. Of my affection for her I shall not speak. If ever there was an angel woman, it was Henrietta. We were at this very place [Florence]. She was then eighteen, and in the most perfect health. One night I dreamed that she was dead; that I was following her hearse; that a few miles from Leghorn, where is the Protestant Cemetery, we came to an inundation, which seemed to preclude the possibility of our reaching a bridge across the Arno. Not six months had elapsed when the first part of my dream was realized. She died. Now hear the second. During that melancholy pilgrimage I recognized the features of the scene as it appeared in my vision. The wide inlet of the Val d'Arno, bounded by the pine forests that stretch along the coast; the stone bridge with its three arches, the colour of the water in the inundation; in fact, all the details of the picture corresponded exactly. Now, if the landscape did not come to me – which is absurd – I must have gone to it . . . does it not establish an entire separation of my body from my soul?[15]

Medwin had very little inventiveness; other details of the story are fairly easy to unravel and the wording often echoes his own account in his 1847 *Life*. While the extract must be approached with caution, there can be little doubt that it is a thinly veiled record of a dream actually recounted by Shelley, and the evidence suggests that this is the 'windmill dream', transposed by Medwin to an Italian landscape. The windmill and the walls, the hedge and the plashy meadows correspond to Medwin's bridge, line of pines, and inundation. 'Henrietta' is Harriet Grove, who was eighteen in 1809–10, and who was described by Medwin as an incomparable woman, a 'Madonna of Raphael'.[16] 'Sister' stands for 'cousin' and her death in the dream is realised in her subsequent loss. This interpretation, incidentally, sheds some light on a curious phrase that Shelley used about her in a letter to Hogg in January 1811: 'She is lost to me for ever – she is married, married to a clod of earth, she will become as insensible herself, all those fine capabilities will moulder.'[17] Harriet was at the time neither married, betrothed to, nor even, to judge by her diary, particularly intimate with her future husband William Helyar. What Shelley seems to mean is that Harriet has abandoned her ideals and has lost her spiritual qualities; she has thus fallen in love with Death, not with another man.

The figure of the corpse of the beloved is a recurrent one in Shelley's poetry and appears as early as in the trashy Gothic of *Victor and Cazire*. A particularly gruesome example is found in *Laon and Cythna*. The lovers, brother and sister, are brutally separated by religious tyranny. Laon, the hero, is tortured in a curious construction, a huge hollow column. He is taken up a 'steep and dark and narrow stair' to the top, and then is thrust outside onto a platform, bound, and tortured by thirst and fever. (It is from this ordeal that he is rescued by the figure of the hermit identified as Dr Lind.) At the climax of his ordeal, he loses his sense of objective reality; an experience occurs which, he says as he recounts it, may or may not have been a dream. Four corpses are hung from the frieze of the platform. Leaning over the platform into the void, crazed with hunger, he sees the decayed body of a dead woman, 'lank and cold and blue'. As he presses his lips to the corpse's cheek it seems to him that Cythna's ghost inhabits it, that it has turned to life and that he has eaten of its now apparently warm flesh (*L. & C.*, 1216–1350).

Linking this 'thrilling horror' to *Sydney* and the 'windmill dream' one sees that the column is in fact a transformation of a windmill. The Eton mill was a common stage-and-fantail one, that is, it had a platform leading out from the top chamber which partly supported the fan-tail and onto which the miller could step when the fan-tail needed adjusting. This sequence represents another attempt of Shelley to solve an artistic problem – how to make a 'tame uninteresting assemblage of objects' transmit the horror they had for him. A windmill does not in itself carry fearful associations; most people would regard it as a useful piece of machinery and a provider of bread.

There is another poem in which a symbolic union with a hanging corpse figures. In it the windmill appears as a gibbet, thus linking private horror with social concerns. The poem is 'Zeinab and Kathema', to which we alluded in Chapter 3, and which we said showed the influence of Sir William Jones. Jones, in his essay 'On the Poetry of Eastern Nations', outlines the dominant motifs of Oriental poetry. One of them is the paradise garden: 'There is a valley indeed to the north of Indostan called Cashmir which . . . is a perfect garden, exceedingly fruitful, and watered by a thousand rivulets.' (This figures later in Shelley's poetry as a beautiful valley in the Indian Caucasus, supposed site of the Garden of Eden and location of the Earthly Paradise.) Jones describes the opening of a typical Eastern love poem. The poet usually bewails 'the sudden departure of his mistress, Haida, Maia, Zeineb, Azza and describes her beauty, comparing her to a wanton fawn'. He then asks others to help look for her and declares his intention of finding her though his path lie through a wilderness.[18] The situation resembles the opening of 'Zeinab and Kathema', which also concerns loss and search. Kathema is discovered on the sands trying to obtain a passage to England, whither Zeinab has been abducted. It has been assumed that Shelley derived the name 'Zeinab' from Southey's *Thalaba*, but in that poem she is a mother, not a lost love; as so frequently occurs in Shelley, there has been a confluence of sources, Southey's poem determining the spelling and choice of name out of the four offered by Jones. Cameron gave 'Zeinab and Kathema' the date of June or July of 1811, when Shelley read Sidney Owenson's *The Missionary* twice, once at Field Place and again at Cwm Elan, the Welsh estate belonging to his cousin, and 'thought strangely'.[19] Like *The Missionary*, 'Zeinab and Kathema' has a Cashmire setting. Cameron's dating is supported by the poem's appearance in the *Esdaile Notebook*. It belongs to a group of four, all of which have the theme of a death wish, and which originally were the last in the book. The third of these, 'The Retrospect', looks back to Shelley's state of mind in the summer of 1811 when, by his own account, he had experienced something like a nervous breakdown. 'Zeinab and Kathema', the second of the group, may offer a further perspective on this breakdown, for Shelley in 1811 was very affected by Southey's *Don Espriella's Letters*, in which the latter described seeing a gibbet at Staines. On the other hand, there are indications that 'Zeinab and Kathema' may have been composed in the spring of 1812, following a reading of James Lawrence's *Empire of the Nairs*. This contains the theme of an idyllic Indian community contrasted with a corrupt English one, discussions about prostitution, and a scene in which the heroine is bound to the headless, putrefying corpse of her lover. Gibbets were also on Shelley's mind in April 1812.[20]

Cameron felt that the raggedness of a number of lines in 'Zeinab and Kathema' bore signs of 'violent emotional involvement' with the subject matter rather than the incompetence of immaturity, and he noticed Shelley's increased politicisation. The poem concerns an Indian youth whose love has been snatched away by Christian missionaries. Its main action takes place on a bitterly cold December evening. This parallels Shelley's situation in December 1810 when his letters to Hogg burst out in vituperations against Christianity for alienating from him the affections of Harriet Grove. In late December, he wrote to Hogg, he had 'followed her' and made a 'vain effort' to win her back.

Kathema on the sands recollects his life in the Vale of Cashmire. These recollections are not altogether happy; he remembers 'life's unveiling morn with all its bliss and care' and 'Passion so prompt to blight, so strong to save'. Zeinab's love has given him 'life and freedom' and mingled joy with pain. But 'just as the veil of hope began to fall / The Christian murderers over-ran the plain', snatching her away. Tracing her to contemporary England, Kathema seeks her through an earthly inferno, where the dominant images are of crippled and mentally deranged *young* men:

> Unquiet death and premature decay,
> Youth tottering on the crutches of old age,
> And, ere the noon of manhood's riper day,
> Pangs that no art of medicine can assuage,
> Madness and passion ever mingling flames,
> And souls that well become such miserable frames.   (103–8)

The young are the victims of the Napoleonic wars; one reason that they are on crutches is that they have lost their limbs. But in the last lines of the poem Shelley sums up the world which Christian morality has created: 'A universe of horror and decay, / Gibbets, disease, and wars, and hearts as hard as they'. The young are also tottering on crutches because they are syphilitic victims – and the entire verse could refer to that social scourge alone. It is related to war, because war has always been the means whereby the venereal diseases are most rapidly spread. (On this subject more will be said in Chapter 8.) It is important for the effect of the poem that the reader should relate to one another the gibbets, disease, war and hard hearts.

On a dark December evening, weak with 'cold and unappeased hunger', Kathema finds a gibbet on a wild heath (manuscript cancellations suggest that originally this was to be a city).[21] Hanging by a chain from it and swinging in the moonlight is a dark-haired 'dead and naked female form', its facial bones 'half mouldered' – Zeinab's.

> Yes! in those orbs once bright with life and love
>   Now full-fed worms bask in unnatural light:
> That neck on which his eyes were wont to rove
>   In rapture, changed by putrefaction's blight,

Now rusts the ponderous links that creak beneath
Its weight and turns to life the frightful sport of death.   (145–50)

She has turned to prostitution and crime as a result of her abduction, becoming a 'Comet, horrible and bright / Which wild careers awhile then sinks in dark-red night'. The comet image suggests both her wild career as a criminal and her role as the spreader of pestilence – a role traditionally attributed to comets. Twining the rusting gibbet chains around his neck, Kathema hangs himself.

The poem is, among other things, a mythopoeic rendering of the creation of a prostitute class through Christian morality and could be entitled 'The Fall of Woman'. The beloved is the prostitute because for Shelley as for Blake 'Every harlot was a virgin once'; the prostitute is an innocent woman who has 'followed the impulses of unerring nature' and been criminalised by the infamy and scorn with which society treats her 'error'. The moral of the poem is the same as that expressed in a note to *Queen Mab* (1813) – 'Even love is sold':

Society avenges herself on the criminals of her own creation [prostitutes] ... Young men, excluded by the fanatical idea of chastity from the society of modest and accomplished women, associate with these vicious and miserable beings, destroying thereby all those exquisite and delicate sensibilities whose existence cold-hearted worldlings have denied; annihilating all genuine passion, and debasing that to a selfish feeling which is the excess of generosity and devotedness. Their body and mind alike crumble to a hideous wreck of humanity.   (Hutchinson, p. 808)

Kathema seeks his innocent love and finds a dead prostitute instead. The image of the young man placing his neck into the chains binding a dead prostitute, his former love, is an emblem of his intercourse with a prostitute, 'diseased and insensible', when sexual fulfilment with an amiable woman is denied him. The emblem is made more specific by the detail of the putrefaction transferred from one neck to another through the chain; entwined necks are used elsewhere in Shelley as a symbol of mating.[22] The act of love has become a means of transmitting disease; the 'sport of death' is not merely the swinging corpse but also the hideous union. The poem was called 'romantic ghastliness' by Dowden, which is a good way of drawing its sting and abstracting the situation from social reality. It is obscene, in the strictly Shelleyan sense: 'I should consider obscenity to consist in a capability of associating disgusting images with the act of the sexual instinct.'[23] The power felt by Cameron lies in Shelley's ability to suggest these images while veiling them in the idiom of Gothic terror writing. One begins too, to understand better what Shelley meant when he assured Hookham that some of the later Esdaile poems had the merit of conveying a meaning in every word.

Shelley's intention is polemical. Unlike the harlot in the 'Even love is sold' note, who, society insists, is a 'tame slave' who 'must make no reprisals',[24] Zeinab in her revenge becomes a real criminal and Kathema is given a high-minded motive for enchaining himself to the corpse: 'My love! I will be like to thee, / A mouldering carcase or a seraph blest / With thee corruption's prey, or Heaven's happy guest' (154–6), as young men in 'Even love is sold' consort with prostitutes under the compulsion of an 'excess of generosity and devotedness'. Kathema hopes that the death of his body will bring about the release of his soul and union with Zeinab's spirit, but the poem's total mood is of hopelessness, shot through with anger. Its rhetorical strategy is to use suicidal self-degradation to discredit Christianity. The nobler the souls of the lovers and the more repulsive their fate, the greater the fury aroused against the 'codes of fraud and woe' that have brought them to this dread pass. Thus victory is snatched from dissolution's void.

Shelley used several sources for 'Even love is sold' – Trotter, James Lawrence's *Empire of the Nairs*, Godwin's *Political Justice* and Mary Wollstonecraft's *Vindication of the Rights of Women*. In conflating them, he frequently changed the emphases and added his own ideas, all the time heightening the stress on prostitution as the most horrible result of marriage and its resultant disease as the worst effect of prostitution. When he wrote congratulating James Lawrence on *The Empire of the Nairs* he professed himself to have long been aware of the evils of marriage, thanks to Mary Wollstonecraft: 'But I had been dull enough not to perceive the greatest argument against it, until developed in the "Nairs", viz., prostitution both *legal* and *illegal*.'[25] This illustrates well Shelley's propensity to deflect the thrust of an author's work in the direction of his own concerns. Lawrence listed six reasons for the abolition of marriage, of which the creation of prostitution was one, but he laid more stress on the hatred and suspicion which arises between the sexes when Love is fettered. For him, the worst result of chastity which drives the young Briton into 'low intrigues and vulgar connections' with prostitutes – whom he calls 'courtesans' – is a decline in refinement of manners. 'Wherever the women are prudes, the men will be drunkards.' He makes no mention of venereal disease, an even more striking omission when he actually describes the wretched life of a prostitute. For Lawrence, the prostitute risks dying of starvation in an attic. For Shelley, her death is owed to that disease to which she is 'irrecoverably doomed'. Similarly, Trotter says of syphilis that 'hideous deformity of body' is a frequent result in the disease's later stages. Shelley has heightened the sense of total decrepitude and added the detail about the mind's decay. At the same time, if accused of an abnormal interest in the subject, he could have claimed with a superficial plausibility that he was merely repeating other authorities.[26]

'Zeinab and Kathema' and 'Even love is sold' demonstrate how deeply Shelley's hatred of Christianity was bound up with contemporary standpoints regarding sexual morality. This must not be exaggerated. His chief charges against Judæo-Christianity were its creation of the fear of Hell, fanaticism and, above all, its faith in the qualities of 'omnipotence, and benevolence, and equity in the Author of an Universe, where evil and good are inextricably entangled'.[27] Yet the sexual question is important, and can be clearly seen in the series of letters which he wrote to Hogg during the Christmas vacation of 1810–11.

Shelley was later to tell Hogg that he looked back with regret to 'our happy evenings at Oxford, and with wonder at the hopes which in the excess of my madness I there encouraged'.[28] Yet these letters show that he was far from happy during the vacation; after the end of his engagement to Harriet, Elizabeth used to watch him 'narrowly' and accompany him in his walks with his dog and his gun – presumably in case he attempted suicide. Charles Grove, who was with him for part of the Christmas holidays, said that after the spring of 1810 he never saw Shelley without some care on his mind.[29]

Shelley was at Field Place from 10 December 1810 to 20 January 1811. During this period he had much to agitate him. He was trying to curb Hogg's passion for his sister Elizabeth, with whom Hogg had fallen in love through Shelley's description, and encouraging him to publish. His religious position was shifting from deism to atheism. Running through the correspondence of this period are other themes: he is very worried about selfishness; his misery over the loss of Harriet is being converted into a fury against Christianity. It is also clear that he is not being candid with Hogg.

On 20 December he writes 'Oh! I burn with impatience for the moment of Xtianity's dissolution, it has injured me; I swear on the altar of perjured love to revenge myself on the hated cause of the effect which *even now* I cannot help deploring. – Indeed I think it is to the benefit of society to destroy the opinions which *can* annihilate the dearest of its ties.' He repeated this idea more emphatically in a letter of 3 January: 'I am convinced too that it [Christianity] is of great disservice to society that it encourages prejudice which strikes at the root of the dearest the tenderest of its ties.' Some two years later he was to pinpoint this thought: 'Chastity is a monkish and evangelical superstition . . . it strikes at the root of all domestic happiness.'[30]

Letters to Hogg become more agitated and disordered. On 26 December he hints that he dare not be completely candid with Hogg; he is speaking in riddles. (Unfortunately this is one of the letters which Hogg patently doctored and for which no original has been found.)[31] On 28 December he promises to come to London to see Hogg on 31 December but fails to do so. Instead he makes an 'inefficient effort', and reproaches Hogg: 'Why do you my happy friend tell me of perfection in love, is she not gone and yet *I* breathe *I* live – but adieu to egoism; I am sick to death of the name of self.' Following this his letters get wilder. 'Never will I forgive Christianity! It is the only point on which I allow myself to encourage revenge . . . It has injured me, she is no longer mine, she abhors me as a Deist, as what *she* was before. Oh Christianity when I pardon this last this severest of thy persecutitions [sic] may God (if there be a God) blast me!' At the same time as declaring his intention to dedicate his life to Christianity's destruction he wishes that he could expire in the struggle to repress his feelings. 'Is suicide wrong?' He sleeps with a loaded pistol and poison. His letter of 6 January hints that the 'inefficient effort' was an attempt to win back Harriet: 'She is gone, she is lost to me forever, forever. There is a mystery which I dare not to clear up, it is the only point on which I will be reserved to you. — I have tried the methods you recommend. I followed her, I would have followed her to the end of the earth but — .'[32] Most biographers doubt that Shelley actually paid a visit to Fern in Dorset, where Harriet was living, a journey of about 115 miles from Field Place and involving several changes of coach, though the time scale between 28 December and 1 January (when he was back at Field Place) makes it just possible. On the other hand he could have started out and given up after reaching London — or Southampton, if he went by the shorter Lewes—Bath road.[33] Shelley moves in agitation from one subject to another. He explains this as dizziness owing to tiredness from 'pacing a churchyard' most of the night. He wishes he could be with Hogg at Oxford (11 January) but cannot return for a fortnight 'for reasons which I will tell you at meeting'. The next day he writes that he is 'rather confused'. He fears that 'in consequence of a fever they will not allow me to come on the 26 [to Oxford], but I will.'[34]

These elements — a period which includes the twenty-seventh of December, a self-destructive mood, a sweetheart lost to Christianity, a claim to have endeavoured to win her back — all have counterparts in a poem in which loss of a beloved is linked to a symbolic sexual fall. While this does not prove a case it does undermine the view that Shelley was in no mood to have visited a prostitute during the Oxford period. That Shelley was simultaneously writing to Hogg vehemently declaring his belief in 'the spirit of universal imperishable love' does not go against this. If he had acted against his principles — and his suicide attempts show that he was capable of doing so — he was not likely to confess this openly in a letter to Hogg, whom he did not completely trust and whose libertine creed he resisted, both in these letters and later in his review of Hogg's novel *Prince Alexy Haimatoff*; indeed, there would be good reason for wishing to maintain his self-respect by insisting on the separation of matter and spirit and the purity of his sexual ethics. Nor does his espousal of a social mission — to annihilate Christianity — preclude behaviour that would have imperilled the realisation of that mission. The letters show that this vow was muddled with a wish to give up the struggle and die. Moreover the theme of the victim of tyranny who injures himself further in the struggle to destroy the demon and whose attempts to discredit his enemy become in themselves a means of self-punishment and self-contempt is so recurrent in Shelley's work that this consideration hardly amounts to evidence against the hypothesis.

This is a convenient point at which to show how Shelley sought to use the image of the mill in his later poetry. Images of grinding and crushing by heavy weights, stones and hard hearts are extremely frequent. So is the iron work of a machine, notably chains and wheels, which of course also form part of a windmill. We consider that the prevalence of these is only partially accounted for by the fact that they are 'natural' metaphors for tyranny and misery. That Shelley was obsessively haunted by windmills and their associations is indicated by some references in *Nightmare Abbey*. The book is a *mélange* of elements suggested by the life of Shelley and his circle, and defies all attempts to slap on it the title of *roman à clef*. However, as we have shown, Peacock's work does sometimes contain recondite local and private allusions.

Scythrop Glowry lives in a tower which commands a view of another tower 'ruinous and full of owls', a garden terrace grown over with ivy and a few amphibious weeds and 'a fine monotony of fens and windmills'.[35] The landscape is an image of Scythrop's mind; contemplating it has filled him with thick-coming fancies and pessimism. His father seeks to make a prudent match for him, reminding him of his duties as heir to this barren estate. But Scythrop has already fallen in love with his cousin, Marionetta. 'What are dykes and windmills to Marionetta?' he replies. 'And what, sir, is love to a windmill? Not grist, I am certain' answers his common-sensical father. The message that Peacock intended to convey to Shelley (and *Nightmare Abbey* was written as a serious pill to purge melancholy, an alternative way of looking at the world) was, in our view, that once windmills are seen simply as windmills they lose their power to terrify as symbols. At the end of the book, Scythrop, unable to decide between two women, resolves to commit suicide with a pistol 'on Thursday evening, twenty-five minutes past seven', but sends his servant, Crow, up to the turret as a watchman, whence the latter sends this message 'The wind blows, and the windmills turn, but I see nothing coming.'[36] One notes that 27 December 1810 was a Thursday: Thursday is the only day of the week mentioned in the book; the point is that Peacock wishes to rectify the habit of mind that allows the mythic associations of particular days (Thursday is the day of Jupiter, the tyrant of *Prometheus Unbound*) to invade everyday life.

Despite the fact that Scythrop loses both women the book ends in a victory for common sense – of a sort. Scythrop calls for Madeira and lives, but wine for him is not what it usually is in Peacock, a stimulus to conviviality. He drinks alone. For all its verve and high spirits, *Nightmare Abbey* is in the end a sombre book. Scythrop has fallen back on an anodyne akin to laudanum, like it a ruby-coloured liquor, and one which Peacock later described as Shelley's refuge from intolerable pain.

Mary, too, seems to have tried to exorcise the associations of Shelley's fearful dream with playfulness. When Shelley was embroiling himself with Lord Eldon and the Chancery suit for custody of his children, she wrote a supportive letter, indulging the fancy that Shelley had been a Don Quixote in a former existence, '& fought with Windmills'.[37] She is not implying that Shelley was crazy, though the Don Quixote parallel was suggested by their reading of Cervantes' novel the previous December. She is drawing on the Romantic reading of Quixote – a Spenserian knight genuinely born out of his time and passing for a fool in a world without ideals. At the same time she is cheering him up: the giants – Lord Eldon and Eliza Westbrook – will prove to be merely windmills. They did not, of course, and Eldon became for Shelley a focus for his feelings about a monstrous social engine designed to create human misery.[38] He used much the same language about Eldon's judgement as he had about Christianity: that it had destroyed the dearest and tenderest of ties. Among his charges against Eldon was his 'complicity with lust and hate'.[39] Peacock wrote that the two subjects on which he heard Shelley express himself with the greatest abhorrence were his persecutions at Eton and Lord Eldon.[40] How Shelley expressed his abhorrence in poetry was to use an image that was accessible to everyone but at the same time charged with his private associations.

> Next came Fraud, and he had on,
> Like Eldon, an ermined gown;
> His big tears, for he wept well,
> Turned to mill-stones as they fell.
>
> And the little children, who
> Round his feet played to and fro,
> Thinking every tear a gem
> Had their brains knocked out by them.   (*The Mask of Anarchy*, 14–21)

By isolating the millstones from the mill Shelley has excluded all ideas of a mill's productivity. The concept of 'weeping millstones' he found in Shakespeare.[41] In his savage *Swellfoot the Tyrant* (1820) they appear again, associated with a building, the 'swineherd's tower' – the Chancery court, and perhaps also the Tower of London. Like the column in *Laon and Cythna* this is a transmutation of the mill. (The 'smock' mill is a variant of the 'tower' mill.) Dakry – Eldon – ascends to the garret (the chamber at the top of the mill which opens out onto the fan-stage), and harangues the 'pigs' – the people of Britain. He weeps at his own eloquence:

> And every tear turned to a mill-stone, which
> Brained many a gaping Pig, and there was made
> A slough of blood and brains upon the place,
> Greased with the pounded bacon; round and round
> The mill-stones rolled, ploughing the pavement up,
> And hurling Sucking-Pigs into the air,
> With dust and stones.   (I, i, 334–40)

Here one finds millstones, tower and the word 'slough', the site of the 'Two

Sisters' mill. 'Slough' comes in naturally enough, pigs being the subject, yet Shelley was capable of inserting riddles into a poem ('Passion'), and it is quite possible that the association of ideas was conscious, and intended for Mary's appreciation. Possibly, too, the madman's black tower in *Julian and Maddalo* (the Slough mill was tarred, which was common), the 'deformed and dreary pile' which Maddalo declares to be the 'emblem and the sign' of our mortality, is another variant of the mill, as is the recurrent imagery of the earth's shadow, the 'cone of night', a magnified projection of a cone-shaped black mill-tower.

The last appearance of the mill is in a fragmentary poem as haunting as the last song of Schubert's *Winterreise* cycle, 'The Organ Grinder'. It almost certainly started life as a personal lyric, but we believe that Shelley intended to place it in a context which would have related its concerns to public ones.

> A widow bird sate mourning for her love
> Upon a wintry bough;
> The frozen wind crept on above,
> The freezing stream below.
>
> There was no leaf upon the forest bare,
> No flower upon the ground,
> And little motion in the air
> Except the mill-wheel's sound.[42]

When Shelley wrote this, he was beginning to adopt the poetical persona of Ariel, who for disobeying the witch goddess Sycorax had been imprisoned in a cloven pine, and whose groans, before his deliverance by Prospero, were vented 'as fast as mill-wheels strike'.[43] It could hardly have escaped Shelley that Ariel's imprisonment lasted for twelve years. 'A Widow Bird' was written either late in 1821 or early in 1822. In the winter of 1821, 27 December fell upon a Thursday.

5

Love and vegetables 1811–13

After Shelley's expulsion from Oxford, he lived for seven weeks in London, mostly at 15 Poland Street. Holmes believes that it was either then or at Oxford that he had his first sexual experience.[1] Certainly Shelley was very lonely there before returning to Field Place, and Hogg seems to have perceived that he was in a dangerous mood. He gave an account of a conversation he had with Timothy Shelley on 7 April in which the latter is supposed to have asked Hogg: 'Tell me what you think I ought to do with my poor boy? He is rather wild, is he not?' 'Yes, rather,' Hogg replied, and advised marriage as a cure. Even Rossetti had to admit that this did tend to support Thornton Hunt's claim, but concluded on the basis of Hogg's stress on Shelley's purity at Oxford that he must have meant 'hare-brained' or 'unmanageable'.[2] We have already shown that Hogg should be read with reservations on this point, and in any case this anecdote comes in the portion which was written specially for the 1858 *Life* when he began to be less discreet.

Without wishing to take issue with Holmes on this matter, which, like the time scales that we have tentatively mapped out to support our hypothesis, cannot be proved and which in any case need not contradict Holmes, we would draw attention to an experience which was sufficiently disturbing for Shelley to have talked about it years later to Medwin. This was his visiting of the wards of St Bartholomew's. Medwin said of this that Shelley

became familiar with death in all its forms, – 'a lazar house, it was', – I have heard him quote the passage –

> wherein were laid
> Numbers of all diseased – all maladies
> Of ghastly spasm, or racking torture – qualms
> Of heart-sick agony – all feverish kinds;
> and where
>
> Despair
> Tended the sick, busiest from couch to couch.[3]

At that time St Bartholomew's had a well-known Lock ward, which was the eighteenth- and early nineteenth-century equivalent of the in-patient V.D. clinic.[4] If Shelley literally became familiar with death in all the forms that St Bartholomew's could demonstrate, then he would actually have seen syphilitic patients in the last stages of the disease. (In chapter 6 we shall give an additional reason for believing that he did.) Knowing Shelley's tendency to allegorise his life and to see himself as in some sense re-enacting the experience of characters in literature and history – his adoption of the nickname of Spenser's 'Elfin Knight' is an example – one cannot help noticing the following circumstance: Shelley was quoting from that passage in *Paradise Lost* where, after the Fall, Adam is shown a vision of the world as it will be in the future, and realises for the first time the terrible and enduring consequences of his action.

Shelley attended the lectures of Abernethy, Hunter's heir. It has been suggested that it was then that he first met William Lawrence, Abernethy's protégé and the demonstrator at his lectures. Lawrence, atheist and radical, was later to become Shelley's doctor.[5]

The medical profession was in a transitional state at this time. Then as now, it was split between the branches of medicine and surgery, though not quite in the same way that it is today. Roughly speaking, physicians had traditionally been in charge of internal diseases and the administering of medicine. They had been the more prestigious branch, and had looked down on the surgeons, whose provinces were 'cutting', blood-letting, wounds and skin conditions. In practice such division of labour could not be rigidly maintained, but training continued to reflect it. During the latter part of the eighteenth century the situation changed fast; surgery became a profession for a gentleman; the absurd and dangerous consequences, moreover, of supposing that diseases could be divided into two kinds were becoming manifest.[6] Nowhere was this more true than in the case of syphilis, which was the province of both surgeon and physician, and often instanced when deploring this artificial division.

Foremost among those attempting to break down divisions in the medical profession was Abernethy. His entire cast of mind was, like Shelley's, a synthesising one. He also tried to dissolve yet another artificial division – that between constitutional and local diseases. His lecture courses always began with the most basic axiom, from which his entire theory and practice ensued: that the whole body sympathises with its parts. The world was permeated by a 'subtile substance of a quickly powerfully mobile nature' which 'appears to be the life of the world'. Whether this fluid should be called electricity, magnetism or 'caloric' he left to scientists to determine. The conduit for this fluid through the human body was of course the nervous system, which was thus the means whereby one part of the body sympathised with another. Abernethy was not being original – he was using a key-word of his age. 'Sympathy', which of course is originally a medical term, was the point at which Romantic medicine touched on physics, chemistry, philanthropy and literature; 'sympathy' related man to nature and man to man.[7]

From this first axiom, Abernethy derived another: that 'local disease, injury or irritation may affect the whole system, and conversely . . . disturbance of the whole system may affect any part'. This in turn opened the way for another of his key principles: the reciprocal influence between the nervous system and the digestive organs. One of his favourite illustrations was *teething*, in which local irritation to teeth and gums is accompanied by diarrhoea and nervous disorder (convulsions). Since the digestive organs were almost invariably involved, whatever the original cause of the disease, it followed that treatment should always take account of diet. This was true even of cancer, a position which seems less eccentric now than it would have done twenty years ago.[8]

Shelley picked up a smattering of medical jargon either from Abernethy's lectures or from hob-nobbing with Abernethian doctors.[9] But there were some more marked and immediate effects of his brief encounter with the medical profession: in the summer of 1811 he started to refer to his 'nervous' illness in letters to Miss Hitchener (the school mistress 'soul sister' who was finally expelled from his household as 'The Brown Demon'), and later to Godwin.[10] Today such talk inevitably conveys the idea that Shelley was being something of a *malade imaginaire*, and one must agree that even in his day the medical concept of 'sympathetic affection' was perceived to offer wonderful opportunities for the hypochondriac. But 'the passions of the mind' were only one of the ascribed causes of 'nervous illness'. Trotter, for instance, wrote 'if any fact more than another has been proved in my own practice, it is that spiritous liquors and all wines with tea, opium, mercurial courses and the sexual indiscretions are the chief causes of the acquired predisposition that equally engenders both [gout and nervous] diseases.'[11]

It must not be supposed that Shelley meant his correspondents to think that his illness was all in the mind. He means, following Aberbethy, that his digestive organs are involved, and probably refers to the abdominal spasms which figured so largely in his later medical history. Chief among the examples of nervous illnesses given by Trotter are 'cramps and spasms' which particularly affect the 'stomach, bowels, kidnies, ureters and bladder'.[12] At the same time Shelley means that he does not know the cause of his illness; it manifests itself as digestive disorders, but the real seat of the disease might be elsewhere.

From London Shelley went back to Field Place and thence to Cwm Elan. Of this period Cameron has written 'What probably happened is that the shattering events of the previous months . . . all of which he had suppressed by keeping continually active – burst upon him at once amid the quiet of Cwm Elan.' A year later he recalled his feelings at the time in 'The Retrospect':[13]

> Then would I stretch my languid frame
> Beneath the wild-wood's gloomiest shade
> And try to quench the ceaseless flame
> That on my withered vitals preyed;

> Would close mine eyes and dream I were
> On some remote and friendless plain,
> And long to leave existence there
> If with it I might leave the pain
> That with a finger cold and lean
> Wrote madness on my withering mien.   (39–48)

What had reduced him to this suicidal state was not 'broken vows', not absence of sympathy and not a life-disdaining pride. Yet each factor has disposed him towards death: 'each one sorrow gave / New graces to the narrow grave' (63–4). Cameron took this to mean that it was not a single cause but all three causes in combination which produced this feeling. But this is a rather strained interpretation of 'new graces'. The more natural meaning of the words is that there was an antecedent cause not mentioned, to which the other causes were contributory. In other words, Shelley *already* had a reason, *not* stated, for wishing to be dead, something which preyed on his 'withered vitals' and which threatened him with madness.

Shelley describes in detail the three factors which, according to him, are not the anterior cause of his wish to die, thus deflecting the reader's attention from this loose end. Forty-five lines later he picks it up again, invoking the meadows of the Welsh landscape which he declares to have been witnesses of 'The sunken eye, the withering mien / Sad traces of the unuttered pain / That froze my heart and burned my brain'. By then the reader assumes that Shelley must mean that the woe is 'unuttered' only in the sense that he kept quiet about it in 1811, and not that he is still keeping the reader in the dark. If this seems excessively artful of Shelley, one should recall the letter to Hookham where he states that the later *Esdaile* poems are simultaneously obscure and pregnant with meaning.[14]

Most commentators have assumed that the 'withering mien' is merely an outward projection of a state of inner despair, like the pale cheek of the knight in 'La Belle Dame sans Merci'. Of course the speaker in the poem is despairing. But Shelley's poetic idiom – like Gray's in 'Ode on a Distant Prospect of Eton College'[15] – could also be describing physical illness.

Five years later Dr John Polidori took notes on a conversation he had had with Shelley about his marriage with Harriet in August 1811. 'Gone through much misery, thinking he was dying; married a girl for the mere sake of letting her have the jointure that would accrue to her; recovered; found he could not agree.'[16] Obviously Shelley was giving a rationalisation of how he squared his marriage to Harriet with his anti-matrimonialism, though this does not mean that his account was untrue, merely that it was not the whole story.[17] Polidori's testimony is consistent too with Shelley's letter to Godwin in which he says that his life until his marriage had been a series of illnesses, and with a sentence from Mary's 'Note on *Queen Mab*'. Mary was evidently going by what Shelley had told her of his state of mind during the period 1811–12: 'Ill-health made him believe that a year or two was all he had of life.'[18]

It seems, therefore, that Shelley was probably giving a true account to Polidori of what he had thought at the time. The evasiveness of 'The Retrospect' then begins to make sense. The anterior sorrow, not mentioned, would be the conviction that he is facing the prospect of a lingering death from the results of an unmentionable complaint, whose horror is mingled with feelings of self-loathing.

A leading venereologist of the period 1800–20 gives a vivid description of the terrors attendant on anyone who had ever had syphilis:

There are some patients who have adopted an unfortunate opinion, that the syphilitic virus when it has once penetrated into the body can never be totally eradicated. They believe in consequence, that a person who has the misfortune to be infected can never consider himself as radically cured; and this absurd opinion makes them very unhappy . . . Such persons are truly deserving of pity, and it is but just to examine their situation exactly, and bestow the most attentive care upon them; for can there be a more dreadful state than that of being perpetually a prey to such terrors?[19]

The venereologist quoted above, it should be noted, is not denying that syphilis can remain in the body for years. In fact his book reveals a knowledge that it very often did.[20] Much of Shelley's behaviour from this point until the end of his life can be explained by his being not 'perpetually' but at certain times a 'prey to such terrors' and, even when able to lay them to rest, overshadowed by illness resulting from having permanently damaged his health, whether through doctors' prescriptions or self-medication. Syphilitics, even when they believed themselves to have been cured (Schubert is an example) suffered from a conviction that they could never be healthy again.[21] At the same time there is a strong impulse in Shelley to surmount self-blame and to place responsibility either on a corrupt society or on something inherent in the nature of things.

Yet 'The Retrospect' is ostensibly a poem designed to show that Shelley has undergone a transformation since his marriage to Harriet, his 'purer mind' as he called her in the dedication to *Queen Mab*. She has given him 'friendship and passion' and beamed a 'reviving ray' upon him. Yet even as the poem asserts this, it betrays a fear that his present state may be only a momentary respite:

> The gloomiest retrospects that bind
> With crowns of thorn the bleeding mind,
> The prospects of most doubtful hue
> That rise on Fancy's shuddering view
> Are gilt by the reviving ray
> Which thou hast flung upon my day.   (163–8)

In another poem, probably written about the same time,[22] the hopes that Harriet will restore him to physical as well as moral health are more overt:

> Will not thy glowing cheek,
> Glowing with soft suffusion, rest on mine
> And breathe magnetic sweetness thro' the frame
> Of my corporeal nature, thro' the soul
> Now knit with these fine fibres?   (*Esdaile*, p. 85, 13–17)

He is appealing to her to transmit her health to him though the electric current that flows from her body. (Ten years later, Shelley was again to use 'animal magnetism' as a medicine, also with a beautiful woman, Jane Williams, as the agent.) As well as her love, 'The thirst for action, and the impassioned thought / Prolong my being' (64–5). The word 'prolong' suggests hope clouded by fear of an early death which he intends to avert.

Love-as-healing is one of the stock metaphors of erotic poetry and the language of mystical experience. But for Shelley love is not merely the cure for the absence of love or for soul sickness; love, when it is not the passion of 'feverish, false desire' but combined with sacred and sympathetic friendship, is a medicine worthy to be included in a physician's armamentarium. 'I have found these sort of beings [beautiful ladies and friends] especially the former, of infinite service in the maladies to which I am subject' he wrote only half-jokingly to Thomas Medwin in 1820. 'I have no doubt, if it could be supposed that anyone would neglect to employ such a medicine, that the best physicians would prescribe them, although they have been entered in no pharmacopoeia.' Nor was Shelley the only Romantic poet to cherish the idea that love could stimulate the body's auto-immune system. Witness Keats' outburst when departing for Italy to die, leaving Fanny Brawne forever, 'Oh Brown, I should have had her when I was in health, and I should have remained well.'[23]

It is true that love figures in 'no pharmacopoeia', but Erasmus Darwin in *Zoonomia* had included 'the passions of love, joy and anger' as one of his six categories of *Incitantia* or Brunonian 'stimulating remedies'. The other five correspond rather well with procedures actually followed by Shelley. They are: 1. Intoxicants and narcotics; 2. Heat in the form of warm baths and electricity; 3. Ether and essential oils; 4. Oxygen gas – there is no record of his using this, but oxygenated medicines were supposed to have the same effect; 5. Labour, play, agitation, friction as with a brush, swinging and horse riding. The warm baths and horse riding will appear in Chapter 7. Shelley was reading Darwin – whether his botanical poetry, his medical work or both is not clear – at Cwm Elan in July 1811.[24]

Amid the complex of emotions which culminated in Shelley's elopement with Harriet, it looks as though one must make room for the following: a desire to enjoy some happiness before he died, if he were to die young, and a hope that he would not die young after all but have his health restored by virtuous love. Perhaps his love for Harriet was bound up with a diminution of his 'nervous symptoms' – which would not be very surprising – and an improvement in health seemed to him to be both the effect and the evidence of genuine passion.

Of course Shelley must be convicted of irresponsibility if he married suspecting his body to be harbouring syphilis. This would be true irrespective of the facts of the matter. But 'harbouring syphilis' does not mean 'infectious'. Whether he had real syphilis, 'pseudosyphilis' or a gonorrhoeal infection it must have been arrested at an early stage. Under such circumstances a man in 1811 could regard himself as damaged in health but not infectious to his wife. He may have been given some kind of assurance by John Grove, with whom he was in correspondence until the latter moved to Edinburgh, when his letters were destroyed.[25] Doctors were extremely ignorant about the transmission of both venereal diseases and allowed marital relations between infected partners to continue in a way that, by today's standards, is amazing. (The same is true of other diseases. In 1815 Shelley and Mary conceived a child despite the fact that Shelley had been told six weeks before that he was rapidly dying of a consumption.) Hunter actually believed that a husband with gonorrhoea was not infectious provided that he took care with his personal hygiene.[26] At the same time, it was thought that a man could pass on effects of his 'intemperance', even if not infectious, by 'seminal weakness', and that his children would be constitutionally enfeebled. 'Fornication perpetuates a disease, which may be accounted one of the sorest maladies of human natures, and the effects of which are said to visit the constitution of even distant generations' said *Nicholson's British Encyclopaedia*, a work which Shelley ordered in 1812, and which there is some evidence that he knew from as early as January 1811.[27] It was believed that the reason for the enervation of the Portuguese was that syphilis was endemic among them. By constant exposure to it they had, as a nation, acquired a certain immunity to its worst ravages, at a cost of degeneracy.[28]

Shelley's first child, Ianthe, was not born until twenty-two months after his marriage – a long interval for those days. During this interval he became extremely interested in taking practical steps to improve his health. There are indications that this was in turn bound up with concern for the future well-being of his family.

Some time late in 1811, Shelley wrote a now lost letter to Gibbons Merle outlining his plans for adopting and educating 'two young persons of not more than four or five years of age; and should prefer females, as they are usually more precocious than males'. Shelley had many singular schemes in life and was always attracted to the idea of adopting children. Nevertheless it is an odd proposal to come from a newly married man and suggests that he was not expecting to have any children of his own in the immediate future. A month later he wrote again complaining of being 'much troubled with dyspeptic symptoms and . . . tormented by visions'.[29]

At Keswick he wrote to Hogg that he had made himself ill with the poison of cherry laurel (*prunus laurocerasus*) leaves, the active ingredient of which is prussic acid. This may have been a suicide attempt. In the last weeks of his life he was trying to obtain prussic acid in order to commit euthanasia if necessary.[30] The Hogg letter contains a declaration that it is his concern for Harriet's happiness which is keeping him alive – otherwise he might as well throw himself off a rock. However, the sentiment could just as easily indicate the reverse – that he had *not* attempted suicide. Secondly, he may have regarded the plant as an aid to poetic inspiration. He *was* writing poetry at this time, much of it centring round images of passion, poisonous plants and the uncertainty of his health. Thirdly, and most likely, he could have been trying to find an opium substitute. This last reason does not rule out the second: Shelley might have been attracted to laurel leaves feeling them to be a particularly poetical sort of cure. In Darwin's *The Loves of the Plants* he would have found the two functions – medicinal and inspirational – brought together in a footnote on the cherry laurel:

The Pythian priestess is supposed to have been made drunk with an infusion of laurel leaves when she delivered her oracles . . . the distilled water from laurel leaves is perhaps the most sudden poison we are acquainted with in this country . . . In a smaller dose it is said to produce intoxication. On this account there is reason to believe it acts in the same manner as opium and vinous spirit but that the dose is not so well ascertained.[31]

By *Zoonomia*, Darwin had become more confident that the drug could be safely used and gave the cherry laurel a prominent place among the intoxicating plants in his *Incitantia*. Trotter lists it as a narcotic drug along with opium.[32]

After the poisoning experience, Shelley started taking laudanum, but 'very unwillingly and reluctantly'. On 29 January, about ten days before setting off for his political mission in Ireland, he wrote: 'I hope to be compelled to [have] recourse to laudanum no more.' Letters of January and February of 1812 touch on Shelley's prospects for a family. He wrote to Miss Hitchener disabusing her of the idea that Harriet was pregnant, 'a piece of good fortune which I could not expect', but added 'I hope to have a large family of children.' He did not anticipate the coming of a 'little stranger' except 'at some distance' – 'years perhaps', according to Harriet. Miss Hitchener was most probably supposed to infer from this that his health did not permit him to consider beginning a family in the immediate future. A little over a month later, in Ireland, he became a vegetarian.[33]

It is impossible that Shelley's reasons for becoming a vegetarian were ethical alone, and that the hope of recovering his health did not affect this decision. Even assuming that he had not yet read those vegetarian writers who were to play so important a part in his thought during late 1812 and 1813, he would still have had his attention directed towards the importance of diet by his encounter with Abernethian doctors. Although not a vegetarian himself, indeed, if Hogg is to be believed, actually hostile to strict vegetarianism, Abernethy did mention it as a possibility in a passage which

urges readers to discover the diet best suited to the individual constitution.[34]

Diet did not have immediate good results. In June appears the first intimation
(from Harriet) of a plan to go to Italy for his health. (Shelley is sometimes
accused of devising this as a later excuse to escape from Godwin's importunities,
but Harriet's letter shows that the idea had been present in Shelley's mind years
before Godwin became a problem.) In July he ordered *Medical Extracts* and listed
medicine among the disciplines more profitable than the classics.[35]

This is the first medical book that Shelley is recorded as owning. Six
months later he was to place some large orders with his bookseller. He
wanted background reading for his first long poem *Queen Mab*; it seems also
that he wanted to build up a basic library. Among his orders were several
medical books: the works of Cabanis, French revolutionist and doctor, whose
Rapports contained much information about the nervous system, the relationship between physique and temperament, sex differentiation, aging and mental illness; *Zoonomia*; the works of the physiologist Spallanzani; Trotter's
View of the Nervous Temperament and *On Drunkenness*; two works of ancient
medicine, Hippocrates and Celsus.[36] To these may be added *Nicholson's
British Encyclopaedia* of which the sections on Pharmacy, Medicine, Surgery
and Midwifery provided generous amounts of medical information,
Theophrastus, one of the chief repositories of ancient medical botany, and
Plutarch whom he saw as an authority for vegetarianism. Other books, such
as Sir William Jones' works, had the odd medical article and he was alert to
the medical information to be culled from travel books such as Sir George
Mackenzie's on Iceland. There are other medical works that Shelley may be
presumed to have read during this period. In the vegetarian pamphlets that
he was to write he cited Dr William Lambe's *Reports on Cancer* and *On Constitutional Diseases*, Abernethy's *My Book*, Cheyne's *Essay on Health*, Joseph
Ritson's *Essay on the Abstinence from Animal Food*, and John Newton's *The
Return to Nature*.[37]

It is from his meeting with John Newton in November 1812 that Shelley's
proselytising vegetarianism dates. From Newton's book he drew many of the
arguments in his *A Vindication of Natural Diet*, the pamphlet which he probably began the same month. Newton, in turn, had derived them from Dr
William Lambe. Though not a doctor, Newton regarded *The Return to
Nature* principally as a work of medicine; he had himself found relief from
chronic asthma through vegetarianism and was anxious to impart to others
the knowledge of its benefits in a number of diseases.

Having told the reader that 'anyone descended from a long line of ancestors
who had lived as Dr Lambe would have us all live, could scarcely be liable
to contagion of any kind' since 'his frame would be an unfit receptacle for
this artificial poison', Newton exclaims, in what is one of his most surprising
and emphatic passages:

What a prospect does it open to mankind, should it be no irrational hope that the monster syphilis with all its gorgon terrors, may yet be driven from the earth. This scourge of the human race, respecting the origin of which there has been so much dispute, arose in all likelihood from an exacerbation of the arsenical state of the fluids produced about the year fifteen hundred by the heat of the southern climates on unhealthy bodies, which were unaccustomed to the ardent sunshine of South America. The afflicting malady appears to have first broken out among the Spaniards three centuries ago, when they acted in those regions that dreadful tragedy which will be an eternal stain upon our species; a refinement of cruelties which the conscious historian has been unable to veil, and for which no sufferings can atone – a scene of horror, that has called down from its heavenly mansion the spirit of Montezuma, to hover o'er the blood which long shall deluge the guilty peninsula.[38]

Nowhere else in the book does Newton look forward to the conquest of a disease with such enthusiasm or paint its terrors in such vivid colours. There is much else that is interesting about this passage, not least its mythologising of the sixteenth-century epidemic of syphilis and the atrocities of the Peninsula War into a tale of retribution for sins committed by the conquistadores upon the New World. We shall return to this theme in Chapters 6 and 8. For the present, we notice the attempt to explain the origin of the disease in terms not only of myth but of a scientific theory. According to this, arsenic was not the cure for but actually the cause of the disease.

Newton probably deduced his theory from Lambe's diatribe against arsenic:

Is this not the very daemon which for so many ages tortured mankind, and which, usurping the sensorium, has corrupted, under a thousand forms, both the mind and body? the evil spirit which has augmented the wants of man, while it has diminished his enjoyments? Which has exasperated the passions, inflamed the appetites, benumbed the senses and enfeebled the understanding? Which has converted his true form into a storehouse of diseases, has blasted the flower of his offspring, and has brought even the strongest of his name to an untimely grave?

(*On Constitutional Diseases*, p. 17)

Lambe had a dire warning for arsenic users and reading him must have confirmed Shelley's fear that he possessed only a limited life span:

Those who escape immediate destruction are frequently reserved only for a more lingering fate, and sink after an illness of a few months, or sometimes of two or three years. The constitution has less powers of restoration after suffering from arsenical poisoning than from others.   (p. 44)

It was because arsenic and other toxic substances productive of disease had been discovered in the water supply that Dr Lambe would allow his patients to drink only distilled water. Today with more exact data on the level of contamination in drinking water, and with the present controversy surrounding lead levels in the blood, one might commend such caution; in his day Lambe was a well-respected physician, not regarded as a crank.[39] Hogg, however, treated him as a figure of fun and has a ludicrous description of him embarking on an 'arsenic hunt', in an extemporised laboratory in his front parlour, luting his retorts with pipe-clay which he then wiped over his clothes so that 'he was barred and brindled all over with white stripes on a dark ground', and looked more Tiger than Lambe.[40]

Hogg's jokes, Peacock's novels, and, until recently, confidence in an age of technology have all encouraged one to join in the laughter at both Lambe and his followers. Yet Hogg was himself as serious a vegetarian as any at the time, and may even have been responsible for introducing Shelley to the Boinville circle of which Lambe and Newton were leading members. Notwithstanding his determination to present the vegetarians as cranks, even he makes it clear that they were taken seriously by open-minded members of the medical profession, among whom must have been William Lawrence. Hogg reported that medical people 'swarmed around' the 'meek followers of vegetable diet' who encouraged their attentions.[41]

Shelley's vegetarian writings have been ably defended, while at the same time their absurdities have been conceded, by several critics, notably Cameron, who pointed out that Shelley was being no more far-fetched than Rousseau when he affirmed his belief in the ability of vegetarianism to eliminate aggression. ('It is impossible had Buonaparte descended from a race of vegetable feeders that he would have had either the inclination or the power to ascend the throne of the Bourbons.') Justice has been done to the economic and moral force of his arguments. Rather than traverse that ground again, we will focus on Shelley's detailed attention to the conquest of disease, a theme from which his arguments never stray far. For instance, after the sentence about Napoleon quoted above, in which Shelley shows himself to be delightfully unaware that 'power' could be taken to mean physical strength, he continues 'The desire of tyranny could scarcely be excited by the individual, the power to tyrannise would certainly not be delegated by a society neither frenzied by inebriation nor rendered impotent and irrational by disease.'[42]

The story of Adam and Eve eating of the tree of evil, was, Shelley writes, an allegory founded in the reality of some great change in the conditions of life whereby man became dependent upon eating animal flesh. From this original deviation from 'rectitude and nature' flowed all subsequent diseases and crime. ('Crime is madness, madness is disease.') The myth of Prometheus, the first to 'apply fire to culinary purposes' records a similar event:

His vitals were devoured by the vulture of disease. It consumed his being in every shape of its loathsome and infinite variety, inducing the soul-quelling sinkings of premature and violent death. All vice rose from the ruins of healthful innocence. Tyranny, superstition, commerce, and inequality were then first known, when reason vainly attempted to guide the wanderings of exacerbated passion.

(*Prose*, pp. 82-3)

Clearly, animal flesh and the arousal of bad passions are closely allied. Shelley was later to transcend this interpretation of the myth, though he would keep the link between disease and Prometheus' sufferings.

Since all disease stems from meat-eating, 'there is no disease, bodily or mental, which adoption of vegetable diet and pure water has not infallibly mitigated, wherever the experiment has been fairly tried'. A reform in diet 'strikes at the root of the evil'. He does, however, sound a *caveat*; too much must not be expected of the system. 'The healthiest among us is not exempt from hereditary disease.' All that is claimed is that 'from the moment of the relinquishing all unnatural habits, no new disease is generated; and that the predisposition to hereditary maladies gradually perishes'. He enjoins the reader to make a fair trial: 'Reasoning is surely superfluous on a subject whose merits an experience of six months would set forever at rest.' It is perhaps significant that Ianthe was conceived just six months after Shelley's conversion.[43]

So far, Shelley has not mentioned venereal disease among maladies which will yield to the system, but his resounding peroration refers to it obliquely:

The elderly man, whose youth has been poisoned by intemperance, or who has lived with apparent moderation, and is afflicted with a variety of painful maladies, would find his account in a beneficial change produced without the risk of poisonous medicines. The mother, to whom the perpetual restlessness of disease and unaccountable deaths incident to her children are the causes of incurable unhappiness, would on this diet experience the satisfaction of beholding their perpetual healths and natural playfulness. The most valuable lives are daily destroyed by diseases that it is dangerous to palliate and impossible to cure by medicine. How much longer will man continue to pimp for the gluttony of Death, his most insidious, implacable, and eternal foe?   (*Prose*, pp. 89–90)

When Shelley reprinted this essay as a 'Note on *Queen Mab*' in May 1813 he inserted a passage which linked it to the 'Even love is sold' note and enabled him to strike a blow for other causes even at the risk of ruining his own point about vegetarianism attacking the root of all evil. He seems to have seen a possible conflict between his anti-matrimonialism, which held that marriage must be abolished if the institution of prostitution and its concomitant diseases were to wither away, and his dietary creed, which if followed would abolish the diseases, but leave the hated institution still standing. He therefore adopts a belt-and-braces approach:

It is true that mental and bodily derangement is attributable in part to other deviations from rectitude and nature than those which concern diet. The mistakes cherished by society respecting the connection of the sexes, whence the misery and diseases of unsatisfied celibacy, unenjoying prostitution, and the premature arrival of puberty, necessarily spring; the putrid atmosphere of crowded cities; the exhalations of chemical processes; the muffling of our bodies in superfluous apparel; the absurd treatment of infants: – all these and innumerable other causes contribute their mite to the mass of human evil.   (Hutchinson, pp. 827–8)

In February 1813, Shelley experienced a mysterious night attack at Tanyrallt, the house where he was staying at Tremadoc, which caused him to flee Wales. Scholars are still not agreed whether he had a hallucination, staged the attack himself as an excuse to flee the area without paying his debts, or was genuinely set upon because he had made powerful enemies. Thornton Hunt said that when he first knew Shelley he suffered from 'physical causes' which he (Hunt) then 'only in part understood' – evidently alluding to the 'college' experiences. At the same time he was definite that Shelley traced this physical suffering to the attack at Tanyrallt and that he ascribed the painful seizures that were to become so marked a feature of his later years to 'the pressure of the assassin's knee upon him in the struggle'.[44] As Hunt elsewhere points to what he regarded as a characteristic habit of Shelley's mind – to 'discard the minor considerations', he seems to have been of the opinion that Shelley mentioned only what he saw as the chief reason for the seizures and disregarded the possibility that there might be other factors involved. (Both Hunts were very resistant to the idea that Shelley was capable of telling a lie.) A blow to the kidneys sustained during the Tanyrallt attack (staged or genuine) might well have been an important contributory cause to Shelley's 'spasms' later in life, but in view of the earlier history of 'nervous illness' it is unlikely to have been the only one, and the possibility does remain that Shelley was being disingenuous.

The Shelleys eventually returned to London in April. There in the following June their daughter Ianthe was born. Of the succeeding period in 1813 Hogg was to write that it was 'auspicious, beneficial and happy'.[45] Yet he tells a number of anecdotes which point to continuing health worries, all of them involving diet.

Shelley, says Hogg, became inordinately fond of panada. He would pour boiling water on bread, flavour it with sugar and nutmeg, and relish the resulting pap. 'Why,' said Hogg, 'you lap it up as greedily as the Valkyries in Scandinavian story lap up the blood of the slain!' 'Aye!', shouted Shelley with grim delight, 'I lap up the blood of the slain!'[46]

Hogg suggests that Shelley was so taken with this phrase that he ate panada in order to say it, and implied that it was a rather exotic dish. Shelley, he says, was taught to make it by a French lady. In fact it was a stock item of invalid food. Sir William Jones, for instance, in a letter quoted in the 1807 edition of his Life and Works, wrote of the nation 'being fed like a consumptive patient, with chicken-broth and panada'. Panada figured in the 'cooling regimen' prescribed to hasten recovery in gonorrhoea.[47] That Shelley enjoyed an excuse to indulge bloodthirsty feelings with impunity has the ring of truth, but it seems an unconvincingly feeble reason for making panada.

Another peculiarity Hogg dwells on is his love for 'common pudding raisins', which he would buy in 'some mean little shop', put in his waistcoat pocket and consume with dry bread. Again, this particular combination, though thoroughly sanctioned by Newton, who took dried fruits and toast for breakfast, had a strong connection with actual treatment of disease, and was not merely a prophylactic. Erasmus Darwin in *Zoonomia* recommended a 'diet of raisins and bread' along with 'Bath or Buxton water drank in large quantities' for leprosy. Bread alone or with raisins was the standard diet allowed to patients taking the 'sweating cure' for syphilis with guaiacum, according to Ulrich von Hutten. Jar raisins and biscuits were among Astruc's remedies for gleet.[48]

Strangest of Hogg's stories relating to Shelley's diet is the following:

Shelley used to pick the turpentine off fir-trees, and eat it with a relish, or in walking through a pine wood he would apply his tongue to a larch, and lick it as it oozed in a liquid state from the bark. I never met with any one else who had the same taste. I have expostulated with him on the subject, and of course in vain; and I once related to him a little apologue, which was rather more efficacious. I was once at a ball, a very pleasant one it was, and we were all dancing away merrily, but we were obliged to desist, for all on a sudden the fiddlers stopped in the middle of a tune; we told them to play on, but they answered, 'We cannot; we cannot go on with our music, because that rascal, Bysshe, has eaten up all our rosin!' Sometimes when he was creeping stealthily up to a fir-tree, that he might lick it, my fable of the poet and the fiddler would come into his head, and he would turn aside laughing. The broken up ball, the interrupted country dance, the enraged musicians, the whole scene appeared in a moment before his eyes.   (Wolfe, II, pp. 49–50)

Here the Divine Poet conducts himself in truly mad style, yet even this behaviour has a more down-to-earth explanation. Turpentine was a medicine and, according to Woodville's *Medical Botany*, was derived chiefly from the two trees mentioned by Hogg: the Scots pine – then commonly called a fir – and the Common White Larch Tree (*pinus larix*), which yielded the best 'terebinthina larigna or Venice Turpentine'. Sometimes the name 'turpentine' was restricted to the essential oil extracted from the oozings, but the *Pharmacopeia Londiniensis* of 1809 included the resin as well. Taken by mouth, its main use was to banish gleets of all kinds whether caused by gonorrhoea or not. It was not recommended for urethritis as it could provoke inflammation, but could be given 'for cleansing the urinary passages, for healing internal ulcerations in general and in laxities of the seminal and uterine vessels'. It also helped to discharge mucous matter from the kidneys and ureters and lent an odour of violets to the urine. Turpentines and resins were recommended in gonorrhoeal complications by Boerhaave, Cullen, Darwin, Hunter and many other famous doctors whose works were the standard text books of their own and of Shelley's day.[49] Hogg seems to be warning Shelley against indiscriminate ad-hoc self-medication.

Shelley was fascinated by pine trees from an early age and would 'scrawl in his school-books – a habit he always continued – rude drawings of pines and cedars, in memory of those on the lawns of his native home'.[50] The pine forest (as opposed to the single pine) frequently has in his poetry associations of soothing and balm to hurt minds and bodies. The hermit who restores Laon to health takes him, after applying a potion to his lips, to a cove edged with 'ebon pines'. In 'The Pine Forest of the Cascine' (1822) Shelley experiences a rare moment of calm. (As there are also roots 'like serpents interlaced' in this Eden, one remembers that after the Fall Adam called for the cedars and pines to cover him.) Without discounting the emotional associations of pine trees, we would suggest that the fact that Shelley actually imbibed their medicinal gum and did not merely *walk* in the forests has some bearing on the appearance of the image in his poetry.

In October 1813 Shelley went to Edinburgh where he possibly met again his cousin John Grove. Although the Brazilian friend he made there, Bernardino Pereira, cordially detested the profession of medicine, they discussed vegetarianism and Shelley converted him to the creed. Pereira wrote a laudatory sonnet on *Queen Mab* in Portuguese, of which Peacock later remembered two lines.[51] It was there, the editors of *Shelley and his Circle* believe, that Shelley wrote a second vegetarian tract, *Essay on the Vegetable System of Diet*.

The latter has variously been described as 'a more perceptive treatment' than the *Vindication* and 'one of his most peculiar and crochety productions'.[52] Both views contain a measure of truth; the second essay is both more coherently thought out *and* revelatory of personal anxieties. It is less sanguine. The use of animal foods is stated definitely to be one of several unnatural habits which produce disease. An adoption of vegetarianism would only 'in some degree' diminish the accumulation of disease in the world. The essay also emphasises the threat of disease to 'those of the strictest individual temperance' and the unborn. 'Beings to whom nations have turned anxiously as to their expected saviours, whom families have regarded as their only comfort and support' are 'abruptly swept away by that mysterious principle which visits the sins of the fathers on the children.' (*Prose*, p. 93) Here Shelley is recalling a passage from Trotter's *View of the Nervous Temperament*:

The sexual appetite is prematurely excited by the numerous hordes of unfortunate women that are permitted to range our streets. The powers of procreation are thus weakened beyond recovery, before the body has acquired its full stability and growth and the vigor of constitution as well as the faculties of mind are shook to the very centre. When such debilitated beings have progeny, the sins of the father are visited upon the children, and they appear a race of invalids from their birth.

(p. 43)

Trotter does not specify how the body is weakened; clearly his description could include masturbation and nocturnal emissions – both believed to lead to 'seminal weakness' – as well as actual resort to the 'unfortunate women'.

It must have been about this time that Ianthe developed a tumour which, according to Hogg, was excised in the New Year.[53] Shelley's marriage, too, was about to break up. With hindsight one can see a pattern of mounting anxiety centred around ill-health in this beneficial and happy year. What happened next marked the climax of this anxiety. It is widely regarded as the most absurdly bizarre event of his life.

6

Elephantiasis

One day – Hogg tells the story – Shelley, in a crowded stage coach, sat opposite a drowsy old woman with very thick legs. He imagined that she was suffering from elephantiasis and 'presently began to discover unequivocal symptoms of the fearful contagion' in himself. Not satisfied with such discoveries, he began to suspect his friends, and many others, of being infected too.

His imagination was so much disturbed, that he was perpetually examining his own skin, and feeling and looking at that of others. One evening, during the access of his fancied disorder, when many young ladies were standing up for a country dance, he caused a wonderful consternation amongst these charming creatures by walking slowly along the row of girls and curiously surveying them, placing his eyes close to their necks and bosoms, and feeling their breasts and bare arms, in order to ascertain whether any of the fair ones had taken the horrible disease.

(Wolfe, II, p. 39)

Fearing that his friend had caught elephantiasis, he would 'stealthily' open the front of Hogg's shirt 'several times a day' and inspect his skin, 'his distressed mien plainly signifying that he was not by any means satisfied with the state of my health'. This examining of his friends and total strangers lasted for several weeks; then the strange fancy 'was forgotten as suddenly as it had been taken up'. (p. 40) Hogg 'never saw him so thoroughly unhappy as he was, whilst he continued under the influence of this strange and unaccountable impression'. Coming from Hogg, who had been with Shelley after the Harriet Grove crisis and his expulsion from Oxford, this is saying much.

Peacock, reviewing Hogg, gives a more sober account. The old woman's legs are not mentioned; she is merely 'fat'. He omits Shelley's impression that others as well as himself were suffering from the disease, and implies that Hogg had got this bit of the story wrong. When Shelley scrutinised others, it was only to reassure himself that such 'symptoms' as he discovered in his own person were likewise present in a healthy constitution. 'He would draw the skin of his own hands, arms and neck very tight, and if he discovered any deviation from smoothness, he would seize the person next to him, and endeavour by a corresponding pressure to see if any corresponding deviation existed.' He did examine 'young ladies in an evening party', but the process 'was as instantaneous as a flash of lightning'. As the days rolled on, 'the delusion died away' (Wolfe, II, p. 326).

85

Peacock plays down the incident, as can be seen when the two friends recall the methods they employed to rid Shelley of his obsession. Hogg made the most of the opportunity to ridicule him:

His female friends tried to laugh him out of his preposterous whim, bantered him and inquired how he came to find out that his fair neighbour had such thick legs? He did not relish, or even understand their jests, but sighed deeply. By the advice of his friends, he was prevailed upon to consult a skilful and experienced surgeon, and submitted to a minute and careful examination: the surgeon of course assured him, that no signs or trace of elephantiasis could be discerned. He further informed him, that the disease is excessively rare, almost unknown, in this part of the world; that it is not infectious, and that a person really afflicted by it could not bear to travel in a crowded stage-coach. Bysshe shook his head, sighed still more deeply, and was more thoroughly convinced than ever, that he was the victim of a cruel and incurable disease.   (p. 39)

Peacock's laughter is gentler; his remedy simple and surprisingly effective. Remembering Shelley's love of Lucretius, he quoted to him the following lines from *De Rerum Natura*:

> Est elephas morbus, qui propter flumina Nili
> Gignitur Aegypto in media, *neque praeterea usquam.*

'The elephantiasis is a disease bred in the heart of Egypt, on the banks of the Nile, and nowhere else.' Shelley told Peacock that these verses were 'the greatest comfort he had' (p. 326). A fear which could be alleviated merely by quoting a few lines of Latin could not, one is bound to feel, have been entertained very seriously in the first place.

There is a third version of this delusion. It does not support the details given by Peacock and Hogg, nor is it definitely an eye-witness account, but it does confirm that Shelley claimed to have elephantiasis. Madame Octavia Gatayes, one of Newton's daughters and a little girl at the time, later communicated this account to Dowden:

As he was sitting in an armchair talking to my father and mother, he suddenly slipped down to the ground, twisting about like an eel. 'What is the matter?' cried my mother. In his most impressive tone Shelley answered, 'I have the elephantiasis.'
                                                                   (Dowden, I, p. 373)

There is no other single anecdote that is more embarrassing to those wishing to take Shelley seriously. Some sympathetic critics have justifiably omitted it from their accounts. Others, such as Holmes, emphasise Shelley's overwrought state at the time, attributable to his financial worries and the imminent break-up of his marriage, while at the same time suggesting that he was behaving like a 'pet eccentric, a drawing-room poet indulging himself, a charade'. Sylva Norman charitably ascribed his behaviour to his special kind of creativity: 'Comic, ridiculous, poignant, it is something that happens to defenseless genius in a body-haunted mind.' Carl Grabo, forgetting for a moment the ludicrous circumstances in which Shelley acquired his notion and the monstrous nature of the disease in question, wrote 'This is a familiar form of fear, common in varying degrees to everyone.' Many are content simply to agree with Peacock that this was one of Shelley's 'most extraordinary delusions'.[1]

The anecdote has been crucial in establishing Hogg's essential credibility. Hogg, it is generally agreed, is incurably farcical and insensitive, and, on occasion, actually deceitful. Yet here his least plausible story is corroborated independently by two others. It follows that Hogg must be a more reliable memoirist than appears from his style; if only one can separate this style from the facts which he relates, one can accept other improbable anecdotes as authentic as well. Such seems to have been the chain of reasoning employed by White when discussing this episode.[2] But of course, in accepting the authenticity of Hogg's particulars, one is drawn into assent to his general portrait, and to such conclusions as 'Shelley lived and moved and had his being under the absolute despotic empire of a vivid fervid fancy.'[3] The episode has had its repercussions on the estimate of Shelley's poetry, and is probably the first biographical instance that occurs when one considers Arnold's 'The man Shelley, in very truth, is not entirely sane, and Shelley's poetry is not entirely sane either.' An ingenious modern variant is the following: 'It is hardly surprising that when Shelley suffered from a delusive illness, it was elephantiasis. His poetry suffered from it too.'[4]

The argument that we are about to put forward maintains that Shelley's delusion was not unaccountable, that it certainly was not funny – though his friends' attempts to dispel it with humour are understandable – and that there was even rationality in it.

The story is the only major one in which Peacock diverges from Hogg in material particulars without drawing attention to the fact. Elsewhere, where narratives overlapped, Peacock either courteously corrected Hogg, as in the matter of whether Shelley loved Ianthe, or, more often, quoted directly from him and added a gloss or amplification. It seems as if Peacock was taking care here to correct Hogg as unobtrusively as possible. His corrections also tend in a certain direction – towards omitting the sexual element from Hogg's description. To appreciate the extent of this one must look at details which Peacock omitted. After describing Shelley's survey of the young ladies, Hogg continued:

He proceeded with so much gravity and seriousness, and his looks were so woebegone, that they did not resist, or resent, the extraordinary liberties, but looked terrified, and as if they were about to undergo some severe surgical operation at his hands. Their partners were standing opposite in silent and angry amazement, unable to decide in what way the strange manipulations were to be taken; yet nobody interrupted his heartbroken handlings, which seemed, from his dejected air, to be preparatory to cutting his own throat. At last the lady of the house perceived what the young philosopher was about, and by assuring him that not one of the young ladies, as she had herself ascertained, had been infected, and, with gentle expostulations, induced him to desist and suffer the dancing to continue without further examinations.

(Wolfe, II, pp. 39–40)

A little further on he wrote:

Nor did females escape his curious scrutiny, nor were they particularly solicitous to avoid it; so impressive were the solemnity and gravity, and the profound melancholy of his fear-stricken and awe-inspiring aspect, that there could be no doubt of the innocence and purity of his intentions: and if he had proceeded to more private examinations and more delicate investigations, the young ladies would unquestionably have submitted themselves with reverence to his researches, which, however, were arrested by authority in the case of the fair dancers before they had greatly exceeded the bounds of decorum.   (p. 40)

The tone is unmistakable; it is a pastiche of the elegantly pornographic 'novel of gallantry'. Hogg is describing the scene as if it were a brothel and Shelley a terrified client, torn between fear and lust.[5] If one were to substitute 'syphilis' for 'elephantiasis' this would become quite plain. The 'lady of the house' who 'had herself ascertained' that none of the 'fair ones' had been infected by the horrible disease would be the proprietress, and the 'country dance' would be both a euphemism and a bawdy pun. (Shelley himself had used the word 'dance' with sexual overtones in his 'Old Killjoy' verse letter to Graham.) Finally, his dissatisfaction with Hogg's health would be explained by his fear that his friend, as a frequenter of brothels, was taking the same risks. By opening Hogg's shirt, he would be looking for the rash which tends to appear first on the chest.

Of course Hogg is saying that, in spite of appearances to the contrary, Shelley was really pure in heart and that it was respectable women whom he was treating in this unseemly way. Yet the more he insists on this, the more forcibly one is reminded of the comparison. There is an over-emphasis on Shelley's modesty. He is said not even to understand what his female friends are implying when they ask how he happened to know that the old woman had such thick legs. That the Shelley who could make an arch remark about Coney Street was incapable of understanding such a mild indelicacy passes belief.

It is possible that Hogg, following his methods elsewhere, is importing the memory of a visit to a brothel paid by Shelley and himself during the Poland Street period, perhaps, when Shelley was 'rather wild'. (Hogg switches very abruptly after the elephantiasis story to one belonging to April 1811, involving someone identifiable as Charles Grove in an amorous entanglement with a mad woman.) But let us assume that the occasion is just what it purports to be: an innocent dance at, most probably, the Newtons'. (Mrs Newton, as an ethical nudist, might well have been able to convince Shelley that she had 'nakedized' with the young ladies and thus could vouch for their health.) One still has to account for the association of ideas that has prompted Hogg to link Shelley's behaviour with brothel imagery.

There is another divergence between Hogg's account and Peacock's. In contrast to Medwin's, Hogg's memory for dates and times was good and often very precise. It is unlikely that he should have forgotten when Shelley suffered this extraordinary terror. Yet he placed the episode in one of the most inconsequential and digressive portions of his narrative; readers (Holmes, for instance) have been led to suppose that it occurred some time during the summer of 1813. Peacock, on the other hand, is quite definite: it happened 'about the end of 1813' and he seems to think the chronology important. The significance of this becomes clearer when one realises that Hogg, by editing letters, had made it appear that Peacock got to know Shelley only in the autumn of 1813, and had effectively barred him from speaking with authority on any matter relating to Shelley previous to this. (One of the unobtrusive aims of Peacock's *Memoir* was to set the record straight on this point without exposing Hogg.)[6] Since Hogg is more likely to be duplicitous than Peacock, one can assume that the latter's date was the correct one, but also that Hogg had some purpose in his vagueness. That purpose was to obscure, with the minimum of downright lying, any connection between Shelley's terror and the breakdown of his marriage. Peacock, who maintained strenuously that there had been no hint of a separation between Shelley and Harriet before June 1814, could afford to be accurate about the date.

There is another feature that Hogg has obfuscated by his method of narration. He says much about thickened skin and mentions 'a whole Iliad of woes', but it is the grotesque detail of the huge swollen legs that is the most prominent. No biographer, to our knowledge, has ever asked the question 'What disease was the subject of Shelley's delusion?', probably because everyone has taken it for granted that this was what is now known as *filiaris*, a disease of the lymph caused by a minute worm and accompanied by swelling of the affected leg. In Shelley's day its Latin name was *Elephantiasis Arabum*, and it was familiarly known as Barbadoes Leg or 'elephantiasis of the moderns'. There *are* accompanying skin complaints. Bateman's *A Practical Textbook of Cutaneous Diseases*, published in 1813 and the most up-to-date manual at the time, observed that the skin becomes 'dark, rough and sometimes scaly'; sometimes the disease appears on the 'arms, and even on the ears, breasts, scrotum etc.'[7]

Yet there is one detail which makes it certain that this was not the disease which Shelley supposed himself to have contracted. This is Peacock's Lucretian quotation. For by 'elephas' Lucretius did not mean *filiaris*, of which Roman and Greek classical writers were ignorant, or at any rate were believed to have been ignorant in the early nineteenth century.[8] He is referring to a disease which in 1813 had the Latin name of *Elephantiasis Graecorum*, elephantiasis of the ancients, or, simply, leprosy. Today this is classified as one of the forms of lepromatous leprosy. 'Leprosy' was the word used by John Mason Good to render Lucretius' *elephas* in the translation which Shelley bought in 1815 and which he had known since at least 1810.[9] Shelley could hardly have been comforted by a quotation referring to leprosy if he thought his disease was Barbadoes Leg.

In every respect, descriptions of *Elephantiasis Graecorum* to be found in Shelley's reading tally with his fear. Bateman even supplies a reason why Shelley would have thought it infectious whereas the surgeon, who almost certainly was Lawrence, could in good faith assure him that it was not. (Lawrence knew Bateman's book and regarded it as authoritative.) Bateman cites several authorities to show that, contrary to received wisdom, modern experts were coming round to the belief that elephantiasis was only slightly infectious. The description given by Bateman is indeed of an 'Iliad of woes': tubercles on face, ears and extremities, thickening and rugous flesh, a 'diminution or total loss of sensitivity of the skin' – it seems likely that Shelley was testing for this when he pulled his friends' skin tight – suppurating ulcers all over the body, destruction of the palate and nose from which a stench issues, and swellings of the joints of hands and feet, ending in gangrene.[10]

There are several references to elephantiasis in Shelley's known reading before 1814, but undoubtedly one of his sources was Celsus' *De Medicina*, from which he would have derived the belief that *Elephantiasis Graecorum* included among its symptoms swollen legs, not merely swollen extremities. Celsus, after mentioning the skin tubercles, has it that 'the trunk wastes; the face, feet and calves swell'. But Celsus, though making it clear that it is a dangerous disease, describes a method of treatment (bleeding, diet and purging). He does not say that it is infectious.[11] Erasmus Darwin's *Zoonomia* states that it is contagious, but not that it is fatal.[12] There is, however, one work that Shelley had owned since the beginning of that year and probably read years before, which contains every feature of his supposed disease apart from the detail of the legs, and which paints its contagiousness and fatality in vivid terms. This is the essay and translation by Jones cited earlier. It was entitled 'On the cure of the elephantiasis' and is to be found in Volume IV of the cheap edition. Next to Volume X, this is the volume which, of all thirteen, gives the most signs of having been closely read by Shelley.[13] A study of it also explains the tone of Hogg's description of Shelley's delusion and Peacock's sanitising of Hogg.

Jones introduces his subject as follows:

Among the afflicting maladies, which punish the vices and try the virtues of mankind, there are few disorders, of which the consequences are more dreadful or the remedy in general more desperate than the *Judham* of the Arabs or *khorah* of the Indians: it is also called in *Arabia* daul'asad, a name corresponding to the leontiasis of the *Greeks*, and supposed to have been given in allusion to the grim distracted and *lionlike* countenances of the miserable persons, who are affected with it. The most common name of the distemper is *Elephantiasis*, or as LUCRETIUS calls it, *Elephas*, because it renders the skin, like that of an *Elephant*, uneven and wrinkled, with many tubercles and furrows; but this complaint must not be confounded with the *daul'fil*, or *swelled legs*, described by the *Arabian* physicians, and very common in this country [India]. It has no fixed name in *English*, though HILLARY, in his *Observations* on the *Diseases of Barbadoes*, calls it the *Leprosy of the Joints*, because it principally affects the extremities, which in the last stage of the malady are distorted and at length drop off; but, since it is in truth a distemper corrupting the whole mass of blood, and therefore considered by PAUL of *Aegina* as an *universal ulcer*, it requires a more general appellation, and may be named the *Black Leprosy*.   (Jones, IV, pp. 367–9)

Jones said that while the milder sorts of elephantiasis might yield to hemlock, in the case of a 'malignant or inveterate judham, we must either administer a remedy of the highest power, or, agreeably to the desponding opinion of CELSUS, *leave the patient to his fate, instead of teasing him with fruitless medicines*, and suffer him, in the forcible words of ARETAEUS, *to sink from inextricable slumber into death*' (p. 369). The remedy of the highest power which Jones proposed, and which to Shelley in 1813 would have been as good as a death sentence, was arsenic.

Jones considered Lucretius to have been mistaken in his belief that the disease was confined to the Nile. 'It has certainly been imported from *Africa* into the *West India* Islands by the black slaves, who carried with them their resentment and their revenge.' Jones' Hindu doctor had assured him that it 'rages with virulence among the native inhabitants of *Calcutta*' (pp. 368–9); the doctor's essay carried the warning that it is 'extremely contagious', hence the saying of Mahomet: 'Flee from a person afflicted with the *judham* as you would flee from a lion' (p. 376).

But this was not the end of the matter. The Hindu doctor, in listing the causes of the elephantiasis (inheritance, faulty diet) added the following: 'The *Persian*, or venereal, fire generally ends in this malady' (p. 377). Jones singled out this sentence for comment: '[The doctor's] observation, that it is frequently a consequence of the *venereal infection*, would lead one to believe that it might be radically cured with *Mercury*' (p. 369). It was the ineffectuality of this remedy with leprosy which led to Jones' encouragement of experimentation with arsenic, both for elephantiasis and for 'the venereal'.

By his favourable publicity, Jones was endorsing the view of the Hindu doctor that the most common terminal stage of syphilis was a combination with and degeneration into leprosy. As he believed that the disease was 'peculiar to hot climates and has rarely appeared in *Europe*' presumably he thought, though he does not say so, that this happened only in places like India, Africa and the Caribbean. However he was not introducing a new idea. That leprosy of any kind could combine with syphilis, indeed *had* combined with it and in Europe as well as in the tropics, was a theory which was as old as the sixteenth century and received frequent airings throughout the eighteenth. Jones gave it a new respectability, thanks to his authority as an encyclopaedic sage.

Ulrich von Hutten (1519) wrote that 'these diseases [elephantiasis and syphilis] are Neighbours each to the other, by reason of some Affinity between them; those who are seized with the Pox, frequently becoming Lepers'. Paracelsus alleged that 'The French Disease derived its Origin from the Coition of a Leprous Frenchman with an impudent Whore, who had venereal Buboes, and after that infected every one that lay with her; and thus from the Leprosy and venereal Bubo, the French Disease arising, infected the whole World with its Contagion.' Jacobus Cataneus, according to an eighteenth-century citation, 'tells us 'tis not only possible there may be a transition from one of these Diseases into the other, but that he saw two persons in which the Pox was changed into the Leprosy'. There were numerous other stories in which leprosy was linked with the origin of syphilis: the French disease originated from coition between a leprous knight and a lady of Valencia, from lying with leprous women on the road to Mount Salvi, from the blood of lepers mixed with wine, and so on.[14] Shakespeare and Donne both use 'leprosy' as a substitute for 'syphilis'. When Scarus castigates the faithless Cleopatra as 'Yon ribaudred nag of Egypt / Whom leprosy o'er take!' he is so furious that the usual 'a pox on her' will not do; he wishes upon her the last extremity of the pox – elephantiasis.[15]

In the eighteenth century the question of whether syphilis was a kind of elephantiasis became a key piece of evidence in the debate as to the origin of the disease. On the whole, those who were inclined to believe that it was, held to what is now known as the 'unitarian' theory: that the disease has always existed under another name and that the epidemic of the late fifteenth century just happened to coincide with Columbus' voyages. They evolved something like a theory of mutation and combination with another disease to account for its sudden virulence in the sixteenth century. Their speculations were not essentially very different from the sophisticated modified unitarianism which is the prevailing orthodoxy today.[16] The other school, now known as the Columbian, believed that the two diseases were entirely different, and that syphilis had been unknown in Europe until Columbus' voyages. The chief spokesman for the 'unitarian' point of view was William Beckett, for the 'Columbian', Jean Astruc. Even a 'Columbian' like Astruc, however, did not deny that syphilis could amalgamate with other diseases; he believed, for instance, that it had mutated with gonorrhoea. Rees' *Chambers' Cyclopaedia*, a widely used reference book which Shelley drew upon for *Queen Mab*,[17] summed up the confusion, listing the various authorities under its heading 'Venereal':

Mr Beckett has attempted to show that it is the same with what among our forefathers was called the leprosy and which in many of our ancient English writings, characters etc is called brenning or burning ... As to the leprosy being the same with this venereal disease it must be owned that there are a good many symptoms in the one disease which quadrate well with those in the other, but then the symptoms in each are so precarious that a great deal of stress cannot be laid thereon.

Rees is guarded about whether syphilis could have combined with leprosy. Not so Franz Swediaur, probably the most respected venereologist in the world during the period 1800–20.[18] He had lived for fifteen years in Britain, mostly in Edinburgh, during which time he wrote *Practical Observations on Venereal Complaints* (1788). This became one of the chief rivals to Hunter's work. But it was the revision and amplification of Swediaur's work, made ten years after he moved to Paris, that he regarded as his magnum opus and which established his European reputation. Known as the *Traité Complet*, it was eventually translated into English in 1819, but in one or another of its French versions it was available in England from at least 1806. It was used by H. H. Southey (the brother of Robert) for his doctoral thesis on the origin of syphilis, though as a Columbian himself he disagreed with Swediaur.[19] Swediaur was determined to prove in the *Traité* that syphilis was a cyclical disease which had existed 'from time immemorial' and he leaned heavily upon Jones' essay ('this precious work' as he called it), which he had obtained direct from Calcutta. It would not be exaggerating much to say that elephantiasis was to him what the orang-utan was to Lord Monboddo, a King Charles' Head. There is no reason to think that Shelley had read or had even heard of Swediaur, unless Pereira mentioned him. (Swediaur was translated into Portuguese and Pereira's doctoral thesis was on a skin disease.) He is brought into this narrative only to make the point that Jones was taken seriously among certain doctors and that the connection between syphilis and leprosy was still very much a live issue in 1813.

The link between sexual disease and leprosy is preserved, consciously or not, in some of the poetry of the Victorian era. It is found, for instance, in Swinburne's 'The Leper' and in Browning's 'Childe Roland to the Dark Tower came' (xiii–xiv). The half-crazed narrator knight, pursuing his mission through a wasteland littered with emblems of a sick society and soul, comes upon a decrepit blind horse 'thrust out past service from the devil's stud!' amidst grass growing 'scant as hair / In leprosy'. He reacts with a *Schadenfreude* – 'I never saw a brute I hated so / He must be wicked to deserve such pain' – which seems inexplicable until one recognises it to be the vindictiveness of a flawed Sir Galahad, and the horse a symbol of an ungovernable sexual appetite which has incurred its appropriate punishment.

There are several possible reasons for the association of leprosy and syphilis. One is that the symptoms do resemble one another. Even today there is some doubt as to whether some forms of so-called leprosy have been rightly classified, and whether they are not, like yaws and bejel, varieties of endemic (non-venereal) syphilis, the result of poverty and poor hygiene. Another is the puzzling coincidence that leprosy declined as one of the chief scourges in Europe at about the same time that syphilis appeared as an epidemical disease. Today this can partly be accounted for by the virtual certainty that any scaly or gangrenous skin disease tended to be classified as leprosy in medieval times, and the numbers of true lepers would thus have been vastly exaggerated. It still remains possible that much medieval leprosy was actually endemic syphilis. One such form – 'the sibbens' – died out in Scotland only in the early nineteenth century.[20] A third reason for connecting leprosy and syphilis was the supposed relationship between leprosy and lechery. Almost every writer on the subject, including Cabanis, felt compelled to mention that an invariable concomitant of elephantiasis was an 'inexplebilis impudentisque coeundi libido', 'a raging with insatiable irresistible desire for venery', which is why another of its names was 'satyriasis'. Jones alludes to the belief obliquely in his reference to elephantiasis as a punishment for the vices of mankind. (This was another piece of received wisdom that Bateman felt bound to cast doubt upon. So far from lepers being more libidinous than other human beings, Dr Adams in his observations of the elephantiacs of Madeira had found that the disease had rendered them impotent.)[21]

Bateman in 1813 wrote of the disease as being 'almost unknown in this country', and added that he had never seen a case. Almost immediately his words became out of date. Two cases of elephantiasis appeared in England, one of them a boy, Charles Uncle, of entirely European parentage who had arrived from the Bahamas in the autumn, and the other a 'Miss N.', almost the same age as Shelley, 'the daughter of an English officer by a Hindoo woman'. She was admitted to the Middlesex Hospital on 4 January 1814, and Charles Uncle went into St Bartholomew's the following April. Each was treated by a doctor who had some connection with Shelley. 'Miss N.' became the patient of H. H. Southey, while Charles Uncle became that of William Lawrence. Lawrence also saw 'Miss N.' twice. These rare cases caused some stir in the medical profession. Lawrence and Southey jointly wrote a paper for the London Medico-Chirurgical Society, the body to which they and most leading London doctors belonged, including Lambe, Abernethy, and Harriet's accoucheur Dr Sims, and of which Bateman was the librarian.[22] The coincidence in time of the appearance of these cases, especially the admittance of Miss N., with the onset of Shelley's panic – 'about the end of 1813' – is so striking that there can be no reasonable doubt that they were connected in some consequential way.

At the same time, Hogg and Peacock's total silence on this matter indicates that Shelley did not entertain the idea that he picked up the disease from contact with Miss N., who could not have been a fat *old* woman.

Neither Hogg nor Peacock speaks of having been on the coach with Shelley and one can assume that if either had he would have said so in order to add authenticity to his version. They must therefore have received the account from Shelley himself. The possibility must exist that Shelley invented the 'fat old woman' and that, if he did, he had something to hide. That there were actually two elephantiacs in Britain, seemingly contrary to received opinion that the disease was peculiar to hot countries, would also have triggered off, in his already depressed and anxious state, the fear that syphilis had started to behave as it did in India and degenerate into elephantiasis. At the same time 'symptoms' might have appeared which it was easy enough to construe as evidence of the disease – 'irresistible desire for venery' and numbness of skin – the first sign, according to Jones – would have been sufficient for this. That Shelley believed himself to have latent syphilis which had flared up in its final and worst mutation is an explanation which accounts for everything we have hitherto mentioned, especially the visible signs of concealment and obfuscation in Hogg and Peacock's accounts. Lucretius would have been a comfort because, although not conclusive, his general point was that climate is responsible for the behaviour of a disease, and he specifically contrasts Egypt with Britain in this respect.[23]

At the same time it is not the only explanation. Assuming that Shelley was telling the truth about the old woman, he was also hinting that her legs were visible, and thus that the woman was an immodest one, that is to say, a whore.[24] The reason why he would have thought an old whore likely to have elephantiasis if she had fat legs is that, already diseased with syphilis – and Shelley by 1812 seems to have thought that all prostitutes became diseased after a time – the prostitute class would be the first to exhibit the new mutation, elephantiasis being the usual end of the Persian fire. Once, however, syphilis had mutated into this form, following Jones' Hindu doctor, it would become pestilential or epidemic and spread non-venereally, infecting the populace, just as the fifteenth-century outbreak of syphilis was believed to have done. This would explain Shelley's fear that all his friends including his female ones, had contracted the disease – not only average sensual men like Hogg.

The parallels between elephantiasis as presented by Jones and AIDS are very striking. Both diseases are endemic to poor or exploited countries, are spread by promiscuity to the dominant culture and threaten to pollute the 'mass of blood' of entire nations. There are attempts to explain them both as retribution: AIDS is supposed by fundamentalists to be God's punishment on a society too tolerant of homosexuals. With elephantiasis, the idea of retribution is present in Jones' view of it as the revenge of the black African slaves and a punishment for 'vices'. The outstanding difference between the two cases is, of course, that Jones' Hindu doctor was wrong. If he had been right, the threat from elephantiac prostitutes would have been as bad in reality as Shelley could have painted it in his imagination, or as the most gloomy forecasts about the spread of AIDS at the present time.

About ten months later Shelley showed panic reactions different in degree though not in kind from those which we have just reconstructed, and under conditions which had this in common with the period of the elephantiasis panic: he was heavily in debt and in London. The letters to Mary of October 1814, quoted in Chapter 2, show Shelley believing himself about to succumb to impurity and vice and writing as if the very breath exhaled by the prostitutes in Covent Garden was capable of subduing him to languor. If he could have behaved so when deprived for a few nights of the physical presence of a loved woman, his reaction the year before when feeling himself to be deprived of love itself would have been considerably more violent.

Shelley's panic has its origins in events much earlier in his life. One can locate his concern with leprosy in June 1811 when writing to Miss Hitchener about Southey's *The Curse of Kehama*. 'I am happy that you like Kehama. Is not the chapter where Kailyal despises the leprosy grand.'[25] Kehama, the god—tyrant, having failed to make the heroine, Kailyal, become his bride, takes revenge. Leprosy spreads to all her limbs, presumably through the agency of Lorrinite, a prostitute—witch in league with Kehama. (Medwin remembered Shelley singling out the description of Lorrinite for recitation during what must have been April 1811.)[26] Too proud to be subdued by such means, Kailyal ripostes that her 'disgrace' carries with it immunity from any worse insult or 'outrage' he might attempt. She then consoles herself with sentiments of a nobler sort; the last two lines, rising to a crescendo, must have been among those which acted so powerfully on Shelley's feelings:

> The immortal Powers, who see
> Through the poor wrappings of mortality,
> Behold the soul, the beautiful soul, within,
> Exempt from age and wasting maladies
> And undeform'd, while pure and free from sin.
> This is a loathsome sight to human eyes,
> But not to eyes divine,
> Ereenia, Son of Heaven, oh, not to thine!   (XIX, 18–25)

These verses contain the transcendent sentiments found so often – though with considerably more distinction – in Shelley. It is not surprising to discover Shelley singling out a case of transcendence of a disease for special admiration when encountering it in literature. (One is reminded of Thornton Hunt's belief that it was towards transcendence that Shelley was most impelled by the horror of his own damaged health.) That this episode was one which Shelley invested with personal significance is suggested by the following: contrary to what one might expect, the 'chapter where Kailyal despises the leprosy' is no sort of climax to the poem, but only one of half a dozen occasions on which the powers of good defy the powers of evil to do their worst; it does not seem to have struck contemporaries as being especially noteworthy. A review for the *Quarterly* which includes copious quotation and which was co-authored by Walter Scott, does not mention it at all.[27]

Related to Shelley's interest in leprosy is his interest in the Book of Job.

This can be seen as early as December 1810, the date, either of composition or of inspiration, of 'Dares the lama', an *Esdaile* poem declaring his powerlessness in the face of religious bigotry and ending with defiant desperation 'What remains but to curse it, to curse it and die?' It was after Job was smitten with boils from head to foot that his wife exhorted him: 'Dost thou still retain thy integrity? Curse God, and die' (Job, 2.9). Mary wrote that Shelley planned to write a lyric drama on the subject, and never gave up the idea. She could find no trace of the project among his papers, though his notebooks do contain odd quotations from Job.[28]

It is not difficult to see why Job would have appealed to Shelley. It is a drama of great beauty. It deals with a question which had always fascinated him: the relationship between evil and divine justice. For Shelley, Christians when worshipping God were really worshipping the Devil, whom he compared in his urbane essay 'On the Devil and Devils' to the junior member of a 'sort of partnership, in which the weaker has consented to bear all the odium of their common actions, and to allow the stronger to talk of himself as a very honorable person, on condition of having a participation in what is the especial delight of both of them, burning men to all eternity.'[29] God is like a king and the Devil a combined judge and government spy. Job, from this viewpoint, furnished a perfect example of this kind of uneasy collaboration between God and Satan. It is the Lord who allows Satan to smite Job with boils in order to test his loyalty. The story, then, provided a suitable framework for Shelley's political and religious views.

But the choice of Job assumes a greater pointedness when one remembers that during the sixteenth century he became, according to popular tradition, the patron saint of syphilitics. This tradition is encountered frequently in the literature of venereal disease, and figures in the *Chambers' Cyclopaedia* article 'Venereal':

Others go much further and suppose [syphilis] to be the ulcers Job complained of so grievously and accordingly, in a Missal, printed in Venice in 1542 there is a Mass in honour of St Job to be said by those recovered of this disease as being supposed to owe their deliverance to his intercession.

'St Job's disease' was another name for syphilis, and 'He is laid up in Job's dock' was a current piece of buckish slang for 'in a salivation'. 'Job's ward' was a nickname for the V.D. unit at St Bartholomew's. Its official name was Lazarus ward, another reminder of the connection that existed between syphilis and leprosy. Most Lock hospitals and wards were converted lazar houses. The term 'Lock' itself was said to derive from the 'logue' or rag used to wipe the leper's sores before the latter's entry to the leprosarium. Thus, when Shelley called St Bartholomew's a lazar house he was being literal, in so far as he was referring to Lazarus (or Job's) ward.[30]

Job was a key figure in the debate on the origin of syphilis. Astruc mentions some who 'deduced the Origin of the Venereal Disease from the Scab which plagued Job'.[31] 'Unitarians' went to the Bible as well as to ancient medicine in order to prove that syphilis had existed since the beginning of the world and could be found disguised as 'The botch of Egypt', 'leprosy' or 'boils'. 'I am inclined to believe, with Gui Patin, that not only Job, David, Solomon and Adam had the pox, but that it was in chaos before creation', as an anonymous writer of 1744 put it.[32] Gui Patin, the seventeenth-century doctor, whose letters were highly celebrated in the 1700s, had even mentioned as a possibility that the Fall of Man was a mythical rendering of the entry of syphilis into the world.

Balduc, a Capuchin and Pineda, a Spanish Jesuit, have written that Job had syphilis. I am willing to believe that David and Solomon had it likewise . . . *Morbus campanus* in Horace, is syphilis. It is found in Catullus, Juvenal and Apulius, and they even say in Herodotus and Xenophon. M. Gassendi said to me that the leprosy of the Bible was syphilis. A libertine said that the serpent in Genesis was a young devil who gave Eve syphilis.[33]

These authorities crop up with monotonous regularity. A short article by Robert Southey's antiquarian friend, William Taylor of Norwich, in the *Monthly Magazine* of August 1812, under the heading 'The Angel Syphilis', cites Pineda again as the author of the view that 'syphilis was known to the earliest ages of human history, to the camp of Moses, to the home of Job . . . As syphilis is the angel of retribution appointed to punish promiscuous intercourse and thus *to diffuse and to perpetuate the sacred ordinances of marriage* [our italics], his commission, it should seem, must have begun with society itself.' It is possible that Shelley saw this piece; it was on the front page and the *Monthly Magazine* had much to interest him in the year 1812, especially Newton's articles on the Zodiac.[34] Columbians such as Astruc considered 'unitarians' to be over-literal in their interpretation of the Bible, and that when David wrote of 'Disturbing of his Bones, the stinking and corruption of his Wounds, and the loathsome Disease of his loins, etc' he did not refer to 'an infirm sickly Body, but to the tortures of a grieved and penitent Mind'.[35] (Astruc is recalling bold Scriptural metaphors such as 'the loins of your mind'.) This hardly satisfied the 'unitarians', since grief and penitence tend to succeed recognition that the sins of the flesh are punished in the flesh.

It is likely that Shelley's projected drama would have developed the implications of the portion of dialogue between Asia and Demogorgon in *Prometheus Unbound* where the former asks 'Who rains down / Evil, the immedicable plague?', and would have contained a confrontation between God and Job in which the latter accused the former specifically as the author of disease and physical affliction. It could also have been a more sophisticated restatement of the 'Note to *Queen Mab*', 'Even love is sold', in which Shelley linked institutional Christianity and its moral teaching with the high incidence of venereal disease.

The incidence of the word 'leper' and 'leprous' in Shelley's poetry is yet
another mark of the elephantiasis episode, a point which we shall amplify
later. Another is an interest in the subject of Egypt as the source of good and
evil, as in his sonnet 'To the Nile'. How Shelley distanced his experience can
be seen in his best-known sonnet 'Ozymandias'.

It is now accepted that Shelley derived the image of the 'two vast and
trunkless legs of stone' that stand in the desert from Richard Pococke's *A
Description of the East and some other countries*.[36] Shelley prophesies the end
of modern tyranny by regarding the ruins of a past empire; it has often been
observed that Ozymandias' huge statuary legs have their counterpart in the
Regent's gout, which Shelley was later to use as an outward sign of his sensualism in *Swellfoot the Tyrant*. Ozymandias, too, is a diseased tyrant. Shelley
has fused Pococke with Celsus. Celsus had written 'The trunk wastes; the
face, calves and feet swell.' Shelley has transformed the *swollen* into the *gigantic*. The trunk has wasted until it has entirely disappeared. All that remains
of Ozymandias is huge crazed stone face ('a shattered visage'), calves and feet,
which are placed in the heart of Egypt, birthplace of elephantiasis. The
statue is 'a colossal wreck', a syphilitic in the last stages of decrepitude on
a stupendous scale, body and mind alike having crumbled into a 'hideous
wreck of humanity', leaving only the imprint of selfish passions on the shattered visage. It is Time the Devourer which has reduced the statue to its
elements, but it is also Time, which in Pope's unpleasant phrase, 'matures
a clap to pox'.[37] In the fullness of time Ozymandias has been revealed for
what he really is. The penumbra of pathological imagery in the poem partly
explains why it is so disturbing and distinctive. The stone legs stand
obstinately, hypostatising the horror, like an inveterate disease or memory of
disease which embeds itself in the boundless and bare sand of consciousness.
Words such as 'which yet survive' and 'Nothing beside remains' take on a
darker significance. The mental traveller, who has come from a land that is
'antic' – bizarre as in *Hamlet* – as well as antique (the words are cognates)
– is obsessed to the exclusion of all else by the persistence of the past, even
in asserting the inevitable overthrow of tyranny. The calm, sardonic
assurance with which he tells his tale is a precariously won triumph. That
Shelley was still remembering Celsus' description word for word four years
after the elephantiasis terror (he may have written 'Ozymandias' as an
anniversary poem in December 1817) is a measure of the indelible impression
of the experience.

Around the end of December 1813[38] Shelley left London for Windsor. In
mid-February he moved to Mrs Boinville's, and a month later wrote a letter
to Hogg saying that he had sunk 'into a premature old age of exhaustion' and
was 'dead to everything' except indulgence of the vanity of hope and a 'terrible susceptibility to objects of disgust and hatred'.[39] To Cornelia Turner,
Mrs Boinville's daughter, with whom he was rapidly falling in love, he con-

fessed that he 'dreaded the visions which pursued him when alone at night'.[40] All this suggests that he had gone through a terrible experience, and when one remembers Hogg's comment that the elephantiasis terror lasted *weeks*, it becomes increasingly clear that this was a major factor in Shelley's collapse and demoralisation. In an autobiographical section from *Epipsychidion* Shelley was to allegorise this part of his life as the time when like a 'hunted deer' he stood at bay, 'wounded and weak and panting'. The image is derived from Cowper's *The Task*, where Cowper writes of himself as a 'stricken deer' who left the herd (the multitude of the metropolis) to seek tranquil death in distant shades (the village of Olney), where he found solace in religion.[41]

This is only one of a number of instances of Shelleyan self-identification with literary or historical characters, and in all cases the self-identification occurs because Shelley has been able to find in the other's story a parallel with his own case. As Cowper had fled to Olney and found Christ, so had Shelley fled to Bracknell and found the divine natures, Mrs Boinville and her daughter, who offered him friendship and discussions concerning sentimental love. But the parallel becomes more striking when one examines what it was that Cowper was fleeing from.

Just before the 'stricken deer' passage, Cowper apostrophises 'Domestic happiness', the 'nurse of Virtue'. He describes what happens when men forsake this, the only vestige of the joy of Paradise before the Fall, for Pleasure, 'that reeling goddess with the zoneless waist / And wandering eyes':

> What shipwreck have we made
> Of honour, dignity, and fair renown,
> Till prostitution elbows us aside
> In all our crowded streets, and senates seem
> Convened for purposes of empire less
> Than to release the adultress from her bond.
> The adultress! . . .   (*The Task*, III, 58–64)

A long passage follows in which Cowper inveighs against the bare-facedness of vice and deplores the decline in public morals. His target is venality of all kinds, but it is sexual depravity which wounds him more than anything else, of which the hordes of prostitutes in London streets are the outward and visible sign, and over which the adultress, 'Cruel, abandoned, glorying in her shame', presides. When Shelley is cut off from hopes of domestic happiness (he wrote to Hogg later of 'struggles and privations which almost withered me to idiotism' prior to his elopement with Mary)[42] he becomes a prey to the thoughts aroused by the 'impures'. Even the coach, scene of the encounter with the fat old woman, has an analogue in Cowper's dismissal of the adultress: 'Let her pass, and *charioted along* / In guilty splendour, shake the public ways' (69–70). Whether Cowper's poem gave him the idea for the stage-coach (if Shelley made up the incident) or a real incident recalled Cowper's poem is a matter on which we reserve judgement.

The elephantiasis episode was no comic eccentricity but a pivotal event, and 'typical' in a sense different from Grabo's: it was an intensification of a nineteenth century nightmare. Harbingers of it can be seen in Shelley's work long before and it was to generate images which he worked into his poetry for the rest of his life. We consider it too as one source for what is, next to Frankenstein's monster, the most powerful image in Mary's writing: the pestilential disease in *The Last Man*. Its universal spread is heralded by rumour of the rising of a black sun in the east,[43] a transmutation of the black leprosy's source in Egypt. It is to the alleviation of this disease that Adrian, the 'tainted wether', dedicates his powers.

7

Pale pain, my shadow 1814–22

What have been called Shelley's 'Golden Years' – the years which saw the emergence of the great poet – coincide with his increasingly chronic and painful ill-health. Three principal diseases were diagnosed – consumption, hepatitis and nephritis. These diagnoses would have provided a disguise if Shelley's illness had been the result of 'tampering with venal pleasures'. All three diseases were considered to be possible effects of the venereal diseases or their treatment, but an outsider would have been quite unable to ascertain whether this was so in any individual case, and no downright lies would have had to be told. And even if Shelley was not thus afflicted, his treatments would have been the same as if he really was, thereby promoting his poetic self-identification with the sufferer from venereal disease, a theme which we shall develop later. A short survey of Shelley's medical history from this point until the end of his life is therefore appropriate.

Having eloped to the Continent on 28 July 1814, Shelley and Mary returned to England in the autumn. For the next ten months they led a debt-ridden, turbulent existence before settling at Bishopgate near Windsor. Of this period Medwin reported that Shelley undertook medical training and 'walked a hospital'. This seems unlikely. True, he was seeing Lawrence in the winter of 1814 and could have visited St Bartholomew's. A reference to the 'reeking hospital' in *Alastor* (1815) may indicate a fresh impression.[1] But it is just as likely that Medwin is reporting an incorrectly remembered or misinterpreted conversation about illness with Shelley in which memories of the April 1811 visits with Charles Grove figured. According to Medwin, Shelley also told him that at one time he expected to breathe his last in that particular hospital, implying that consumption was the disease from which he then believed himself to be suffering. It is not at all clear from Medwin's account that Shelley was referring to the period 1814–15 as far as dying in the hospital was concerned, and in any case it is a little odd that he should have expected to die in a hospital. On the whole, people of Shelley's class did not die of consumption in hospital, and although he was in financial straits, money for private nursing could have been borrowed from Hogg.[2] More likely, Shelley was harking back to elephantiasis which, as a rare disease, would have made him an object of study and experiment at St Bartholomew's, and which in its late stages would have rendered him too loathsome to be cared for privately. Coincidentally or not, during the period to which Medwin assigned Shelley's medical training, Lawrence's elephantiac patient, Charles Uncle, was discharged from St Bartholomew's, somewhat improved. (He would have been placed in Lazarus Ward, and was probably the only genuine leper in it.) This would help explain a connection in Shelley's mind between the year 1815, the lazar house and consumption.

On the same day (28 February) that Lawrence was reading his paper on the newly discharged Charles Uncle to the Medico-Chirurgical Society, Shelley consulted Dr Christopher Pemberton, another member of that learned body.[3] At first sight, his choice of Pemberton is puzzling. Shelley preferred to associate with doctors who were non-conformist in some way (Lind, Lambe, the Quakers Sims and Pope, Bell) and sometimes free-thinkers and republicans as well (Lawrence, Vaccà). Pemberton, however, was a thoroughly establishment figure and, moreover, a doctor to the hated Prince Regent.

The answer is probably that Pemberton was the country's top liver specialist and the author of a famous treatise on the subject. Claire had had an inflammation of the liver diagnosed the previous November by Currie, another specialist.[4] Perhaps the latter had advised Shelley to go to Pemberton. If so, Shelley was probably already suffering from that pain in his side which was to become such a marked feature of his later history. He would probably also have had a cough, then regarded as a common symptom of chronic hepatitis. He had written to Harriet the previous October mentioning trouble with his lungs.[5]

He visited Pemberton twice, but according to Mary's 'Note on *Alastor*', Pemberton diagnosed consumption:

In the Spring of 1815 an eminent physician pronounced that he was dying rapidly of a consumption; abscesses were formed on his lungs, and he suffered acute spasms. Suddenly a complete change took place; and, though through life he was a martyr to pain and debility, every symptom of pulmonary disease vanished.

(Hutchinson, p. 30)

That sounds very odd; relating it to Hogg's scepticism about Shelley's consumption, one is seemingly faced with evidence of hysterical illness. Hogg wrote that Shelley 'coughed at times violently, as many others cough . . . and sometimes felt a pain in his side and chest, and he called it spasms . . . He was encouraged in these chimeras' by self-interested friends (presumably the Hunts).[6]

Yet it is clear that during the first half of 1815 Shelley was seriously ill. Apparently he did nothing to help himself during the six weeks following his visits to Pemberton, but that is not surprising. Mary's and his first baby had just died. He had his hands tied with complicated financial negotiations that were eventually to result in an income of only a thousand pounds a year. But after May one does find Shelley behaving like a man who believes his life in danger. He gave Mary a bank draft with instructions as to what to do should he die. He made a tour of South Devon, the warmest part of Britain, and visited Clifton, rival to Bath, site of celebrated medicinal springs and Beddoes' old stamping ground. According to Chambers, the springs had been famed since 1639 for treatment of 'disorders of the urinary bladder and kidneys' as well as, later, 'consumptions and weakness of the lungs'. In a letter of 1822, Mary spoke of May 1815 as a time when Shelley had been ill, '*al solito*'.[7]

Later in the summer he had another 'severe pulmonary attack', for, according to Mary's 'Note on the Early Poems', it was just after his recovery from this that the Shelleys, Peacock and Charles Clairmont made, in late August, a famous voyage up the Thames. It was intended as a rest cure for Shelley who had been 'advised by a physician to live as much as possible in the open air'.[8] The prescription evidently worked; after the trip Charles wrote to his sister Claire 'In Shelley the change is quite remarkable; he now has the ruddy, healthy complexion of the autumn upon his countenance, and is twice as fat as he used to be.'[9] The apparent discrepancy in Mary's accounts of the disappearance of Shelley's consumption is smoothed over if one assumes that she saw the second, later summer attack as continuous with the first early spring one and that the sudden disappearance did not take place until late summer.

Peacock reported that Shelley was ill both before and during the river trip, but implied that he had run down his health with misplaced vegetarianism; he had been 'living chiefly on tea and bread and butter, drinking occasionally a sort of spurious lemonade, made of some powder in a box, which, as he was reading at the time the *Tale of a Tub* he called *the powder of pimperlimpimp*'.[10] Peacock made no mention of the consumption. What however one can infer from the Swiftian reference is that the 'spurious lemonade' was in fact a medicine and that Shelley had been receiving treatment, an inference supported by a letter written to Hogg just before the river trip in which he said that his health had much improved since he had put himself under Lawrence's care.[11] This aspect Mary has almost completely suppressed. She implies that the cure was spontaneous and that it was due to the healthy open-air life.

A likely reason why she should have been so anxious to play down the role of the doctor and emphasise the benefits of nature is that Shelley had almost certainly been taking mercury, in 1815 a common enough treatment for tuberculosis, and that he was just about to come off it when the river trip took place.[12] Such a trip would have been a doctor's standard prescription for a patient debilitated and rendered 'nervous' by the mercury. (Shelley was in a very depressed state before he embarked on the voyage.) Pearson, a venereologist and Hunterian doctor like Abernethy and Lawrence, advised that syphilitic patients 'should live in the open air as much as possible' to counteract mercurialism. Swediaur warned that mercurial preparations all had a tendency to emaciate the body, but 'this sort of emaciation is not dangerous; for after the mercurial course, patients generally resume their natural *en bon point*, and even sometimes become fatter than they were before'. (Compare Charles Clairmont's remarks.) The 'spurious lemonade' was very likely some antidote to mercury such as Dover's powder.[13] Mary's sensitivity on this point will emerge more clearly later.

It may seem surprising that, given his views on arsenic, Shelley should nevertheless have been willing to take mercury, but one finds him doing so several years later. From 1815 onwards, Shelley's attraction towards experimental practitioners, although it never disappears entirely, becomes less evident. Lawrence, Bell and Vaccà, Shelley's doctors of whom most is known, could be described as pioneering in surgical techniques, or unorthodox in their political and religious views, but they were not antimercurialist as such. Abernethy, Lawrence's mentor, actually had a reputation for being rather too fond of doling out mild mercurials; Hogg called him the 'emperor and autocrat of all the blue pills'.[14]

Peacock attributed Shelley's sudden improvement in health to the 'prescription' he gave him when the party reached Oxford.

I told him: 'If he would allow me to prescribe for him, I would set him to rights.' He asked: 'What would be your prescription?' I said: 'Three mutton chops, well peppered.' He said: 'Do you really think so?' I said: 'I am sure of it.' He took the prescription; the success was obvious and immediate.   (Wolfe, II, p. 340)

This anecdote is usually taken to be a hit at Shelley's vegetarianism, which of course it is, but it is also a double entendre. 'Mutton' as slang for prostitute can be found in Elizabethan and Jacobean dramatists. 'Peppered' meant 'infected with venereal disease', and was an exact counterpart to the French 'poivré', the word used by Rousseau when he thought himself poxed by a Venetian *padoana*. The terms were still current in the Regency. The 1811 *Lexicon Baltronicum*, which included 'Buckish Slang' and 'University Wit', has entries for both 'mutton' and 'peppered' in the above senses. (Both chop-house and brothel catered for the appetites of the Regency man of the town with no wife to cook for him.) A faint echo of the bawdy meaning survives in the vulgarian Hogg, who wrote of Mrs Newton's habits of nudism as 'cooling her unprejudiced mutton', giving the word a sense – naked female flesh – unrecorded by the *OED*.[15] Unless one supposes that Peacock acquired only in later life the taste for double entendres recorded by Buchanan it is impossible that he should not have known, in 1815, that the phrase was an *équivoque*, and as we have shown earlier, Shelley was perfectly capable of understanding it. It was, however, safe for Peacock to record it in a family magazine of 1860, where the context provided an effective disguise; besides, the bawdy sense was by then antiquarian.[16]

Of course Peacock does not mean anything so pointlessly sick as 'What you need is a little debauchery, preferably with diseased women', though the principle of homeopathic Paracelsian medicine – 'the hair of the dog that bit you' – lies embedded in his joke, as does a submerged pun on the word 'appetite'. Literal peppered mutton chops are to undo the ravages of metaphorical peppered mutton chops.[17] The point of the remark would be the same whether Peacock thought Shelley was frightening himself to death with fantasies about diseased prostitutes or needlessly worrying about the delayed effects of 'impure coition' years previously. It is probably significant that Peacock gave Shelley this advice at Oxford where he was 'so much out of order that he feared being obliged to return' from the boating journey, for the Oxford area contained associations of the windmill. Peacock also mentioned that Shelley had consulted a doctor 'who may have done him some good, but it was not apparent'. This seems to be a reference to Lawrence. A mercurial course left patients debilitated and depressed. Peacock would be giving a sensible 'prescription' for someone whose constitution had been weakened by a drastic treatment. (Dr Lambe would have done the same.)[18]

This interpretation of Peacock's remark is further reinforced by the fact that during this period there was a condition to which the name 'venereal consumption' was given. It is not certain what this designated; gummas on the lung is one possibility; another is a delayed side effect of mercury treatment. Contemporary venereologists agreed that syphilis could attack the lungs, and regarded this as a highly dangerous condition, a harbinger of the end, and one which could appear moreover when all other symptoms had seemingly cleared up following earlier treatment. Swediaur wrote that it was characterised by 'a dry cough, or accompanied with puriform or really purulent expectoration, producing a general emaciation of the body with a hectic fever' and called it *Phthisis pulmonalis vel atrophia syphilitica*. Sometimes, wrote Swediaur, this cough is the only sign that the syphilitic virus is lodged in the body, and the patient never goes through the other secondary stages. A venereal consumption may occur even when the sufferer has apparently been cured of the complaint for several years. Sometimes there is not even a cough, but merely sleeplessness and a wasting away. Astruc taught that severe 'gleet' led to venereal consumption and that 'atrophy, marasmus and hectic fever' could be brought on or aggravated by 'venereal taint'.[19]

In the autumn of 1815 Shelley began *Alastor*, the subject of which is a Poet who becomes emaciated and finally dies in the course of a hopeless and feverish quest in search of ideal love. He is the victim of a metaphorical venereal consumption, symptoms of which resemble closely the clinical descriptions of the venereologists, with the exception of the cough.

1816–18 and the move to Italy

On his return from the Continent in September 1816, Shelley's health became a matter of concern to both Fanny Godwin and Claire. In October he started weighing his food, which suggests that he had become emaciated.[20] The Shelley household was now in Bath; somewhere secluded was needed as the birthplace for Claire's illegitimate child by Byron. But, like Clifton, Bath was also a health resort, and one especially associated with the cure of skin diseases, including leprosy. Mary's journal elsewhere has only very scanty records of Shelley taking baths as a health measure, even when they were prescribed; so it is quite possible that he paid unrecorded – though not very beneficial – visits to the baths. 1817 was a bad year for his health; from January dates one of the most vivid descriptions of the 'spasms' mentioned earlier. Thornton Hunt witnessed Shelley suddenly throwing up his book and hands, sliding off his chair, pouring forth loud and continuous shrieks, 'stamping his feet madly on the ground . . . This happened about the time when he was most anxious for the result of the trial which was to deprive him of his children.'[21]

Sentences like the last have been quoted by biographers such as White as evidence that Shelley's infirmities were mostly psychosomatic. It is pointed out that bouts of illness are always accompanied by some emotional crisis. Hogg wrote that Shelley used 'spasms, consumptions, breaking of blood-vessels, veins, and arteries . . . as a pretence for undertaking what he eagerly desired, but felt to be imprudent and improper'.[22] But what is cause and what effect? Quite apart from the fact that one would expect a genuine illness to be exacerbated by stress, and that illness can itself be the cause of an emotional crisis, some of the crises which Shelley was thrown into resulted from measures he took to palliate or cure his illness. Moreover, even when the 'spasms' seem most to be the result of emotional turmoil, some other, purely physical, factor is interacting with them. Such a case occurred during the summer of 1814 when Shelley was agonising over his desire for Mary and his duty to Harriet. According to Hookham, he was suffering from an intense bodily pain which would cause him to 'roll himself suddenly on the ground, pulling the sofa cushions upon him'. But Shelley was also reported by Hookham to be consuming vast quantities of laudanum. He attempted suicide by taking an overdose of the drug and was saved only by the timely intervention of the doctor who forced him to walk up and down the room.[23] After Shelley had eloped with Mary to Europe, and was presumably enjoying a holiday from responsibilities, the spasms still continued.[24]

From the middle of 1817, when the Shelleys were living at Marlow, dates the first definite reference to the 'fixed pain' in his side. In September he went up to London to consult Lawrence. The next day he wrote to Byron: 'My health is in a miserable state, so that some care will be required to prevent it speedily terminating in death . . . they recommend Italy as a certain remedy for my disease.' Mary shared his alarm: 'ah! my love you cannot guess how wretched it was to see your languour and encreasing illness . . . write my love, a long account of what Lawrence says – I shall be very anxious untill I hear'. No one reading the interchange of letters between Mary and Shelley during these last months of 1817 can doubt the overwhelming importance of health as the reason for the Shelleys' emigration: 'Surely,' Mary wrote in exasperation, '[Godwin] cannot be blind to the many heavy reasons that urge us [to go to Italy] – your health the indispensable one if every other were away.'[25] Under the umbrella description 'every other' she was probably including Shelley's fear that his children might be taken away from him, his disgust with the political state of England, threats of arrest for debt and her own natural wish to travel. Peacock later ascribed Shelley's departure to a 'spirit of restlessness'. Yet at the time he considered that Shelley had gone to the Continent for his health above all. Describing the sultry weather of the summer of 1818 he remarked 'If the summer of last year had been like this, you would not, I think, be now in Italy; but who could have foreseen it? Do not think I wish to play the tempter. If you return to England I would most earnestly advise you to stay the winter in a milder climate.'[26]

Thornton Hunt was convinced that the financial burden imposed on Shelley by the importunities of friends contributed to his leaving England.[27] Undoubtedly he did wish to escape from Godwin. Probably Shelley was exaggerating when he told the latter that he had had a 'decisive pulmonary attack' in December. (Mary's *Alastor* note had said that 'every symptom of pulmonary disease vanished' in 1815 and implied that none ever returned.) But this does not mean that Shelley did not seriously think his life in danger. 'Consumption' was a vague term, and covered not just pulmonary symptoms but emaciation as well. Shelley had struck Polidori as consumptive in 1816. Even as late as 1819 Shelley was still worrying about being consumptive. A letter from Claire to Byron in May of 1819 said 'Mr Bell, one of the first English surgeons has seen Shelley (who has been very ill) and he has ordered him to pass the summer at Naples & says if S has any consumptive symptoms left by the approach of next winter he must pass the cold season at Tunis.'[28]

Yet for all these urgent reasons, the Shelleys dithered. Even as late as mid-January it is by no means clear that the decision to go to Italy had finally been taken. Holmes believes that it was a visit from Godwin on 20 January which was decisive: 'It at last brought home to him that it was time to put the Italian plan into operation.'[29] But there was another factor – one which caused Godwin to cut short his visit. On 22 January Shelley contracted ophthalmia for the second time that winter. Mary, conflating the two attacks, wrote that it was contracted after visiting the poor near Marlow. Medwin added that the attack 'nearly deprived him of sight'. (In the winter of 1820–1 ophthalmia recurred even more severely. On the latter occasion Shelley seems to have suffered it during the second half of December and most of January, something not recorded in Mary's journal.)[30]

Lawrence was a specialist in ophthalmology. In 1814 he was appointed surgeon to the London Infirmary for Diseases of the Eye. In 1830 he published a major work, embodying the experience of years, called *Treatise on the Venereal Diseases of the Eye*, one section of which dealt with gonorrhoeal ophthalmia and the other with syphilitic iritis. He was not the first to recognise the connection between ophthalmia and sexually transmitted diseases. Both Swediaur and Abernethy had reported ophthalmia as a possible complication of gonorrhoea. Surgeons at St Bartholomew's had observed cases of what they called 'syphilitic ophthalmia'.[31] There is no record that Shelley consulted Lawrence specifically about ophthalmia, but, given Lawrence's interests, expertise, connection with St Bartholomew's and closeness to Shelley, it seems likely that the attack of ophthalmia was the final straw, the factor which decided him to quit England, where he was a prey to continual alarms, false or otherwise. The Shelleys left on 12 March 1818, never to return. The last poem published by Shelley before leaving England was 'Ozymandias'. It contains as good an explanation for his exile as any.

Images of hollow, consumed and staring dead eyes are frequent throughout Shelley's poetry. But these, together with the themes of eyelessness and blindness, become more frequent after the ophthalmia. *The Colosseum*, a fragmentary story begun in Rome in the autumn of 1818, is about a blind old man whose lack of sensual sight is compensated for by the eye of his imagination and inward vision. It is as if Shelley were trying to write a counterpart to Milton's 'On his Blindness' before the event. Sometimes 'blindness' appears metaphorically, as when Prometheus speaks of himself – or is it of his oppressor Jupiter, or both? – as 'eyeless in hate'. This persistent concern surely has something to do with his choice of Euripides' *The Cyclops* as a subject for translation.

The sole clue to the dating of the translation is Shelley's testimony that he wrote it only when he could do nothing else, which suggests that the exercise was a distraction from personal misery. Timothy Webb, the first to direct attention to the extraordinariness of Shelley's having selected a frequently gross satyr play out of all other available ones, suggested that he wrote it in the summer of 1819, after the death of his son William. January 1819 is another likely time. Shelley went through some crisis in Naples in the winter of 1818–19, and was reading Euripides then.[32]

Ulysses is the hero, a wanderer who lands on a foreign shore expecting to find succour and relief; the parallel with Shelley is obvious. He finds instead Polyphemus, a selfish phagedaenic monster, who vies with Count Cenci for the distinction of being the most purely evil creature in the Shelley canon.

Without a scrap of reverence for Jupiter, Polyphemus nevertheless behaves as he does because the god has first provided the model. (He rapes Silenus in a parody of Jove's rapture of Ganymede.) The climax of the play is the horrific blinding of Polyphemus with a red-hot stake by Ulysses, who has been forced into cunning and subterfuge in order to save his own life. For Shelley the story is a revenge fable; the savage relish with which the blinding is described channels the rage against what was for Shelley an obscene social system, buttressed by bad morality, which had literally threatened *him* with blindness. Ulysses carries Polyphemus' curse with him on his further wanderings. Shelley knows well that such hate, however justified, carries with it a penalty, and that the wrongs done Ulysses have exasperated him to a revenge that will incur the further wrath of the cruel gods.

In *The Last Man* a little group of survivors, including Adrian and Verney, leave a plague-stricken England and cross the Alps. In the vale of Chamounix the plague burns itself out and vanishes from the earth. 'For seven years it had had full sway upon earth . . . her barbarous tyranny came to its close here . . . From this moment I saw plague no more. . . . I cannot say whether the knowledge of this change visited us, as we stood on this sterile spot. It seems to me that it did; that a cloud seemed to pass from over us. Yet we did not hope. We were impressed by the sentiment, that our race was run, but that plague would not be our destroyer.'[33] If 'plague' in *The Last Man* has something to do with Shelley's illness, and we consider it does, then this passage suggests Mary's belief that exile finally laid to rest, though not immediately, those fears which had culminated in the elephantiasis terror. Certainly Shelley gave health as the first reason for not returning to England even when urged by Peacock to do so, and despite bouts of guilt and frustration at his consequent political impotence.[34]

Most morbid conditions were held to improve in a mild climate; a spell in Southern Europe was the standard prescription for delicate constitutions and mysterious ailments. Coleridge and Southey went to Malta and Madeira respectively on doctor's advice. But there were only a few for which residence abroad was considered essential. The most favoured places were Madeira, the South of France, Portugal or Italy. British health resorts such as Hastings were considered second best. Tuberculosis was one such serious disease; obstinate syphilis was another.

Syphilitics were renowned for feeling the cold more intensely than others. Cold not only made the body more recipient to the infection, but also, according to Hunter, 'in warm climates the disease seldom or never arises to such heights as in cold climates; it is more slow in its progress, and much more easy to cure'. Pearson declared that patients who moved abroad 'with Lues Venerea in their constitution' found that they could do without medical assistance during their stay. The idea persisted beyond Shelley's lifetime. A medical textbook of 1829 suggested that the day might come when Barbados and Jamaica would become syphilitic resorts. The seaside was especially recommended. Naples, Montpellier, and Lisbon, three resorts mentioned by Swediaur as outstandingly successful in curing syphilitics, were coastal or nearly so. Lawrence mentions 'residence at the seaside and warm bathing as being especially advantageous to the lingering arthritic ailments of syphilitic patients'.[35]

Shelley was very sensitive to cold, and, by contrast, blossomed in the heat. 'The extreme heat,' wrote Mary, 'always put Shelley in spirits.' In July and August of 1819, when the Shelleys were at Livorno, he 'basked in the dazzling heat and sunlight' which to others was 'almost intolerable'. At one time his doctors advised him to go somewhere even warmer — Spain and, as mentioned earlier, Tunis.[36]

However, heat favoured the spread of other diseases such as worms and dysentery. The expatriate English in Italy, whether there for their health — as so many were — or not, tended to be itinerant, following the climate of their choice from one residence to another. When the weather turned cold at a fashionable spa like the Bagni di Lucca, they would move south to Rome and then to Naples. When it became too hot there they would move north once more, timing their return to Lucca to coincide with the opening of the season. The Shelleys' numerous domestic upheavals during the Italian years are sometimes presented as the result of a demonic wanderlust of Shelley's, on whose altar he sacrificed the health and happiness of his family. In fact, the typical pattern of the itinerant English family in Italy can be discerned.[37] In 1818 after a spell at the Bagni di Lucca he went south to Naples in October and north to Rome in the spring. In his case the pattern was disrupted. There was the need to negotiate with Lord Byron about the future of Allegra, his daughter by Claire. On one occasion the Shelleys were unable to return to the Bagni di Lucca because of scandal spread by their servant Paolo.

The heat agreed with Shelley, but not with the children; both William and Clara died of conditions indirectly due to it. This was to become a major cause of estrangement between him and Mary, who wrote despairingly after William's death at Rome in June 1819: 'We came to Italy thinking to do Shelley's health good — but the Climate is not any means warm enough to be of benefit to him & yet it is that that has destroyed my two children . . . [William's] malady appeared of so slight a nature — and as arising simply from worms inspired no fear of danger . . . we had a most excellent English surgeon to attend him and he allowed that these were the fruits of this hateful Italy — '.[38] After the birth of the Shelleys' last child, Percy Florence, in November 1819, they never again seriously considered moving south, in spite of doctors' recommendations, the danger to the baby being the major reason.[39] Another complicating factor was the desire to have a trustworthy surgeon (John Bell) as Mary's accoucheur, which resulted in several changes of plan as they tried to track *his* movements – vainly, as it happened. Finally there was the pull of Pisa, presided over by the world-famous Vaccà and containing one of the most illustrious medical schools in Europe. Shelley had been recommended to spend the winter there as early as May 1819 and in fact moved there in January 1820, driven out of Florence by the hardest weather for seventy years. Thereafter, the Shelleys spent most of their time in that city, the nearby Bagni di Pisa and the littoral towns of the Bay of Spezia – Livorno and finally Lerici. For most of the last four years of his life, Shelley was living either at a watering place, the seaside or a centre of medicine. (These were probably the attractions for many of the other English colonists as well; at salon gatherings in Pisa doctors and professors of medicine were lionised as often as poets and writers.) Without denying the existence of other motives for the Shelleys' wanderings – captivation by the scenery, antiquities and works of art, the need for congenial society – one cannot ignore the constant pressure of illness. Shelley's principal pursuit was health.

Continental practice in treating syphilis was very different from its counterpart in England. There the physician directed his patients to the country's natural resources – mineral waters, hot springs, vapour baths – and played down mercurials. Swediaur reported that mercury had actually been banned in the hospitals of Italy and Portugal until a few years before he wrote. He singled out Naples as a place where those who had suffered from syphilis for twenty or thirty years, afraid of using mercury, would go regularly every year, their objective being the natural stoves (*stufe*) of the *Sudatorio di San Germano*, where a few weeks' treatment would set them up for the next year. The Naples area abounded (and abounds) in medicinal springs, one of the best-known being Castellamare, of which a Victorian traveller–doctor, Madden, reported that it was especially used in cases of 'obstinate gout', 'rheumatism', 'chronic skin diseases', and 'arthritic affections'. Behind these phrases one can discern that among the patients were old bucks suffering from the infirmities bred of youthful intemperance, gonorrhoeal rheumatism being the 'rake's disease'. There is no record that Shelley attended any Naples baths, though he considered taking a house in Castellamare for June 1819.[40] The imagery of medicinal steam did, however, work its way into *Prometheus Unbound*, on which he was working while at Naples and directly afterwards at Rome.

At two other places Shelley certainly did use the baths. One was the Bagni di Lucca, where he stayed for three months in the summer of 1818, possibly on the recommendation of a Dr Beilby of Livorno. According to Madden these baths were sulphurous and were particularly used for 'chronic rheumatism, leucorrhoea, catarrhal affections of the urinary organs [gleets], dyspepsia, and certain cutaneous eruptions'. Later in 1820 and again the following year Shelley went to the Bagni di Pisa (San Giuliano), the calcareous hot waters of which were used for 'the treatment of gout and rheumatism, impaired power and enlargement of the joints and also in certain chronic ulcers and skin diseases'. He very likely used the Casciano baths as well. Mary wrote to Maria Gisborne in December 1819 that the pain in Shelley's side was taking on 'so rhumatic an appearance' that a course of warm baths in the following May was envisaged; she mentioned Casciano, famous for its rheumatic cures. Shelley did go there in May and June of 1820, had a respite from his 'nervous symptoms', and talked to a doctor at the baths.[41]

Carriage exercise and horse riding were highly recommended in all the conditions from which Shelley is supposed to have suffered – consumption, hepatitis and kidney disease. They were also appropriate for venereal complaints, especially chronic gonorrhoea.[42] Horses were relatively cheap in Italy, and as soon as he arrived at the Bagni di Lucca Shelley began to explore the countryside in this way. No doubt he enjoyed this fashionable gentlemanly pursuit for its own sake, but the activity also had a medical purpose. 'We keep horses as this kind of activity is absolutely essential for my health' he wrote to Peacock in January 1819 at a time when he was taking mercury, and he explained to Claire in 1821 that his reason for going in for sailing was that it was cheaper than the horse riding prescribed by Vaccà, his Pisan doctor.[43]

The hepatic phase: December 1818 – February 1819

Mary wrote that during their sojourn in Naples Shelley 'put himself under the care of a medical man who promised great things and made him endure severe bodily pain without any good results. Constant and poignant physical suffering exhausted him.' It was during this period that he wrote some of his 'saddest verses'. The medical man was a Doctor Roskilly, of whom practically nothing is known. From letters to Peacock, one learns more about what Shelley suffered. 'I am under an English surgeon here who says I have a disease of the liver which he will cure & have been using mercury and Cheltenham salts with much caution and some success for this last ten days.' Later he added that caustic had been laid on his side.[44]

These, especially the use of Cheltenham salts, were standard treatments for chronic hepatitis. The caustic suggests that Roskilly was opening an issue in the hepatic region, a drastic but logical development of blistering. A hangover from the 'humoral theory' when disease was thought of as a deep-seated poison, issues were artificial suppurations created by lunar caustic and kept festering with the insertion of peas or gentian root, supposedly purging the poison. To keep an issue open – and the process could go on for six months – was a lucrative part of a surgeon's practice.[45]

In the back of Mary's journal, surrounded by jottings dating from 1818, some in Shelley's handwriting, is a prescription for balsam of copaiba to be taken in a gum arabic mucilage with *Liquor Potassae* (a diuretic) as an adjuvant. This was a ferocious medicine producing headache, with flushing of the face, dryness in the mouth and redness of the lips and tongue. The *Encyclopaedia Britannica* for 1911 wrote of it that 'its distinctive features are its disagreeable taste and the unpleasant eructations to which it may give rise, its irritant action on the intestine in any but small doses, and its exceptionally marked stimulant action on the kidneys. In large doses, this last action may lead to renal inflammation.' It also left a 'characteristic odour on the breath' which had to be disguised. The reason why one might want to disguise it, apart from the unpleasantness, was that, like turpentine, the first use almost invariably attributed to the acrid resin in the dispensatories was for urethral discharges. (By 1911, its only use was in treating the gleets of chronic gonorrhoea.) It seems most likely that the medicine was meant for Shelley; Mary's journal was the repository for prescriptions for the whole family, and one knows of no condition for which the others might have taken it. Occasionally it was used for hepatitis but it is not certain that the prescription dates from late 1818; it could have been one of Beilby's or even Lawrence's.[46]

When the actuality of Shelley's treatments is brought home, one begins to feel that Mary has played his sufferings down rather than up. His assurance to Peacock that he is using mercury with 'extreme caution' suggests that Peacock had seen him suffering a mercury treatment on a previous occasion, and would have wanted such assurance. (One of the effects of taking mercury was that the patient became sensitised to it, and salivation was excited by increasingly smaller doses.)[47] It obviously debilitated him further. A young traveller who met Shelley during his last days in Naples noticed his emaciation and 'read on his countenance and in the whole of his delicate excited frame the words "Death, early death!" ' It was during this period and at Rome when he was still 'suffering his cure'[48] that he worked on *Julian and Maddalo*, a poem whose imagery of burning, stamping, sealing and, above all, immediate sense of frenzied pain, owe something in our view to Shelley's actual suffering from a running sore during its composition.

Liver damage is a common result of secondary syphilis, though this was not universally recognised. Astruc reported that a latent venereal taint could cause 'obstructions' in various organs, including the liver. On the other hand Hunter declared that syphilis did not attack the liver. As someone who trusted English rather than Continental doctors, Shelley is more likely to have been of the Hunterian persuasion, and seems to have welcomed the diagnosis, for chronic hepatitis was regarded as curable. Yet despite the fact that Shelley was being given orthodox if severe treatment for a complaint not in itself disgraceful, when Mary published a selection of Shelley's letters in 1840, she left in the doctor's diagnosis of a liver condition, but omitted the remedy, except for the horse riding![49] There were many innocent reasons for taking mercury; even William's worm powders contained it in the form of calomel. (One suspects that this and drastic purges must bear some responsibility for his death.) The only plausible explanation for this omission is that Mary considered that the mere mention of mercury would invite inferences that Shelley had really been suffering from a shameful disease. It shows that early suppressions in the Shelley record were in part directed towards obviating this charge and reveals the hypersensitivity of Mary on the matter.

At Rome Shelley came under the care of John Bell (1763–1820), one of the most brilliant anatomists of his day. One surmises that he countermanded Roskilly's treatment. Mary's comment on the latter shows she lost faith in him, but she never did in Bell. At any rate, Shelley's health improved in Rome. As well as William's vermifuges, he prescribed a strong cordial, an opiate which seems to have had the same formula as the 'black drop', and a diuretic mixture, the latter apparently intended for Shelley.[50] There is no knowing what Bell diagnosed, apart from the consumptive symptoms referred to by Claire, though one small clue exists: if he disagreed with Roskilly, he probably thought that the fixed pain might be nephritic. Bell had extensive experience in lithotomy (cutting for kidney stone) and it could have been he who encouraged Shelley to consult Vaccà, another acknowledged expert, who in the early 1820s published three lithotomical treatises.

The nephritic phase: Pisa and elsewhere 1820–2

Andrea Vaccà Berlinghieri (1771–1826) had established his reputation with his *Traité des maladies vénériennes* (1800). It was not unusual to combine expertise in lithotomy with venereology, kidney damage being a frequent result of gonorrhoea. Benjamin Bell (no relation to John Bell) had the same spread of talents.[51]

Mary was retrospectively to write of Shelley's consultation with Vaccà: 'He, like every other medical man could only guess at [the cause of Shelley's suffering], and gave little hope of immediate relief. He enjoined him to abstain from all physicians and medicine and to leave his complaint to Nature.' But in July he did commit himself to a diagnosis – nephritis and, from October on, references to this come thick as autumn leaves, especially in letters to Claire. 'Vaccà says his disease is entirely nervous and nephretic' wrote Mary. Shelley was showing concern about drinking water in August 1821 and Jane Williams reported to Rossetti in the 1870s that Shelley was still having spasms when she knew him, though not to any alarming degree. Yet when Trelawny saw Vaccà after Shelley's death, the latter told him that Shelley's disease had not been nephritic, though it is unclear whether Vaccà had changed his mind in Shelley's lifetime or as a result of examining a piece of what Trelawny alleged was Shelley's kidney.[52]

Despite these indications that Vaccà was genuinely puzzled, bided his time before diagnosing, and even then was prepared to change his mind, some commentators have assumed that '[Vaccà] had at once wisely diagnosed

Shelley's ill-health as nervous in origin, recommending the relaxation of the baths and a relief from medicines'.[53] From this one might infer that Vaccà was giving a dummy prescription to a hysteric.

But what else should Vaccà have done? Here was a patient who had been thoroughly 'messed' by one doctor after another, who had over the years taken arsenic, nitric acid, laurel leaves, diuretics, including powerful resins, opium and mercury, drugs known or believed to damage the digestive organs and the last especially a cause of chronic nephritis which is listed in medical dictionaries even today. Was his infirmity constitutional or drug-induced? The only way to find out was to eliminate one variable. It was in line with good medical practice of his day – Abernethy would have done the same – to have 'earnestly interdicted medicine in all its forms'.[54] It was advice consistent with Vaccà's practice elsewhere. He was, for instance, exceedingly cautious about giving any prophylactic mercury for gonorrhoea, believing that the disease 'guérit d'elle-même' and would yield to 'les forces de la nature', especially 'le bain général'. Like Abernethy, he believed that many so-called syphilitic symptoms would yield to diet, and his prescriptions of baths and horse riding were standard treatments for pain, rheumatism, urethral and nephritic disorders. Shelley's use of resinous medicines and diuretics certainly suggests a chronic urinary condition, consistent with kidney damage, and his spasms would have suggested kidney stone to contemporary doctors. At the same time it is no wonder that Vaccà's diagnosis did not reassure him, despite the latter's insistence that his nephritis was of a type 'not mortal'. A lithotomy, which Shelley saw in prospect – a major operation even today – was in 1821, even when carried out by a skilful surgeon (without anaesthetics), an often fatal ordeal.[55]

During the winter of 1820–1 Shelley suffered the recurrence of ophthalmia, mentioned earlier, and boils 'which got worse while his face swelled dreadfully'.[56] 'He was a martyr to the most painful complaint, Nephritis,' reported Medwin, '. . . and now was trying Scott's vitriolic acid baths, much in vogue.' No patent medicine of this name existed, nor can we find a precedent for using vitriolic (sulphuric) acid for nephritis. The 'Scott' can only be Beddoes' Helenus Scott, who had come home from Bombay a few years previously and set up a fashionable practice in London; he began to treat hepatitis (not nephritis) and, to a lesser extent, syphilis, with a mixture of dilute nitric and hydrochloric acid. Medical journals are full of references to 'Mr Scott's Nitro-muriatic acid baths' for a few years from 1817 onwards; they were indeed in vogue.[57] But we can find no reference to his using sulphuric acid. On the other hand, sulphurous baths were a standard remedy for diseases of the skin, gout, diseased joints, rheumatism and pain of all sorts. The hot waters of Italy were held to be effective because of the 'excess of vitriolic acid in the ferruginous waters'. (They were also held to cure venereal eruptions.)[58] It looks as though Shelley, deprived of the benefits of

Hogarth's *The Harlot's Progress*, Plate V (detail). 'She dies – and from the
terrible consequences of pandemonial love' (Lichtenberg's 1799
commentary). The eighteenth-century image of the prostitute's end. The
fallen teeth on the handkerchief next to the spittoon are signs of mercury poisoning.

Silhouette of Dr Lind.

Chalvey Well, Slough, c. 1850

The Windmill Inn, Salt Hill, during the early railway era.
Shelley and Mary stayed there in April 1815.

Charles Kirkpatrick Sharpe as a
young man, by Thomas Fraser.

Self-caricature of Charles
Kirkpatrick Sharpe in later life.

The Jones memorial by Flaxman, University College Chapel,
Oxford. Jones learns Sanskrit and codifies Indian laws.

Abernethy delivering his anatomical lectures (engraving after Thomas Lawrence).

Thomas Trotter in the uniform of a naval surgeon.

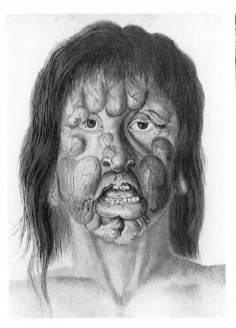

Gonsalves, an elephantiac of
Madeira, c. 1807.

The Syphilitic by Albrecht
Dürer (1495), showing
Scorpio in the ascendant.

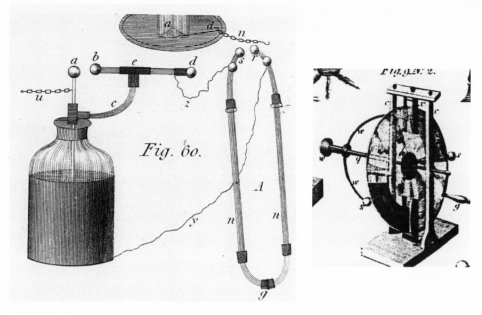

Electrical apparatus recommended by Adam Walker, probably resembling that owned by Shelley at Eton and Oxford. i. Leyden jar accumulator. Electricity is applied through the jaws *s* and *r* of the forceps to the part requiring treatment. ii. Generator, used for 'increasing the circulation of the blood'. When the glass disc is rotated, thin leather pads at top and bottom produce a charge. This is collected by segments of black silk and makes sparks to the brass armature (s, s).

Electrical experimentalist on glass-footed stool, c. 1790.

Goblet said to be the original of the bowl of mercury in *Letter to Maria Gisborne* (approximately 9 × 9 cm).

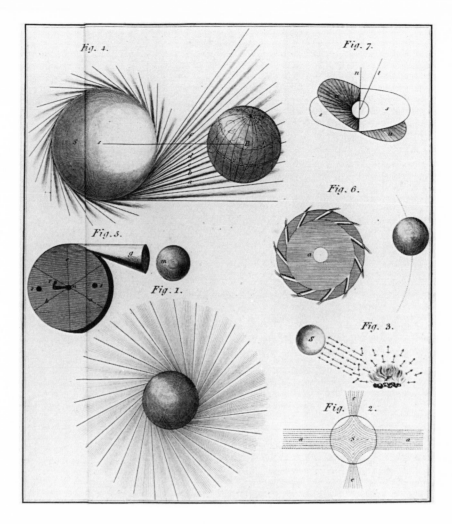

Light represented by Adam Walker as whirling spokes
(*P.U.*, IV, 254).

Asphyxiating a dog in the vapours of the Grotta del Cane, late 18th century. Visited in February 1819 by the Shelleys, who refused the exhibition (*P.U. III*, iii, 124–30).

Entrance to the Grotto of Posilipo, Naples, c. 1798. Visited by the Shelleys in December 1818 and a likely source for the cavern in *The Triumph of Life*.

the Bagni di Pisa, both by floods and the cold, was making himself an artificial bath to treat both the pain in his side and the boils. Medwin, who had recently returned from India where he is likely to have heard of Scott, is here parading his (inaccurate) knowledge of 'medical acids'.

It was during this period that Medwin introduced Shelley to mesmerism, which seems to have worked, though this was probably due as much to the soothing presence of Claire and, subsequently, of Shelley's last infatuation, Jane Williams. Both Jane and Mary later 'magnetised' him.[59] Thus one of Shelley's final treatments was with electricity, the sympathetic fluid pervading the universe, which he regarded as sometimes analogous to, sometimes synonymous with, love. Out of this experience came the poem 'The Magnetic Lady to her Patient'. Jane asks her subject 'What would do / You good when suffering and awake? / What cure your head and side?' The sleeper replies 'What would cure, that would kill me, Jane' and asks her not to tempt him to 'break my chain'. Medwin thought that Shelley's reply referred to his fear of lithotomy; more probably, he was talking both of breaking his marriage bond, as Judith Chernaik suggested, and of suicide.

Shelley's best winter in Italy was that of 1821–2; all reports agree that there was an improvement in his health, especially after he went to Lerici in April. Thornton Hunt, who saw him just before he drowned, reported that his chest had filled out since 1818. Thornton wanted to counteract the impression of effeminacy left by Trelawny, who had written that study had contracted Shelley's chest. But Trelawny and Thornton agree about his robustness, the former declaring that he could outwalk all the Pisan circle.[60]

Yet there are signs that Shelley was haunted to the very end of his life by the fear of progressive degeneration and the more estranged he was from Mary's love, the more he felt that his strength to resist disease was undermined. Medwin often heard him express the wish to die young and 'escape from the decay of mind and body that must soon be my portion'. Gronow meeting him shortly before his drowning reported that he looked careworn and ill; he avoided answering any questions about himself, his way of life and his future plans.[61] This reluctance to discuss the future is expressed in a letter of 18 June: 'If the past and the future could be obliterated, the present would content me so well that I could say with Faust to the passing moment, "Remain, thou, thou art so beautiful."' On that same day he asked Trelawny to procure him prussic acid, in order to 'hold in my possession that golden key to the chamber of perpetual rest'. 'His physical suffering was often very severe,' Peacock commented, 'and this last letter must have been written under the anticipation that it might become incurable.' Shelley's strange dreams and behaviour during the last weeks of his life and the nightmarish clarity of his last poem *The Triumph of Life* suggest that he was using laudanum heavily once more, despite Vaccà's prohibition.[62] Then there is the business of Marianne Hunt's portrait bust of him. Based on memories of these last days, it depicts a weary and sick-looking man, yet the Hunts thought it an excellent likeness.[63]

It is not germane to our purpose to speculate that Shelley's behaviour towards the end of his life was a harbinger of neurosyphilis and that intuiting this he engineered his own death by drowning on 8 July 1822; for one thing, since neurosyphilis appears in only a quarter of all untreated and unsuccessfully treated cases, the chances were in favour of any syphilitic avoiding this fate. Secondly, while the onset of neurosyphilis is very various, the only points of resemblance between Shelley's symptoms during the last years and that of a fairly well-documented case such as Guy de Maupassant's are that each was diagnosed as having a 'nervous' condition; Maupassant suffered for years from eye complaints before the condition finally declared itself. Medwin reported that Shelley was suffering from myopia and a line from 'The Magnetic Lady to her Patient' could be taken as meaning that he had headaches as well as a fixed pain in his side. Maupassant took up sailing during the years preceding his final collapse because he had a passion for it. (It was also a healthy activity which he could pursue long after he became too feeble for other exercise.)[64] Curious as such parallels might at first appear, they clearly have many possible explanations, and are in any case tenuous. Thirdly, all the indications are that it was Edward Williams who was impatient to embark on the last voyage, against all advice.[65] Finally, and most importantly, the speculation leads nowhere; there is ample evidence of a continuing working-over of the theme of sexually transmitted disease in Shelley's poetry after the move to Italy without the need for recourse to it.

It is to the mythologising of Shelley's experience that we now turn, in which we include not merely his personal life story, but his understanding of the social history of his age. 'You know I always seek in what I see the manifestation of something beyond the present and tangible object' he wrote.[66] He believed that 'almost every youth in Britain' had endured a sexual experience with a 'diseased and insensible prostitute' – in other words, that it was a *typical* story, and thus a poetical circumstance. With Yeats he could have said 'These masterful images . . . grew in pure mind, but out of what began?'[67] That masterful images should emerge from such a rag-and-bone shop should be a source of admiration, and also a reminder of how firmly the ladders of Shelley's poetry are grounded in the mundane.

8

The myth of syphilis

The readings which follow are supported by the examination of Shelley's biography attempted in the previous chapters, but they are not, ultimately, dependent on total acceptance of our hypothesis. That is, they could be 'right', yet be registering vicarious experience on Shelley's part.

Cultures reveal their traumas in their art. In Western Europe, the far-reaching effects of the epidemic of syphilis which swept the continent after 1494 was one such trauma. A perception of this is to be found in D. H. Lawrence's *Preface to These Paintings*. He attributed the 'extra morbidity' that appeared in Europe at the end of the Middle Ages to the realisation that 'the very sexual act of procreation might bring as one of its consequences a foul disease, and the unborn might be tainted from the moment of conception'. 'By the end of the sixteenth [century], its ravages were obvious and the shock of them had just penetrated the thoughtful and imaginative consciousness.' The 'secret awareness of syphilis and of the utter secret terror and horror of it' had 'struck a blow at our feeling of communion . . . we have become ideal beings, creatures that exist in idea of one another, rather than flesh and blood kin . . . we are afraid of the instincts . . . the reason being some great shock to the procreative self.'[1]

Lawrence's ideas are intuitive, and dubiously applicable to an entire culture, at least to the extent to which he pushes them. But there is a particular relevance in using them as a reference point from which to consider the effect that a venereal disease might have had on Shelley. For not only did Lawrence instance him as an example of an artist who had responded to the impact of syphilis on the consciousness by escaping into idealism, but his insight is an unwitting development of one which Shelley himself had had concerning the effect of venereal disease on English literature:[2]

The earlier dramatic English writers are often frightfully obscene, exceeding even the Romans . . . Luxury produced for the Romans what the venereal disease did for the writers of James, and after the redeeming interval over which Milton presided the effects of both were united under Charles II to infect literature.

(*Prose*, p. 223)

Lawrence was not concerned with whether Shelley actually had contracted venereal disease: his point was that between the sixteenth-century epidemic and the discovery of the arsenic and bismuth treatment of the early twentieth the fear of syphilis had lain 'potent and overmastering' for everyone:

> I am convinced that *some* of Shakespeare's horror and despair, in his tragedies, arose from the shock of his consciousness of syphilis. I don't suggest for one moment Shakespeare ever contracted syphilis. I have never had syphilis myself. Yet I know and confess how profound is my fear of the disease, and more than fear, my horror.
>
> (Lawrence, p. 57)

Secret horror is not, however, the only possible response of an artist to a communal shock of this sort. An alternative reaction is to mythologise the experience, to dignify it and thus assert man's control over it. In the case of syphilis such an attempt was made within forty years of the epidemic. This was Girolamo Fracastor's *Syphilis sive Morbus Gallicus* (1530), a didactic Latin poem which gave the disease its incongruously euphonious name. Its models were Lucretius' *De Rerum Natura* and Virgil; much admired in its day, the poem is arguably among the finest of its genre – the Renaissance Latin Georgic. It is hard to think of a better poem on a more unlikely subject.

Fracastor's latest translator has revealed the work to be an allegory in that Renaissance tradition whereby pagan characters could function as saints and types of the Christian divinity; Pan could represent Christ, Diana the Virgin Mary and so on.[3] However, what strikes a modern reader is not so much its orthodoxy as its humanism. Like Chaucer's *The Knight's Tale* it proclaims man's dignity in an irrational universe. Human sinfulness as a cause of the disease functions surprisingly little in Fracastor, considering the subject and the apocalyptic feelings it engendered in contemporaries such as Sebastian Brant and Albrecht Dürer. Fracastor believed that the Renaissance epidemic was inevitable, a result of a conjunction of certain planets. He gives several mythological accounts of the disease's origins, in some of which impiety features, but the punishment is no more proportioned to the offence than that of the man in the *Arabian Nights* who blinds a genie's son by carelessly throwing around date shells. Yet, though man is subject to these whims, the world is not a thoroughfare of woe; gods can be appeased through ritual purification; nature has not turned against man, but contains at once the evil and the cure, yielding both a healing mineral (mercury) and vegetable (lignum vitae). As well as offering practical help (according to the best lights of his time) Fracastor's poem arouses horror and sympathy, especially on behalf of the stricken young.

Nahum Tate made a famous translation; Pope included the poem in his *Selecta Poemata Italorum* of 1740. And at least one English poem drew on its myth of the discovery of lignum vitae. As Fracastor's poem bears on this study it is worth some examination.

Certain sailors, wrote Fracastor, venturing into unknown waters on their way to the New World, driven beyond their destination, were guided to the island of Ophyre, where, armed with arquebuses, one of their first acts was to kill several of a host of brightly coloured birds (parrots), which inhabited the 'untrodden mazes' of the forest. The birds were sacred to Apollo, who, speaking through one of the flock that had survived, decreed that 'Discord herself' should arise among the sailors, 'bringing in her train madness and the sword' and encounters with the Cyclopes. In addition their bodies would become 'loathsome with an unknown disease' until such time as they repented and implored help of the very woods that they had violated. On hearing this verdict, 'a sudden numbness seized their bones, and all their blood paled and ran icy-cold with fear'.[4]

Features of this myth can be seen quite clearly in *The Ancient Mariner* of Coleridge, who admired Fracastor. (The most likely time for Coleridge to have read the latter was 1794 when he was projecting an unrealised 'Imitations' of Renaissance Latin poets.)[5] There is a sea voyage to the west, ingratitude towards providential powers, wanton and inexplicable shooting of a 'pious bird of good omen', the albatross,[6] and the aftermath of a living death which comes in the shape of a harlot associated with a loathsome disease whose supposed involvement in the origin of syphilis we traced in Chapter 6:

> *Her* lips were red, *her* looks were free,
> Her locks were yellow as gold:
> Her skin was as white as leprosy,
> The Night-mare LIFE-IN-DEATH was she,
> Who thicks man's blood with cold.

The antithesis to this leprous white harlot-figure in Coleridge's poem is the red-rose healthy bride, from whose marriage the unlucky wedding guest has been diverted by the Mariner. The tale imparts fatal knowledge that makes him a 'sadder and a wiser man'. Whatever this knowledge is, it has made him recoil from a world in which people unthinkingly and happily continue to get married. On the Mariner's recommendation he has 'turned from the bridegroom's door'. The Mariner says that praying together is far sweeter than a wedding feast – in other words, it is preferable to seek community in spiritual rather than in sexual congress – and he has been able to transmit the sense of a 'great shock to the procreative self', whereby interrelatedness 'as ideal beings' is exalted above flesh and blood kinship, to revert to Lawrentian terms.

This reading is not offered as a solution to the shooting of the albatross and what this 'means', but as an additional corrective to the popular impression that Coleridge's poem is all about personal guilt and has no wider social application. On one level, *The Ancient Mariner* is a parable, felt by a sensitive person, of the punishment inflicted on Europe for its rapacious exploitation of other continents – the new twist given to the Biblical proverb that the sins of the fathers are visited upon the children.

Coleridge's use of Fracastor is an example of Romantic mythologising of the awareness of syphilis. Shelley's work supplies others, some of which, we are satisfied, involve allusions to Fracastor, as well as imagery drawn from a variety of sources.

Around 1800 the older name 'lues venerea' started being replaced by 'syphilis' in England, largely, we suspect, through the influence of Swediaur. Interest in Fracastor's poem also seems to have increased. In 1808 it was reprinted in England for the first time in sixty years. The publishers were Slatter and Munday of Oxford, the booksellers whose premises were practically opposite University College, and to whom Timothy Shelley introduced his son, begging Slatter to 'indulge him in his printing freaks'. (They published the *Margaret Nicholson* volume.)[7]

The book, therefore, was readily available in the Oxford of 1810; Good's translation of Lucretius, which Shelley had read before the *Margaret Nicholson* poems, quoted from Fracastor, at a point which for Shelley would have been a conspicuous one (Book VI, the episode on diseases, including elephantiasis).[8] In addition there are passages in Shelley which are so striking in their parallels as to convince us that he did read the poem as a whole, even when due allowances are made for the fact that both he and Fracastor had common models in Lucretius, Virgil and Ovid.

In 'Lines written among the Euganean Hills' Shelley laments the enslaved state of Italy under the brutal Celt (the Austrian Emperor). Fracastor similarly laments the state of Italy, once so prosperous, now suffering the 'foreigner's yoke', the 'Euganei' having been subdued by the Austrian Emperor. Shelley's lament is followed by an apostrophe to Padua, formerly a famous centre of humanist and medical studies, in whose halls the lamp of learning is extinguished. The allusion is chiefly to Petrarch, but Fracastor had also been a luminary of the university and had made an important contribution to both literary critical theory and medicine. It was during his tenure that the university was closed owing to the league of the Emperor and Pope against Venice. No other poem of Shelley's contains so many direct allusions to *The Ancient Mariner* as this; among them is a reference to the dice game between Death and Life-in-Death. If, as we believe, Shelley perceived that Coleridge had made use of Fracastor's fable, the parallels with these two poets' works would not be coincidental. Both 'The Euganean Hills' and *Syphilis* contain the image of the spark which becomes a blaze consuming an entire forest. In Fracastor the spark is compared to disease spread by contagion (*contagis*) (I, 45–52), in Shelley to the inextinguishable spirit of revolution, which he elsewhere calls a 'contagion'.

More evidence of Shelley's reading of Fracastor is found in *Letter to Maria Gisborne*, which contains a picture of gnomes working in liquid mercury mines situated beneath volcanoes. In this case, however, Darwin's *The Botanic Garden* (Part I, Canto III, vii) is likely to be the primary source.

Fracastor depicts Ilceus' transportation to a river of mercury in the volcanic area of the Lipari Islands. Yet another passage bearing signs of Fracastor's influence (combined with that of Spenser's Cave of Mammon and Milton) occurs in *Alastor* where the Poet wanders among

> the secret caves
> Rugged and dark, winding among the springs
> Of fire and poison, inaccessible
> To avarice and pride, their starry domes
> Of diamond and of gold expand above
> Numberless and immeasurable halls . . .
> . . . Nor had that scene of ampler majesty
> Than gems or gold, the varying roof of heaven
> And the green earth lost in his heart its claims
> To love and wonder.   (87–92, 95–8)

Fracastor's Ilceus sees 'vast and rugged chambers of that timeless world, the huge caverns where no light ever breaks and the rivers winding far below the ground'. Here, says his conductress, is the 'womb of all those metals you mortals, who look upon the realms of the sky, so keenly desire'. The idea of inaccessibility to avarice and pride, and the glittering underworld having its counterpart in the star-hung dome above, are both present in Fracastor's poem. Liquid mercury and volcanic fires are coupled in *Alastor*, if we are right in identifying the former with the 'springs of poison'. As in *Alastor*, Fracastor's underground caverns have roofs glittering with gold – 'aurea tecta'. His halls trickle with dross – 'rorantesque domos spodiis' – 'domos' suggesting both 'domes' by homophony and 'halls'.[9] There are other reminiscences of Fracastor which will be mentioned in due course.

Another area from which Shelley drew imagery relating to venereal disease is the Bible. Such scattered remarks as his jotting: 'Loathsome diseases, the cause of modern obscenity, exceeding the worst of antiquity in hideousness and horror' suggest that as far as science went he inclined either towards a Columbian or combination theory of the origin of syphilis. For mythopoeic purposes, however, he used Biblical plague imagery to give an archetypal perspective on the disease which was widely regarded as a *type* or modern counterpart of leprosy, and which for him epitomised the evil resulting from the idea of the God of the Bible. One passage particularly lodged in his mind:

The Lord shall smite thee with the botch of Egypt, and with the emerods, and with the scab, with the itch, whereof thou canst not be healed. The Lord shall smite thee with madness, and blindness, and astonishment of heart: and thou shalt grope at noonday . . . Moreover he shall bring upon thee all the diseases of Egypt, which thou wast afraid of; and they shall cleave unto thee.   (Deuteronomy, 28.27–9, 60)

It is from the Bible, too, that some of Shelley's imagery of harlot-figures derives, particularly from the passage in Proverbs where a young man is warned against seduction by a 'strange woman' – a passage which eighteenth-century Biblical commentators interpreted as simultaneously allegorical (a warning against 'whoring after strange gods') and literal (an exhortation to chastity):[10]

> The lips of a strange woman drop as an honeycomb and her mouth is smoother than oil: but her end is bitter as wormwood, sharp as a two-edged sword . . . for by means of a whorish woman a man is brought to a piece of bread . . . I discerned among the youths, a young man void of understanding, passing through the street near her corner; and he went the way to her house. In the twilight, in the evening, in the black and dark night: and behold, there met him a woman with the attire of an harlot, and subtil of heart . . . so she caught him, and kissed him . . . with her much fair speech she caused him to yield, with the flattering of her lips she forced him . . . He goeth after her straightway, as an ox goeth to the slaughter . . . till a dart strike through his liver; as a bird hasteth to the snare, and knoweth not that it is for his life . . . for a whore is a deep ditch; and a strange woman is a narrow pit.
>
> (Proverbs, 5.3–4; 6.26; 7.7–10; 13, 21–3; 24.27)

We shall have occasion to refer to these two passages later. At this point we are using them to illustrate how in 'The Wandering Jew's Soliloquy' Shelley used Biblical allusions eclectically to emphasise the role of the Almighty as the author of disease and especially of a disease which tended 'more than any other to the destruction of the human species' thus betraying his desire to abolish his own work.[11]

The Jew tauntingly challenges God to kill him by one of his usual methods:

> Where is the noonday pestilence that slew
> The myriad sons of Israel's favoured nation?
> Where the destroying minister that flew
> Pouring the fiery tide of desolation
> Upon the leagued Assyrian's attempt?
> Where the dark earthquake demon who ingorged
> At thy dread word Korah's unconscious crew?
> Or the Angel's two-edged sword of fire that urged
> Our primal parents from their bower of bliss
> (Reared by thine hand) for errors not their own,
> Yes! I would court a ruin such as this,
> Almighty Tryant! and give thanks to thee. –
> Drink deeply – drain the cup of hate – remit; then I may die.
>
> (*Esdaile*, pp. 161–2)

As Cameron noted, the Biblical details are not exact, although Shelley had a wide knowledge of the Bible. There is, in the original, no *noonday* pestilence or *fiery tide* or *two-edged* sword.[12] In the Bible, too, it is the eating of the fruit which brings death into the world, and one would expect the Jew to name that as the 'ruin' he would court, rather than the angel's sword. The pestilence is a noonday one because as in 'Zeinab and Kathema' it strikes in manhood's prime and because it is associated with the 'groping at noonday' of blindness. Disease is here a *fire*, because it consumes the body; this is why certain diseases went by such names as 'St Anthony's fire' or 'The Persian fire'. The disease is called a 'fiery tide': Shelley has fused the account of the destruction of Sennacherib (II Kings, 19.35) with Isaiah, 30.30–3, where the Lord threatens a 'steam of brimstone' upon the Assyrians. In Numbers, 16, Korah is engulfed for disobedience, to the accompaniment of fire and plague. The angel's fiery sword, sometimes glossed as a comet, is two-edged and sharp, like the 'harlot's end'. The desperation of the Jew's desire to be relieved of the role of undying mortal may be gauged by his seeking 'ruin such as this' – the worst kind of death imaginable. Six years later Shelley made his Prometheus recall a curse in which he had invited Jupiter to smite him with disease: 'Rain then thy plagues upon me here / Ghastly disease and frenzying fear.' His purpose in so invoking the divine malevolence is to allow Jupiter to heap crimes upon his own head until he reveals himself to be externally what he is internally, like Ozymandias, and to become an object of scorn 'through boundless space and time'. (*Scorn* is often associated for Shelley with the idea that disease may make the sufferer an object not of pity but of contempt.) Similarly, the death of the Jew will be yet another indictment of God. 'Remit' has the obvious meaning 'lift this curse of immortality'. But the ambiguous punctuation also allows the sense that the Jew will 'remit', that is, hand back the cup of hate to God, who will be left holding it, unable to disclaim responsibility.[13] The thanks will be ironic, since God will have discredited himself.

The Fall of Man is a dominant motif in Shelley's poetry, and one which he constantly reworked while remaining agnostic concerning the ultimate origin of evil. Under the influence of John Newton, he was introduced to a framework on which a non-Christian version of the myth could be developed. This schema, which was Zoroastrian and based on the Zodiac of Dendera, was in Newton's case used for vegetarian propagandist purposes. Peacock, who in 1860 regarded the system as absurd, described Newton's schema as dividing the Zodiac into two hemispheres, that of Oromazes (good) and Ahrimanes (evil). Each hemisphere contained six Zodiacal signs. In Oromazes were Taurus (eternal light), Cancer (celestial matter) 'sleeping under the all-covering water on which Brahma floated in a lotus-flower for millions of ages', and Gemini, who typified the union of light and celestial matter. From this union issued Leo (Primogenial Love)

who produced the pure and perfect nature of things in Virgo, and Libra the balance denoted the coincidence of the ecliptic with the equator and the equality of man's happy existence . . . the first entrance of evil into the system was typified by the change of celestial into terrestrial matter – Cancer into Scorpio. Under this evil influence man became a hunter, Sagittarius the Archer, and pursued the wild animals, typified by Capricorn. Then, with animal food and cookery, came death into the world, and all our woe.

But Aesculapius or Aquarius the Waterman rose from the sea, typified by Pisces, 'with a jug of pure water and a bunch of fruit' and universal happiness under the Ram returned (Wolfe, II, p. 325). Shelley would have found the Fall of Man related to astrology in Milton as well: Libra, 'betwixt Astraea [Virgo] and the Scorpion sign' (*P.L.*, IV, 998), contains the head of the Serpent constellation (Anguis), which extends through Scorpio to Sagittarius. Satan, identified with Anguis, 'enters the world in Libra but leaves it between Scorpio and Sagittarius'.[14]

Traces of the details of this cyclical myth can be seen in Shelley's poetry right up to *Charles the First* and the *Triumph of Life*. As always, he did not simply take over another person's reading of a myth, but adapted it in his own highly individual way, as he did for instance in his development of Newton's vegetarian gloss on the Prometheus story.

One respect in which Shelley reshaped the Zodiac myth was in the treatment of Scorpio, which for Milton, as for Newton, is the crucial turning point in mankind's history. But for Shelley the turning point does not have an exclusively general meaning (the descent of spirit into matter) nor a narrowly specific one (eating animal food). The Fall of Man is for him both a metaphysical truth and a mythologised account of a real incident in history; it is also repeatedly re-enacted in the individual human life. One of the applications of the transition of Cancer into Scorpio is the entry into the world of a predatory principle, Selfishness, the opposite of sympathy and love; this predatory principle is exemplified by lust, one of the results of which is disease.

The ancient system of 'correspondences' linked each sign of the Zodiac with a part of the human body. Traces of this system remain in speech; one still speaks of being 'lion-hearted' or 'bull-necked'. The scorpion was assigned to the genitals. The bite of the scorpion, according to Pliny, whom Shelley had read at Eton, filled man with an ungovernable raging pain which he could assuage only by sexual intercourse, which in turn hurt the woman. Furthermore, according to the *Chambers' Cyclopaedia* article 'Venereal', the scorpion was yet another of the supposed causes of syphilis; this was actually offered as a scientific possibility!

Lister and some others take [syphilis] to have had its first rise from some of the serpentine kind, either from a bite thereof or from some of their flesh taken as food. This is pretty certain, that men, bitten or stung by scorpions, are greatly eased by coition, but the woman, Pliny assures us, receives a great deal of damage thereby ... what proves a remedy to the wounded person proves a disease to the woman, and from women thus infected, other men, they say, become infected in their turn, and thus has the disease been propagated.

It was from this superstition, probably, that yet another name for syphilis derived: the Serpentine Evil. Fracastor repeatedly alludes to it as 'serpens' (creeping); cleansing the body of the disease is like sloughing off a dead skin.

That there was a similarity between syphilis and the poison of stinging invertebrates and reptiles was often noted.[15]

Venereal disease, then, is woman's revenge on man for his violation and abuse of her. The idea is present in 'Zeinab and Kathema'. Another place where revenge is linked to syphilis is to be found in the *Chambers'* article:

> By communicating this dreadful malady, the severest scourge with which, in this life, Heaven chastens the indulgence of criminal desire, the Americans, says an excellent historian, have not only amply revenged their own wrongs, but . . . have perhaps more than counterbalanced all the benefits which Europe has derived from the discovery of the New World.

That syphilis is the punishment for the enslavement of a race has already been encountered in Newton and Jones; it was a commonplace of the period and can be found elsewhere in Shelley's reading.[16] Revenge and venereal disease are thus related by both myth and history. When Shelley in 'Lines written among the Euganean Hills' speaks of the 'bitter woe' that 'love or reason cannot change / The despot's rage, the slave's revenge' (234–5), he has a specific instance in mind: the tyrants of Italy and their rebellious subjects. But in context it also has the force of a general reflection and embraces every kind of despot–slave relationship, or alliance between Death and Sin, including that between men and women – the words 'despot' and 'slave' are those repeatedly used by Mary Wollstonecraft to characterise power relationships between the sexes – and between the masters and slaves of the West Indian colonies (where Jones had said elephantiasis was raging). The 'revenge' takes many forms, including bloodshed, as well as the one recognised as appropriate punishment for lust.

The scorpion also figures in the mythology of the fifteenth-century epidemic. According to astrological lore, the outbreak was signalled by an unprecedented conjunction of planets with Scorpio in the ascendent; one emblem of this concept is Dürer's print *The Syphilitic*. In Shelley the scorpion is used for many purposes: sometimes it is simply a goad of misery, the chastisement of God or, in his most famous allusion to Pliny, self-consuming desperation. 'And we are left, as scorpions ringed with fire / What should we do but sting ourselves to death?' (*Cenci* II, ii, 70–1). But it is also associated with lust as early as *Zastrozzi*, where Verezzi recoils from Matilda's bosom 'as if stung by a scorpion', and in *Laon and Cythna*. In *Queen Mab* when Shelley was using Chambers and the influence of Newton was at its height, the scorpion is associated with the Diseased Tyrant, a monster of sensualism who transmits a universal pestilence. At some points it is explicitly identified with 'Falshood', a complex word for Shelley. Falshood may simply mean 'lying' (*Prose*, p. 71); it may be false religion, Voltaire's *l'infâme* ('Falshood and Vice'); it may be associated with sexual vice ('Passion'); or it may be a fusion of all of these.

There are other cases where Shelley takes a dead metaphor like 'scorpion' and invests it with a literal pathological force.[17] A good example is the word 'canker' which suggests to most people a disease of roses, in which sense Shelley does use it once. But the word, cognate with 'cancer' and 'chancre', originally signified an eating, spreading gangrenous sore. When Shelley writes that the name 'King' 'has poison in it, 'tis the sperm / Of what makes life foul, cankerous and abhorred' he is thinking of venereal disease, for which 'the foul disease' was another common name.[18] He is also making use of a primitive germ theory, precursor to that of Pasteur; found in Lucretius, Fracastor owes his place in medical history to his development of it.[19] A second example concerns the words 'pestilence' and 'plague'. Since 'the pox' was considered by many to be the worst of all nineteenth-century scourges and so widespread as to partake of the nature of an epidemic, 'pestilence' and 'plague' should be understood to include syphilis, along with other diseases such as typhus, diphtheria, cholera, and yellow fever. The old-fashioned name 'lues venerea', often shortened to 'lues' (plague), indicates that syphilis had been classed as a kind of plague, the root meaning of the word being a 'stroke' or a 'wound', especially as dealt by divine anger. 'Plague' was the English Biblical translation of the Vulgate 'plaga', a word used to describe the infliction of leprosy and the diseased spots.[20] *Sickness* by William Thompson (1747), a didactic poem which Shelley knew and used in *Queen Mab*, calls syphilis 'a subtle fiend that mimics all the plagues'.[21] In the fifteenth century the disease was thought to be literally pestilential, that is, spread by the air, as well as contagious, and this attitude was preserved through language. Cowper calls it *pestis venerea*. When Shelley writes of 'pestilence' and 'plague' one should assume, unless there are indications to the contrary, that the idea of what Shelley called 'the pestilence that springs from unenjoying sensualism' is present. And that quotation, in turn, shows that sometimes in Shelley this may be the primary meaning.

The context from which Shelley gathers his allusions and mythology is frequently part of the meaning of the poem. In saying this we realise that we are disagreeing with Earl Wasserman, who maintained that Shelley completely 'new-models' his sources and that when he uses myths they 'are to be understood as really having no inherited contexts at all'. This is not the place at which to engage with Wasserman's thought-provoking argument, except to observe that it rests on the assumption that Shelley wrote for a 'pure' reader, who even when an underlying source is brought to light allows it promptly to recede into the shadows in order to experience the work 'as though it is autonomous'. Our assumption is the Empsonian one that a work of art is not autonomous.[22]

Here we may conveniently make overt some of our other assumptions and list what we consider to be the characteristics of Shelley's poetry most relevant to our argument at this point. Some of these are commonplaces of Shelley criticism; others are more contentious.

First of all, the allusiveness mentioned above is highly eclectic; there is almost never one source only for a name or image in Shelley's poetry. Moreover, the sources are seldom exclusively literary. Almost invariably there proves to be a fusion between events in Shelley's life and sources in his enormously wide reading. The use of elephantiasis in 'Ozymandias' is a good illustration, but the habit also displays itself in the most apparently trivial of cases, as, for instance, in *Letter to Maria Gisborne*. Shelley pities Maria, who has exchanged the delightful Italian countryside for sordid London. She must listen to the curse of a drunken prostitute – 'a wretched woman reeling by' (269) – instead of a melodious serenade or 'yellow-haired Pollonia murmuring / To Henry, some unutterable thing' (272–3). 'Pollonia' (spelled with one 'l' in Shelley's draft)[23] has long been identified with Apollonia Ricci, daughter of the Gisbornes' Livornese landlord; Apollonia, Mary used to tease Maria's son Henry, was dying of love for him. But 'Polonia' is also a character in Calderón's *St Patrick's Purgatory*, where she figures as a princess driven mad by passion. As well as a private joke, the name is a delicate compliment to Maria, who had introduced Shelley to Calderón, regarded by him as a liberating author. The unifying theme of the poem – Spanish freedom – mingles with the theme of friendship since Maria and Shelley are drawn together through shared sympathies on the subject. Clearly it is ridiculous to ask 'Which Pollonia did Shelley mean?' Both are appropriate for different reasons. Hence even a name can supply a glimpse of the associative powers of Shelley's imagination.

The point is important, because some readers may become impatient with what seems to them unnecessary source-hunting, and ask 'Why multiply explanations of why a line is as it is and not otherwise when a good reading already exists?' Our answer is that reading Shelley has forced us to the conclusion that he almost never used an image until he was satisfied that it belonged to an authentic part of his own experience *and* that it was also to be found in myth and great writers of the past. A great deal of head-scratching over what was the primary source of this or that allusion or image in Shelley can be avoided once this is accepted. For instance, is the presence of 'the ash and the acacia' in line 437 of *Alastor* determined by euphony (Shelley had a fondness for arrangements like 'Blue thistles bloomed' and 'The Brescian shepherd breathes'), or by the fact that both ash and acacia have deciduous, light, pinnate leaves which are among the first to fall, and are thus contrasted with the gloomy evergreen conifers above them? Or, again, because in a list of deciduous trees in *Nicholson's British Encyclopaedia*'s section on gardening, the first two are 'acacia, ash' which thus impart a taxonomic nuance to the line, in keeping with the eighteenth-century Miltonising evident in the poem at this point? Or because the acacia was believed to be a kind of mimosa and is thus a sensitive plant; or because (likely enough – the acacia was a very popular tree then) these two trees grew in Windsor Great Park, said by Mary to be the immediate inspiration of the passage? The answer surely is that the cumulative force of all these reasons made the line seem inevitable and *ben trovato*.

Secondly, in Shelley a disconcerting literal-mindedness frequently coexists with the abstract or intangible. This is particularly true when he touches on matters of sex or death. The habit of mind is sometimes exhibited on the minutest scale, as for instance in his description of sodomy as an 'operose and diabolical machination'. In the space of two words he has moved from a clinical, Gibbonian consideration of the practical difficulties confronting homosexual intercourse to a shudder of revulsion at the unspeakable. Another example is furnished by the fragment beginning 'Thy little footsteps on the shore'. Matthews has shown that the footsteps are those not of William Shelley but of Fanny Godwin, who committed suicide in 1816, and that the line 'Where now the worm will feed no more' refers specifically to the breasts of Mary Wollstonecraft, mother of Fanny, and dead for twenty years. Not only will the infant Fanny no longer twinkle infant hands on her bosom, but the bosom itself has been completely consumed. There is also present a reminiscence, conscious or unconscious, of Cleopatra applying the asp to her bosom, which suggests the idea of worms feeding where a baby should – an example of how Shelley's reading interacts with personal concerns.[24]

Yet another example is found in an *Esdaile* poem, 'A Tale of Society as it is from Facts'. It describes the plight of two beggars, mother and son, the latter an 'impressed' soldier for whom 'the stern control / That ruled his sinews and coerced his soul / Utterly poisoned life's unmingled bowl / And unsubduable evils on him wrought'. Now a 'shadow of the lusty child' who had once been the breadwinner to his mother, the young man is unable to partake of the pleasures natural to youth.

> And is it life that in youth's blasted morn
> Not one of youth's dear raptures are enjoyed,
> All natural bliss with servitude alloyed,
> The beating heart, the sparkling eye, destroy'd,
> And manhood of its brightest glories shorn
> Debased by rapine, drunkenness and woe . . .
> His health and peace insultingly laid low,
> Without a fear to die or wish to live,
> Withered and sapless . . .   (*Esdaile*, p. 65)

The concept of brightness 'shorn' gained currency, as did so many eighteenth-century poeticisms, via Milton, and in particular through two passages in *Paradise Lost*: Satan before he has lost all original brightness is compared to the sun 'shorn of his beams' (I, 596), and Adam, after giving way to lust, rises like 'Samson from the harlot-lap / Of Philistean Dalilah, and waked / Shorn of his strength' (IX, 1060–2). The soldier has lost moral integrity and physical strength, and thus resembles both the fallen archangel and Samson. The brightest glories of which he has been shorn are his godlike powers to act according to the creed of Liberty, Equality and Fraternity, but he also resembles Samson literally, because being a soldier his hair would have been shorn. For Shelley at Oxford, wearing long hair was a symbolic act, the growth of a meteoric or lion-like mane proclaiming his solidarity with the spirit of 1792 in contradistinction to the close-clipped haircuts of the private soldier (the lowest rank) which were the fashion among undergraduates in 1810. Hogg particularly mentions this, though he tactfully omits any ideological reason for Shelley's long hair, presenting it as a mere eccentricity.[25] The cutting of hair is thus an outward and visible sign of inner degradation. But that the soldier has also lost all capacity to enjoy the dear raptures proper to youth, and has been shorn of manhood's glories ('manhood' is used synonymously with 'virility' elsewhere in Shelley),[26] when taken with the Samson quotation and the historical moment at which the poem was written, activates still further the literal meaning of 'shorn'.

In 1811–12 when this poem was begun, the chief British theatre of war was Portugal; in all likelihood it was finished just as Wellington was poised to take the border fortress of Ciudad Rodrigo. It was very shortly after this that the Inspector General of Hospitals to the Portuguese army wrote 'In the British army, it is probable, that more men have sustained the most melancholy of all mutilations, during the four years that it has been in Portugal through this disease, than the registers of all the hospitals in England could produce for the last century.' He was referring to a particularly virulent form of syphilis, a feature of which was the Black Lion, an encircling penile chancre which could destroy the glans in a matter of months, necessitating amputation, the 'melancholy mutilation'.[27] Thus the young man is impotent in a literal way, unable to perform the act which was for Shelley the expression of the 'highest in our nature'. Shelley also recognises war as one of the chief agents of the spread of venereal disease, as it had been in the 1490s; this is of some importance elsewhere in his poetry, especially in *Laon and Cythna*.

Thirdly, while it must never be forgotten that Shelley is always trying to turn the private into the universal, there is a dimension to his poetry which is arcane, secret. This does not mean, however, that his work is a vast esoteric system like Blake's.

Peter Butter wrote, 'There are a number of images [in Shelley] which constantly recur and which seem to have special significance for him.' Butter quoted Shelley's own words: 'Every human mind has what Bacon calls *idola specus*, peculiar images which reside in the inner cave of thought. These constitute the essential and distinctive character of every human being.' These favourite images, Butter commented,

constitute a symbolic shorthand language for expressing ideas as well as feelings. This is not to say that he started with a number of philosophical ideas, and then cast about

for metaphors by which to convey them; . . . Rather, the starting point is more likely
to be a vivid sensuous experience; for his senses, especially of sight, were abnormally
acute. Then round the natural objects which he loved – such as streams and caves,
islands and clouds – there crystallised his emotions, intuitions and thoughts, so that
they came to have an ever richer meaning.[28]

The examples adduced by Butter to support his fine argument do not
altogether bear out Shelley's words about the 'idols of the cave' since streams,
islands, rocks and clouds could be said to belong to the Universal Mind which
Shelley appears to have believed in and thus be directly accessible to
everyone.[29] Shelley seems to be talking about a grey area which is personal to
the individual but which is not a sealed book to the outsider, provided that an
inquirer into the secrets of another's cave possesses the necessary insight. A
most suggestive note to *Hellas* speaks of Ahasuerus' ability to intuit the Sultan
Mahmud's guilt and induce him to connive at his own downfall as 'a sort of
natural magic, susceptible of being exercised in a degree by any one who should
have made himself master of the secret associations of another's thoughts'.[30]
Shelley sometimes invites readers to be Ahasueruses inasmuch as he challenges
them to read the 'secret associations' of his thoughts and become fellow-adepts.
This is in keeping with his fascination with concealment, secret societies like
the Illuminati, anonymous publication, disguise and hoaxes.

There are many reasons why Shelley might have been led to communicate
in this way. The following we consider to be the most probable: that the
peculiar circumstances of his situation made him uncertain about who his
audience was, and that at times he wrote for himself and sympathetic friends
(who might include fellow-spirits unknown to him personally); that he also
regarded an image in a poem as being like the end of a thread handed to the
explorer of a labyrinth – it had the capacity to lead the reader through the
windings of the cave. Relevant here is his remark that almost all familiar
objects were signs, 'standing not for themselves but for others in their capacity of suggesting one thought, which shall lead to a train of thoughts'. One
thinks in particular of the windmill.[31]

But readers are in other respects more like Mahmud than Ahasuerus, for
the work to which they expose their imagination is, by their receptivity,
enabled to act on them in a way that they cannot reciprocate, that is to say,
subliminally, like an unsettling dream. The half-realised image, the latent
pun, the apparently unfocussed obsession – these in Shelley merit the
description which T. S. Eliot applied to Shakespeare, Donne, Webster and
Tourneur: 'Their words have often a network of tentacular roots reaching
down to the deepest terrors and desires.'[32] For Shelley this was also a
strategy of political subversion, especially in *Prometheus Unbound*.

Fourthly, Shelley is the nearest to a Renaissance poet that the Romantic age
produced. We have mentioned his literal-mindedness, but that is only a part-
truth. His art, like that of Dante and Spenser, is typically 'polysemous, that

is, having many meanings', to use Dante's famous description of the method of the *Divine Comedy*.[33] In Dante and Spenser the first class of meanings is the literal, including the historical. The second is the allegorical, and includes the moral or anagogical. *The Faerie Queene* is an evocation of a chivalric world which never existed, a political allegory, a history of the Christian Church and a philosophical poem dramatising the struggle between virtue and vice. Shelley may have regarded the 'ideal' – allegorical – as the more important dimension of his poetry, but the literal can never be discounted. Keats, in *Adonais*, becomes the type of the Poet, killed by 'contagion of the world's slow stain', the beloved of the Muse, yet one never forgets that there was a poet who did die and that critics really were malignant (even if Shelley was mistaken in supposing that their venom killed him), and that but for these facts, *Adonais* would not have been written.

Fifthly, in Shelley no clear dividing line can be drawn between public and personal poems. This is true even of political satires like *Swellfoot the Tyrant*.

Having declared and partly explained some of our assumptions, we will now consider the story which Shelley constructed out of the major events of his life. Essentially, it is the story of *Paradise Lost*. This myth provides a patterning for the work of many of the other major Romantics; indeed it is arguably the quintessential Romantic myth, and related to the Romantic exaltation of the state of childhood.

Shelley's myth of the Fall operates both on the societal and personal level. The following elements repeatedly appear, and can be connected to form a coherent fable. A youth, in early spring or May, has a moral awakening, which is closely associated with an erotic arousal, the experience being rendered in terms of dedication to a social mission and subsequent or concomitant encounter with a female deity. The moment of transcendence passes, leaving the youth desolate and/or in the grip of a feverish passion. He is driven by an inner compulsion out into the world, envisaged as a forest or wilderness, where he stumbles heedlessly or rashly. At this point he has a blighting experience which, after an interval, makes him prematurely old, in pain, frail, grey-haired and like a stricken deer. (Cowper is here fused with the Newtonian Zodiacal schema.) The experience has established an archetype; it sets the pattern for shadowy re-enactments of the first trauma. The youth is rescued by a woman who takes him to a cave or private solitude and lulls him to a sleep which is neither life nor death; alternatively he does die. There is sometimes a sequel: a rude awakening from this sleep and further misfortunes.

This is a conflation of many poems, some of which contain only one of these elements. They include the early poem 'I will kneel at thine altar', *Alastor*, 'Hymn to Intellectual Beauty', *Laon and Cythna*, *Rosalind and Helen*, *Prince Athanase*, *Julian and Maddalo*, *Epipsychidion*, *Adonais* and *The Triumph of Life*, plus the prose fragment *Una Favola*. It has never been doubted that some of the fable's elements correspond to actual events in Shelley's life. In particular the moral awakening by the divinity is generally taken to be an account of a mystical experience at puberty, though it is doubted that Shelley actually shrieked and clasped his hands in ecstasy (as he said he did in his most celebrated statement of this experience, the 'Hymn to Intellectual Beauty'). It has sometimes been denied that this experience included the erotic, on the grounds that 'intellectual' means 'of the mind'. But the spirit is also the 'messenger of sympathies / That wax and wane in lovers' eyes'. When Intellectual Beauty manifests itself on earth it never, in Shelley, addresses the intellectual faculties alone, but is always united to 'requisitions' (Shelley's term in the Preface to *Alastor*) of the imagination and the senses.

The arousal of sexuality at puberty was recognised in Shelley's day to be inseparable from moral, intellectual and imaginative development, as the following quotation from Cabanis, whose work Shelley ordered in 1812, makes very clear. Cabanis also tellingly describes an intermixture of religious feeling and erotic imagining:

The physical circumstances peculiar to adolescence are naturally interlinked; they form a system to which certain accessory phenomena . . . come to be related; and since the most remarkable of all such circumstances, by which I mean the development or new action of the organs of generation, exerts a great influence over the moral being, since it suddenly creates other ideas and other inclinations, we cannot doubt that the new moral state is inseparable from these circumstances . . . it is also the moment when the imagination exerts its greatest sway; it is the age of all romantic ideas, of all illusions; illusions which no doubt one should beware of exciting and artificially nourishing, but which only a false philosophy would wish entirely to dissipate indiscriminately and peremptorily. It is then that the loving affections so easily transform themselves into a religion, a cult! One adores invisible powers as one would a mistress, perhaps solely because one adores, or because one needs to adore a mistress; because everything stirs the now extremely sensitive fibres, and because that insatiable need for sensation by which one is tormented cannot always be satisfied with real objects.[34]

Many Romantics also dwell on the theme of premature blight and in many cases make some attempt to explain this either in fictionalised autobiography or in private confessions. Whether they were right or consistent in their self-analysis is not the point; the salient fact is that they presented this theme as having its sources in decisive events in their own lives. De Quincey wrote of a 'horror of life' which had descended too early upon him; this horror can be traced to the indelible memories of beautiful, calm deathbed scenes associated with loved members of his family, particularly his sister. Byron ascribed the premature arousal of his passions, from which he derived much of his sense that life's springs had been poisoned, to a servant girl's excessive freeness with his person when he was about ten years old.[35] In Shelley's poetry the figure of the blighted poet, especially in *Epipsychidion*, has been accounted for by the experience of puberty itself, and the concomitant arousal of sexuality, a distraction from his imaginative development. This is a view difficult to square with Shelley's belief that sexual intercourse was the type or symbol of all other kinds of love. Another view relates the blighted poet to the shock of expulsion from Oxford and encounter with real opposition from authority. A third – and probably today the most common – cites the experience of being crossed in first love, specifically, by Harriet Grove. A fourth refers to Shelley's injudicious marriage to Harriet Westbrook. With the last three views we have no essential quarrel – it is no part of our argument that these did not contribute to the poet's griefs, 'wrecked hopes' or the recurring motifs of life's 'great cheat' and 'youth's smooth ocean smiling to betray'. What we are maintaining is that crucial components of this blight were a replacement of love by lust and the discovery of the horror of prostitution, and that the Poet figure in Shelley is almost invariably not merely heartbroken, but marked by disease. The next step in our argument is an interpretation of a certain important cluster of images in his work.

9

Nightshade, well, forest

Of all the Romantics, with the possible exception of Blake, it is Shelley who has the most paradoxical cast of mind. The sign which is the thing signified, the cause which is the effect, the spoiler spoiled, the self-propelled chariot and the two-headed snake – no reader of Shelley can proceed very far without encountering such paradoxical and self-reflexive images.[1] Related to them is a Shelleyan peculiarity first discussed by Matthews. The latter developed Butter's 'idols of the cave' thesis, pointing out that Shelley's symbols do not simply ' "stand for" anything in the systematic manner in which the Cross, for example, stands for Christianity' but are collecting points for several of his 'political, scientific or philosophical perceptions of reality'. Moreover, Shelley's concepts may be called on to illustrate opposite qualities. 'A *veil* is now of ugliness concealing beauty, now of beauty concealing ugliness . . . so too with *lightning, cloud, labyrinth, meteor* and the rest.'[2] (In 'Ode to Naples' (145–6) cruel carnivores prey on the corpse of beauty, while in *Letter to Maria Gisborne* (40–3) beautiful carnivores prey on the corpse of cruelty.) Many words have this double potential – indeed this quality is the source of indeterminacy of meaning, according to Derrida, who gives as an instance the word *pharmakon*, which can mean both cure and poison.

Shelley's exploitation of this potential is pervasive, and confusing until it is recognised as a conscious strategy, not thoughtless muddle. It is allied to one of his key precepts: 'All things exist as they are perceived'[3] and the Godwinian belief that Good and Evil spring from the same sources. One would not go so far as to say that Shelley constructed a system of fearful symmetry by which the same image or concept always functioned as both good and evil; sometimes he used the more familiar method of *antithesis*: the vulture is always 'evil'; its counterpart, the kingfisher, always 'good'.[4] Yet the habit is so marked as almost to amount to a Shelleyan imprint and has a medical dimension. It reveals what could be called a homeopathic bias of mind.

The two great systems of medicine are the allopathic and the homeopathic. Allopathy cures through antidotes; homeopathy operates on the principle that like cures like.[5] The homeopathic principle expresses itself in a number of famous apothegms: 'The wounder heals' (ascribed to the Delphic Oracle); 'Ubi venenum, ibi remedium'; 'arsenic cures arsenic' (a saying of Paracelsus).[6] Such a simple paradox has many manifestations; it lies behind

136

Hotspur's 'Out of this nettle, danger, we pluck this flower, safety' or Brutus' 'As fire drives out fire, so pity, pity', as well as Peacock's mutton chop joke. With Shelley this principle is not merely immanent, but overt too. It appears in *Julian and Maddalo*:

> . . . some perverted beings think to find
> In scorn or hate a medicine for the mind
> Which scorn or hate have wounded – o how vain!
> The dagger heals not but may rend again . . .   (354–7)

Shelley refers here to the homeopathic principle, but warns against a simple-minded application of it. It is a perversion of the maxim 'The wounder heals' to attempt to cure a wound by stabbing another with the offending dagger; that is not the true meaning of the Delphic Oracle. (The correct Paracelsian remedy would have been to anoint the weapon with 'wound salve', healing the wounder, which thus becomes a healer.)

In Shelley there are many homeopathic emblems. One is electricity: lightning can blast and blight; under different circumstances, electricity is a panacea. The snake, regarded as a venomous reptile, is evil, but in as much as it sheds its skin it symbolises self-renewal. Another important emblem is the nightshade.

This was one of the poisonous plants which had been made a popular remedy in the eighteenth century through the work of Stoerck and especially through Thomas Gataker, whose *Observations on the Internal Use of the Solanum or Nightshade* (1757) continued to influence medical opinion until well into the nineteenth century. Noting that the garden nightshade had been formerly looked upon as 'an excellent Remedy for inflammations of the venereal kind, and for ulcers' he recommended all nightshades for the complaint. One of them, the woody nightshade, *did* catch on as an anti-syphilitic. This was supposed to work, like opium, through its narcotic properties, 'hence rendering the system inirritable to the syphilitic virus'; Woodville, the authoritative medical botanist, lists its use in venereal disease among its most important applications. Like arsenic, woody nightshade was admitted to the *London Pharmacopeia* in 1809.[7] It is this nightshade that features in Shelley's poems, for there it is variously described as 'blue', rambling in habit, and having berries which resemble a 'quenchless fire' (that is, red berries), but which are also amber. Only the woody nightshade fits this description; the other nightshades have white flowers and black berries. Furthermore, its Latin name, *dulcamara*, which was the name of the drug derivative, and its common English name, Bittersweet, are in themselves oxymorons and fitted the plant well for Shelley's purposes.

That love has a dual bitter-sweet nature is at least as old as Lucretius' 'Medio de fonte leporum surgit amari aliquid quod in ipsis floribus angat' (From the heart of the fountain of delight rises a jet of bitterness which torments even amidst the flowers). Even more ancient is the connection of the bitter and sweet with the harlot: 'The lips of a strange woman drop as an honeycomb . . . but her end is bitter as wormwood.' In Shelley the Lucretian, Solomonic and contemporary medical associations of 'bitter-sweet' are fused.[8]

The nightshade first occurs in *The Wandering Jew* where it seems to be just a piece of Gothic décor. Its first important use as a symbol is in one of the *Esdaile* poems, 'Passion'. This has the same rhetorical structure as Southey's 'The Holly Tree' (also about a red-berried plant), in which the poet selects a natural object, in this case the nightshade, and 'moralises' it.

Since it has been questioned whether the plant in 'Passion' is the nightshade, this point must be cleared up first. As Cameron noted, two lines in *Queen Mab* recall this poem: 'Like passion's fruit, the nightshade's tempting bane / Poisons no more the pleasure it bestows' (VIII, 129–30). And this ought to settle the matter, but for the following considerations: the plant of 'Passion' is said to have a 'chequered stalk of mingling hues'. Secondly, the poem is subtitled 'To the — ' (with a blank), which Dowden considered a curious omission if Shelley was indeed thinking of a plant as common as the nightshade. Perhaps, Cameron suggested, Shelley was not sure of the plant's name. But his own counter-proposal, the *arum maculatum* or Lords and Ladies, is open to the same objections without any corresponding advantage, for the stalk of this plant is an unmottled green. There is also the sheer improbability of Shelley's ignorance; if Mary's claim that he 'knew every plant by name' is an exaggeration, he could nevertheless recognise a dried milkwort, not the commonest of plants.[9]

It is a waste of time to comb botanies for plants with chequered stalks; this is a case where one sort of accuracy overrides another. 'Chequered', a favourite word in the *Esdaile Notebook*, is required to supply Shelley with an image of the juxtaposition in life of good and evil, pleasure and pain. He tries to cancel out the pictorial effect of 'chequered' by the word 'mingling'. (Purple and green do indeed 'mingle' in a nightshade's stalk.) Milton's 'L'Allegro' had made 'chequered' a stock epithet, immediately eliciting the stock noun 'shade'. An almost pedantic care for correctness also obliged Shelley to bring in the odd word 'stalk', for, uniquely among the plants listed in the *London Materia Medica* and reproduced in *Nicholson's British Encyclopaedia*, it was the stalk (*caulis*) from which 'decoctions' were derived, though stalk and berries contained the same active ingredient. As for the second objection, it disappears when one recognises the genre of poem that Shelley was writing. It is a *conundrum*, such as were then collected in ladies' albums, but of a serious kind. The reader is meant to guess the name of the plant. Shelley has hidden in the text – not too abstrusely – the answer to his riddle. The very sight of the unnamed poisonous plant is enough to evoke a Gothic atmosphere (another clue) and an 'awful feeling', 'As if I stood at *night* / In some weird ruin's *shade*' (29–30, our italics).[10]

There is no reason to dispute Cameron's dating of the poem (November 1811). Thus there could be two events which prompted it: Harriet Grove's marriage that autumn and Shelley's discovery that Hogg had tried to seduce Harriet Shelley. This suggests that the poem is neither just about the contrast between the sweetness of love when fulfilled and its bitterness when thwarted, nor about the treachery of a friend. Rather, Shelley is reviewing his entire experience and making a general reflection on the very different effects which a good, reciprocated and an evil, unshared, sensual passion can produce. In order that the nightshade might serve as an image of both kinds simultaneously, he sets out to exploit the ambivalent character of the plant itself – that it is beautiful but conceals a deadly poison, and that this poison can be harmful or, used as a medicine, beneficial. The attempt to draw out all the implications of the image at once is rather cumbersome; it also leads him into a series of linguistic ambiguities. The poem begins:

> Fair are thy berries to the dazzled sight,
> Fair is thy chequered stalk of mingling hues,
>> And yet thou dost conceal
>> A deadly poison there
>> Uniting good and ill.   (1–5)

Are the berries actually beautiful, or only to the beholder, whose judgement might be swayed by his desire to taste? Does the 'good' reside in the appearance of the plant and the ill in its poison, or does he mean that the 'deadly poison' itself can have both good and ill effects? As the poem proceeds, Shelley uses first one meaning and then another as suits his purpose.

Next he goes through a pretence of searching for some representative human type with which the plant may aptly be compared. He thinks first of the lawyer, the tyrant, the 'Christian' extortionist landlord and the professional soldier. All are conceived as predators who lay claim to some spurious achievement or distinction, and the force of the comparison relies on the contrast between fair appearance and sordid fact.

In each case, however, the comparison with the nightshade is dismissed as inappropriate, for whereas the plant can inspire awe, the predators merely arouse contempt. The nightshade is more exactly suited, he decides, to serve as the emblem of human passion:

> Thou art like youthful passion's quenchless fire
> Which in some unsuspecting bosom glows
>> So wild, so beautiful,
>> Possessing wondrous power
>> To wither or to warm.   (31–5)

So far, the nightshade's beauty has been merely treacherous; if it is to symbolise the ambiguous nature of passion, there will need to be a sense also in which it is genuine, one could even say 'innocent', a sense in which it does not mask an evil so much as advertise a good. Nor will this good be visual only, for to limit it in this way would give to the subject of passion the status of a mere onlooker, and not of a participant. The power to 'wither or to warm' possessed by both the nightshade and passion must reside in the poison or 'bane', which also has healing properties. This reading is supported not only by the ambiguity pointed out in stanza one, which enables one to think of the poison itself and not merely the poison and the visual beauty of the plant combined, as 'uniting good and ill', but also by the next stanza, where passion is described in almost pharmacological terms as the '*Essence* of Virtue blasting Virtue's prime,[11] / Bright bud of Truth, producing Falshood's fruit' (36–7):

> Prime source of all that's lovely, good, and great
> Debasing man below the meanest brute,
> *Spring of all healing streams*
> *Yet deadlier than the gall*
> Blackening a monarch's heart.   (41–5. Our italics)

In the final stanza, Shelley names the force which can convert a healing and ennobling passion into a withering poison, the source not just of heartbreak but of vice. It is 'Custom':

> Why art thou thus, O Passion? Custom's chains
> Have bound thee from thine heaven-directed flight
> Or thou wouldst never thus
> Bring misery to man
> Uniting good and ill.   (46–50)

'Custom's chains' refers, of course, to the sacred institution of marriage, the barrier erected by society against 'consentaneous love'. A year later, in his 'Notes to *Queen Mab*', Shelley was to write:

Not even the intercourse of the sexes is exempt from the despotism of positive institution. Law pretends even to govern the indiscriplinable wanderings of passion, to put fetters on the clearest deductions of reason, and, by appeals to the will, to subdue the involuntary affections of our nature. Love is inevitably consequent upon the perception of loveliness. Love withers under constraint: its very essence is liberty . . .

(Hutchinson, p. 806)

Passion (which is regarded as an essential component of Love in this passage) can wither and die under the constraints of marriage; it can also 'wither' actively, and it is in the active voice that the verb is employed in the poem. Fundamental to Shelley's views on marriage and his concepts of 'passion' and 'reason' is his belief that young men are frustrated in their relationships with women by a false value placed on chastity, either as a means of 'saving oneself for marriage' or of remaining tied to one partner. The result of this tyranny over the affections is that the young men 'formed for love' turn in despair to the company of prostitutes, thereby debasing the divine part of their nature to a selfish appetite and risking infection. One of the reasons why the nightshade is said to be not like the tyrant is that whereas the tyrant withers up the soul, the nightshade merely 'mayst kill the body' and thus seems 'sweet' in comparison. For the nightshade, therefore, to function as an emblem of passion, passion must be seen as having the power of killing the body.

Passion, then, is synonymous with sexual desire or excitement, and the nightshade is an image of that excitement vitiated by lust and the prospect of disease. Passion itself glows in the 'unsuspecting bosom', that is, the adolescent is caught unawares by the novelty and strength of the emotion, and is ignorant of the ruin to which it can lead. The idea that a youth may unwittingly risk his future sexual happiness recurs in Shelley's later, mature poetry, where there is a strong note of self-excuse and regret.

The poem also contains a contradiction reflecting a matter over which Shelley was profoundly divided. He claims that the tyrant is worse than the nightshade, yet in the penultimate stanza the nightshade is apparently worse than the tyrant, for Passion is there stated to be 'deadlier than the gall / Blackening a monarch's heart'. Shelley seems to want to say that tyranny is more evil than lust. But he ends up saying that lust is more evil than tyranny, and indeed suggests that it is antecedent to tyranny and implies that the body's degradation as a result of lust is as bad as any soul-withering effects. One recalls his remark to Claire ten years later: 'Ill health is one of the evils that is not a dream, and the reality of which every year, if you neglect it, will make more impressive.' Physical pain was always for Shelley a challenge to the philosophical position that he worked out in *On Life*: that 'the solid universe of external things is "such stuff as dreams are made of" '.[12] A poem written at the same time as 'Passion' shows that his own health was very much on his mind: apostrophising a 'premature' spring-like day in winter, he enquires if it is an emblem of 'Passion's rapturous dream' which when 'many chequered years are gone' leaves behind only 'life's blasted springs'. Whatever the day symbolises, he declares, he will love its 'vernal glow', whether 'Health with roseate wreath / May bind my head, or creeping Death / Steal o'er my pulse's flow'.[13]

The nightshade reappears in *Queen Mab*, Shelley's longest early poem, with its meaning extended. Here the poison connected with pleasure is not a predatory passion only, but also disease, the venereal poison. In *Queen Mab* evil is expelled from the Universe and a 'gradual renovation' is in progress throughout Nature. This change is brought about by the rule of Love, exemplified by reciprocated love between man and woman: 'All things are recreated, and the flame / Of consentaneous love inspires all life' (VIII, 107–8). It is imaged very largely in terms of a recovery of physical health: 'Health floats amid the gentle atmosphere, / Glows in the fruits and mantles on the stream' (VIII, 114–15). Man abandons meat-eating, source of the quarrel between Reason and Passion and ruin of healthful innocence. (Vegetarianism preserves natural temperance and renders the body immune to the syphilitic virus.) Love brings to an end the conflict of interests in Nature, and even the predatory nightshade has lost its poison:

> Like passion's fruit, the nightshade's tempting bane
> Poisons no more the pleasure it bestows:
> All bitterness is past; the cup of joy
> Unmingled mantles to the goblet's brim.   (VIII, 129–32)

The repetition of the word 'mantles', coming soon after the lines extolling health, indicates that the poison of the nightshade is the antithesis of both 'Love' and 'Health'; 'the cup of joy' may now be expected to brim with both.

The connection between sexual pleasure and disease is given a more explicit formulation as Shelley continues his description of the beautiful future:

> Peace cheers the mind, health renovates the frame;
> Disease and pleasure cease to mingle here,
> Reason and passion cease to combat there.   (VIII, 229–31)

It would be possible, of course, to regard these as merely general reflections: 'Life's pleasures are often destroyed by illness; on the other hand much of its difficulty results from the conflict between our desires and the dictates of reason; in the millennium neither will be the case.' Such an interpretation would do much to weaken the rhetorical force of the lines; nor would it do justice to the pattern of intricate statement in the poem. The words are being used in a precise sense.

There is an obvious parallel between the poisoned pleasure conveyed by the nightshade and the diseased pleasure that results when passion and reason are opposed. It was the Law that tried to 'govern the indisciplinable wanderings of passion and to put fetters on the clearest deductions of reason', thus bringing the two into disharmony and causing young men to seek out prostitutes. The 'mingling' of disease and pleasure refers back to the 'unmingled' joy which 'mantles to the goblet's brim' when the nightshade's poison becomes inactive. This in turn recalls other lines in the poem in which 'the unmingled joys which sense and spirit yield' are contrasted with the evils of 'unenjoying sensualism'. What emerges clearly from *Queen Mab* is that lust and disease are inextricably related, while the nightshade's poison or 'bane' functions as an image of both. Moreover, 'bane' is explicitly linked to prostitution and syphilis. In Canto V, referring to the state of society when still governed by oppressive institutions, Shelley laments that

> Even love is sold . . .
> And youth's corrupted impulses prepare
> A life of horror from the blighting bane
> Of commerce; whilst the pestilence that springs

From unenjoying sensualism, has filled
All human life with hydra-headed woes.   (V, 189, 192–6)

'Commerce', while possessing the larger meanings 'any sort of venal transac-
tion', 'intercourse, chiefly immoral, between the sexes', was also, in the eighteenth century, a synonym for 'prostitution', and indeed the general and the
specific meanings merge here.[14] But in the 'dawn of love'

> No longer prostitution's venomed bane
> Poisoned the springs of happiness and life;
> Woman and man, in confidence and love,
> Equal and free and pure together trod
> The mountain-paths of virtue.   (IX, 87–91)

'Prostitution's venomed bane', then, is a purely evil component of the
nightshade's *tempting* bane. It is now linked to the image of a *well* – the
springs of happiness and life.

A passage in Shelley's review of Hogg's *Memoirs of Prince Alexy Haimatoff*
(1814) shows him again associating the nightshade with prostitution, as well
as with other kinds of 'sensualism', such as seduction, one of its root causes.
He criticises the novel severely for its encouragement of 'loveless intercourse
of brutal appetite' through the character of Bruhle, Alexy's tutor. 'No man
can rise pure from the poisonous embraces of a prostitute', he protests, and
his general verdict is that the book is 'an unweeded garden where nightshade
is interwoven with sweet jessamine'.[15]

The nightshade next appears in *Rosalind and Helen* (1817–18):

> Like the autumn wind, when it unbinds
> The tangled locks of the nightshade's hair,
> Which is twined in the sultry summer air
> Round the walls of an outworn sepulchre,
> Did the voice of Helen, sad and sweet . . .
> Unbind the knots of her friend's despair.   (207–11, 214)

Even here there is a connection between *nightshade, disease* and *prostitution*. Rosalind and Helen are two friends who have both suffered from
society's tyranny, but whereas Helen's marriage was one of 'consentaneous
love' with a young idealist, Rosalind's love was sold. To please her dying
mother she has married a tyrannous man 'loving only gold'. Upon becoming pregnant she considers aborting her child, fearing that her offspring will
find the earth a charnel house as she has done. The 'outworn sepulchre'
around which the nightshade twines is an emblem of her mind, in which
hateful memories of her dead husband persist. He has been consumed by a
mysterious ailment: 'Whether his ill were death or sin / None knew, until
he died indeed / And then men owned they were the same' (433–5). The imagery and situation strongly recall the following address to the Tyrant in
Queen Mab:

> Dost thou desire the bane that poisons earth
> To twine its roots around thy coffined clay,
> Spring from thy bones, and blossom on thy tomb,
> That of its fruits thy babes may eat and die?   (IV, 262–5)

Rosalind's husband has been 'a tyrant to the weak' – that is, a petty one, a small-scale Ozymandias, his sepulchre as enduring a stone monument to evil passions as Ozymandias' huge legs.

Friendship between women is able to dissolve such horror with its paregoric calm and the dissolution is symbolised by the unwinding of the nightshade's stems. One finds here, too, one of the first adumbrations of the *autumn* wind as healer, driving out the disease that comes with the 'sultry' air. (Shelley has here made the nightshade purely malevolent. In *Laon and Cythna*, in some respects a companion poem, he gave the bryony, a red-berried plant associated with white magic, the innocent functions of the nightshade, which it resembles to some extent.)[16] However the experience of living with such a man has left a permanent mark on Rosalind's psyche and health. Despite the happy ending, 'Rosalind, for when the living stem / Is cankered in its heart, the tree must fall, / Died ere her time' (1292–4).

The scene of this loving sisterly encounter is a well in the middle of a forest, which is the obverse of life's springs poisoned by prostitution in *Queen Mab*. The emblem of the poisoned well now purified is developed in a beautiful and intricate image belonging to the lyric drama *Prometheus Unbound* (1819).

In that poem, the Spirit of the Earth, a child on the threshold of puberty, remembers that before the overthrow of the tyrant Jupiter

> toads, and snakes, and loathly worms,
> And venomous and malicious beasts, and boughs
> That bore ill berries in the woods, were ever
> An hindrance to my walks o'er the green world.   (III, iv, 36–9)

The wood or forest represents life, as it does in Dante, Spenser and Milton, but here it is also more specifically sexual experience and experimentation. It is so used in *Queen Mab*, where, in the renovated world

> Reason was free; and wild though Passion went
> Through tangled glens and wood-embosomed meads,
> Gathering a garland of the strangest flowers,
> Yet like the bee returning to her queen,
> She bound the sweetest on her sister's brow,
> Who meek and sober kissed the sportive child,
> No longer trembling at the broken rod.   (IX, 50–6)

The 'garland of the strangest flowers' (there are hints here of incest and lesbian love) are sexual delights previously considered unlawful. Passion's wanderings are paralleled by those of the adventurous Spirit of the Earth,

who, after the overthrow of Jupiter, re-encounters the formerly ugly denizens
of the forest, which have been apotheosised with little apparent change of
shape or colour; this suggests a change in the attitude of society towards sexuality. 'All things had put their evil nature off' including the 'ill berries':

> I cannot tell my joy, when o'er a lake
> Upon a drooping bough with nightshade twined,
> I saw two azure halcyons clinging downward
> And thinning one bright bunch of amber berries,
> With quick long beaks, and in the deep there lay
> Those lovely forms imaged as in a sky.   (III, iv, 78–83)

These halcyons are antitheses to the *vulture* which had torn Prometheus' heart
with its beak 'dipped in poison not its own'. The birds' abandonment of their
normal fish-eating habits is usually regarded as Shelley's ultimate piece of
vegetarian propaganda, which is true up to a point. But Shelley encountered
the idea of vegetarian kingfishers in Paracelsus; they had a particular
significance for alchemists, who conceived of them as their own counterparts in
Nature. A halcyon possessed a unique form of digestion which gave it the
power of repeating some of the processes of alchemy. When it ate 'the bodies of
herbs or of seeds or the like', it 'restored and renovated' the flesh after death.
Whatever food it ate − and it was trained from birth by the parent birds to eat
only that which itself restored the body − was reduced to 'first entities' and
thereby contained all the virtues of the elixir. As for the alchemists, kingfishers
symbolised the hope of immortality, so for Shelley they represent the conquest
of disease and the renovation of the flesh; their 'azure' counteracts the 'blue' of
plague and of nightshade flowers.[17]

The halcyons are also a mating pair, evoking the legend of the faithful lovers
Alcyone and Ceyx; the activity of eating the berries together is a metaphor for
the couple's sexual intercourse. The 'one bright bunch of amber berries' which
the birds 'thin' between them is sexual pleasure shared equally and temperately
between two partners. ('Unshared pleasure' is one of the vices of the tyrant
(*Q.M.*, V, 35) and what is sought when visiting a prostitute.) The berries are
amber because that resinous jewel is associated with healing both in Paracelsus
and folk medicine.[18] The lucid water represents the purity of a sexual life no
longer poisoned at its source, but a mirror of the eternal. The elixir which con-
quers disease and death, and mutual, fulfilled sexual love are the same. Poison
has become food.

The last poem Shelley wrote which mentions the nightshade is *Epipsychidion*
(1821). This contains the passage which Thornton Hunt believed to bear out
his accidental discovery and is a passionate love poem, addressed to Teresa
('Emilia') Viviani, daughter of the governor of Pisa, who was being kept in a
convent until a suitably rich husband could be found for her. It is also of all
Shelley's volumes the one whose publication was shrouded in the greatest
anonymity, 'to avoid the malignity of those who turn sweet food into poison,

transforming all they touch into the corruption of their own natures'.[19] The poem falls into three distinct sections: a dedicatory address to Emilia, in which Shelley openly declares his love for her, a passage of veiled autobiography, and a final section describing an imaginary elopement, too solemn in tone to be entirely playful and containing passages of unusual erotic intensity. The word 'epipsychidion' was coined by Shelley himself. It is usually rendered as the 'soul within our soul', a phrase taken from Shelley's prose essay fragment *On Love*. Although the love depicted in the essay is not exactly intellectual, the generally metaphysical character of *On Love* has encouraged many critics to interpret *Epipsychidion* as describing an asexual love, or to maintain that its subject matter is 'essentially . . . the role of poetry as the most appropriate object of human desires'.[20]

Although these readings are still very influential, other critics such as Cameron, Holmes, and Brown have stressed the essentially sexual nature of the love celebrated in the poem, a view with which we are in agreement. Brown makes some interesting points about the contradictions between Shelley's *Advertisement* to the poem and the 'high-powered erotic rhetoric' of the poem itself. Ostensibly, Shelley presents sexual connection as 'a convenient metaphor, much in the manner of the medieval mystic, for conveying something altogether beyond the sense . . . The trouble is that because Shelley really did want Emilia sexually, the scene takes on a reality, a literalness, impossible to ignore.'[21]

Critics who 'Platonise' the poem also tend to play down the autobiographical element, citing Shelley's concern lest it be reduced to the level of 'a servant girl and her sweetheart'[22] and his description of the poem as 'an idealised history of my life and feelings'. But the context in which the last remark occurs, a letter written to John Gisborne almost a year after the infatuation had ended, makes it clear that he did fantasise about a physical union with Emilia, as the reference to the Ixion myth shows, and that 'idealised' does not mean 'not factual' but 'transcending the *merely* personal':

The *Epipsychidion* I cannot look at; the person whom it celebrates was a cloud instead of a Juno; and poor Ixion starts from the centaur that was the offspring of his own embrace. If you are anxious, however, to hear what I am and have been, it will tell you something thereof. It is an idealised history of my life and feelings. I think one is always in love with something or other; the error, and I confess it is not easy for spirits cased in flesh and blood to avoid it, consists in seeking in a mortal image the likeness of what is perhaps eternal. *(Letters, II, 434)*

Shelley hints to Gisborne, moreover, that he is in love again ('what I am and have been') and that this new love might be added to the record of past loves to be found in *Epipsychidion*. Before finishing the letter he virtually admits that his new love is Jane Williams. In his *Advertisement* to *Epipsychidion* he tells the reader that a 'matter of fact' history does lie behind the poem and, while insisting that the poem is unintelligible unless understood on a moral and philosophical level, declares that he would deserve reproach were he not able to give an account of the facts veiled by figures of speech and rhetorical colours.[23]

The 'veiled autobiography' section treats of the same set of events as *Una Favola*.[24] It begins with a description of the poet's moral, intellectual and sexual awakening in early adolescence. This takes the form of an authentic religious experience, the four essential marks of which, according to William James, are 'ineffability', 'a noetic quality', 'transiency' and 'passivity'.[25] All of these are present in Shelley's description of his encounter with the female deity who manifests herself in nature 'Robed in such exceeding glory / That I beheld her not'. The lines in which Shelley expresses his sense of the arousal of his sexuality and the intensity of his yearning are among the most inspired in the poem:

> Then, from the caverns of my dreamy youth
> I sprang, as one sandalled with plumes of fire,
> And towards the lodestar of my one desire,
> I flitted, like a dizzy moth, whose flight
> Is as a dead leaf's in the owlet light,
> When it would seek in Hesper's setting sphere
> A radiant death . . .   (217–23)

But mystical states must fade into the light of common day or, in this case, the gloom of common night. Shelley's is no exception: 'But She, whom prayers or tears then could not tame, / Passed, like a God throned on a winged planet . . . / Into the dreary cone of our life's shade' (225–6, 228). There is a strong suggestion that it is the very intensity of his passion which has caused the vision to depart. At this point he seeks to find her again in a mortal form and it is here, in the rough commerce of everyday life, that the novice is likely to make mistakes.

> And therefore I went forth, with hope and fear
> And every gentle passion sick to death,
> Feeding my course with expectation's breath,
> Into the wintry forest of our life;
> And struggling through its error with vain strife,
> And stumbling in my weakness and my haste,
> And half bewildered by new forms, I passed,
> Seeking among those untaught foresters
> If I could find one form resembling hers,
> In which she might have masked herself from me.   (246–55)

He is driven not only by hope and fear but also by lust; this is the point of his *haste* and of his saying that every *gentle* passion was sick, that is, too weak to restrain his tigerish ones. Now comes the disastrous encounter:

> There, – One, whose voice was venomed melody
> Sate by a well, under blue nightshade bowers;
> The breath of her false mouth was like faint flowers,

> Her touch was as electric poison, – flame
> Out of her looks into my vitals came,
> And from her living cheeks and bosom flew
> A killing air, which pierced like honey-dew
> Into the core of my green heart, and lay
> Upon its leaves; until, as hair grown gray
> O'er a young brow, they hid its unblown prime
> With ruins of unseasonable time.   (256–66)

The strategic placing of these lines suggests that this was a turning point in the poet's life and one that brought a lengthening concatenation of pain and guilt. Afterwards he progressed from one unsatisfactory love relationship to another but without ever truly realising his vision of a perfect love until he met 'Emily'.

Not included among the 'many mortal forms' but mortal nevertheless are two leading figures of Shelley's ménage: Mary, symbolised by the Moon, which 'warms but not illumines', and Claire, usually identified as the 'Comet, beautiful and fierce / Who drew the heart of this frail Universe / Towards thine own' (368–70) – a reference to Shelley's earlier love for her. These brought partial deliverance until he met Emily, represented by the Sun. All the loves symbolised by celestial phenomena are 'divine' in that they embody in a lesser degree the ideal most truly represented by Emily. Shelley was 'rash' only when he sought love, spiritual and sexual, among women who lacked this quality.

The most problematic identification is the 'One whose voice was venomed melody'. She is presented as a harlot figure who communicates a sexually transmitted disease. The image of the nightshade hanging over the water and thus poisoning the springs of life is reinforced by other details. The 'venomed melody' recalls 'prostitution's venomed bane'. The details of the woman's breath, redolent of faint flowers, and the killing air, allude to the belief that syphilis was originally spread by exhalations.[26] But the disease also spreads by contact: 'Her touch was as electric poison'. These details, taken with others discussed below, furnish as precise a description of a disease which is the province of both surgeon and physician as it is possible to accommodate within the metaphoric conventions that Shelley employs.

Imagery of flames feeding on the vitals was used to describe a wide variety of diseases, including syphilis (Tate's translation of Fracastor's poem employs it throughout).[27] In *Epipsychidion* the disease invades the poet's constitution – it pierces into the core of his green heart. But honey-dew also lies upon its leaves (external symptoms). The honey-dew image is an instance of the precision of Shelley's language. The compound denotes the gummy excrement left on leaves by aphids, which have sucked out the plant's own sap 'during the vernal or midsummer sap-flow' and which is followed by a black mouldy powder,[28] withering the plant. It is thus an antithesis to honey-dew meaning *nectar*, in which sense it is used to describe the liquid murmur that falls from Emily's lips as from a *blue* hyacinth. Shelley makes use of the two theories of infection: the older humoral one and the primitive germ theory of 'animal contagion'. The use of honey-dew as a pathological image is, as far as we can discover, Shelley's own invention. However, it is reminiscent of another poem in which the sufferer is compared to a plant and the symptoms of disease are the gummy oozings which emanate from its own vital juices as if the plant were weeping – Fracastor's *Syphilis*:

As often either on the cherry or on Phyllis' mournful tree you have seen a thick fluid seep from the moist bark, then harden into a sticky gum, in just the same way, where this disease holds sway a mucus usually flows all over the body, then at last it solidifies into an ugly scab.   (I, 360–4)[29]

('Phyllis' mournful tree' is the almond, which appears in *Prometheus Unbound* and of which we shall have more to say.) As usual with Shelley, however, the honey-dew image has more than one source. It also occurs in *Titus Andronicus*, a drama which Shelley ranked with Michaelangelo's *Day of Judgement*:[30] Lavinia's tears 'stood on her cheeks, as doth the honey-dew / Upon a gathered lily almost withered' (III, i, 112–13).

Lavinia is a chaste woman whose very pride in her virtue and scorn of sensuality make her the chosen victim of the evil characters. She meets a lustful Roman empress in the 'ruthless, vast and gloomy woods' where she is raped by her sons. (Shakespeare's woods contain a 'swallowing womb' – an open grave; in Shelley's draft there are cancelled lines about falling over a 'yawning grave'.)[31] She is found wandering 'as doth the deer / That hath received some unrecuring wound' (ibid, 89–90). Her hands and tongue have been cut off so that she cannot tell what has happened to her except by picking out from Ovid's *Metamorphoses* the tale of Philomela – like herself a 'tongueless nightingale' whose history has been a pattern of her own. Only when her allusions have been 'read' can she name her rapists. The parallels with *Epipsychidion* suggest that, like Lavinia, Shelley describes a terrible experience which the actual words on the page cannot express except obliquely and allusively; draft cancellations at this point include 'dumb words hid what ?you cannot tell'.[32]

Finally, the image in *Epipsychidion* of greying hair (264), which in another context could be the result of grief alone, considered alongside the other pathological imagery recalls the contemporary superstition regarding premature greyness. It has been objected that Shelley refers to a purely psychological state and uses grey hair as a simile – '*As* hair grown grey'. Were the poet anyone but Shelley, this might be a weighty objection, but it is one of his better-known peculiarities that his comparisons are often statements of what the object for comparison actually is or will prove to be in the course of time. A good example, from *Prometheus Unbound* (II, iii, 2–3), is supplied by

Matthews: 'The mighty portal / Like to a volcano's meteor-breathing chasm', where the mighty portal *is* a volcano's chasm, though the onlookers do not yet realise it. Given this habit and that Shelley actually was prematurely greying at the time that *Epipsychidion* was written, it seems perverse to deny that the ruins include literal hairs.[33]

Similarly, 'pierced . . . into the core of my green heart' which could be a conventional Renaissance trope expressive of the pangs of despised love,[34] gives rise to interpretative problems in Shelley because of his habit of blurring the distinction between the body and mind. An instance is furnished by the following passage from *Julian and Maddalo*. The Maniac recalls that his scornful lady once wished that he had castrated himself:

> That like some maniac monk, I had torn out
> The nerves of manhood by their bleeding root
> With mine own quivering fingers, so that ne'er
> Our hearts had for a moment mingled there
> To disunite in horror.   (424-8)

It would be difficult to delimit the meaning of 'hearts' in the above passage.[35]

Of course Shelley does refer to a psychologically damaging event – he could hardly do otherwise. In Thornton Hunt's opinion, the effect of his 'college experiences' was much greater on his mind than on his body. When moralists write about lust they usually stress its soul-withering results. 'Not only love – love that ought to purify the heart, and first call forth all the youthful powers, to prepare the man to discharge the benevolent duties of life, is sacrificed to premature lust, but all the social affections are deadened by the selfish gratifications, which very early pollute the mind, and dry up the generous juices of the heart.'[36] Thus Wollstonecraft on the pernicious effects of sending boys away to boarding school, in a passage which contains some suggestive verbal parallels with the episode under consideration in *Epipsychidion*. Similarly, Milton writes in *Comus* that when lust 'by lewd and lavish act of sin / Lets in defilement to the inward parts / The soul grows clotted by contagion'.

However this does not mean that the One is a particular prostitute. Thornton Hunt did not say that she was. She could be a personified abstraction: false religion is a whore in the Bible and in Spenser, and Hunt responded to the Spenserian element in *Epipsychidion*, as his illustration of the False Florimel shows. Envy in Dante is *la meretrice*. Fortune is proverbially a strumpet. In *Epipsychidion* the similarity to the corresponding figure of Life in *Una Favola* makes it virtually certain that the One is Life, whom one might reasonably expect to preside over the wintry forest of 'our life'.

In *Una Favola*, Love appears to the Youth 'at the dawn of the fifteenth spring of his life' accompanied by a troop of veiled and garlanded forms, and conducts him to a gloomy labyrinthine garden. This corresponds to the period in *Epipsychidion* when the protagonist meets the Being in his youth's dawn. The garden in *Una Favola* matches the *Epipsychidion* landscape of whispering woods, fountains and flowers; it becomes a 'lonely wood', upon Love's desertion, which has its counterpart in *Epipsychidion*'s 'wintry forest'. The Youth of *Una Favola* is fed upon a bitter and sweet fruit, the One is met under nightshade bowers; Life in *Una Favola* 'had the reputation of an enchantress' but proved 'more false than any Siren', the One utters a 'venomed melody' from her 'false mouth'. The Youth's hair is whitened and the flower of his body withered as a result of the pains ensuing upon Life's falsity.

In *Una Favola*, Life persuades Love to abandon the Youth 'in that savage place', which suggests that the Youth has been deserted by a loved woman who has succumbed to 'the prejudices of the world', or that Love has deserted the Youth's heart, returning to the realm of the ideal – the third sphere – allowing Lust to have full sway – or both. Life hides with Death, leaving the youth alone with the veiled troop which had accompanied him into the labyrinth. 'And whether those forms were the spectres of his dead thoughts or the shadows of the live ones of love no one can clarify.' Shelley becomes evasive here, allowing his hypothetical reader to intepret the forms as people, thoughts, or both. Upon the desertion of Love, they unveil themselves to the 'astonished' youth, proving to be the companions of Life, not of Love. 'Their horrible aspect and gloomy faces so overcame his heart with melancholy and for many days he wept so much that the herbs upon his path, fed with tears instead of dew, became like him, pale and bowed.' The forms dance around him wherever he goes, mocking and screaming menacingly, and when he seeks repose, process in front of his couch, each more 'schifosa' (filthy, obscene, loathsome) and terrible than the last. The imagery is appropriate to a sexual lapse followed by shame and the terror engendered by the prospect of a horrible death or, at the least, a lifetime of damaged health. The troop of mocking, screaming forms is very reminiscent of the chorus of Furies in *Prometheus Unbound*, whose torments include 'foul desire round thy astonished heart' and infection of the blood.

This does not of course mean that the chorus of forms is to be identified *exclusively* with these terrors any more than the Furies are; 'wrecked hopes' of all kinds, including political, are suggested. But that the threat of venereal disease is an important element among them is indicated by the following: after the most loathsome form has unveiled itself, the Youth seeks refuge in the cave of Death, an enchantress who sings sweetly over a slow fire of cypress wood. This figure is an imitation of Maimuna in Southey's *Thalaba*, and is thus associated with Mrs Boinville, whom Shelley called Maimuna.[37] The culmination of the torment inflicted by the forms thus corresponds, in Shelley's life history, to the elephantiasis terror, and the retreat to Death's cave to his retreat to Mrs Boinville's. (The figure is also conflated with Mary who does not otherwise appear in *Una Favola*; she, too, is a Maimuna – a Maie Moon: 'Maie' was Shelley's pet name for her in 1815 and the Moon his recurrent symbol for her.) Death in *Una Favola* corresponds, like Life, to a period of time and a number of associated experiences.

In *Epipsychidion* what Shelley has done is to incorporate the desertion by Love and the unveiling of the forms into the encounter with the One, who carries the full charge of the menace and horror of the unveiled forms. Whereas in *Una Favola* the nourishment by the bitter and sweet fruit suggests a kind of apprenticeship in passion which prepares the Youth for his 'fall', something akin to the period remembered by Kathema as 'life's veiling morn with all its bliss and care . . . Passion so prompt to blight, so stong to save' (24,28), in *Epipsychidion* the plant is named as the nightshade and thus given the associations of prostitution that it has acquired in the rest of Shelley's poetry. In *Epipsychidion*, according to this reading, Life is presented as a prostitute who transmits venereal disease, rather than as a conventional false enchantress such as Keats' *La Belle Dame Sans Merci*, because she is emblematic of a number of experiences which include 'the usual intercourse endured by almost every youth of England', actual infection or the very real threat of it, and the consequent misery and loss of self-esteem.

This reading gets round the difficulties which arise from identification of the figure with any of the known women in Shelley's life. (These difficulties do not arise from the supposition of the unknown one posited by Cameron and Holmes.) It is improbable that he would have disguised Harriet Grove as a seductive harlot. Harriet Shelley is a more likely candidate for the following reasons: Medwin, who was close to Shelley during the 1820–1 period, said that the One was an allegory of her, and Peacock, for all his championship of Harriet, never challenged him directly on this point.[38] A draft passage of the *Dedication* to *Laon and Cythna* refers to two figures in Shelley's life before he met Mary, one 'dear but false' and the other a 'heart of stone' whose touch withered him until his revival by Mary. These seem to correspond to the two Harriets respectively.[39] Moreover, Shelley regarded a loveless marriage as legal prostitution and had undoubtedly ceased to love Harriet by the beginning of 1814.

However, the figure of the poisonously beautiful siren does not fit Harriet Shelley very well either. Medwin in this area is particularly suspect. As Peacock pointed out, Medwin tampered with the evidence in order to elevate the status of Harriet Grove at the expense of Harriet Shelley, and he was opportunist enough to have misinterpreted this passage in order to support his thesis. The identification with Harriet Shelley also runs up against a difficulty of chronology. After the fatal encounter in *Epipsychidion* the Poet rashly seeks 'the shadow of that idol of my thought' in 'many mortal forms' – the fair, the wise and One who is said to be 'true – oh why not true to me?' (267–71) If the 'heart of stone' (Harriet Shelley) of the draft *Dedication* to *Laon and Cythna* is the same as the poison lady of *Epipsychidion*, then logic induces one to equate the 'dear but false' woman (Harriet Grove) with the *Epipsychidion* one who was true, but not to him. But this would make his love affair with Harriet Grove come long after his marriage to Harriet Shelley. The matter is further complicated by the fact that Shelley, in his final version of the *Dedication*, conflated both Harriets with other unsatisfactory love relationships, and summed them *all* up as 'false to me / Hard hearts, and cold, like weights of icy stone / Which crushed and withered mine'(51–3).

The period of the poet's search for the 'shadow of the idol' after encountering the poisonous One, has no exact equivalent in *Una Favola*. In theory it could have begun at any time after 1807, as argued in Chapter 2. The parallel with *Una Favola* and the reference to the 'golden prime of my youth's dawn' indicates that the autobiographical passage begins during the Eton period where the poet's struggles with 'vain strife' against the errors of the world commenced. The symbolic landscape of *Epipsychidion*, if based on a real one as so many of Shelley's landscapes are, also suggests that the moment of encountering Life occurred at Eton rather than Oxford. He calls his companions 'untaught foresters'; Eton abuts onto Windsor Forest. There is even a prototype of the well: Chalvey or Queen Anne's Well, Adrian's favourite 'bubbling spring' in *The Last Man* and a well-known beauty spot.[40] The gloomy garden of evergreens in *Una Favola* might have had a non-literary as well as a literary origin – the grounds of the Windmill Hotel which stretched down to the Chalvey brook.

On the other hand there are contra-indications that the actual encounter with the 'Life' figure of *Epipsychidion* is set in the Oxford period. There was a wood too, at Oxford – the wintry garden of evergreens which Shelley declared to be the abode of the 'two sisters'. The honey-dew image appears for the first time in *Rosalind and Helen* (1817–18). Lionel, Shelley's most sentimentalised self-projection, is subjected to the hatred of priests which resembles 'the unseen blight of a smiling day / The withering honey-dew, which clings / Under the bright green buds of May / Whilst they unfold their emerald wings'. He is punished for irreverent verses and laughter-provoking tales, including one called 'Banquet in Hell' (*R. & H.*, 676–90). This could refer to the *Margaret Nicholson* volume, which contains a few lines where Satan welcomes despots to his domain, though no banquet is mentioned. But here again the evidence is not conclusive; Shelley had already gained the reputation of a subversive at Eton, and it is known that he wrote poems and plays there which have not survived.[41] The association of the honey-dew with the hatred of priests, incidentally, does not conflict with its association with venereal disease in *Epipsychidion*. For Shelley, as for Blake, brothels were built with bricks of religion, and prostitution was the direct consequence of Christian sexual morality. This point will be developed further in the next chapter.

Nor is it clear which, if any, or the fair, wise or untrue 'mortal forms' are to be identified with the two Harriets.[42] As with *Una Favola*, however, there is a point where the miseries following the fatal encounter reach a climax, and this point can be given a date. This is the Cowperian passage, discussed in Chapter 6 and established as referring to the flight to Bracknell after the elephantiasis panic, where the Poet, like a 'hunted deer' turned upon his thoughts 'wounded and weak and panting'. In *Epipsychidion* it is Mrs Boinville's turn to disappear, though cancelled draft lines about 'angels' who lifted him and 'kept at bay' the hours when 'life is worse than death' suggest that he originally intended a specific reference to her and to Cornelia.[43] Immediately after the 'hunted deer' passage, he encounters 'Deliverance' in the shape of Mary, the Moon, who leads him into a cave of sleep.

Ever since Rossetti, the objection has been levelled that Thornton Hunt's reading of the passage was 'servile' and over-literalistic. Another objection is the common sense one that no matter how reckless Shelley was or how naive his faith in the impenetrability of anonymous authorship, he would surely never have risked publishing such a confession, least of all at a time when he was becoming increasingly tender about his reputation. The reading we put forward takes account of both objections because it proposes a Shelley who has exactly balanced the literal against the allegorical, and the claims of frankness against those of prudence. He is just specific enough and just vague enough for both purposes. His poem is aimed at 'the sacred few', 'the unprejudiced' who will be able to strip the veil from his allegory, but who will place the blame not on him but on 'the mistakes cherished by society respecting the connection of the sexes, whence the misery and diseases of . . . unenjoying prostitution necessarily spring'. At the same time, he has provided himself with an egress should enemies seize on the confession as confirmation that his poems are emanations from the diseased imagination of a debauchee. If it be urged that this reading confuses tenor with vehicle, the symbol with the symbolised, it should be remembered that this is exactly what Shelley's poetry characteristically does. In *Charles the First* the ragged and diseased beggars supplying an anti-masque are 'at once the sign and the thing signified' (I, i, 168). They represent the 'beggary of England' – England's moral bankruptcy – and are also literally the beggary of England – her beggar class. In the same way, the prostitution of the youth of England is represented by an encounter with a prostitute.

Shelley presents Emily as Love, the elixir of True Life, who will redeem him from the consequences of encountering the poisonous One. She is described in terms that contrast almost point for point with the latter's baleful physical features. The honey-dew example has already been given; in addition, Emily's voice, cheeks, perfume, breath and eyes are presented in the same way. A symbolic sexual union with her, imaginatively realised through poetry, will restore his body and mind from the delayed results of seduction by the poisonous One. The well over which the One presided and which the nightshade polluted becomes the fountain of delight in the last section of the poem:

> Our breath shall intermix, our bosoms bound,
> And our veins beat together; and our lips
> With other eloquence than words, eclipse
> The soul that burns between them, and the wells
> Which boil under our being's inmost cells,
> The fountains of our deepest life, shall be
> Confused in Passion's golden purity,
> As mountain-springs under the morning sun.   (565–72)

The wells, fountains and springs are not only a source of life, joy and inspiration but the means by which the deepest instincts of nature are expressed; they represent the surges, the active energy, the intensity of sexual feeling as expressed in the genitals.

In a cancelled preface to *Epipsychidion*, Shelley wrote, quoting Byron's *Manfred*, that the fate of the author of the poem was 'an additional proof that "The Tree of Knowledge is not that of Life" '[44] thus indicating the centrality of the encounter in the wintry forest. 'Knowledge' here corresponds to the False Life of *Una Favola* and carries associations of the eating of the apple in the Garden of Eden and a descent into concupiscence. This concept receives its most complicated development in Shelley's last poem, *The Triumph of Life*, discussed in Chapter 12.

10

White hair and frail form

One of the most problematic features of Shelley's poetry is the 'recurrent figure of the frail Poet, pale of hue and weak of limb, consecrated to his youthful vision of Beauty, but incapable of realising or recreating it, driven at last to death by unassuageable desire for he knows not what'. For some readers, this figure confirms their sense of Shelley's immaturity; one form of defence has been to deny the existence of any important autobiographical element in the poetry, urging that 'it is a mistake to identify a lyric protagonist as the voice of the poet, or to read a prayer, elegy, or ode, which has its rhetoric in part determined by tradition, as primarily confessional'. Mediating between these two extremes, Judith Chernaik placed Shelley in a tradition of allegorised biography represented by Dante and Milton, and argued that the images of the poet's weakness 'suggest original or potential strength even as they assert failure'. Even in making this defence, however, she was concerned to play down the sources of the image in the actual circumstances of Shelley's medical history; hence, speaking of the Poet figure in *Adonais*, she wrote that loss of strength 'though imaged in physical terms, is clearly mental and spiritual'.[1]

Nearly two decades after Chernaik's important essay, and in a changed climate of opinion – which she has done much to create – it should be possible to admit that the Poet's psychic weakness is inseparable from his physical weakness without being accused of selling the pass, just as it is possible to concede that some of his attempts at transforming his autobiography into allegory are unsuccessful, and to trace his developing artistic and emotional maturity through examination of this figure.

The most commonly mentioned characteristic of the Poet, under which title for convenience we include all Shelleyan self-projections of this kind, is his prematurely grey hair. It has an emblematic quality or significance. It is a badge of the suffering bought by experience, and in its final appearance, in *The Triumph of Life*, a badge of infamy as well.

'Sadak the Wanderer', a fragment dated 1810–12 by Neville Rogers and which, like 'Zeinab and Kathema', has for its theme the quest for a lost love, has a protagonist with 'withered brow' and 'lank', 'scattered' – either 'thin' or 'blown' – hair.[2] But *Alastor* (1815) marks the first certain appearance of this figure, and is Shelley's first full-scale attempt at an 'idealised' life history.

156

The last statement is contentious. The orthodox view is that although personal concerns are no doubt reflected in the poem, it is autobiographical only in the most general way: 'Shelley wrote the poem precisely in order to *distance* himself from his own lived experience.'[3] *Alastor* is variously said to be about sollipsism, narcissism, the relationship between the older and the younger generation of Romantic poets, the Romantic quest for experience beyond the humanly possible. With much of this one can agree: Shelley probably intended interpretation of the poem to be open-ended. There is no doubt that he portrays the *Alastor* Poet's history as representative, not merely personal. At the risk, however, of incurring the charge of being retrogressively and reductively Victorian – Victorian Shelleyans are frequently accused of acknowledging no truth but the biographical – we would argue that these interpretations are grounded upon a disguised narrative of events in Shelley's life, almost in their exact order. Of course he shapes, omits, simplifies, and is highly subjective in his choice of incidents.

A number of puzzles concerning the poem are cleared up once this is recognised; one which may be mentioned is the apparently arbitrary nature of the changes of locale. Why does the scenery change from the Oriental to the (nearly) British? Why does the poet go to the Vale of Cashmire (Eden) instead of beginning his life there? Why a forest here, a whirlpool there, a green recess elsewhere? The reason is that the poem's shape has been dictated by Shelley's own wanderings, and these have been interwoven with numerous literary allusions.

This claim we intend to substantiate elsewhere in detail. Full-scale treatment would not be appropriate here as *Alastor* is not central to our argument; we regard it as one of the re-enactments of the archetypical story of vision and betrayal described in Chapter 8. However, we will say enough to indicate the lines along which such a full-scale argument would be developed; readers may care to anticipate this argument by filling it out and deciding whether they agree with it. It opens with the assumption that the start of the Poet's wanderings corresponds to either Shelley's entering Oxford or his expulsion from it.

The action of *Alastor* begins for the Poet 'when early youth had passed' and he has 'left his cold fireside and alienated home'. It is thus different from the idealised biographies dealt with in the last chapter and those discussed later on in this one, for they commence their spiritual history with awakening at the dawn of youth.[4] Shelley has completely omitted the loss of Harriet Grove from the narrative, for reasons that are artistic as much as personal.

The poet is a vegetarian and a student of the culture of ancient civilisations, including the Zodiac. He is accompanied by an Arab maiden who provides him with food from her father's tent, but whom he otherwise totally ignores. The reader is never sure how long she continues to follow him, though at a later point ministrations to the Poet's bodily needs pass to some cottagers, whom we identify with the Newtons. Eventually the Poet's wanderings take him to the Vale of Cashmire, embowered with odorous plants.

This part of the story corresponds to Shelley's actual wanderings in the Lake District, Ireland, Wales during 1811–12, his espousal of vegetarianism, and his intellectual adventures among such books as Volney's *Ruins of Empire*. The Arab maid is Harriet, whose daily return to her father's tent represents her subservience to the Westbrooks. Cashmire is Nantgwyllt in the Elan Valley, an all-but 'perfect Heaven' where Shelley and Harriet hoped to settle in May 1812.[5]

There the Poet, up to this point happy, has a vision which leaves him in a state of erotic agitation and despair. He dreams of a 'veiled maid', a poet, whose voice is 'like the voice of his own soul'. She brings knowledge, truth, virtue, and political awareness – 'lofty hopes of divine liberty'. Sent by the 'spirit of sweet human love' as a punishment for the Poet's spurning of her 'choicest gifts' – the Arab maid – , she also arouses him to a pitch of sexual excitement only to fade away at the point of a dream consummation. Awakening from his trance, the Poet finds the world vacant, cold and garish, 'lost, lost, forever lost. . . that beautiful shape!' Now in the grip of an irresistible and corrosive passion he flees through a tangled, swampy and precipitous wilderness, 'startling with careless step the moonlight snake', after which point his health begins to suffer.

We believe Shelley to be allegorising here his awakening militant feminism and realisation that he needed more than an 'amiable female' in his life, whereas other youthful 'awakenings' in his poetry relate to puberty and the discovery of sexual passion. The woman of surpassing mental powers and poetical imagination does not appear in his poetry or prose fiction before *Queen Mab*, which he began in 1812. Stimuli were James Lawrence's feminist *Empire of the Nairs* which he read in the spring of 1812, his correspondence with Godwin and his reading – or re-reading – of Mary Wollstonecraft. He ordered her *Vindication of the Rights of Women* at Lynmouth in July 1812.[6] The figure of the veiled maid undoubtedly owes much to the 'divine Luxima', the heroine of Sydney Morgan's *The Missionary*, which Shelley had read in the Elan locality almost exactly a year before, but inasmuch as she is also the recreation of a feminist like the youthful Mary Wollstonecraft, and thus had actually lived, there was hope of finding her reborn, as it were, on earth.

The poet now wanders 'day after day' through places identifiable as Tremadoc and Ireland (spring 1813), undergoing an 'autumn of strange suffering' which leaves him emaciated and with his scattered hair 'sered'. Now it is winter; he amazes the cottagers and terrifies their children with his 'wild eyes'. Certain 'youthful maidens', however, are able to interpret 'half his woe'. Shelley has now arrived at the elephantiasis terror; the maidens are those who sympathised with him; Fanny Godwin and Claire Clairmont are the likeliest candidates.

Henceforth the Poet is the only remaining character. The poem approaches the point corresponding to Shelley's meeting with Mary, where a closer veil becomes necessary because it records Shelley's disillusionment with her in 1815;[7] for all her virtues she has proved not to be a reincarnation of her illustrious mother. Mary wrote that *Alastor* was written in a different spirit from *Queen Mab* because 'a very few years' had 'checked the ardour of Shelley's hopes'. The poem is about the failure of a luminary to find a woman who will sustain and inspire his revolutionary passion. Hence the Poet dies – Shelley's 'best self' is extinct; *Alastor*'s Narrator is one who has accommodated himself to the world, including domestic life, but who mourns with ever decreasing detachment as the poem advances, the fate of his *alter ego*.

Shelley's mental exhaustion at the Boinvilles has its counterpart in the Poet's finding himself amid 'a waste of putrid marshes'. Intending to seek death, he embarks in a boat on a 'sunny' day. At midnight on the same day he is drawn by a fierce current into the 'slant and winding depths' of a cavern. As he enters he cries 'Vision and Love! . . . I have beheld / The path of thy departure. Sleep and death / Shall not divide us long!' (366–9) This is a journey into what Shelley elsewhere called the 'caverns strange and fair / Of far and pathless passion, while the stream / Of life, our bark doth on its whirlpools bear' (*L. & C.*, 2588–90) – in other words, an embarkation on a relationship with a real woman, a recovery of the Vision from the realms of sleep and death, and not a journey into those realms as some critics have argued.[8] The next passage (369–420) allegorises the stormy early months of Shelley and Mary's relationship, including the imbroglio with Claire – the whirlpool in the poem.

At two other points the Poet's hair is mentioned; each corresponds to a time when Shelley believed his life to be in immediate danger. He wishes to deck his 'withered hair' (413) with daffodils; the poem has by then moved to the spring of 1815, the period of Pemberton's diagnosis and the escape to Salt Hill. Later, in a forest landscape which, according to Mary, was inspired by Windsor Great Park,[9] he gazes in a well at the now 'wan light' of his eyes 'through the reflected lines / Of his thin hair' (470–1). The poet is beckoned by the 'starry eyes' of the Vision, unable to find happiness in the spirit of the natural world which stands beside him. His despondency answers to Shelley's just before commencing the Thames voyage which followed his second pulmonary attack. He wrote to Hogg 'Who is there who will not pursue phantoms, spend his choicest hours in hunting after dreams, and wake only to perceive his error and regret that death is so near?' The Poet follows the path of a winding stream which ends in a waterfall – the void (the Thames voyage was planned by Shelley to end with the Falls of Clyde).[10] He dies in a late autumnal season amid barren mountains, alone.

Alastor is a highly allusive poem and, as far as we can see, the allusions usually have a polemical point – Shelley differentiates himself from his source in some way while invoking similarities. For instance there are several places at which the legend of Narcissus is recalled; Shelley's Poet has not fallen in love with himself, but with someone who can respond to his ideal self, a nice but essential difference. Similarly, echoes of *Peter Wilkins*, the eighteenth-century science fiction novel which, according to Medwin, profoundly influenced Shelley,[11] are present because Peter, who has fled from an unsatisfactory marriage, finds an uplifting winged wife after a voyage through a cavern, whereas the Poet does not.

One of Shelley's sources, we believe, is *Syphilis*, the influence of which on the description of the Poet's underground wanderings was argued in Chapter 8. ('Fracastor', oddly, is one of the only true rhymes for 'Alastor'; this may be pure coincidence, but it points to the poem's being on Shelley's mind at the time.) Shelley had occasion to be reminded of it in 1815, for it was in April of that year that he bought Good's translation of Lucretius, where he would have found in two places a citation from Fracastor's episode of the youth of Brescia.[12]

The youth is highborn, illustrious and beautiful. He has some un-Shelleyan accomplishments such as prowess at the chase, but resembles the *Alastor* Poet in many respects, including his great promise and attractiveness to women. Shelley says of his Poet that 'Virgins as unknown he past have pined / And wasted for fond love of his wild eyes' (62–3). As for Fracastor's youth, 'Him all the goddesses of Ollius and maidens of Eridanus desired, the goddesses of the groves and the girls of the countryside. All these wooed him with sighs. Perchance one of them was spurned (*'neglecta'*) and called the High Gods to avenge her; and not in vain for the good powers heard her prayers. The wretched man, too confident to fear such dire mischance, was attacked by this disease.'[13] One of the most horrific images in the whole of *Syphilis* is to be found in this episode: 'Foul ulcers (shame on the mercy of heaven) began to devour the fair eyes which the light of heaven loved.' Good singled out these lines twice as an especially egregious example of bad taste.

Both youth and Poet are punished for spurning human love. Unlike the youth, however, the Poet has a metaphorical 'venereal consumption' and it is that, not ulcers, which gradually extinguishes the light of his eyes. Like syphilis, though, the Poet's disease follows the presumed bite of a vicious reptile (the snake which the Poet has carelessly aroused and which is the antithesis of the gentle squirrels that took food from his hand before the onset of his passion). The Poet's 'wild eyes' frighten the cottager's infant; this has its equivalent in the *'oculis torvis'* of Fracastor. That phrase in turn comes from lines immediately preceding the youth of Brescia episode, where Fracastor writes of another young man who 'looking with wild eyes on his distorted limbs, on his loathsome joints and swollen face, has often in his misery denounced the cruelty of heaven and of fate'.[14] This is virtually what Shelley was doing in his imagination during the winter of 1813, the period corresponding to the episode with the cottagers. In this section, too, is to be found a striking verbal parallel between the two poems. Speaking of the inability of the young syphilitics to find rest, Fracastor wrote:

> Fugerat: iis oriens ingrata Aurora rubebat.   (I, 372)

Compare

> He fled. Red morning dawned upon his flight.

Shelley's line is not a translation. In *Syphilis* the subject of 'Fugerat' is *sleep*. Nevertheless the lines have a marked rhythmic similarity and this, coupled with similar ideas of flight, inability to sleep and an unwelcome red dawn, is, as far as we can find, without another parallel.[15] There is, however, a *double* allusion in Shelley's image, which also recalls the following lines from Wordsworth's *The Excursion* (probably the greatest single influence on *Alastor*). They describe a hermit's motives for fleeing society:

> Not always from intolerable pangs
> He fled; but compassed round by pleasure, sighed
> For independent happiness.   (III, 379–81)

Unlike the hermit, the Poet *is* fleeing from intolerable pangs, and seeks not independent happiness but sympathy, rapture and a cure for his disease. In the next line Fracastor writes of the 'phantom of the Night' (*noctis imago*) being hostile to the venereal sufferers, which is very close to the 'fierce fiend of a distempered dream' which drives the Poet. Shelley's preface says that he has been deluded by a 'generous error'; in 'Even love is sold' it is an 'excess of generosity and devotedness' that induces young men to consort with prostitutes.

Enough has been said to illustrate how the spectre of syphilis haunts a re-enaction of the archetype. We now turn to passages that prefigure the grey hair image in *Epipsychidion*.

In *Rosalind and Helen* (1817–18), the friends meet deep in the centre of a 'vast and antique wood' approached by a winding path which leads to a spring. Tradition attaches a spectral tale to this spot:

> That a hellish shape at midnight led
> The ghost of a youth with hoary hair,
> And sate on the seat beside him there,
> Till a naked child came wandering by,
> When the fiend would change to a lady fair!   (150–4)

Here again are the forest and well, with a protean foul/fair lady and the prematurely aged youth. The fiend 'sate' by the well, ready to deceive any vulnerable, errant ('naked', 'wandering') child. Seated by her and forced to look on and witness the eternal recurrence of his terrible story is a previous victim of her wiles, whose suffering has occasioned his early death. That story, Shelley says, is only a legend; the truth is worse:

> . . . here a sister and a brother
> Had solemnized a monstrous curse,
> Meeting in this fair solitude:
> For beneath yon very sky,
> Had they resigned to one another
> Body and soul. The multitude,
> Tracking them to the secret wood,
> Tore limb from limb their innocent child,
> And stabbed and trampled on its mother;
> But the youth, for God's most holy grace,
> A priest saved to burn in the market place.   (156–66)

Obviously the two youths and the child are all manifestations of the same character, and they, in turn, are related to the 'withered' Lionel, Helen's husband. But what is this worse truth?

Brown has cogently traced the source of the theme of incest in Shelley (where, between brother and sister, it is *always* portrayed approvingly), to the memory of 'his own youthful engagement to his first cousin Harriet Grove, with whom he was nearly as intimate in childhood as he was with his own sisters, and with whom he shared a startling facial resemblance, making the two appear almost twins'. An engagement between cousins is transformed into the closest kind of consanguineous union, in order that it may function as a 'paradigm of sympathetic connection between the sexes, like mated to like, in perfect harmony'.[16] Such a union is a revolutionary force, because the brother–sister partnership confronts Christianity (social anthropology in Shelley's day had discovered that brother–sister incest was not a universal taboo), and because it is inherently feminist. The 'monstrous curse', then, is a vow that the brother and sister have made to defeat tyranny, especially the tyranny of Christian sexual morality; the motif of sexual union with a sisterly co-revolutionary appears as early as the Margaret Nicholson 'Epithalamium': it would have been pure wish-fulfilment on Shelley's part which cast Harriet in that role, though according to him she was at one point a Deist.

The story is a highly metaphorical account of the defeat of the wished-for partnership. The sister has been 'stabbed and trampled' by the multitude (convention). This reflects Shelley's outburst on Harriet's loss and reversion to Christianity: 'She is married, married to a clod of earth, she will become as insensible herself, all those fine capabilities will moulder.'[17] Images of bright sparks of humanity being *trampled* into the dust, or *kneaded* into a mass, crowd Shelley's pages. The murder of the child represents the prevention of a race of little scions of infidelity which the incestuous union would have realised. The fate of the Shelley figure would seem to refer specifically to his expulsion from Oxford following the *Necessity of Atheism* pamphlet; burning for atheism figures in *Queen Mab* (VII, 1–13), and Shelley is probably identifying with Giordano Bruno or Spinoza whose philosophical position was very near to his own and of whom *Nicholson's British Encyclopaedia* erroneously declared that he was burnt as an atheist.[18] But there are other associations with 'burning in the marketplace' in Shelley's poetry which interact with the atheist's punishment and which are here activated by the context of virtuous love thwarted by priestly law.

In *Rosalind and Helen* the marketplace is the opposite of the 'fair solitude' of the union between brother and sister. (There are echoes of St Leonard's Forest, where Shelley went walking in January 1811.)[19] Whereas the lovers' sylvan solitude is the most private, the market is the most public of places. Another marketplace occurs in *Laon and Cythna*, which Shelley finished just before beginning *Rosalind and Helen*. Laon leaves the private solitude – the cave – where he and his sister Laone/Cythna have just made love. Descending back to the war-desolated countryside in search of food, he enters a 'village in a wood' and dismounts 'Beside the fountain in the market-place':

> No living thing was there beside one woman,
> Whom I found wandering in the streets, and she
> Was withered from a likeness of aught human
> Into a fiend, by some strange misery:
> Soon as she heard my steps she leaped on me,
> And glued her burning lips to mine, and laughed
> With a loud, long, and frantic laugh of glee,
> And cried, 'Now, Mortal, thou hast deeply quaffed
> The Plague's blue kisses – soon millions shall pledge the draught!
>
> (2758–66)

Although a real woman, in her crazed mind she personifies disease 'I am Pestilence; – hither and thither / I flit about, that I may slay and smother: – / All lips which I have kissed must surely wither' (2772–4). Holmes was so struck by the similarity between this and the 'venomed melody' passage that he thought it might be dealing with the same incident, and drew his readers' attention to the 'odd placing reference of the "well"' and similar images of 'blue nightshade' and infectious poison.[20] Of course there is no nightshade in the above lines. What Holmes registered is the similar association of the colour blue and sexually transmitted disease. The collocation of the habitations of man, poisonous creatures, raging appetite, the colour blue and sex appears again in the following lines from *Prometheus Unbound* describing the world of Jupiter's reign, where, after volcanoes and floods: 'Blue thistles bloomed in cities; foodless toads / Within voluptuous chambers panting crawled' (*P.U.*, I, 170–1). The lines suggest at once toads seeking corpses as food in Pompeian cemeteries and defilement of nuptial chambers which the toads treat as cisterns to knot and gender in.

The crazed female has cast herself as the Proverbial 'whorish woman'. As in the Bible the sexual assault takes place at night. Further details confirm her self-identification as a harlot. Her lips are 'burning' – obviously with both disease and lust – indeed with the disease that is the result of lust, and which had been referred to as 'the burning' from medieval times. 'Burnt' was an alternative to 'poxed' or 'clapped' in the Regency though Shelley is as likely to have known this from his miscellaneous reading[21] and his study of seventeenth-century drama, most notably from a passage very familiar to him, the invective of the mad Lear against women: 'But to the girdle do the gods inherit, / Beneath is all the fiend's. / There's hell, there's darkness, there is the sulphurous pit; burning, scalding, stench, consumption' (IV, vi, 123–8). 'Glue' was another name for 'the pox'; in Shelley's poetry it always has overtones of sexually transmitted disease.[22]

However, the woman is merely an impersonation of the Harlot; when Laon asks for food she takes him to a pile of loaves, a literal-minded fulfilment of the admonition 'By means of an whorish woman a man is brought to a piece of bread'. Laon and Cythna, surprisingly, do not contract disease from Pestilence's bread, but are on the contrary physically sustained. The reason is that 'to the pure all things are pure'. Potential poison becomes food, as the kingfishers converted the nightshade into their own nature. Strengthened by his love, Laon is unassailable, just as Shelley felt that Mary's love protected him from 'the impure' in 1814. The episode records a resistance to prostitution, not a succumbing to it.

The episode has another function, being the first intimation of the Plague which will overwhelm the country. In the story the Plague arises later, as the aftermath of war, but this adumbrative episode makes the point symbolically that the epidemic is in origin transmitted by sexual outrage. It is thus doubly the product of the Tyrant, one of whose chief instruments of power is the rape and enslavement of women, so that 'life is poisoned in its wells' (3315). The Plague first strikes the animals – Shelley is conflating several descriptions of epidemics – since it is the 'brutish' that are first affected; the disease then moves on to the 'noble animal' who is not a creature of mere appetite.

Laon makes a second journey to the countryside, now famine-stricken as well:

> There was no corn – in the wide market-place
> All loathliest things, even human flesh was sold;
> They weighed it in small scales.   (X, xix, 3955–7)

Then the 'blue Plague' strikes man (3964). 'Each well / Was choked with rotting corpses' (3973–4), and corpses are also piled up in a 'crumbling pyramid . . . near the great fountain in the public square' of the Golden City (3992). The marketplace, then, is the public place of commerce, where the fountain of life is polluted and where all things are sold. Shelley's words here evoke both the note 'Even love is sold' and the corresponding lines of *Queen Mab*. A public square is frequented by public women, like the disreputable piazzas of Covent Garden, also a *market* in the usual sense of a place where food is bought and sold. London is, of course, the paradigm of the Golden City of the poem. (Just as Shelley saw in St Bartholomew's the type of Milton's lazar house of the world, so he probably saw in Covent Garden the type of the Garden of Eden which had become the world's brothel. 'Hell is a city much like London.')

The prophecy of Pestilence does come true for Laon in a punning sense. Laon's lips wither when he and Cythna are literally burnt in the marketplace, the pyramid of their bonfire representing the obverse of that of the piled-up corpses. They have been offered up as sacrificial victims in order to rid the land of the Plague; it is not only their revolutionary atheism which has singled them out but their sexual code, Shelley's cure for the social evil of prostitution. Their *Liebestod* is a moral victory over all aspects of tyranny, but especially sexual obscenity. Fire drives out 'fire'; their burning confirms the truths that have been spoken by their pure lips.

A third fountain in the public or market square occurs in *Prometheus Unbound*. It is the hiding place from which the young Spirit of the Earth watches the transformation of relationships between the sexes and the shedding of their evil nature by poisonous plants and animals: an episode that culminates in the emblem of the halcyons thinning the nightshade berries and the Spirit's happy anticipation of his own sexual awakening.

There is, then, a very strong association between the marketplace, fountains, burning, prostitution, disease and Christian sexual ethics. In *Laon and Cythna*, after the brother and sister are joined 'body and soul' they resist sexual pollution but are literally burnt. In *Rosalind and Helen* the brother and sister are separated, which leaves the brother open to the fate of being sexually 'burnt'. Irrespective of whether the episode in question is a covert confession on Shelley's part, the above interpretation, so far from being extraneous to the poem, is intimately bound up with Shelley's free love code, propagation of which is one of the chief raisons d'être of *Rosalind and Helen*.

Disaster strikes Laon too when he is separated from his sister, which happens early in the poem, before their sexual union in the cave. It is this sequence which was discussed earlier in Chapter 4 and related to 'Zeinab and Kathema' and the Oxford windmill. Bound with cankering 'chains that eat into the flesh', his 'parched skin' is 'split with piercing agonies' and thirst rages within him 'like a scorpion's nest / Built in mine entrails' (1189–1359). Newton's astrological system can be discerned in the poem: Laon is Leo, Cythna (Cynthia, Cytherea – the name combines associations of both Venus and Diana) is Virgo; their separation (which imagery of briony berries, ruined vineyards and harvests suggests takes place under the sign of Libra)[23] ushers in the reign of Ahrimanes; hence the scorpion. The scorpion's nest, as in *Zastrozzi* (following Pliny), represents lust. Raging thirst eventually reduces Laon to craving even the formerly spurned water from a 'putrid pool' offered by his captors. His ordeal climaxes in the eating of the corpse's flesh – where Laon takes on momentarily the role of the predatory Sagittarius. It is at this nadir that the hermit (Dr Lind) rescues and restores him to health. Seven years later, Laon, gazing at his reflection in a lake, sees 'My thin hair / Was prematurely gray' (1668–9).

A hoary-headed youth weeping over 'an open grave' appears in the poem of 1817 entitled 'Death'. This is the only poem in which white hair operates as an emblem of bereavement alone, though even here the mourning for dead 'kindred, friend and lover' is bound up with lost hopes and 'my pain'. A grey-haired figure is the hero of the unfinished *Prince Athanase* which, according to Mary, was begun in the same year at Marlow. However, scholars such as Reiman have concluded that nothing survives of a Marlovian *Ur*-text and that the existing poem was written entirely in Italy and worked on even as late as mid-1819. The first part was prepared for publication along with *Julian and Maddalo*, with which Shelley seems to have associated it. But when *Prince Athanase* finally appeared, it was after Shelley's death and with some of his notebook drafts added.[24]

The first part tells the story of an idealistic and gifted young prince, 'weak and gray before his time', who is pursued from land to land by restless griefs. The nature of these griefs is hidden from even the young luminary himself. He has no secret crime on his conscience; he is devoid of evil passions: 'Not his the thirst for glory or command / Baffled with blast of hope-consuming shame / Nor evil joys which fire the vulgar breast / And quench in speedy smoke its feeble flame' (9–12). No one could have a purer heart or a more innocent mind. He has no fear of 'what religion fables of the grave'. He scorns all disguise and speaks his mind frankly and fearlessly, but mildly. Although this paragon has thousands of foes, their arrows of mortal hatred pass by him harmlessly. Yet in spite of this

> . . . like an eyeless nightmare grief did sit
> Upon his being; a snake which fold by fold
> Pressed out the life of life, a clinging fiend
> Which clenched him if he stirred with deadlier hold; –
> And so his grief remained – let it remain – untold.   (120–4)

This is a very violent 'grief'; clearly the word means something a great deal stronger than 'bereavement' or 'sorrow'. 'Grief' would seem to be a collecting point for a number of concepts, including several obsolete meanings of the word. This frequently occurs in Shelley. 'Stern', for instance, more usually carries the force of the old sense 'cruel' than the modern 'severe'. According to the OED, 'grief' can mean 'hardship', 'suffering', 'wrong or injury', 'a sore, wound, disease of the skin, a disease', 'anger', 'physical pain', 'mental pain', 'keen or bitter regret or remorse'. It seems likely that some, if not all, of these meanings are present here.

The poem as prepared for the press by Shelley stopped there, at the point where it had become incumbent to explain Athanase's grief. Shelley's notebook drafts show, however, that Athanase was about to unlock his heart and that some sort of explanation would have emerged. Some of these drafts (corresponding to fragments I, II and III of Hutchinson's text) deal with the prince's relationship with his tutor Zonoras, a Dr Lind figure, who is able to draw Athanase out more effectively than his other friends. The image of the honey-dew on the green leaves is again prefigured:

> And when the old man saw that on the green
> Leaves of his opening [deleted *manhood*] ?spring a blight had lighted
> He said: 'My friend, one grief alone can wean
>
> A gentle mind from all that once delighted:-
> Thou lovest. . .   (230-4)

The old man is wrong; Athanase is not love-sick. His pupil's response is a wry smile – some cancelled words read 'in scorn':[25]

> And Athanase. . . then smiled, as one o'erladen
> With iron chains might smile to ?talk of bands
> Twined round her lover's neck by some blithe maiden
> And said. . .   (236-9)

Athanase's story of his wanderings, told in a flash-back, would have ensued, as the immediately following draft cancellation 'Then I will tell thee all I know' indicates.[26] He would then have died, probably after more vain journeys.

Mary supplied a few details of the plan of the poem. How far she had been in Shelley's confidence and how far she had inferred the story from his notes is not clear.

The idea Shelley had formed of Prince Athanase was a good deal modelled on *Alastor*. In the first sketch of the poem, he named it *Pandemos and Urania*. Athanase seeks through the world the One whom he may love. He meets, in the ship in which he is embarked, a lady who appears to him to embody his ideal of love and beauty. But she proves to be Pandemos, or the earthly and unworthy Venus; who, after disappointing his cherished dreams and hopes, deserts him. Athanase, crushed by sorrow, pines and dies. 'On his deathbed, the lady who can really reply to his soul comes and kisses his lips.'   (Hutchinson, p. 159)

When Zonoras makes his well-meaning diagnosis, the fatal encounter with the Pandemian Venus would seem to have already taken place, and it is this encounter that is ultimately responsible for Athanase's emaciation and grey hair.

At this point one needs to know what Shelley meant by Uranian and Pandemian love. The terms are taken from Pausanias' speech in Plato's *Symposium*, but in one respect Shelley departs from Plato, for whom Uranian love is exclusively homosexual; taking a tip from this, Edward Carpenter made out a case that Athanase's grief was unrecognised homosexual passion. While the argument which we are about to put forward could be used to support this, Shelley's writings — notably the introduction he wrote to his own translation of Plato's *Symposium* — do not suggest that he would have regarded a homosexual orientation as an 'eyeless nightmare'; he was even prepared to speculate on how its physical expression among the ancient Greeks was rendered compatible with love of intellectual beauty.[27]

'Uranian' and 'Pandemian' have often been equated with 'spiritual' and 'physical' love respectively. But this is to misunderstand not only Shelley but Plato too, for whom the physical is an essential ingredient of Uranian love. Moreover the Pandemian lover is not merely 'earthly' but sensual and concerned only with his immediate physical gratification. Here is the relevant passage in Shelley's own translation of the *Symposium*. Pandemian love is

common to the vulgar, and presides over transient and fortuitious connexions, and is worshipped by the least excellent of mankind: the votaries of this deity. . . seek the body rather than the soul, and the ignorant rather than the wise, disdaining all that is honourable and lovely, and considering how they shall best satisfy their sensual necessities.[28]

The Uranian lover, on the other hand, although no less admiring of the beloved's physical beauty, is chiefly drawn to him by virtue of mental and spiritual qualities. Uranian Love

exempts us from all wantonness and libertinism. Those who are inspired by this divinity seek the affections of that sex which is endowed by nature with greater excellence and vigour both of body and mind.[29]

The distinguishing feature in the response of the two kinds of lovers to physical beauty is that whereas for the Pandemian lover it was the 'sole object of desire' for the Uranian it was the preliminary step leading to the contemplation of the supreme beauty itself, and played a part even in the final stages of this mystical ascent. According to Shelley, even though 'the gratification of the senses. . . soon becomes a very small part of that profound and complicated sentiment which we call love', the sexual impulse 'serves from its obvious and external nature as a kind of type or expression of the rest, as common basis, an acknowledged and visible link'. The sexual act 'ought always to be the link and type of the highest emotions of our nature' (*Prose*, pp. 220, 222).

'Earthly and unworthy' therefore do not accurately convey to a modern ear the full force of Plato's disgust for the Pandemian Venus, though 'unworthy' in the nineteenth century still had the stronger meaning 'despicable'. Gross, promiscuous, libertine — that is what should be understood. Pandemian love corresponds very closely to the sensualism, in Shelley's mind always associated with tyranny and exploitation, of the gallant. Pandemian love at its best easily lapses into lust and thence into loveless brute appetite. It is an encounter with a deity of this sort of love that Prince Athanase has experienced.

Despite Mary's remark that *Pandemos and Urania* was modelled on *Alastor*, it does not appear to be the same story, though it contains the same motifs of the sick hero and a quest for love ending in death. In *Alastor* the only personage who deserts the Poet is a dream-vision whom he has not been seeking but who comes into his mind unawares; the Arab maiden cannot be said to have deserted him since, on the contrary, he spurns her. Rather, *Prince Athanase* seems to be an attempt to deal with the material which was eventually to be shaped into the autobiographical section of *Epipsychidion*. But with only Mary's note to go on it is impossible to be more definite.

Examination of the meaning of Pandemian love does, however, cast a new light on the character of the Prince. He has been tainted by Pandemian love in some way, yet his purity of heart and mind is stressed. Shelley has created a description of repression; the 'grief' which strangles Athanase is a Gordian knot of emotions which amount to a dark second self, a Doppelgänger whose existence he denies so effectively that he is unaware that he *is* denying it, but which is capable of all the vile deeds of which his higher princely self knows nothing. Hence, the possibility exists that the Prince has wished for 'glory and command' and has experienced 'hope-consuming shame', does have a secret crime on his mind, is deeply wounded by the enmity of men and cherishes bitter and revengeful feelings towards them, is not candid with his friends and is afraid of 'what religion fables of the grave' – not necessarily a Christian hell, but some sort of life of pain after death. (Any belief in the immortality of the best self carries with it the possibility that the worst self will also survive.) Shelley once declared to Hogg his creed that the immoral never escaped from the fetters of the diseased body: 'For the immoral "never to be able to die, never to escape from some shrine as chilling as the clay-formed dungeon which now it inhabits" is the future punishment which I believe in.'[30] Shelley took this quotation from the Schubart 'fragment' on the Wandering Jew, which is another clue to Athanase's 'grief'. Athanase (deathless) has an imperative mission to denounce tyranny, and his 'griefs' – injuries – entitle him to do this; – yet in as much as he is crippled by his 'grief' at the hands of the Pandemian Venus his unfulfilled mission itself fuels further guilt. Moreover, this Doppelgänger is actually the product of the high ethical standard which he has set himself; any deviation from rectitude further disqualifies him in his own eyes from being the one whose pure lips will utter truths that will bind the scorpion falsehood with a wreath of everlasting flame. Lilies that fester smell far worse than weeds.

We are, of course, arguing that the portrait of this split personality was created from Shelley's own experience; he described himself as having been an 'assemblage of inconsistent & discordant portions' before he met Mary, who, he said, enabled him to feel for the first time 'the integrity of my nature'.[31] Even if this fragment of self-analysis had not survived, one could still deduce it from the disjunctive response to a situation that Shelley sometimes exhibits: 'Everyone will recollect Mrs Shandy's clock; and, after the customary smile has passed, cannot but be shocked at the picture it affords of the brutal prostitution of the most sacred impulses of our being' (*Prose*, p. 222). A similar Shelley ends the invective of 'To the Lord Chancellor' with the words 'I curse thee – though I hate thee not' (61), or (to take an absurd but revealing example) in the midst of his vegetarianism suddenly embarks on an orgy of bacon-eating and complains bitterly when the inn-keeper runs out of the article.[32] That the 'evil joys' which 'fire the vulgar beast' have left 'their dark unrest' within the soul of Shelley's Athanasian persona is not only possible but indicated by the centrality given to the encounter with the Venus of the vulgar, ('Eyeless nightmare' is another of the images of blindness alluded to in connection with Shelley's ophthalmia and *The Cyclops*. The latter seems to have been linked in some way with *Prince Athanase*, for a fragment of Shelley's translation is found among the *Prince Athanase* drafts.)[33]

'Ode to the West Wind' (1819) adds to the image of thin or grey hair that of falling hair. The Poet's address to the West Wind includes the plea 'Make me thy lyre, even as the forest is: / What if my leaves are falling like its own!' Falling leaves are compared to hair in a fragment which Neville Rogers recognised as a preliminary version of the 'Ode':

> 'Twas the 20th of October
> And the woods had all grown sober
> As a man does when his hair
> Looks as theirs did, grey & spare
> When the dead leaves
> As to mock the stupid
> Like ghosts in—.[34]

These leaves anticipate the image of dead leaves in Shelley's opening invocation to the West Wind: 'Thou from whose unseen presence the leaves dead / Are driven, like ghosts from an enchanter fleeing' (2–3). The leaves are represented as diseased: 'Yellow, and black, and pale, and hectic red, / Pestilence-stricken multitudes. . .' (4–5) The West Wind to whom he prays for strength is a renovating force, as was historical necessity in *Queen Mab*. It will not only bring the Bourbons hurtling from their thrones, but like some mighty enchanter – or alchemist – expel the stale and infected air of Europe and replace it with its own purity. It is an image of potentiality; in Paracelsian code, 'wind of the west' was the secret name for the philosopher's stone when it had reached the 'red stage' and the 'Great Work', that is, the creation of the Panacea, was just about to be accomplished.[35] The idea had both a mystical and a practical appeal for Shelley. As a nineteenth-century radical he was aware that many diseases flourished as a result of iniquitous social

conditions. At the same time disease is for him a metaphor for the 'immedicable plague' of evil; all its differing aspects, both natural and man-made, are
diseases too:

> The fiend, whose name was Legion; Death, Decay,
> Earthquake and Blight, and Want, and Madness pale,
> Winged and wan diseases, an array
> Numerous as leaves that strew the autumnal gale. (*L. & C.*, 379–82)

The personal dimension to the 'Ode' has often been remarked upon, especially its connection with domestic concerns, namely the deaths of Clara and
William and Shelley's hopes for the baby which Mary was then carrying;
these are surely included in the 'new birth' which he prays may be quickened
by the action of the wind. However the link between the theme of regeneration and Shelley's thoughts concerning his own present and future health is
just as close. The yellow, black, pale and red of the diseased leaves correspond exactly to the colours of the body's 'humours' – yellow bile, black bile,
phlegm and blood. Disease infects not only the 'body politic' but the
individual human body as well.

Among the lines which have gained Shelley the opprobrium of being 'self-
absorbed' and 'narcissistic' are those in which he compares his strength and
swiftness as a boy to that of the wind itself:

> If even
> I were as in my boyhood, and could be
>
> The comrade of thy wanderings over heaven,
> As then, when to outstrip thy skiey speed
> Scarce seemed a vision. . .
>
> A heavy weight of hours has chained and bowed
> One too like thee: tameless, and swift, and proud.   (47–51, 55–6).

An important source here is William Thompson's *Sickness*, the source also
of Shelley's similar description of himself in *Adonais* ('a pardlike Spirit,
beautiful and swift') and of some of the imagery of *Queen Mab*, *Laon and
Cythna* and *Prometheus Unbound*. Thompson describes his recovery from an
illness in which 'each intellectual spark and fiery seed / Of reason, mem'ry,
judgement, taste and wit' had been 'scarce animated', having been 'extinct
and smother'd in unwieldy clay'. Whereas now

> . . . (O blessing!) now
> I seem to tread the winds; to overtake
> The empty eagle in her early chase,
> Or nimble-trembling dove, from preyful beak,
> In many a rapid, many a cautious round,
> Wheeling precipitant: I leave behind,
> Exulting o'er its aromatic hills,
> The bounding Beher-roe. . .   (IV, 372–9)

Shelley's description is perhaps the more modest in that it portrays him not as he now is but as he once was. To employ Thompson's language, his purpose is to reclaim the 'intellectual spark', the 'fiery seed' of 'scarce animated' thought, from the 'unwieldy clay' in which at present it lies 'extinct and smother'd', that he may thereby herald the rebirth of the revolutionary ideal. Thus he prays to the fierce wind to

> Drive my dead thoughts over the universe
> Like withered leaves to quicken a new birth!
>
> And, by the incantation of this verse,
> Scatter, as from an unextinguished hearth
> Ashes and sparks, my words among mankind!   (63–7)

Shelley was expecting to die young; his thoughts are 'dead' in that their influence will be felt posthumously. That this was the meaning he intended is indicated by another notebook fragment connected with the 'Ode':

> And this is my distinction, if I fall
> I shall not creep out of the vital day
> To common dust nor wear a common pall
> But as my hopes were fire, so my decay
> Shall be as ashes covering them. Oh, Earth
> Oh friends, if when my [blank] has ebbed way
> One spark be unextinguished of that hearth
> Kindled in—.[36]

The idea of a 'fiery seed', a spark which generates life, is to be found too in Paracelsus, and continues the alchemical metaphor. In the phrase 'ashes and sparks', the ashes correspond to the dead leaves, and in turn to the Poet's thoughts, which will even in their decay act as a fertilising compost. Shelley's meaning could be rendered: 'Just as withered leaves fertilise the barren earth, though of course without being able to determine the variety of growth, so my thoughts will nurture, even if they do not define, the new age towards which they point the way.' The 'sparks' on the other hand, correspond to the seeds, which as well as the dead leaves are being carried along by the wind (5–12), and represent that part of Shelley's thought which will, he hopes, prove truly regenerative on its own account. The ashes/sparks dichotomy is an analogue of the body/spirit dichotomy; the human body serving as compost had its hopeful aspect for Shelley as for other Romantic poets.[37]

A valetudinarian source for these famous lines is suggested by Mary Shelley's words in her 'Note on *Queen Mab*' concerning the relationship of the poet's health to his desire to 'awaken mankind', believing that 'his written thoughts would tend to *disseminate* [our italics] opinions which he believed conducive to the happiness of the human race':

Ill-health made him believe that his race would soon be run; that a year or two was all he had of life. He desired that these years should be useful and illustrious. He saw, in a fervent call on his fellow-creatures to share alike the blessings of the creation, to love and serve each other, the noblest work that life and time permitted him.

(Hutchinson, pp. 836–7)

By applying these words to Shelley's 'Ode' it will be seen that the Poet's description of himself as 'tameless, and swift, and proud' expresses not so much self-pity or self-delight as regret for, and pride in, the energies of pre-pubertal boyhood lost through ill-health. It is in this context that one should look for a relation between the private and public concerns of the poem. The cry 'I fall upon the thorns of life! I bleed!' is of too personal a nature to have to do with politics directly. On the other hand, as a response to bereavement or the pain of rejection, it would seem to have too little bearing on the revolutionary hopes proclaimed in the final section. The key to both these areas of concern lies in the image of the 'thorns of life', which is a composed allusion to that symbolic landscape of painful error encountered in *Epipsychidion* and elsewhere. It was suffering encountered in the 'wilderness' involving the tragic loss of his health, that both confirmed his mission – the moral reformation of society – and determined its means, that is, the Word, the 'fervent call on his fellow creatures', the 'trumpet of a prophecy'.

Another distinguishing mark of the Poet is his 'frail form', sometimes transformed into or compared with a gentle, sensitive, swift-footed herbivore – llama, fawn, or antelope, but most often a deer. This being, pursued by predatory tigers, hounds, ounces or wolves, has already been discussed in connection with Cowper's 'stricken deer' passage and the elephantiasis terror, and mentioned as an emblem in Newton's Zodiac. Undoubtedly, too, it owes something to the common Renaissance pun 'venery' (both love and hunting) and to the homophony of 'hart' and 'heart'. A third source is to be found in the legend of Actaeon.

In *Adonais* (1821), Shelley's elegy on the death of Keats, among the mourners is 'one frail form', Shelley himself. One has here a short-hand version of the Poet's history as told a few months previously in *Epipsychidion*.

> he, as I guess,
> Had gazed on Nature's naked loveliness
> Actaeon-like, and now he fled astray
> With feeble steps o'er the world's wilderness,
> And his own thoughts, along that rugged way,
> Pursued like raging hounds, their father and their prey. (274–9)

The hounds are, of course, his own guilt and sense of failure.

Actaeon, after surprising Artemis at her bathing, was changed by the goddess into a stag and torn to pieces by his own hounds. To gaze on Nature, even in her 'naked loveliness' would seem a perfectly normal activity in a Romantic poet. Indeed, eighteen months earlier, in *Peter Bell III*, Shelley had satirised Wordsworth as a 'kind of moral eunuch', his fault being that he had merely 'touched the hem of Nature's shift' and had never dared to lift the garment and reveal Nature's naked loveliness. Had he tempted her 'deepest bliss' Nature would have yielded 'love for love, frank, warm and true'. This she has done for Burns whose 'errors prove it' (313–27). Why then should Nature revenge herself on the Poet by turning his own thoughts against him? Why has she not treated him like Burns?

The reason must be that Burns' boldness and sexual errors are merely infringements of Custom and do not offend against Nature; the Poet, however, *has* offended Nature, despite the latter's normal generosity to her lovers, quite unlike the implacable virgin pride of Artemis.

A clue regarding the nature of the Poet's offence was suggested to us by Matthews' refusal to accept that the Poet figure was Shelley at all. He was inclined to believe, following Shelley's draft, that the figure was based on Rousseau.[38] Matthews' suggestion has not found general acceptance, but his observation was an unwitting testimony to something related: Shelley's self-identification with Rousseau, which reaches its apogee in *The Triumph of Life*, the implications of which will be developed more fully in Chapter 12. If one accepts that Shelley had Rousseau in mind here, the next step is to ask what incident from Rousseau's history or fictions might have contributed to the image of 'gazing on Nature's naked loveliness'.

In Rousseau's *Confessions* there is an episode which he introduces with the words 'Whoever you may be that wish to know a man, have the courage to read the next two or three pages and you will have complete knowledge of Jean-Jacques Rousseau.'

In Venice he went into the chamber of a beautiful courtesan, Giulietta, 'as if it were the sanctuary of love and beauty; in her person I felt I saw the divinity'. But suddenly he began to weep 'like a child' at the following reflection: 'This thing which is at my disposal . . . is Nature's masterpiece and love's. She is not only charming and beautiful, but good also and generous . . . yet here she is, a wretched streetwalker, on sale to the world.' He concluded that either his senses were deluding him or that she must have some secret flaw. Because of her sweet breath and fresh complexion, 'It did not so much as occur to me that the pox might have something to do with it.' The secret flaw, Rousseau discovered as he was on the point of sinking upon her breast, was that she had a malformed nipple. 'I beat my brow, looked harder' and 'was struck by the thought that it resulted from some remarkable imperfection of Nature'. He felt that he was holding in his arms 'a sort of monster'. Noticing his revulsion, Giulietta scornfully gave him his congé: 'Give up the ladies and study mathematics.'[39] The episode was ever thereafter associated with shame in Rousseau's mind.

Shelley was acquainted with *The Confessions* as early as 1811. The Giulietta story appears to be present in *Adonais*, with Giulietta transformed from 'Nature's masterpiece' into Nature herself. Like the Poet, Rousseau gazes upon the naked loveliness of a beautiful deity. There is even a correspondence between Rousseau's beating his brow and the emphasis on the wounded brow of the Poet. Rousseau sees Giulietta as simultaneously the goddess of love and the lowest sort of prostitute, and discovers deformity and monstrosity at the heart of the fountain of delight. The poet has made a similar discovery about Nature; she punishes him for his revelation of her deformity, the punishment being that he must live with the consequences of his fatal knowledge, like the Ancient Mariner, who saw that 'the very deep did rot'.

The Giulietta passage seems to us to lie behind the Swiss episode of June 1816 when, after hearing *Christabel* recited, Shelley 'ran out of the room, suddenly shrieking and putting his hands to his head'. The verse that had sparked off this reaction was that describing the witch's deformed breast. It had suddenly produced for him a vivid mental image (*not* a delusion) 'of a woman he had heard of who had eyes instead of nipples, which taking hold of his mind horrified him'.[40] In Rousseau the actual words of which 'malformed nipple' is the translation are 'téton borgne'; normally 'borgne' means 'one-eyed', which is how a native English speaker would first translate it before realising that Rousseau is using the word in a peculiar sense. Hence the idea of nipples actually *being* eyes presents itself to the volatile imagination. (There is ample evidence that Shelley's imagination was of this kind.)[41] Shortly after this incident, Shelley and Byron toured the landscape of Rousseau's *Julie*, a book which was the product of a different Rousseau, the poet of sentimental love, and an exorcism of the troubling and problematic Rousseau of the *Confessions*.[42]

The question must now arise as to whether the Poet is a mere gazer or someone who has tempted Nature's deepest bliss and discovered from experience that she can be a sister to Wordsworth (who when *he* gazed, as in 'The Daffodils', laid up treasures in his mind), a warm lover to Burns, and a monster to himself. The parallel with Rousseau is again suggestive; Rousseau declared that he never for a moment considered that Giulietta might have had the pox – though in denying this strenuously he puts into the reader's mind a possibility which might otherwise not have occurred. On the contrary, 'I even felt some qualms about my not being wholesome enough for her', the reason being that he had recently paid a visit to a *padoana*. So certain was Rousseau that he had caught the pox from this encounter that he had immediate recourse to a surgeon. 'Nothing can equal the uneasiness I felt for a whole three weeks, without any real discomfort or any obvious symptom to justify it. I could not imagine that anyone could leave the embraces of a *padoana* unscathed.'[43] (Compare Shelley's 'No man can rise pure from the poisonous embraces of a prostitute.') Here one has, surely, an explanation for Rousseau's behaviour with Giulietta. He has not emerged unscathed from the embraces of the *padoana* for it has coloured his attitude towards 'Nature's masterpiece' and sexuality in general: the sense of his own unwholesomeness is projected onto a 'good and generous' woman so that he sees her as a 'wretched streetwalker' and discovers her deformity.

The Actaeon parallel suggests, however, that the Poet is a completely innocent victim of divine cruelty. 'Destiny was to blame for Actaeon's misfortunes, not any guilt on his own part; for there is nothing sinful about losing
one's way.'[44] Yet, like the *Alastor* Poet, he is presented in terms which
indicate both his guilt and his innocence and the impossibility of disen-
tangling one from the other. When Urania (in *Adonais* not merely the Muse
of astronomy but the Venus Urania, Intellectual Beauty) asks the mourning
Poet to identify himself, he does not answer

> but with sudden hand
> Made bare his branded and ensanguined brow
> Which was like Cain's or Christ's — oh! that it should be so!
>
>   (304–6)

Here Actaeon, Christ, and Cain are fused together in the emblem of the
'branded and ensanguined brow'. The brow bears the mark of Actaeon's
antlers (a grotesque horn of infamy), Christ's crown of thorns, and the curse
of Cain. The Poet's gesture in revealing his wound is ambiguous —
deliberately so, we consider. He is displaying his injuries — the movement
being theatrical, an 'Ecce homo!' It also suggests shame, as if he has committed some crime against Urania's law, an abuse of the sexual instinct; the
gesture is thus confessional, an admission of guilt. To have suffered in the
cause of universal love makes him like Christ, a scapegoat; yet the comparison with Cain makes him a criminal. (Crime was for Shelley, as James
Rieger pointed out, always an abuse of some 'passion of the mind'.)[45] Cain
has committed an unnatural act. The suggestion is that the Poet has also done
so and that he has partaken of the nature of the tyrant by abusing the passion
of love; in connection with this one recalls Shelley's dictum 'Nothing defeats
and violates nature . . . [more] than prostitution' (*Prose*, p. 223). Both Cain
and Actaeon are punished far in excess of their offence. Cain's crime is the
product of a moment of rashness under provocation rather than of an evil
disposition. He is a kind of Wandering Jew and a victim of God's injustice.

The imagery surrounding the Poet combines the erotic with the political.
He is carrying the phallic thyrsus, 'topped with a cypress cone', the cypress
being sacred to Venus and a concomitant of Adonis' funeral rites. It is one
'Round whose rude shaft dark ivy tresses grew / Yet dripping with the
forest's noonday dew' (291–2). Ivy is a female symbol in Shelley; it is almost
always present among the twining plants which form part of the description
of the cave or forest solitude where true lovers perform their mysterious rites,
and the noonday forest and the dew similarly have sexual connotations.[46]
This spear 'vibrated, as the ever-beating heart / Shook the weak hand that
grasped it' (294–5). The Poet is declaring his intention to continue to write
erotic poetry in spite of social ostracism and vilification in the literary
reviews, but he is also declaring specifically his undiminished sexual potency

and defiance of the 'hounds of the mind' which continue to torment him with guilt for sexual error, and strive to implant in him a 'horror of life'. It is the pulsing of the blood that shakes the rude shaft. The narrator at the end of *Adonais* leaves 'the contagion of the world's slow stain' and is borne 'darkly, fearfully afar' into the Infinite, leaving behind his *alter ego* to continue the struggle on earth.

The image of the hounds of the mind pursuing the deer is also in *Prometheus Unbound*. The Furies (Jove's hounds) are 'the ministers of pain and fear / And disappointment and mistrust and hate / And clinging crime'. Their role is to 'track all things that weep and bleed and live' as 'lean dogs pursue / Through wood and lake some struck and sobbing fawn'. They howl to one another: 'Leave the self-contempt implanted / In young spirits, sense-enchanted / Misery's yet unkindled fuel' (I, 452–6; 510–12) so that they may the better punish Prometheus. Although they have been given a wide brief, there is a strong component here of imagery of sexual guilt and their threats are of *physical* torture inflicted at the time or at some future date. They have 'hydra tresses', that is to say, they are 'hydra-headed woes' in the sense that they have not 'many heads' but 'heads of hydras':

> *Furies*: Thou thinkest we will live through thee, one by one,
> Like animal life. . .
> That we will be dread thought beneath thy brain
> And foul desire round thine astonished heart,
> And blood within thy labyrinthine veins
> Crawling like agony?
> *Prometheus*:   Why, ye are thus now.   (I, 483–4, 488–91)

Controlling the Furies is Jupiter's minister, Mercury, who carries an ambiguous 'serpent-cinctured wand'. As the caduceus, this is his badge of authority, but it was frequently confused with the Wand of Aesculapius, and as such offers a promise of healing. Mercury is, however, a quack doctor and the cure he offers – submission to Jupiter – rots the soul; he declares himself very sorry to have to inflict further pain, but his task is in fact to 'execute a doom of new revenge' – despair. His role corresponds to the effects of medicinal mercury, which causes brain damage and madness while producing many of the same symptoms as the disease it claims to cure. Prometheus rejects this 'cure' preferring to face the terrors of the hydra-headed woes and confront them with his strength of mind and constitution. On the political level, Mercury is the turncoat and the timeserver. In his exhortation to Prometheus to repent and 'bend thy soul in prayer' he prefigures the reaction of the laureate Robert Southey who, when Shelley referred in a letter to 'the wretched state of his health', replied

You rejected Christianity before you knew – before you could possibly have known – upon what evidence it rests . . . Look to that evidence while you are yet existing in Time, and you may yet live to bless God for any visitation of sickness and suffering which, by bringing you to a sense of your miserable condition, may enable you to hope for forgiveness.[47]

The worst torments that the Furies can inflict are of course psychological: the spectacle of Christ's words being turned into an instrument of oppression and the fate of the French Revolution. They try to cure Prometheus of imagining a new world by building on the 'the self-contempt implanted' in a young spirit. Once the undaunted courage of a virgin mind has been lost, the rest follows.

Mercury, the mineral, appears too in that graceful tribute to friendship, *Letter to Maria Gisborne* (1820), which Shelley wrote after investing in what he considered a philanthropic venture, the building of a steamboat designed by Maria's engineer son Henry. This deceptively discursive poem is unified by the theme of the magical transformation of evil into good and the redemption of the past. It pivots on a number of analogous polarities: instruments of torture are contrasted to the ironwork of the beneficent steamboat; the 'powdery foam of salt abuse' of the literary reviews to the sea churned up by the boat's paddle wheel. Similarly there is a 'bad' mercury and a good one. The bad is

> that dew which the gnomes drink
> When at their subterranean toil they swink,
> Pledging the demons of the earthquake, who
> Reply to them in lava – cry halloo!
> And call out to the cities o'er their head, –
> Roofs, towers, and shrines, the dying and the dead,
> Crash through the chinks of earth – and then all quaff
> Another rouse, and hold their sides and laugh.   (58–65)

These gnomes are obviously evil anti-alchemists who pervert the ancient mystical meaning of the marriage of mercury and sulphur. Instead of working to produce the panacea, they stir up its opposite – universal pestilence – and the poisonous quicksilver they quaff helps their labours along, as mere palliatives can actually strengthen a disease.[48] (Laughter and pledging a draught are associated with Pestilence in *Laon and Cythna*.) Shelley opposes the mercury in the gnomes' cup of life to that in a walnut wood goblet on the table before him.[49] On this is floating serenely a model steamboat – a re-enactment of an innocent boyhood pleasure, before the storms of passion beset him. These contrasting mercuries have later an analogue in the prostitute/Polonia opposition mentioned in Chapter 8.

Like Marvell's 'The Garden', the *Letter* is set in a retreat (Henry's workshop) in which reminders of the outside world and the past with its strife and misery have their stings drawn. Marvell stumbles on melons and falls on grass, but he is quite safe; he is not re-enacting the Fall of Man but displacing it. Similarly the alchemy of the *Letter* converts disaster into health, light-heartedness and hopes for the future. A china cup on Shelley's table was once a thing 'from which sweet lips were wont to drink / The liquor doctors rail at' (87–8), but the disturbing possibilities that the cup once contained laudanum and the 'sweet lips' were those of a suicide are quickly dispelled with a joke: the 'liquor' turns out merely to be tea and the sweet lips are those of the absent Maria. Laudanum returns however at the end of the poem, in what, if this were a conventional letter, would simply be health news; here it is a unifying motif. Shelley promises that he will no longer feed his nervous condition by sipping the laudanum 'from Helicon or Himeros' – that is to say, he has foresworn poetry – the trumpet of a prophecy – in favour of a modest but practical mission, and sexual desire in favour of friendship. Aiding this resolve is the study of geometry, with which he proposes to 'strangle' his nerves. He is, in short, adopting a humorous version of Giulietta's advice to Rousseau upon his discovery of her deformity: 'Give up the ladies and study mathematics.'

Even when Shelley uses illness as a metaphor for a state of mind, the starting point is likely to be some physical pain or illness of his own. An example of this is his poem to Jane Williams, 'The Magnetic Lady to her Patient' (1822).

> Sleep, sleep on! forget thy pain;
>   My hand is on thy brow,
> My spirit on thy heart, poor friend;
>   And from my fingers flow
> The powers of life, and like a sign,
>   Seal thee from thine hour of woe;
> And brood on thee, but may not blend
>   With thine.   (1–8)

'What would do / You good when suffering and awake / What cure your head and side?' Jane asks her patient. The image of the suffering Christ fleetingly appears again, but it is the actual symptoms of Shelley's disease that are in the foreground. In this poem, too, a clear associational link is displayed between Shelley's lost health and his experience in early youth. Jane tells her patient to 'Forget lost health and the divine / Feelings which died in youth's brief morn.' Evidently Shelley had been telling her, either actually or in fantasy, something of his life history. It was in the 'clear golden prime of his youth's dawn' that he had encountered the Being, Intellectual Beauty and sexual passion (*Epips.*, 192). The divine feeling which had died when the experience ended and the lost health which resulted from his fatal encounter in the thorny wilderness are related to each other by proximity. Jane tells him to 'forget thy pain'. She is referring both to the physical pain associated with lost health and to the pain of being in love with someone whose own affections are taken up with Edward Williams.

> Sleep, sleep on! I love thee not;
>   But when I think that he

Who made and makes my lot
As full of flowers as thine of weeds,
  Might have been lost like thee;
And that a hand which was not mine
  Might then have charmed his agony
As I another's – my heart bleeds
  For thine.   (10–18)

'Lost' can mean simply 'lost in love' but here there are suggestions of error
and of going astray which link up with the lost health. If both meanings are
allowed, the stanza becomes at once more complex and more relevant to the
interacting themes of illness and unrequited love, while Shelley's need for
physical as well as spiritual solace is balanced against a corresponding need
in Williams or the Williams-who-might-have-been.

11

Evil, the immedicable plague

Disease is one of the oldest metaphors for, or synonyms of, evil. Evidence that they were once equated survives in such terms as 'The King's Evil' and Spenser's 'The foul evil' as well as the word 'ill'. 'War is a disease' wrote William Thompson in *Sickness*, voicing an eighteenth-century commonplace.[1] Shelley's particular contribution, as Clutton-Brock pointed out, was to image disease as the result of celestial tyranny, rather than of divine displeasure or man's innate depravity, and to depict the whole world as suffering from it.[2]

In Shelley, nature as well as society is infected. Natural evils include earthquakes, drought, extremes of temperature, poisonous plants, predatory animals and shipwreck-causing tempests. Nature contains a spirit of evil – 'a pitiless fiend' (*Q.M.*, IV, 30). Man-made evil includes the interlocking manifestations of tyranny – war, priestcraft, kingship and vice of all kinds. Disease is common to both categories for it is inherent in the degenerate natural world, but it is also man-made because spread by man. Hence disease is a convenient synecdoche for 'Evil, the immedicable plague' as Asia in *Prometheus Unbound* calls it. There is a continuum. The 'pitiless fiend' is not seen as separate from the evil of sensualism and tyranny in human society and the individual human mind and body. This is all of a piece with Shelley's propensity for using imagery drawn from natural disasters – wrecked ships, blasting by lightning, polar ice, the spasms of earthquakes, the venom of snakes – to represent bodily and mental affliction on a personal and societal level. Since he also has a tendency to merge tenor and vehicle, it is not surprising to find that not only is disease used as a metaphor for both natural and man-made disasters, but that man-made and natural disasters will be used as metaphors for disease or aspects of it, at the same time as disease imagery is also employed literally.[3]

That the type of all diseases from which Shelley sees man and nature suffering is syphilitic has been perceived by several critics, notably James Rieger and Stuart Curran with respect to *The Cenci* and Brown with respect to *Queen Mab*.[4] This chapter seeks to develop their observations, particularly in relation to *Prometheus Unbound*. But before doing so, it will be necessary to make some observations about Shelley's attitude to the body and the material world.

It is tempting to infer from the prevalance of the frail poet figure that Shelley regarded ill-health as a necessary condition for writing poetry, as apparently A. E. Housman did.[5] Shelley came in at the end of the eighteenth-century cult of sensibility, which encouraged the belief that robustness of constitution was inimical to poetic genius; the sentiment is found in Cowper's letters, for instance, and one might expect to find it in Shelley too. Yet surprisingly one does not; still less are there any grounds for thinking that he would have agreed with the following thought of Wolfgang Hildesheimer: 'Great minds . . . have always preferred to have sickly, delicate unassuming bodies, so that they might confront their physical weakness and overcome it again and again.'[6] In Mary Wollstonecraft, Shelley would have found a spirited challenge to such an idea. She acknowledged that men of genius frequently impaired their constitutions and 'the violence of their passions bearing a proportion to the vigour of their intellects, the sword's destroying the scabbard has become almost proverbial'. Superficial observers 'have inferred from thence that men of genius have commonly weak . . . delicate constitutions'. But 'I find that strength of mind has in most cases been accompanied by superior strength of body, – natural soundness of constitution.' Indeed, poets 'must have had iron frames' in order to resist the violence of the poetic frenzy. 'Shakespeare never grasped the airy dagger with a nerveless hand, nor did Milton tremble when he led Satan.'[7]

Shelley seems to have shared her view that the excitement of writing poetry impeded convalescence, and he suspended work on *Rosalind and Helen* in obedience to Lawrence's 'edict against the imagination'.[8] He did of course see himself as one who felt pain and pleasure more intensely than the mass of mankind, and considered that this took its toll on his body. But there is little doubt that Shelley would have agreed with Wollstonecraft that the greatest genius was characterised by the greatest vigour of constitution; for a man of genius to be ill like Tasso or Rousseau was a misfortune. Where he appears to differ from her is in his stress on the ability of the imagination to operate despite bodily weakness and suffering. This ability was a compensation, an escape route which he could adopt when his real desires seemed unrealisable. (The same applies to his frequent fantasies of release through death.) 'Health is the greatest possession, health of body and mind – as this writer weak enough in both too well knows' he wrote to Claire in 1821. ' "Be strong, live happy and love" says Milton.'[9] That was his best dream. Although suffering is the subject matter of so much of Shelley's poetry, running through his work is a conviction that this ought not to be; it is significant that in *Julian and Maddalo* it is Maddalo, the Byronic character, not Julian, the Shelleyan, who says 'Most wretched men / Are cradled into poetry by wrong, / They learn in suffering what they teach in song.' (544–6) It is an 'inexplicable defect of harmony' in the constitution of human nature that it finds that 'the pleasure that is in sorrow is sweeter than the pleasure of pleasure itself' (*Prose*, p. 292).

Shelley feels bound to add that there is nothing necessary in this linkage of the highest species of pleasure and pain, for 'the delight of love and friendship, the ecstasy of the admiration of nature, the joy of the perception and still more of the creation of poetry is often wholly unalloyed'. In the song of the skylark he finds the 'keen clear joyance' and 'harmonious madness' to which poetry should aspire.

Shelley's 'thought' is sometimes described as if it exhibits a straightforward transition from early Utopianism to a retreat into metaphysics as he came to despair of the possibilities for the improvement of society. For D. H. Lawrence, the image of this late Shelley was the essential one. 'Shelley is pure escape;' he wrote, 'the body is sublimated into sublime gas . . . why should he insist on the bodilessness of beauty, when we cannot know of any save embodied beauty?'[10] Lawrence is being obtuse for once about Shelley, whose attitude is nothing so consistent. More acute are the readings of critics like Wasserman and Webb, who see Shelley as oscillating between two contraries, 'neither of which he could abandon and neither of which he could accept with conviction', that is, 'how to combine his belief in the necessity for improving the state of society with his deep-seated conviction that there was a continuing and infinitely more important life after death'.[11]

Shelley always had a bent towards transcendence. In 'The Retrospect' he wrote of having early learned to 'Scorn the chains of clay' which bound his aspiring soul (71–2); from first to last his writings are liable to yield stock metaphors of the *contemptus mundi* tradition, whether Neo-Platonic or Christian: the world is a dunghill, a charnel house, a morass or swamp; the body is the dungeon or coffin of the soul. Yet working against this imagery is his keen and sensuous delight in the natural world and what William Empson called the 'feeling of being accepted by the universe, such as is immensely conveyed by Shelley'.[12] The body is not only a prison, but the lyre on which the divine music of love is played, the lamp that nurtures the flame. Even in the Platonic passages which occur so frequently in his later poetry he does not so much denounce the body as lament its transitory nature, and this, as in *Adonais*, he usually does in the form of a compliment to some physical beauty. He makes the lament seem all the more moving by his affirmation of the soul's immortality. And there is plenty of evidence from his poetry that he regarded the evil represented by the body's chaining of the soul as not absolute but conditional, and that the interdependence of matter and spirit was seen by him as a good, provided that evil no longer held power in the material world, or alternatively, that the human condition, in spite of its limitations, could nevertheless offer free rein to the spirit. One of Shelley's most vivid symbolisations of the latter idea is the benign meteor which rises from the morass; kindled by 'divine' power, the fire is nevertheless generated in nature from matter.[13]

It is misleading to suggest, as James Rieger did, that the dualistic philosophical tradition which Shelley was drawn towards would necessarily have driven him to a logical cul-de-sac from which he could escape only by passive suicide. For Paracelsus, who managed to yoke empiricism to Neo-Platonism, the separation of body and spirit did not lead to this conclusion. While fully adopting the familiar model of the bodily structure as a prison, Paracelsus' solution to the problem of how to free the speculative mind from this clog that it may penetrate into ultimate mysteries of the universe was, paradoxically, to attempt to perfect the body.

Paracelsus took over the Christian doctrine of the 'spiritual body'. Man has two bodies, corporeal and spiritual, 'enclosed in one'. To the corporeal body belong the five organs of sense, to the spiritual the senses themselves, which, Paracelsus maintains, proceed from the immaterial, not from Nature. However, 'the spiritual body does not complete its work in a situation which is badly disposed'. When a man is born deaf, 'this happens from a defect of the domicile in which hearing should be quartered'. Hence the importance of medicine, for it 'acts upon the house by purging it, so that the spiritual body may be able to perfect its actions therein, like civet in a pure and uncontaminated casket'.[14]

The relationship of corporeal to spiritual body in Paracelsus has a counterpart in Shelley's poetry in the relation between an object of sense and its reflection, a recurrent image. The reflection is an image of the material object, but intangible and possessing qualities of intensity which the original object does not have. 'Why is the reflection in that canal more beautiful than the objects it reflects? The colours are more vivid and yet blended with more harmony' (*Prose*, p. 337). Yet in describing what happens to the reflection one is also describing indirectly what happens to the original objects. An example of Shelley's exploitation of this fact occurs in *Hellas*. He who would consult the oracular Ahasuerus must 'sail alone at sunset' and cry out his name 'when the pines of that bee-pasturing isle / Green Erebinthus, quench the fiery shadow / Of his gilt prow within the sapphire water' (165–74). The fiery reflection of the sunset-lit prow is cooled by the green reflection of the pines in the water, yet the reader takes away the impression that it is the pines themselves which offer soothing balm to the inflamed prow of the lonely seeker.[15] Nor is this impression wrong, for the pine forest is the source of the reflection and also of the wind which will pilot the helmsman to the oracle (176–81). Reflection and substance merge.[16]

Paracelsus would have pulled Shelley in two directions: towards contempt for the world and towards its purification. Of course any literal belief Shelley may have had in Paracelsianism did not survive his Eton schooldays, but, as we have been arguing, it continued to give direction to his emotional life and to supply images in his poetry. Its continuing influence also accounts, in part, for the propensity mentioned in Chapter 9 to confound mental and physical events. A comparison between Shelley's procedure and Milton's in

Samson Agonistes makes this point clearer. Samson protests that his torments are not confined 'to the body's wounds and sores' but are mental too, preying on the purest spirits of the mind 'as on entrails, joints and limbs'; his griefs pain him 'as a lingering disease', and 'nor less than wounds immedicable / Rankle, and fester and gangrene / To black mortification' (606–22).

> Thoughts, my tormentors, armed with deadly stings,
> Mangle my apprehensive tenderest parts,
> Exasperate, exulcerate and raise
> Dire inflammation, which no cooling herb,
> Or medicinal liquor can assuage.   (623–7)

The distinction between bodily and mental pains is made explicit. (The nature of Samson's mental torture is, of course, appropriate to one whose most bitter self-reproach is that of sexual servitude to the harlot Dalila.) No such certain distinction attaches itself to the description of Prometheus' sufferings, as will be seen later. When Shelley writes of mental tortures, these are an intensified reflection of what is happening to the body.

Queen Mab (1813)

In *Queen Mab* Shelley's vision is of the Earthly Paradise *and* the New Jerusalem, both envisaged as existing on our planet. Evil has been expelled from Nature, as well as from the heart of man, and there is no longer an antithesis between a diseased body and a transcendent soul. *Queen Mab* explicitly qualifies a dualistic view; the body is at first seen as 'an useless and worn-out machine' (I, 155), but that is before Mab has shown the soul the potentialities of life on earth. To see the world as a dunghill or mire is a punishment for accepting that Nature and man's body are intrinsically evil and must so remain:

> Man is of soul and body, formed for deeds
> Of high resolve, on fancy's boldest wing
> To soar unwearied, fearlessly to turn
> The keenest pangs to peacefulness, and taste
> The joys which mingled sense and spirit yield.
> Or he is formed for abjectness and woe,
> To grovel on the dunghill of his fears,
> To shrink at every sound, to quench the flame
> Of natural love in sensualism . . .
> The one is man that shall hereafter be;
> The other, man as vice has made him now.   (IV, 154–62, 166–7)

As so often, Shelley employs the language of mysticism in the service of an ideal which is essentially humanistic. The highest good of which man is capable is that body and soul should each contribute, and contribute equally, to the pleasure of the other.

Another aspect of *Queen Mab*'s identification of evil with illness has already been touched on in connection with 'Ozymandias' and *Rosalind and Helen*. The wicked man is also the diseased man. The type of all vice is lust. The tyrant is the arch-sensualist. His youth is 'a vain and feverish dream of sensualism' and his manhood 'blighted with unripe disease', obviously a direct result of this sensualism; his days are 'of unsatisfying listlessness', his nights racked with pain. He in turn infects society with his own evil passions. The influence of tyrants 'darts like subtle poison through the bloodless veins' of the social system that they have monstrously created.[17] This idea is refined in *Prometheus Unbound*, the poem in which Shelley projected himself as he really wanted to be: not gray-haired or frail, but literally titanic in his ability to endure both bodily and mental tortures. Prometheus' unbinding coincides with a recovery of physical and explicitly sexual vitality which he can transmit to others.

Prometheus Unbound

We are not attempting a complete exposition of this complex work nor are we trying to displace such famous readings as those of Pottle, Cameron and Wasserman. Our aims are the more limited ones of stressing the similarities between the poem and *Queen Mab*, especially with respect to its celebration of the 'joys of mingled sense and spirit', and of developing an observation made by Richard Holmes. Quoting the lines in which the Furies threaten to be 'foul desire round thy astonished heart / And blood within thy labyrinthine veins / Crawling like agony' he commented:

The physiological suggestiveness of these lines, the implication of the adrenalin 'shock' to the heart and the literally monstrous invasion of venereal infection through the delicate network of the blood system (an image conceived as long ago as Mont Blanc) gives the Furies of guilt and remorse a wholly new and contemporary presence. The medical basis of this image was to be characteristic of the whole poem, whose other major image sources are also from the natural sciences.

(Holmes, p. 492)

Just as pertinent is the allusion to the 'astonished heart' of Deuteronomy, 28.27–28, quoted in Chapter 8. The contemporaneity is fused with the punishment meted out to dissidents by the Old Testament God of Wrath.

The basic medical metaphor relates *Prometheus Unbound* to *Queen Mab*, whose abstractions – Reason, Passion and Selfishness/Sensualism correspond to the characters of the mature lyric drama – Prometheus, Asia, Jupiter. Of course these are not exact equations. The characters in *Prometheus* represent larger clusters of meaning, and in becoming persons, however shadowy and symbolic, acquire a psychological reality without which they could not function at all as characters in a drama. Nevertheless in each poem the schema is essentially the same. In *Queen Mab* Reason and Passion together constitute reciprocal or 'consentaneous love', while their disunion gives rise to selfishness and sensualism and thus disease. This corresponds to the separation of Prometheus and Asia during the reign of Jupiter. The love between Asia and Prometheus is the same as that celebrated in *Queen Mab* and which was to be the effect of, as well as the pre-condition for, the downfall of tyranny. Again, the concept has been enlarged between 1813 and 1819. Whereas before Shelley called the union of Passion and Reason 'consentaneous love', the uniting of Prometheus ('Intellect', 'forethought') and Asia (Love) would now be thought of as Uranian love. Shelley envisaged that the few 'eminent in virtue'[18] would start to lead the many – would prepare and strengthen themselves by becoming adepts in this higher form of love. It was thus that Shelley's ideas on free love were bound up with his political hopes.

At the beginning of Act I, Prometheus the Titan has been hanging, chained and freezing for three thousand years, on a mountainside in the Indian Caucasus. Asia, previously his inseparable companion, now exiled and in eclipse, lives in a distant valley (Cashmire?) in the same group of mountains. (It is never made clear whether this separation has been the cause or the effect of Prometheus' binding.) Ironically it was Prometheus who had mistakenly placed Jupiter – his captor – in a position of power in the first place. Thenceforward he had tried to check Jupiter's falsehood and force.

Prometheus has the secret of Jupiter's downfall: that Thetis, whom Jupiter has raped, will give birth to a child who will overthrow him. Thinking that Prometheus can tell him when this will happen, presumably so that he can organise a pre-emptive strike, Jupiter sends up bands of Furies to torture him both physically and mentally. Looking on in sympathy are two Oceanides, Panthea and Ione, who act as intermediaries between Prometheus and their exiled sister Asia. That Jupiter is unable to alienate them is probably due to the fact that they represent aspects of inherent sexual love. Asia – Venus and Nature, according to Mary's note – is the realisation of Intellectual Beauty on earth, a fusion of the organic with the ideal which it is the purpose of *Prometheus Unbound* to make credible.[19] She is like Astraea who left the world because of its wickedness, and who is associated by Shelley with pleasure and erotic poetry as Asia is. (Astraea is another name for the Zodiacal sign of Virgo.)[20]

The very probable reason for Shelley's introduction of the Furies (an expansion from a hint in Aeschylus' fragmentary *Prometheus Unbound*) lies in their traditional role in using disease and war as instruments of torture, which Shelley would have known from *Lemprière's Classical Dictionary* and the Abbé Banier's *The Mythology and Fables of the Ancients Explained from History*. They were represented as wreathed with serpents, 'a burning Torch in one Hand and a Whip of Scorpions in the other'.[21] The Furies are essential to the spread of syphilis in Fracastor. They abet the malice of Saturn and Mars, taking ingredients from the Styx and thence unleashing that 'pestem horribilem, famem bellum necemque' (I, 420). (Syphilis is inextricably connected not only with war but with famine as well.) The vulture sent by Jupiter tears at Prometheus' heart rather than the traditional liver, the change suggestive, in Shelleyan terms, of a shift away from the organs of digestion to those of generation. Another detail not found in Aeschylus is that the vulture's beak is polluted by Jupiter's poisonous saliva. Since Jupiter inflicts disease through his saliva – known to be one of the body fluids which could spread syphilis – he should be viewed as virulently infectious, like those similar figures, Count Cenci and the tyrant in *Queen Mab*. (It is worth noting that Malbecco in *The Faerie Queene*, a 'cankered crabbed carle', has a name which literally means 'evil beak' but which also, according to Helena Shire, has associations with cuckoldry, jealousy and sexual disease.)[22]

Other tortures endured by the Titan during his years of 'sleep-unsheltered hours' come from the spears of the crawling glaciers, whose 'bright chains / Eat with their burning cold into my bones' (I, 31–3), pain in the bones being one of the most unequivocal ways in Shakespeare of indicating a syphilitic.[23] The metaphor of the chain does duty for a variety of purposes in Shelley's poetry; it is the 'weight of hours' which bows down the speaker of 'Ode to the West Wind', the restraint on the spirit attempting to transcend mortality, the consuming iron which bites into Laon's flesh, the yoke uniting Kathema and Zeinab, the marriage bond, and a concatenation of events which the doer and sufferer of wrong trails behind him. Often the chain is that of physical pain, including that caused by disease, as in 'The Magnetic Lady to her Patient' and in *Queen Mab*:

> Commerce! beneath whose poison-breathing shade
> No solitary virtue dares to spring,
> But Poverty and Wealth, with equal hand
> Scatter their withering curses and unfold
> The doors of premature and violent death,
> To pining famine and full-fed disease,
> To all that shares the lot of human life,
> Which poisoned, body and soul, scarce drags the chain
> That lengthens as it goes and clanks behind.   (V, 44–52)

The action begins when Prometheus decides to recall his curse pronounced on Jupiter three thousand years before. It is easy to overlook how truly – and understandably – horrible this curse is, imprecation being of all rhetorical forms the one most subject to an automatic mental translation into milder terms, for it tends to be assumed that the language is always exaggerated. In the same reckless spirit as the speaker of 'The Wandering Jew's Soliloquy', Prometheus had invited Jupiter to 'Rain then thy plagues upon me here, / Ghastly disease and frenzying fear' (I, 265–6). (There is far less emphasis on disease in Aeschylus' *Prometheus*.) He then pronounces the countercurse:

I curse thee! let a sufferer's curse
Clasp thee, his torturer, like remorse;
Till thine infinity shall be
A robe of envenomed agony;
And thine Omnipotence a crown of pain,
To cling like burning gold round thy dissolving brain.   (I, 286–91)

He curses Jupiter, that is, with the very plagues that Jupiter had inflicted on him. They are simultaneously physical and psychological; they are 'like remorse' which brings to mind the 'pining regrets and vain repentances, / Disease, disgust, and lassitude', 'the fear of infamy, disease and woe', which torment the selfish in *Queen Mab* (V, 246–7, 255). Allusions to Christ and to 'Luke's Iron Crown', a torture inflicted on a sixteenth-century Hungarian rebel and made familiar by Goldsmith's *Traveller*, flicker in the background. But more distinct are those to classical mythology and to pathology. It is the robe of Hercules, tainted by the blood or, according to Apollodorus, by the semen of the poisoned Nessus, that Shelley principally has in mind here, as well as the frenzied sufferings of Hercules described by Sophocles and Ovid. The same image was used by Thompson in *Sickness* to express *his* agony.[24] The lines about the 'crown of pain' describe the pressure on the brain resulting from necrosis of the cranial bones: excruciating headaches, meningitis and madness are what Prometheus calls down on his tormentor. His curse ends with the wish that Jupiter will one day prove to be outwardly what he is within, becoming the target of lasting scorn – the fate that befalls Ozymandias.

When Prometheus hears his curse repronounced by Jupiter's phantasm he is appalled at himself: 'It doth repent me: words are quick and vain; / Grief for a while is blind, and so was mine. / I wish no living thing to suffer pain' (I, 303–5). These lines have been interpreted as an expression of Prometheus' forgiveness of Jupiter, but it has also been pointed out that the device of making Jupiter's phantasm restate the curse to Prometheus dramatises a psychological truth: one hates at one's own peril. The curse boomerangs on the utterer. Prometheus is repenting a self-inflicted wound. The original stage direction reads '[Prometheus] bends his head as in pain.'[25]

This is the point where Mercury appears, followed by the Furies. After they vanish Earth consoles Prometheus with four good spirits. The last belongs to an idealising erotic poet, a love-adept, but not one who seeks 'mortal blisses'. The objects of his poetry are 'yellow bees' sucking honey from the 'ivy bloom', which are illuminated by the sun's rays reflected from water, an image anticipating the later kingfishers. From these objects he creates 'forms more real than living man' (I, 737–51). These lines are often taken as epitomising Shelley's complete idea of the Poet, without taking account of the dramatic context and Prometheus' particular need at this point to escape from 'the pestilent and abhorrent brutalities which he detected around him in "real" life', to adapt Thornton Hunt's words.

Two sister spirits follow, reminiscent of Mrs Newton and Mrs Boinville, who in real life comforted Shelley after the Furies struck. They bear witness to Love, but Love accompanied by Desolation or Ruin. They come not to torment Prometheus but to assure him of eventual triumph in spite of all calamities. What is noticeable about the verses sung by these last two is the contrast between their hard political meaning and the romantic erotic imagery. The reason for this contrast is that Shelley does not recognise the normal distinction between personal and humanitarian love but, like Wollstonecraft, sees the latter as growing out of the former. Love accompanied by Ruin will have both an interpersonal and a political aspect. The fifth spirit sees 'Hollow Ruin' yawning behind Love's 'planet-crested shape', along with 'great sages bound in madness, / And headless patriots, and pale youths who perished, unupbraiding' (I, 765–9).

The same line of thought is continued by the sixth spirit, though in a more general and allusive vein:

> Ah, sister! Desolation is a delicate thing:
> It walks not on the earth, it floats not on the air,
> But treads with lulling footstep, and fans with silent wing
> The tender hopes which in their hearts the best and gentlest bear;
> Who, soothed to false repose by the fanning plumes above
> And the music-stirring motion of its soft and busy feet,
> Dream visions of aëreal joy, and call the monster, Love,
> And wake, and find the shadow Pain, as he whom now we greet.
>
> (I, 772–9)

The 'planet-crested shape' of Love is the same that inspired Christianity and the French Revolution, both of which brought Ruin and Desolation in their wake. Hence the headless patriots and mad sages. The 'tender hopes' of the 'best and gentlest' turn into the distempered dreams of those zealous 'friends of the people' who, whether from lack of self-knowledge or an inadequate system of morals, are betrayed into actions which ultimately negate and dishonour the ideals for which they stand. At the personal end of the continuum, they are 'sense-enchanted', with the result that through youthful inexperience they prepare their own future unhappiness.

Act II of *Prometheus* opens in the Edenic valley where Asia awaits Panthea. This is the beginning of the long-hoped-for change in society. After the winter of Prometheus' captivity comes the vernal equinox.[26] Spring loosens the icy chains of the glaciers which will finally be lifted from Prometheus by Hercules in the third act. From this point almost all the significant changes in society and nature, including those of political import, are imaged in terms of sexual pleasure and rejoicing.

This is true even of Panthea's first dream in which she foresees Prometheus' regeneration in terms which recall Kailyal's words about the unsubduable beautiful soul:

> his pale wound-worn limbs
> Fell from Prometheus, and the azure night
> Grew radiant from the glory of that form
> Which lives unchanged within.   (II, i, 62–5)

Yet while Panthea insists that Prometheus has divested himself of his body, the soul's dominion is envisaged in bodily terms.

> . . . the overpowering light
> Of that immortal shape was shadowed o'er
> By love; which, from his soft and flowing limbs,
> And passion-parted lips, and keen, faint eyes,
> Steamed forth like vaporous fire; an atmosphere
> Which wrapped me in its all-dissolving power.   (II, i, 71–6)

As Pottle wrote, Prometheus is 'freed, unscarred and rejuvenated, an ardent bridegroom awaiting his bride',[27] an impression reinforced by Panthea's second dream:

> As we sate here, the flower-infolding buds
> Burst on yon lightning-blasted almond-tree,
> When swift from the white Scythian wilderness
> A wind swept forth wrinkling the Earth with frost:
> I looked, and all the blossoms were blown down;
> But on each leaf was stamped, as the blue bells
> Of Hyacinth tell Apollo's written grief,
> O, FOLLOW, FOLLOW!   (II, i, 134–41)

This passage also has a medical context. The Paracelsian 'doctrine of signatures' taught that medicinal plants were in themselves prescriptions, and bore God's 'writing' indicating as much to the initiated. Following Cameron, the almond tree can be interpreted in exclusively political terms: its blossoms contain a message directing Panthea and Asia to the 'cave of Necessity, [where] they will find new revolutionary forces astir'.[28] Or they can be generalised as an emblem of hope, prefiguring the coming of deliverance as in the Book of Jeremiah, and suggested by actual almond trees which Shelley would have seen bursting into flower in any spring. These associations interact with the legend of Phyllis and thus with the theme of the renewal of love. According to Lemprière, when the faithless Demophoön came to Phyllis' tomb and wept, the leafless almond tree into which she had been transformed burst into blossom. But the second dream is more closely connected to the first than these interpretations suggest. The lightning-blasted almond tree is an image of Prometheus' 'wound-worn limbs' touched by electric poison. In the Bible almond blossom stands not only for deliverance but also for hoary hair as in Ecclesiastes, 12.5: 'And the almond tree shall flourish, and the grasshopper shall be a burden, and desire shall fail.' (Trelawny, consciously or not, alluded to this symbol when he wrote that Shelley's hair in 1822 was beginning to 'blossom'.)[29] The fallen almond blossom is thus a permutation of the image of falling hair. Yet the blossoms proclaim the rebirth of Prometheus' love for Asia, obstructed only by Jupiter's continuing rule, and thus symbolise hope which creates itself out of the wreckage, as the fallen leaves of 'Ode to the West Wind' quicken the 'new birth'; they also presage the unbinding and renewal of Prometheus' actual body. The directives to 'follow' bear also the promise of a panacea by means of which Panthea's dreams will come true and the blight on Earth's generative powers be lifted.

As if under a spell, the sisters journey up the slopes of a volcano and descend into its depths, the abode of Demogorgon. Once there, Asia, the Child of Ocean, will awaken the powerful voice of revolution, of which earthquake and volcano are the symbols. Critics have sometimes objected to the undramatic nature of this journey. It ought to be arduous, but the winged sisters float up on a 'stream of sound' scarcely distinguishable from a 'plume-uplifting wind'. (There is a pun on the two senses of the word 'air' – 'music' and 'gas'.) Cameron and Matthews' explanation is that they are being drawn along by the force of historical necessity. Grabo also suggested that the imagery of exhalations from the earth is evidence of Shelley's extensive knowledge of the chemistry of his time and the hoped-for curative properties of 'the elastic fluids'. Since scientific discovery is itself part of the historical process, one may conflate these two readings, and, taking a deterministic view, see the sisters as borne up by the inevitable progress of medical science.

It seems that Shelley did not intend to tie himself down to describing the effects of a particular medicine, pneumatic or otherwise. His approach is eclectic; he gives the 'plume-uplifting wind' a variety of properties. Inasmuch as the terrain is volcanic and the wind is said to 'steam', it suggests the vapour baths of the *stufe* in the Naples area. In that the stream is magnetic and described as drawing the sisters to the top of the sleeping volcano and then downwards into the crater, it suggests the earth's own electro-magnetic force, about which Shelley would have been informed by his first physics lecturer, Adam Walker.[30] In that the wind is probably identical with an 'oracular vapour' which intoxicates the sisters when they arrive at the volcano's summit, it suggests nitrous oxide, one of whose effects was to appear to increase the bodily powers: 'Mrs Beddoes had a uniform pleasurable sensation, frequently felt as though she was ascending in a balloon and found that she could walk more easily up Clifton Hill.'[31] It was Davy's belief that the pleasure produced by inhalation of this gas was not lost but 'mingles with the mass of feelings and becomes intellectual pleasure, or hope'.[32] The gas also produces synaesthesia; as with marijuana, its association with an intensified sense of sound was frequently remarked upon. One subject declared that he felt like the sound of the harp. Moreover it could indeed be 'oracular'; witness Davy's famous utterance under its influence: 'Nothing exists but thoughts! – the universe is composed of impressions, ideas, pleasures and pains!'[33] Although in Davy's opinion nitrous oxide was not produced in nature, Shelley would have had the authority of Adam Walker for believing that laboratory experiments were merely repetitions of what nature had previously accomplished.[34] Nitrous oxide could be produced when vegetable matter, nitre and intense heat were all present, and all three could plausibly meet in the forest-clothed crater of a sleeping volcano; Shelley's inspiration for the landscape of the sisters' journey was the Astroni Crater, which had trees growing within it.[35] However, the operations of the gas were uncertain: in some 'its effects have been unpleasant and depressing; in some it has produced convulsions, and other nervous symptoms', *Nicholson's British Encyclopaedia* reported.[36] Before Davy's experiments it had been an object of intense suspicion, and one American natural philosopher, Samuel Mitchill, even declared that it was a compound of the 'principle of contagion'.[37] While having nothing but good effects on the sisters, this 'oracular vapour' is dangerous to some, for it is that which

> . . . lonely men drink wandering in their youth,
> And call truth, virtue, love, genius, or joy,
> That maddening wine of life, whose dregs they drain
> To deep intoxication; and uplift,
> Like Maenads who cry loud, Evoe! Evoe!
> The voice which is contagion to the world.   (II, iii, 5–10)

Critics differ as to whether Shelley intended 'contagion' to be understood here in a good or a bad sense; precedents for either can be found in his work, and the context does not help. We consider that Shelley is again being deliberately ambiguous here. The voice of the wandering youth might be an inspired revolutionary message based on love, or it might be tainted by the 'egotising folly' of one who cannot repress the mutiny within and merely imagines himself to be one of the 'eminent in virtue'. This figure, a focus for Shelley's profoundest self-doubt, appears again under the name of Rousseau in *The Triumph of Life*.

The sisters' intoxication might also stem from the virtues of the surrounding vegetation, which, as we have said, should be considered as growing inside the sleeping volcano. Cedar, pine, yew and laurel are the forest trees named. The first three provide aromatic resins; the fourth a narcotic substance strongly associated with the Pythian priestess of Delphi. Plutarch, an author well-known to Shelley, thought the fume of burning laurel wood induced her prophecies. Along with the latent fire, all the ingredients for a ritual fumigation are present. Fumigations and incantations played an important part in the magical rites of raising and laying spirits. (Even as late as 1817 Shelley was still displaying an interest in the occult,[38] and his self-poisoning with laurel leaves has been noted.) He seems here to be conceiving the volcano as a *tripod*, a hugely magnified version of the one at Delphi which supported an incense-filled bowl over a central fire.[39] Demogorgon, the deity of the volcano, is a revolutionary's version of the god Apollo, who presided over the Delphic Oracle, but a sort of photographic negative of Apollo, shooting out *dark* rays. What he means to Jupiter is another matter, as will be seen later.

The descent into the crater is followed by Asia's famous questioning of Demogorgon regarding the origin of 'evil, the immedicable plague'. At the climax of the dialogue she asks her momentous question: 'When will the destined hour arrive?' for the overthrow of Jupiter. She is declaring her readiness to unite her powers with those of Prometheus. The question causes an earthquake and volcanic eruption, a geological simultaneous orgasm.[40] It initiates a rush of hours which synchronises the present with the future. They are an image of hope at the moment of its realisation, though for Jupiter they signify the end of all hope. Two chariots appear, one for Asia and Panthea, the other for Demogorgon, now rapidly ascending as a black volcanic cloud. Asia is transported to a cloud on top of a mountain where she is transfigured and becomes the 'Lamp of Earth' – Venus Urania embodied in the natural world.

Jupiter has been eagerly awaiting the incarnation of his 'fatal child, the terror of the earth', the product of his rape of Thetis, which he remembers in terms which show that part of the pleasure for him, as for Count Cenci, lay in infecting the object of his lust. He calls her the 'Bright image of Eternity'. She is a mute sea-nymph, the drama's most telling blank, a type of enslaved women whom 'smiles adorn, as calm decks the false Ocean' (*L. & C.*, 3329–30).[41] He gloatingly recalls her agonised cry:

> God! Spare me! I sustain not the quick flames,
> The penetrating presence; all my being,
> Like him whom the Numidian seps did thaw
> Into a dew with poison, is dissolved . . .   (III, i, 38–41)

The seps, along with the amphisbaena and the dipsas, sprang from the blood of the Gorgon's severed neck; uniquely it consumed the marrow as well as the flesh, thence dissolving the bones.[42] Jupiter intends that his 'child' will trample out the spark of humanity forever, and thus prove mightier than himself, since he lacks that ultimate power. The child proves mightier in a sense which he does not foresee. It turns out to be Demogorgon, who hurls Jupiter into the abyss.

The rape of Thetis, the engendering of the 'fatal child' upon her and the child's identification as Demogorgon are all Shelley's additions to the story. Why Demogorgon should be Jupiter's child and what might be his symbolic function is a question which has exercised commentators more than any other in *Prometheus Unbound*. The reading which we propose interweaves political and philosophical readings with the pathological, and demonstrates one example of the astonishing syncretism of Shelley's imagination.

This reading turns on paradox, wordplay, homeopathy and the ironic reversal of Jupiter's expectations in a series of analogous situations. In each case, Jupiter's understanding of Demogorgon differs from that of the good characters.

Pulos proposed that the rape of Thetis represents the appropriation of the intellectuals by the establishment, and that the 'fatal child' is a resultant monstrous philosophical error, Malthusianism, which threatens to quench the hopes of man forever by providing incontrovertible scientific proof that perfectibilism, were it possible, would be undesirable; if ever realised it would create the conditions most favourable for a population explosion, and rapidly lead to mass starvation. Hence the 'natural' checks on population – war, poverty, disease – are inevitable, and the only proposed palliative is a requirement to abstain from marriage, which Shelley called a separation from 'the soothing, elevating, and harmonious gentleness of the sexual intercourse' (*Prose*, p. 247). Opposed to this fatalistic Necessity is Godwinian Necessity, with which the individual cooperates instead of being blindly driven along; this force has been brought into being by the suffering caused by tyranny itself, and is therefore Jupiter's child. 'The Godwinian necessity of an ascending humanity is thus the true necessity', as Cameron wrote.[43]

Matching the two Necessities are two senses in which Demogorgon is a black cloud. In *The Cenci* a black cloud is a syphilitic pollutant. After Beatrice has been raped by her father she cries

> There creeps
> A clinging, black, contaminating mist
> About me . . . 'tis substantial, heavy, thick,
> I cannot pluck it from me, for it glues
> My fingers and my limbs to one another,
> And eats into my sinews, and dissolves
> My flesh to a pollution, poisoning
> The subtle, pure, and inmost spirit of life!   (III, i, 16–23)

Curran commented on this passage that

The syphilitic imagery . . . lends a measure of verisimilitude to the mythic formulations Shelley draws upon: namely the Manichean legend that the evil legions of Ahriman saw in a blazing corona above them the nude figure of a virgin whose beauty and insubstantiality at once inflamed and frustrated their passion. As a result they ejaculated black clouds that encompassed the earth with pestilence, from which arose the unnatural forms of life into which man is now born.[44]

Jupiter has not clearly envisaged his child; it is still a spirit and inchoate, but a diseased god may be expected to generate a universal disease. Demogorgon proves to be not the disease but its antidote; the black cloud is a purifying sulphurous fumigation, as Wasserman surmised.[45]

Matthews associated Demogorgon with the many-headed rebel giant Typhon, imprisoned, according to Lucan's *Pharsalia* (which supplied the seps image), in the volcano Inarime, and thus with the power of the unrepresented multitude. (Shelley used the phrase 'many-headed insurrection' in *Hellas*. Malthus himself called the insurrectionary hordes threatening the Roman Empire the 'hydra-headed monster'.)[46] Demogorgon can therefore be identified with the force of the proletariat, irresistible because of its 'unvanquishable number' once roused from sleep. The increase in population, held by Malthus to be the reason for keeping the masses in perpetual subservience, is the very means of their self-deliverance.

Jupiter hopes to keep down the hydra-headed monster of insurrection with a hydra-headed monster of his own production, a super-syphilis more terrible than any of his other plagues, which will brutalise man into a condition of permanent slavery.

> The pestilence that springs
> From unenjoying sensualism, has filled
> All human life with hydra-headed woes.

The improved treatment . . . has greatly contributed to disarm this cruel hydra of many of its heads.

The monster syphilis with all its gorgon terrors may yet be driven from the earth.

These antithetical correspondences extend even to Demogorgon's name: he is both a gorgon and an anti-gorgon who 'looks on the Gorgon's head unveiled; he lashes the cowering Fury with her own scourge'.[47] The literal meaning of 'Demogorgon' is 'Spirit of the Earth'. It was Matthews who saw that Demogorgon is also δημοs-γοργω – 'the people monster'. What Jupiter wishes him to be is the Gorgon Demon, the Spirit of Syphilis with all its gorgon terrors. Thus one has a complex of paired meanings: Malthusianism/Revolution; black ejaculation/black fumigation; Demogorgon/δημοs-γοργω; war, famine disease/deliverance from these; hydra-headed woe/many-headed monster. A universal 'syphilis' is to the tyrant as its cure is to the people.

This association of Malthusianism with syphilis, literal and metaphorical, is to be found in *Don Juan*, Canto I, which Shelley read in September 1818 when *Prometheus Unbound* was gestating. Speaking of progress, the narrator observes

> What wondrous new machines have late been spinning!
> I said the small-pox has gone out of late,
> Perhaps it may be follow'd by the great.

> 'Tis said the great came from America;
> Perhaps it may set out on its return –
> The population there so spreads, they say
> 'Tis grown high time to thin it in its turn,
> With war, or plague, or famine, any way,
> So that civilisation they may learn;
> And which in ravage the more loathsome evil is –
> Their real lues, or our pseudo-syphilis?   (I, cxxx, cxxx)

War, plague and famine, the traditional checks on population, are here called a 'pseudo-syphilis' as loathsome as the real thing (a fairly topical reference to Abernethy). Europe's corruption is to be exported to America in fair exchange. Characteristically, what is an aside in *Don Juan* is an integral metaphor in *Prometheus*.

With Prometheus' unbinding, health is transmitted to Earth by physical contact with him and she is rejuvenated. He is the regenerative life-force, reversing the process by which sexual diseases are transmitted from person to person. He has discovered the panacea, which also denotes in alchemy 'the perfect wisdom'.[48] When Asia speaks to Demogorgon of Prometheus' attempts to counteract the evils of Jupiter's reign before his enchaining, she stresses his role as a physician; he had given man, *inter alia*, knowledge of the virtues of plants and medicinal waters, 'Nepenthe, Moly, Amaranth, fadeless blooms'. Instead of prescribing poisonous minerals 'He told the hidden power of herbs and springs / And Disease drank and slept' (II, iv, 61, 85–6). As understood by Paracelsus, the panacea might be a definition of Promethean man himself, or of the human being who in *Queen Mab* 'stands adorning / This loveliest earth with taintless body and mind' (VIII, 198–9).

Upon Earth's restoration to health, she offers Prometheus a cave recognisably located in Greece with a nearby temple dedicated to him.[49] The Promethean influence thus moves rapidly from East and West. It is in this cave that Prometheus may be presumed to be dwelling in Act IV. During Jupiter's reign the cave had been one where the Earth's spirit had 'panted forth in anguish'. Those who inhaled the vapour from this cave 'became mad too, and built a temple there, / And spoke and were oracular, and lured / The erring nations round to mutual war' (III, iii, 125–9). Now, however, it

> fills
> With a serener light and crimson air
> Intense, yet soft, the rocks and woods around;
> It feeds the quick growth of the serpent vine,
> And the dark linkèd ivy tangling wild,
> . . . it circles round,
> Like the soft waving wings of noonday dreams,
> Inspiring calm and happy thoughts.   (ibid., 132–6, 144–6)

This cavern has been identified, by the Norton editors, with Demogorgon's crater into which the sisters had gazed, and from which a maddening oracular vapour had also been fuming; Wasserman suggested that Demogorgon's cavern was also the abyss into which Jupiter plunged to oblivion. 'The deep can exhale either evil or the force which removes evil. It can either be hell or the heart from which the Golden Age emerges.'[50] Although the topography of the poem makes it unlikely that all three caverns are literally the same, they are so in idea.

The 'crimson air' was identified by Grabo with what Davy called 'nitrous acid gas', but which today would be described as a mixture of nitric oxide gas and nitrogen peroxide. The latter gas, actually brown-orange but called 'red' by every contemporary account and 'crimson' by Erasmus Darwin, is formed when nitric oxide gas combines with the oxygen of the air, which it does very readily ($2NO + O_2 = 2NO_2$). From Davy, Shelley would have known that 'crimson air' was produced by 'fuming nitrous acid',[51] the medical use of which in the cure of syphilis we have already described in Chapter 2. ($2HNO_2 = H_2O + N_2O_3 = H_2O + NO + NO_2$.) Such fumes in *Prometheus* could have their source in a deep subterranean well.

Attempts were made to find a medical use for this crimson air. Cavallo recommended it to Lind as a sickroom fumigant, but warned that it damaged the lungs. Davy burned his throat when he inhaled it.[52] It is one of the impurities present in the making of laughing gas (nit*rous* oxide). For years the presence of this contaminant hindered the discovery that it was laughing gas which had the medical use.

Davy attempted to stimulate plant growth with laughing gas. Despite his failure, he maintained for a time that it had the property of 'increasing the powers of life'. However, by the time Shelley read his *Elements of Chemical Philosophy* in 1812, Davy had concluded that the gas was 'not fitted to support life' – an epitome of hopes kindled only to be quenched. Shelley would also have known from Davy that the differences between gaseous compounds of oxygen and nitrogen are entirely a matter of the proportions in which the two gases are combined.[53] Like the bittersweet, the gases contain within them a dual principle, one of life (oxygen, the 'vital air') and one of lifelessness, nitrogen, or azote ('without life'). In Prometheus' world azote and oxygen 'marry' in a passionate tumult of crimson clouds (the image is taken from Erasmus Darwin)[54] and produce a new compound, a benign, oracular vapour which feeds growth.

Prometheus and Asia withdraw to the cave to make love. His fire is converted into the magnetic fluid, and the energy which their love-making releases diffuses itself throughout the world as joy and creativity. Hence they have not really left the world, but are *conceiving* the action of Act IV and creating a 'moment in and out of time'. The need for privacy is the obvious reason for Prometheus' non-appearance in Act IV, an absence which has incurred much criticism and unnecessary apologetics.

Cronin made the happy suggestion that Prometheus and Asia can be identified with different kinds of poetry, the epic and the erotic respectively.[55] We would develop his insight as follows: the split between the two has been a damaging one for poetry, analogous to that between Reason and Passion; lack of harmony between the elements of poetry was deplored by Shelley in *The Defence of Poetry* (*Prose*, p. 286). The union of Asia and Prometheus will bring these lopsided and degenerate elements into harmony once again. Act IV is an attempt at such harmonising. Most readers agree that Shelley fell short of his ideal; Act IV contains some of his worst writing. But it also contains some of his best. Examination of what at first appears to be loose imagery reveals careful conceptualisation, as the following example shows.

The union of Prometheus and Asia conceives two miniature worlds which come speeding along two rivulets from the forest surrounding the cave; the natural inference is that they have originated from the cave itself, which Panthea and Ione, who describe the approach of these orbs, cannot see. They contain the Spirits of the Moon and Earth. As it whirls over the rivulet the Earth's orb 'grinds the bright brook into an azure mist / Of elemental subtlety, like light' (IV, 253–5). How can a 'sphere' be said to grind? Is this a case of fluent muddle?

Panthea remarks that 'vast beams like spokes of some invisible wheel' are flashing from inside the orb. The orb is therefore revolving over the surface of the brook like a paddle wheel, an ethereal version of Henry Reveley's steam boat, and the rays of light – the imagery of spokes derives from Lucretius – which would also be rays of heat, are turning the water to steam. (See the plates for what might have been a visual stimulus for this image.) Shelley deliberately uses the word 'grind' because he is doing here what Milton did in *Paradise Lost*, only in reverse. When Milton wants to express the unfallen quality of Eden, he employs words like 'wanton', 'error', and 'serpent' in their original senses. Hence in Book IV 'error' simply means 'wandering' without connotations of sinfulness. But after the Fall these words acquire the 'bad' meanings which they have today.[56] Shelley, by contrast, takes a word like 'grind' and rids it of the mill-wheel's sound, of all associations with tyrannous machinery, and gives it a redeemed meaning to suit the new world. He does the same with 'knead' a few lines later.

Although children, the Spirits of the orbs quickly mature. The Spirit of the Earth is masculine and exults in a sense of sexual power:

> The joy, the triumph, the delight, the madness!
> The boundless, overflowing, bursting gladness,
> The vaporous exultation not to be confined!
> Ha! ha! the animation of delight
> Which wraps me, like an atmosphere of light,
> And bears me as a cloud is borne by its own wind.   (IV, 319–24)

The Earth spirit becomes the lover of the Moon spirit, fertilising her and causing vegetation to grow on her orb's icy surface. Earth and Moon are both 'interpenetrated' by love, the very 'flame of consentaneous love' which in *Queen Mab* inspired and renewed all life. And here, no less than in *Queen Mab*, the transformation of Nature is celebrated in images of returning health. This 'nuptial masque', this 'ritual mimicry' (the phrases are M. H. Abrams')[57] of the union of Prometheus and Asia takes place on the feminine, maternal earth, which has not dematerialised or undergone a sex change.

Man is also healed by another natural virtue – that of medicinal springs. The Earth spirit tells how 'hate, fear and pain', fleeing before the power of love

> Leave Man, even as a leprous child is left,
> Who follows a sick beast to some warm cleft
> Of rocks, through which the might of healing springs is poured.
>
> (IV, 388–90)

Shelley alludes here to the legendary discovery of the waters of Bath. The figure of the errant child/youth appears again, but this time he wanders *safely*. The word 'leprous' needs no comment.

In the new world, sexual adventurousness is no longer punished by disease, just as investigation of the 'secrets of Nature' is no longer regarded as a violation. 'The abyss shouts from her depth laid bare / Heaven, hast thou secrets? Man unveils me; I have none' (IV, 422–3). The 'abyss' in Jupiter's world was envisaged as a volcanic crater, in which Jupiter was engulfed. In Prometheus' world, the abyss, whether envisaged as sea, sky or crater, is no sulphurous pit whence issue burning, scalding, stench and consumption; it exults in its own exploration and exacts no revenge for outraged modesty. An Actaeon gazing on Nature's naked loveliness would not be hounded, a Ginotti would not become a Wandering Jew. Yet at the very end Demogorgon appears again to warn that the recurrence of evil will always be a threat; it is possible that 'Eternity, / Mother of many acts and hours [will] free / The serpent that would clasp her with his length' (IV, 365–7). There is an analogy between the serpent's uncoiling and Fracastor's view of the cyclical nature of the Serpentine Evil: 'Once again when the Fates shall will it in the course of years, the time will come when the disease lies hidden, consigned to death and night. Later after long centuries this same malady shall arise.'[58]

The Cenci and Swellfoot the Tyrant

The symbolisation of evil as a syphilitic infection has in Shelley a very particular application: the damaging of an apostle of liberty's reputation by hypocrites. We have already mentioned Shelley's description of the 'killers' of Keats as 'literary prostitutes'. Holmes suggested that the poisoned saliva on the vulture's beak 'implies whole dimensions of verbal slander, sneers and rumours' (p. 494), a view with which we agree. In 'Fragment of a Satire on Satire' Shelley wrote of 'the deeper wounds, / The leprous scars of callous Infamy' (18–19).

The link between syphilitic infection and infamy is also present in *The Cenci*. Having raped his daughter, the Count wishes the disease upon her. He hopes she will die 'plague-spotted' and threatens 'I will make / Body and soul a monstrous lump of ruin' (IV, i, 94–5).

> let her food be
> Poison, until she be encrusted round
> With leprous stains! Heaven, rain upon her head
> The blistering drops of the Maremma's dew,

Till she be speckled like a toad; parch up
Those love-enkindled lips, warp those fine limbs
To loathed lameness. All-beholding sun,
Strike in thine envy those life-darting eyes
With thine own blinding beams!   (IV, i, 129–37)

Count Cenci is a kind of vicar to Jupiter, and like him he also hopes to
engender a child by rape. Since he is a mortal, his will be a diseased child
rather than a disease, and he hopes that it will daily grow 'more wicked and
deformed' to bring everlasting disgrace on Beatrice. Beatrice is unable to
accuse her father openly because if her violation is known, her good name
will still be irrevocably damaged. The ideas of rape and infamy are united
in the words in which Beatrice comes nearest to telling her judges what really
happened:

                          a father
First turned the moments of awakening life
To drops, each poisoning youth's sweet hope; and then
Stabbed with one blow my everlasting soul;
And my untainted fame.   (V, ii, 120–4)

The Cenci increased Shelley's reputation for immorality. Charles Kirkpatrick
Sharpe's second letter about arsenic and aquafortis was prompted by its
publication. One reviewer strongly hinted that the tone of the play was the
result of a venereal taint:

There can be little doubt that *vanity* is at the bottom of this, and that weakness of
character (which is a very different thing from what is called weakness of *talent*) is also
concerned. Mr Shelley likes to carry about with him the consciousness of his own
peculiarities; and a tinge of disease, probably existing in a certain part of his constitution, gives to these peculiarities a very offensive cast.[59]

'Vanity' corresponds to the 'consciousness of his own peculiarities', and
'weakness of character' to the 'tinge of disease'. Shelley saw this review,
marked by his publisher Ollier 'John Scott' (editor of the *London Magazine*),
and singled it out for especial comment as having been written 'with great
malignity'.[60] His next letter to Ollier insisted upon the greatest secrecy for
the publication of *Epipsychidion*.
   What is important to note is that for Shelley, as for Blake, 'a truth that's
told with bad intent / Beats all the lies you can invent'. Beatrice has been
raped and has murdered her father, yet Shelley means us to sympathise with
her prevarications and concealments, because the truth would make her 'un-
polluted fame' into a 'stale mouthèd story' (Shelley is using 'stale' in the ar-
chaic sense of 'prostitute') to be told by 'vilest gossips', that is, the hearers
would simply gloat over the scandal and forget the wrongs which provoked
Beatrice into acting as she did. Lying becomes a lawful means of self-
protection, just as it is for Ulysses in *The Cyclops*.

Those who vilify the representatives of progressive elements in society show their bad faith, even when the charges are partly true. If the vilifiers had any integrity, they would not want them to be true. This is the assumption behind the championship of Shelley's unlikeliest heroine – Queen Caroline – in *Swellfoot the Tyrant* (1820).

A savage political lampoon which has often been compared to the cartoons of Gillray, *Swellfoot* deals with the attempts of George IV to divorce the Queen for adultery. Shelley had no illusions about her personal morals, but inasmuch as she was a focus for the hopes of the people of England, those who wished to prove her guilt were tools of the Castlereagh administration. He also saw her plight as analogous to his own. Caroline appears as Iona Taurina, a cow pursued by the gadfly of scandal, yet another permutation of the Zodiacal ungulate chased by the predator. The Gadfly, a member of the Milan Commission which spied on Caroline,[61] is another manifestation of the stinging creature which is the agent of disease. The Gadfly trails 'blistering slime'; it has pursued Iona from Parthenope (Naples) through the 'fortunate Saturnian land' (the length of Italy) to 'the darkness of the West' – Milan, though the phrase is equally applicable to Pisa. The route matches Shelley's between 1818 and 1820, and the scandal applies equally to the *odium theologicum* of the reviews and the blackmailing activities of the Shelleys' ex-servant Paolo. The Gadfly celebrates the driving of its victim 'Far, far, far! / With the trump of my lips and the sting at my hips' and boasts that Iona has been 'dumbed' – silenced – by this trump. It is easy to see here a parallel with the trumpet of Shelley's prophecy, 'dumbed' in a drone of British humbug, but the Gadfly also exults that the venomous sting at his hips will soon literally kill Iona: 'If you had hung her / With canting and quirking, / She could not be deader than she will be soon' (I, i, 253–5).

Shelley gives the Gadfly an ancient lineage, indicating that it is, to adopt Matthews' term, an 'over-determined concept' – in other words 'scandal' is only one of its manifestations. One point of origin is 'utmost Aethiopia'. He provides an inaccurate reference: 'And the Lord whistled for the gadfly out of Aethiopia, and for the bee of Egypt, etc. – EZEKIEL',[62] which is a version of Isaiah, 7.18: 'The Lord shall hiss for the fly that is in the uttermost part of the rivers of Egypt, and for the bee that is in the land of Assyria.' Shelley misquotes in line with his obsession – that the Nile is the source of all disease, yet another link between *Swellfoot* and 'Ozymandias'. In *Laon and Cythna* the 'plague-stricken, foodless' multitudes are driven 'like lean herds pursued by gadflies' of fear to pile up the martyr's pyre for the lovers (*L. & C.*, 4169–70).

Shelley wrote *Swellfoot* under the shadow of Vaccà's diagnosis of nephritis, and the image of Iona being driven 'from city to city / Abandoned of pity' also refers to his pursuit of health. Accomplices of the Gadfly are the Leech and the Rat, false doctors. The Rat, like the Leech, claims to be curing the 'plethory' of the state:

I'll slily seize and
Let blood from her weasand, –
Creeping through crevice, and chink, and cranny,
With my snaky tail, and my sides so scranny.   (I, i, 265–8)

Shelley was mentally preparing to be cut for the kidney stone and to face subsequent death. If the Leech is a blood-letter, then the 'weasand' (windpipe) would seem to be a displacement of the urethra and the Rat a lithotomical instrument, the gorget, to which Vaccà had made several improvements; the name is suggestive of 'gorge', the throat.

Swellfoot, in short, is an exorcism of the terror not merely of infamy but also of painful disease and death. As in *Prometheus Unbound*, the curse becomes a blessing. What Swellfoot and his kind would wish to label as sexual perversion (one of the germs of Shelley's satire was his fancy that scandalmongers would even go so far as to say that Caroline was guilty of imitating Pasiphaë) is converted into a quasi-hermaphroditic image of Iona Taurina pursuing the court of Swellfoot mounted on the back of her consort John Bull, the Ionian Minotaur. He is a man–monster like Demogorgon and, like him, rises from the depths of the earth; Ion and Iona are a matching brother–sister pair, like Laon and Laone. Famine, normally a means of ensuring subservience to Swellfoot, becomes, like over-population in *Prometheus*, a spur to action; the Goddess of Famine cooperates for once with Liberty and provides loaves which turn the 'swinish multitude' into strong bulls.

The Sensitive Plant

The 'dumbing' of the truth of pure lips by the 'leprous scars of infamy' is hinted at in *The Sensitive Plant*, a poem held to be one of pure escape into a Platonic world of ideas. The escape, however, is not quite as philosophic a matter as it appears to be at first.

This poem is a fable so clear that, on one level, even a child could understand it. Adopting the metrical and stanzaic form of one of Southey's moral tales, 'God's Judgement on a Bishop' (which is the same as that of 'Humpty Dumpty'), it tells the story of the decay of a garden after the death, at the end of summer, of its tutelary deity, a beautiful Lady. The reader is led to expect that after winter spring will not be far behind. But instead, the Sensitive Plant, the 'feeblest yet the favourite' in the garden, is a 'leafless wreck' and the 'loathliest weeds' have taken over, a shock all the more devastating because of the level tone in which Shelley announces it.

The poem has reached its nadir, but not its conclusion. At this point Hope creates itself out of the wreck it contemplates. 'In this life / Of error, ignorance and strife, / Where nothing is, but all things seem' (III, 122–4) one is entitled to believe that the beautiful garden still exists, for 'love and beauty and delight' exceed the imperfect senses. The retreat from life's hideousness would seem to be into a world completely beyond experience, which Shelley's sceptical philosophy would have allowed him to entertain as a possibility.

Undoubtedly one of the dimensions of this poem is the political. Shelley wrote it in a state of depression following news of the Thistlewood plot to assassinate the members of the Ministry. 'Everything seems to conspire against Reform' he wrote to Peacock, but he added 'I have a motto on a ring in Italian – "Il buon tempo verra."'[63] The Lady may, accordingly, be regarded as Liberty, and Shelley's Conclusion to the poem an extension of the Italian motto. The Plant is the political radical who can only suffer and hope. But this is only one of many possibilities; the Lady has also been interpreted as Intellectual Beauty united to Nature. She has a 'lovely mind', is reminiscent in other ways of the vision in *Epipsychidion*, and departs as suddenly. This interpretation seems correct too, since, for Shelley, Intellectual Beauty always included political awareness, or 'truth'. The Sensitive Plant has been identified as 'mankind amid natural creation or else the type of the poet with creative sensibility amid general mankind'.[64] And inevitably it has been read as denoting Shelley himself and a proof of his narcissism. (He did of course regard himself as a person of great sensibility and once in a letter to Claire called himself a mimosa – the generic name for sensitive plants.)[65]

However, we are less interested in attempting to establish the primacy of the various readings than in analysing the metaphor within a metaphor which sustains them. It has often been pointed out that the poem is a development of Hamlet's "Tis an unweeded garden / That grows to seed. Things rank and gross in Nature / Possess it merely.' But there is another Shakespearean line behind the poem, Iago's 'Our bodies are our gardens, to which our wills [i.e. sexual appetites] must be our gardeners.' *The Sensitive Plant* is entirely built around the conceit of the body's decline rendered in terms of the loss of Eden. In this scheme, the Sensitive Plant is the branching nervous system, about which Shelley would have learned a great deal from his reading of Cabanis.[66] The Lady remains Intellectual Beauty, whose loss has a catastrophic effect on the body because of the interrelatedness of the psychic and the physical.

The garden is one of love, a *hortus conclusus* in which all the flowers and herbs are breathless and trembling with bliss, but none more than the 'companionless Sensitive Plant' (I, 12) since the nervous system is the agency by which all parts of the body experience sensations.

> But the Sensitive Plant which could give small fruit
> Of the love which it felt from the leaf to the root,
> Received more than all, it loved more than ever,
> Where none wanted but it, could belong to the giver.   (I, 70–3)

It is clear that the sensations which the body is experiencing are those of erotic arousal, but erotic arousal in a context of modesty. The Sensitive Plant is shy, like the timid lovers of *The Witch of Atlas*; its Latin name is *mimosa pudica*, the modest mimosa. The mimosa's habit of closing its pinnate, fan-like leaves at the slightest touch, as if protecting itself from a rude sexual advance, earned it this name. In the West Indies, where the plant grows wild, many of its nicknames, such as 'Shame Lady' and 'Shame Darling', stem from the same idea. The pleasurable sensations are not merely genital ones, that is, 'felt from the root', but radiate through the entire body.

> . . . the Sensitive Plant has no bright flower;
> Radiance and odour are not its dower;
> It loves, even like Love, its deep heart is full,
> It desires what it has not, the Beautiful!   (I, 74–7)

The nervous system is not beautiful in itself, unlike, say, the eyes. But it is through sensation that one first apprehends the Beautiful and falls in love with it. Its full heart indicates yearning for orgasmic release, seen as a generous impulse, an act of giving and of gratitude towards 'the giver' – a deliberately vague word.

The death of the Lady is followed by the sickness of every gentle passion, and the entry of lust with its resultant disease. Many of the obnoxious weeds which spring up after her death directly evoke syphilis. There is the 'leprous scum' (III, 66), accompanied by 'spawn, weeds and filth', which makes the running rivulet 'thick and dumb'. Many are fungi. A *fungus* is a medical as well as a botanical term; it is the name given to 'proud flesh', a spongy morbid growth for which removal by caustics was the standard treatment. Some syphilitic eruptions were fungoid in character; those around the anus acquired the picturesque name of 'mushrooms of St Fiacre'.[67] The atmosphere of sexual obscenity is maintained by the line 'Plants, at whose names the verse feels loath' (III, 58). This somewhat prim turn of phrase suggests that Shelley did have some definite names in mind; one that seems likely is the stink-horn, the carrion-smelling fungus whose apt Latin name, *Phallus impudicus*, which Shelley would have found in a note to Darwin's *The Loves of the Plants*, implies the reverse of all that the *Mimosa pudica* stands for.

'Unctuous meteors . . . burned and bit' the leaves of the tender Indian plants – the garden is clearly located in Cashmire – with a 'venomous blight'. On the social level, these meteors also suggest the Regency gallants, who are as promiscuous (the meteors 'from spray to spray / Crept and flitted') as they are infectious and oily; in *Peter Bell III* Shelley had written that the 'gallant' is a 'thing' 'whose trade is, over ladies / To lean, and flirt and stare, and simper' until he makes women 'cruel, courteous, smooth, inhuman' (III, x).

The effect of this blight on the Sensitive Plant is the nearest thing to a venereal ophthalmia that a plant could be imagined to display:

> The Sensitive Plant, like one forbid,
> Wept, and the tears within each lid

> Of its folded leaves, which together grew,
> Were changed to a blight of frozen glue.   (III, 78–71)

'Glue' here has syphilitic overtones, as in *The Cenci* and *Laon and Cythna*. The leaves of the Sensitive Plant fall, like hair in 'Ode to the West Wind'. The sap 'shrank to the root through every pore / As blood to a heart that will beat no more' and winter comes with a breath like a *chain*. The heart and the root are the last to be affected because, as Shelley says in his apology for erotic writers in *A Defence of Poetry*:

> . . . the end of social corruption is to destroy all sensibility to pleasure; and, therefore, it is corruption. It begins at the imagination and the intellect as at the core and distributes itself thence as a paralysing venom through the affections into the very appetites, till all become a torpid mass in which sense hardly survives. At the approach of such a period poetry ever addresses itself to those faculties which are the last to be destroyed, and its voice is heard, like the footsteps of Astraea, departing from the world.   (*Prose*, p. 286)

This is the plot of *The Sensitive Plant*. The 'root' corresponds to the 'very appetites', the organs of pleasure which are the 'last to be destroyed', the destruction of which realises 'the last triumph of evil'.

The rhythm now changes. Like the tentative-seeming unfurling of a leaf Shelley offers his hope, that in this world of illusion:

> It is a modest creed, and yet
> Pleasant if one considers it,
> To own that death itself must be,
> Like all the rest, a mockery.   (III, 126–9)

The creed is modest yet pleasant, that is to say, it is unpretentious yet comforting; it is also 'modest' in the sense of 'sexually virtuous', yet pleasurable. Thus the poem suddenly reveals itself as belonging to that genre of poetry, of which *Comus* is the great example, which has as its object the reconciliation of Virtue and Pleasure.

Death is a seeming. It is also a 'mockery', a counterfeit, an imitation. Death imitates sexual climax – 'sweet death', 'the death that lovers love'[68], and that in turn is another imitation, for it is the act which ought always to be the link and type of the highest emotions of our nature. The sexual act is an invitation to eternity; in their ordinary swoon lovers experience an annihilation of the sense of time (and, therefore, of mutability): 'Love me my dearest Mary . . . The remembrance & expectation of such sweet moments as we experienced last night consoles strengthens & redeems me from despondency. *There is eternity in these moments* – they contain the true elixir of immortal life.'[69] Gathering conviction, the poet expands his creed:

> That garden sweet, that lady fair,
> And all sweet shapes and odours there,
> In truth have never passed away:
> 'Tis we, 'tis ours, are changed; not they.   (III, 130–33)

He is saying that if we — all or any of us — associate sexuality with the disgusting and obscene then it will become so, for nothing is but as it is perceived. But whenever we make love in tenderness and truth — and Shelley would include here dream and fantasy experiences, 'the complete or partial, actual or supposed fulfilment' of the claims of love (*Prose*, p. 220) — the lost paradise is regained. Imperfect as the senses are, Shelley does not say that human beings can do without them. Beauty, Love, and Delight exceed them: the ladder to the eternal rises higher than the senses can reach but the ladder is grounded ultimately in sense experience.

To a nineteenth-century Frenchman, this creed, so far from being modest, was presumptuous and ludicrous: 'To think of attaining to the Infinite between two sheets!' Of such truths, as Asia said of a different matter, 'Each [heart] to itself must be the oracle.'

12

Egyptian bondage: *Charles the First* and *The Triumph of Life*

One of Shelley's strategies, which he adopted increasingly after the move to Italy, was to employ historical figures as personae. In all cases there is a series of parallels between these characters and Shelley's own life. For Shelley this was a means of escaping from 'self, that burr that will stick to one!' while at the same time remaining in some sense a confessional poet. Such self-identification reassures the isolated individual that he is not a unique personality, trapped in a particular time and place, but a *type* who has existed before and will exist again in history as opposed to myth. As the Indian Youth in the 'Fragments of an Unfinished Drama' says, 'It may be / That Nature masks in life several copies / Of the same lot, so that the sufferers / May feel another's sorrow as their own' (92–5). Beatrice Cenci, Queen Caroline and Keats are three different examples of such personae; Tasso would have been another if Shelley had finished the projected drama of his life. This project eventually materialised as *Julian and Maddalo* in which traces of an origin in Tasso's story can be seen. (One reason why Shelley dropped the Tasso project, we think, is that events in his own life overtook him as he was planning it and made the self-identification unworkable. *Julian and Maddalo* also furnishes an example of the use of a double persona, so that Shelley 'is' both Julian and the Maniac.)[1] In each case Shelley sets himself the task of selecting those features from his chosen persona's life history which, without violating historical fact, will emphasise resemblances and reinforce the sense of his being only one of Nature's multiple copies.

Charles the First

Shelley's two last large-scale works both employ this strategy, though in the unfinished drama *Charles the First*, which Shelley began writing about the turn of the year 1821–2,[2] this is not at all obvious. However we believe, after an examination of Shelley's notes and sources, that one of his *alter egos* would have been Sir Harry Vane the Younger, whose career and character threw up many parallels with his own – extraordinary talents, an irregular life at Oxford, bitterness against the church, enmity towards his father, 'enthusiasm', cunning, and exile.[3] Shelley noted that he was '15 years old 1627' – the same age that figures in *Una Favola* – and altered his sources in order to make him one of the Parliamentarians who tried to escape to America in 1635. (Vane in fact became a controversial governor of Massachussets.)[4] Shelley's interest in the character was probably stimulated by other factors: firstly his name, which combines the diminutive of Henry, Shelley's *alter ego* in *Queen Mab*, with suggestions of luminous wings (vans) – pride, ineffectuality, and a weathercock instability; secondly, the part played by Vane in bringing about the execution of Strafford, which involved the public humiliation of his father, and thirdly, his execution after the Restoration, which made him a Commonwealth martyr.

A foreshadowing of the important role Vane was destined to play occurs when Charles speaks slightingly of him to Archy, his fool, who is prophesying in riddles the downfall of Strafford and Laud. (These speeches have been pigeon-holed as pastiche of the Fool's speeches in *Lear*. Certainly *Lear* is the model, but almost every word of them is instinct with meaning, and has behind it Shelley's reading in Catherine Macauley, Clarendon, Whitelocke and Hume; this mask of an Archy would repay close analysis.) Archy tells the king that in 'the meadows beyond Lambeth' he found something 'instead of a mitre' (i.e., the power of the church). 'Vane's wits, perhaps' replies the king flippantly. 'Something as vain,' ripostes the fool, 'I saw a ? gross vapour hovering in a stinking ditch over the carcass of a dead ass . . . his Grace of Canterbury expects to enter the New Jerusalem some Palm Sunday in triumph on the ghost of this ass' (ii, 434–41). Vane is equated here with the ass and thus with the people of England, the meek and patient adoring multitude. If, however, the Archbishop should attempt to ride in triumph on the ass, some kind of ironic reversal will occur. The ass, like the 'vapour in the vale' of *The Mask of Anarchy*, will be resurrected and grow mighty; it will prove to be Balaam's ass, through whom the Spirit of Liberty speaks.[5] Vane has been assigned the role of a patrician champion of the people.

The unwitting Charles has earlier called Archy a parrot 'Hung in his gilded prison from the window / Of a queen's bower over the public way' (ii, 99–100), thinking of him as an amusing bird-brained pet. But, like Fracastor's parrot, his function is to warn; he is strategically placed to see the social corruption of Charles' London both without and within and to relate private vice to public pest. Normally queens – unless they are painted Jezebels – do not have bowers over public ways; the queen in this case is also a 'quean' – a harlot. Archy is another persona of Shelley; the caged bird (Shelley harks back to his lodgings in Half Moon Street in the summer of 1813, when Mrs Newton compared him to a lark hanging in a cage) makes prophecies to which no one pays attention. In one of his speeches Archy alludes to the Widow Bird song;[6] we think that Shelley was intending that the song should have the same relationship to the play as Beatrice's lyric 'False friend, wilt thou smile or weep?' has to *The Cenci*, that he would have introduced the theme of corruption entering the kingdom when love departs from it, thus making a connection between lost love on the private level and the ravaging of the garden of England.

Charles the First begins with the degeneration of the dramatic arts, an extravagant Roman triumphal masque in which corruption is glorified. 'A troop of cripples, beggars, and lean outcasts, / Horsed upon stumbling jades, carted with dung, / Dragged for a day from cellars and low cabins / And rotten hiding holes' (i, 169–72) is brought on in order that the richness of the preceding chariots should appear by contrast more glorious and divine. The date is 1633, a time when the venereal disease was infecting literature; 'Councils and counsellors' are said by one character to 'hang on one another, / Hiding the loathsome [blank] / Like the base patchwork of a leper's rags' (i, 129–31). The 'red plague' epidemic that raged eight years earlier (1625) casts an ominous shadow over the proceedings. (Eight years before 1821–2 takes one back to the winter of 1813/4 and elephantiasis again.) The 'vanity' of the pageant is supposed to be an exorcism of this memory, but in fact recalls it. Puritans complained that the drama encouraged a decline in sexual morals; the royal family was blamed for this through its encouragement of and participation in dramatic representation; Prynne was mutilated because the subtitle of his pamphlet against the stage, *Women Actors Notorious Whores*, was taken to refer to the queen, who had acted in a pastoral. The masque at the Inn was staged, according to Catherine Macauley, specifically to reassure their majesties that they need not deprive themselves of their favourite amusements.[7]

It seems, then, that Shelley was trying to shape the historical facts into a mythological pattern featuring social corruption intermingled with sexual corruption, a fall from grace and a resurrection, exile succeeded by a triumphant return. We suspect that one reason why Shelley gave up the project was that he found that the facts obstinately refused to fit the framework and was not prepared to do violence to the historical record.

The Triumph of Life

In *The Triumph of Life*, which Shelley was working on shortly before his death, the motif of the chariot which seems glorious but is accompanied by corruption reappears. As before, he uses the device of multiple personality and self-identification with a historical character.

There are three narrative voices. The first is that of Shelley as Narrator, who in the introduction stretches himself beneath an old chestnut tree on an Apennine slope with his back to the morning sun, watching night recede before him. He has a vision. His dreaming self is rather like one of Chaucer's Dreamers, more puzzled, less capable of interpreting his vision than either the Narrator or the reader. This Spectator exists in dream time; there are hints that he is an inexperienced self of the Narrator, about to 'enter life', as the nineteenth-century phrase had it. But he inhabits a post-1821 world, for within the fable of the poem Napoleon has recently died.

The vision is of a dusty highway, through which a torrent of people is busily hurrying, pursuing 'their serious folly'. Through this multitude rushes a chariot containing the dark, hooded Shape of Life, who is, of course, False Life or worldly existence. She sits 'as one whom years deform' — the words could mean that the Shape was deformed either with age or with some kind of aging disease or, most likely, both. Life in the fullness of time is seen no longer as a poisonously beautiful seductress but as a raddled old harlot whose shrouds fail to conceal the marks of her trade. She is the final apotheosis of the fat old woman and her vehicle is both a chariot and a 'stage-coach', a piece of theatrical machinery belonging to the world's 'show', just as the Gadfly, a bug that hums, is humbug.

The car is guided by a four-faced, blindfolded charioteer, often identified with Destiny. Chained to this car is a captive multitude, composed of almost all the great leaders of history. A few are exempt, including Christ and Socrates; nor are they among the crowd of people, now identified as a *ribald* one. The swarming of the crowd has become a lustful dance, 'fierce and obscene'. In front of the chariot are young men and women, 'tortured by the agonizing pleasure' who 'fling their wild arms in air' and 'as they glow / Like moths by light attracted and repelled, / Oft to their bright destruction come and go' (136–60). The chariot ruthlessly passes over them. Behind it 'Old men, and women foully disarrayed / Shake their grey hair in the insulting wind, / Limp in the dance and strain with limbs decayed / To reach the car of light' (164–8). For them desire has outlived performance.

The Shape seems as if 'crouching within the shadow of a tomb', a phrase reminiscent of the lament that 'grace and power were thrown as food / To the hyaena lust, who, among graves / Over his loathèd meal, laughing in agony, raves' (*L. & C.*, 88–90). Grace and power in *The Triumph* are thrown to Life, leaving behind 'the action and the shape', a mere husk of being.

'Struck to the heart by this sad pageantry', the Spectator turns away and is aghast to see the decayed shape of Rousseau, who describes the progress of the chariot and then offers to recount 'how and by what paths' he has been brought to 'this dread pass'. The phrase has at least three possible meanings: 'this fearful road', 'this terrible reputation', and 'this dreadful predicament'.

Rousseau, the third narrative voice, identifies many of the captive multitude, then describes his own youthful experience. He encountered a 'Shape all light' who offered him a cup 'mantling with bright Nepenthe'. As his lips touched the goblet a vision of the Car of Life burst upon him. He was swept into the multitude and joined in the ghastly dance. Eventually wearying of it he fell by the wayside where the Spectator found him. 'Then, what is Life?' asks the Spectator. Rousseau begins to reply. Here the poem breaks off.

The poem's unfinished state has given rise to several problems of interpretation. Why, for instance, is there such an emphasis on lust in a poem which has the whole of Life as its ostensible subject? (Matthews estimated that there were fifty-six lines dealing with the erotic to 108 dealing with the political, a very high proportion.) What determined the choice of Rousseau as the chief guide? Is the Shape all light intended to be evil or good? And finally, is the poem – which as it stands is deeply pessimistic – really optimistic in conception? These problems are interrelated.

It is sometimes said that for Shelley the personal morality of a poet was irrelevant and that he made a total separation between man and artist. His remark that the poet and the man are two different natures is often cited in evidence,[8] as is the following passage from *A Defence of Poetry*.

Let us assume that Homer was a drunkard, that Virgil was a flatterer, that Horace was a coward, that Tasso was a madman, that Lord Bacon was a peculator, that Raphael was a libertine, that Spenser was a poet laureate . . . Their errors have been weighed and found to have been dust in the balance; if their sins were as scarlet, they are now white as snow: they have been washed in the blood of the mediator and the redeemer, Time.   (*Prose*, p. 295)

But Shelley's edgy, bitter joke about Spenser betrays an unease with this statement, which comes after an assertion that the poet 'ought personally to be the happiest, the best, the wisest, and the most illustrious of men . . . the greatest poets have been men of the most spotless virtue, of the most consummate prudence'. He cuts the argument short with the facile *tu quoque* tactic: 'Judge not, lest ye be judged.'

And offsetting the above quotation are such remarks as this to Peacock: 'Do you think Wordsworth could have written such poetry if he had ever had dealing with moneylenders?'[9] Shelley was certainly attracted by the idea of a simple match between the private life of a poet and the moral value of his work. In this he had for company Milton, who believed that he who hopes to write well 'in laudable things' ought to be 'a true poem, that is, a composition and pattern of the best and honourablest things'.[10] Shelley's uncertainty as to how to deal with examples of disparity between 'the man' and 'the work' shows that this was a problem that bothered him greatly, and one for which, like the problem of how to be angry without sinning, he never found a satisfactory solution. And one of the writers around whom Shelley's uncertainty centred was Rousseau, regarded by him as a poet.

In a letter to his father of February 1811, Shelley argued that ethics were independent of Christianity. He numbered the Deist Rousseau with Hume and Voltaire, men who had been of the 'strictest morality . . . all of whom whilst they lived were the subject of panygeric, were the directors of literature & morality'. He must have been trying to score debating points (or was in for a rude shock), for a letter to Hogg in May shows him well aware of Rousseau's reputation after the *Confessions* were published: 'The Confessions of Rousseau are either a disgrace to the confessor or a string of

falsehoods, probably the latter.'[11] In 1812, echoing Wollstonecraft, he pronounced this judgement: 'Rousseau gave license by his writings to passions
that only incapacitate and contract the human heart. So far hath he prepared
the necks of his fellow beings for that yoke of galling and dishonorable servitude which at this moment it bears.'[12]

Yet in 1815 and 1816 he discovered the Rousseau of *The Rêveries* and *Julie*.
This is the Rousseau of whom he was to write that he 'celebrated the dominion of love, planting as it were trophies in the human mind of that sublimest
victory over sensuality and force'.[13] The second view of Rousseau coexisted
with but never superseded the first, which coexistence gave rise to the question: how could the same man be simultaneously the author of two such
morally different books? Both *The Confessions* and *Julie* lie behind *The
Triumph of Life*, though it is the influence of the second that has received
the greater attention, notably from Reiman.[14]

Clearly, Shelley regarded Rousseau's 'trumpet of a prophecy' as impugned
by the revelations about his private life. Like Hogg he subscribed to the old-
fashioned view, grounded in classical rhetoric, that, in order to persuade, an
author should have *pathos* (emotion), *logos* (rationality), and *ethos* (credibility,
that is, he should be seen as a person fit to urge a certain line of moral conduct). In turn this problem – the relationship between a poet's private life
and his public influence – was bound up with Shelley's own self-
identification with Rousseau.

The tendency towards self-identification was spotted as early as 1860 when
Peacock's correspondent, the former John Cam Hobhouse, suggested that
Shelley had staged the Tanyrallt attack of 1813 in order to imitate the episode
of the stoning of Rousseau's Motiers house in *The Confessions*: 'I have no
doubt that Shelley copied that obscene worthy.'[15] (Shelley, Mary and Claire
visited Motiers during their 1814 Continental excursus.)[16] Be that as it
may, there certainly are some striking parallels. Rousseau and Shelley had
in common certain traits – eccentricity of dress and a love of childish sports
which continued into adulthood. Shelley's paper boats can be matched by
Rousseau's cup-and-ball. Like Rousseau, Shelley lived in a retreat from the
world which he called the Hermitage, and both had a reputation for being
mad. Shelley's renewed interest in 'herborizing' (a Rousseauesque term) in
1821 probably owes as much to Rousseau, a botanist, as to Hogg.[17] In their
defects there were also parallels between the two. One of the most notorious
of Rousseau's pieces of self-incrimination is his account of sending his
children to orphanages. And Shelley was guilty of a similar neglect, for
despite fighting tooth and nail for custody of his children by Harriet, and
supporting them financially, he made no attempt to see either after his elopement with Mary. More excusably, in February 1819 he left Elena Adelaide
in Naples, a child for whom he had undertaken responsibility. Although he
did not intend the abandonment to be permanent, he felt very guilty when

she later died. The *Alastor* poet also bears resemblances to the Rousseau of
the *Rêveries* as, we argued in Chapter 10, does the 'frail form' of *Adonais*.

There are, of course, many respects in which Shelley was not like
Rousseau, the most important being, firstly, the former's feminism and
secondly, the fact that Rousseau's voice really had carried 'contagion to the
world' whereas Shelley, particularly towards the end of his career, increasingly despaired of making any impression at all. But he tried his very best
to be 'contagion': one of the last acts of his life was to help found a journal
which he hoped would give him a voice. Critics have noticed that in *The
Triumph of Life* Rousseau functions as the Spectator's mirror image, and that
there is a strong suggestion that the Spectator is being given the choice of
repeating Rousseau's career. Matthews pointed out that the Narrator (whom
he does not differentiate from the Spectator) begins his trance thus: 'in a conviction of *déjà-vu* . . . what the Spectator is obscurely recollecting in the *déjà-
vu* passage are Rousseau's birth and young manhood as if they were his own:
that is, a metaphor or re-incarnation is used so to emphasise the parallel between their two careers as to suggest virtual identity'.[18] Rousseau says to the
Spectator that 'even thou mayst guess' how he has been brought to the 'dread
pass'. 'Even' has the same ambiguity as the French 'même': 'Even you may
guess, naive dream person that you are and ignorant of history', or 'You are
the very one most likely to intuit the truth (because you are my *alter ego*).'

There is another complication to Shelley's self-identification with
Rousseau. When the decayed Rousseau appears he is mistaken for an 'old
root which grew / To strange distortion out of the hill side' but the Spectator
soon realises his error, and learns that

> . . . the grass which methought hung so wide
> And white, was but his thin discoloured hair,
> And that the holes it vainly sought to hide
>
> Were, or had been, eyes.   (185–8)

Later Rousseau is called a 'cripple'. In creating this figure, Shelley has taken
elements from both Dante's *Inferno* and Spenser's *The Faerie Queene*. From
the former he derived the figure of the blind man imprisoned in the shape
of a gnarled tree; this is the punishment after death of the suicide Pier de
Vigne. As a result of 'the harlot envy', his master, Frederick II, was falsely
persuaded that he had been unfaithful and commanded him to be blinded.[19]
From Spenser come hollow eyes and various elements of the hair. Despair,
whose 'griesie locks, long growen, and unbound, / Disordred hong about his
shoulders round, / And hid his face; through which his hollow eyne / Lookt
deadly dull', attempts by subtle sophisms to persuade the Elfin Knight to
commit suicide (*F.Q.*, I, Canto ix, xxxv). 'The Elfin Knight' was one of
Shelley's sobriquets in the Leigh Hunt circle; in *Alastor* the Poet is both
Elfin Knight and Despair as he peers into the well and sees his wan eyes

through his own thin, faded hair. Rousseau's death was mysterious; as late as 1822 *Blackwood's Edinburgh Magazine* was repeating the rumour that he had committed suicide.[20] In *The Triumph of Life* one of his functions is to persuade the Spectator that the world is a waking hell where everyone either does or suffers wrong; there can be no cure, only oblivion. (This statement will be qualified later, but at this point we are concerned to stress the similarities between Rousseau and Despair.)

But in conflating these two figures, and thus creating a character who may or may not have eyes, Shelley produced something other than the sum of the parts. Rousseau in the poem has terminal syphilis. He is thus an embodiment of the Hollow Ruin that yawns behind Love, and the Terror which succeeded 'Nature's sacred watchwords' – the ideals of the French Revolution. There can be no doubt that this was Shelley's intention. That Rousseau was syphilitic was a notorious accusation made by Voltaire who (Rousseau said) spread the rumour that he was 'worn out with debaucheries, rotten with the pox'.[21] And, one remembers, Rousseau had undergone a period of three weeks in which he was terrified of actually having contracted the disease.

Rousseau indignantly denied Voltaire's charge in the *Confessions*. He declared that he had never contracted the pox and had been assured by a doctor that, owing to a physical malformation, he was incapable of doing so. (Medically speaking, this is less than convincing, especially since Rousseau also claimed to have fathered children.) He insisted that he had always been 'timid and modest as a virgin' – despite admissions elsewhere of lapses from his high ideals. He freely confessed to being diseased, but said that the disease was nephritis caused by a urinary disorder which he claimed to have had from birth. For this condition he had been forced to lay in an enormous stock of bougies at huge expense.[22]

Rousseau closely relates the temperature of his urine to the ardour of his political philosophy. After a violent attack of nephritis during the blazing summer of 1749 when he was walking daily to Vincennes, he received a *coup de foudre*: he read of a competition for a prize essay on the relation between civilisation and morals, and 'beheld another universe and became another man'. Shortly after winning the competition the nephritis struck again. Given six months to live, he 'determined to spend the little time I had . . . in independence and poverty and put all the strength of my soul into breaking the fetters of prejudice, courageously doing what seemed to me right, without in the least worrying what men might think'. The parallel with Shelley's writing of *Queen Mab* in the belief that he had only a few years to live will readily be seen, as well as Shelley's disregard for prudential considerations, not to mention nephritis.

Rousseau's syphilis is obviously the infamous reputation which clings to him after he dies, the 'deep scorn' and the 'dread pass' to which he has been led. (Since there is no possibility of actually meeting the illustrious dead, one can only know their fame or infamy and infer their character from their writings.) The question arises, is the reader meant to consider (for the purposes of the poem at any rate) that the historical Rousseau really was shamefully diseased or is the disease a mere metaphor for calumnies which have been advanced against him?[23]

In favour of the latter, this passage from *A Defence of Poetry* may be cited:

> In the intervals of inspiration, and they may be frequent without being durable, a poet becomes a man and is abandoned to the sudden reflux of the influences under which others habitually live. But as he is more delicately organized than other men and sensible to pain and pleasure, both his own and that of others, in a degree unknown to them, he will avoid the one and pursue the other with an ardour proportioned to this difference. And he renders himself obnoxious to calumny when he neglects to observe the circumstances under which these objects of universal pursuit and flight have disguised themselves in one another's garments.
>
> But there is nothing necessarily evil in this error, and thus cruelty, envy, revenge, avarice, and the passions purely evil have never formed any portion of the popular imputations on the lives of poets.   (*Prose*, p. 296)

It is therefore the passions not purely evil which have been imputed to poets; though the description is sufficiently wide to include bibulousness and excessive love of fame, Shelley is obviously referring here principally to sexual errors. The reference to pleasure and pain disguising themselves in one another's garments recalls the Sixth Spirit's song in *Prometheus Unbound* where the 'best and gentlest' dream visions of aërial joy and call the monster Love, but wake to find its shadow, Pain. A cancelled passage has Rousseau inveighing against a fickle world which dispenses both 'fame and infamy'. He, who had once 'sought both', prizes 'neither now', for he knows how transient reputation is except for the supreme truth-finders:

> I know the place assigned
> To such as sweep the threshold of the fane
> Where truth & its inventors sit enshrined. –
>
> And if I sought those joys which now are pain,
> If he [i.e Voltaire] is captive to the car of life,
> Twas that we feared our labour wd be vain.[24]

This also relates Rousseau to the popular imputations against poets. Realising that he fell short of the rank of the very greatest, he could have chosen to be a doorkeeper at the shrine of truth, but fearing that he might lose both lasting fame and the pleasures of this life, he 'sought the joys which now are pain' – in other words delusive sexual relationships; as the Maniac in *Julian and Maddalo* says 'There is one path / To peace, and that is truth, which follow ye! / Love sometimes leads astray to misery' (347–9). (This is a plausible explanation of a none-too-clear passage, but does not shed much light on whether Rousseau is calumniated or diseased; both may be the results of following Love rather than Truth.)

Again Rousseau says that if the spark with which Heaven had lit his spirit had been supplied with 'purer nutriment' by Earth, 'Corruption would not now thus much inherit / Of what was once Rousseau – nor this disguise / Stained that within which still disdains to wear it' (201–5). There is an alternative uncancelled reading: 'Stained that which ought to have disdained to wear it'. The word 'disguise' is a suitable metaphor for a bad reputation, and either reading could make sense: Rousseau still disdains the infamy which a corrupt society foisted on him, or (alternative reading) ought to have denied calumnies against himself more unequivocally and vigorously, and not to have taken a perverse pride in exaggerating his misdeeds. This last would square with Shelley's remark to Hogg that the *Confessions* were probably 'a string of falsehoods' and, in the cancelled passage, that Rousseau *sought* infamy.

Neither reading, however, takes into account the implication of the spark–nutriment images: that Rousseau himself is corrupt and not merely calumniated. Again, if Rousseau's disguise was merely the creation of malignant tongues, it is difficult to see why Socrates escapes unscarred. Shelley knew very well that Socrates was accused of pederasty; he was grieved to find a notable scholar giving respectability to this slur.[25] Yet Socrates is one of the few who has escaped enchainment to the car of Life, and he is contrasted with Plato, who is still thus bound, owing to his infatuation for a beautiful youth called Aster.

Moreover, the word Shelley uses throughout *The Triumph of Life* is not 'calumny' but 'infamy', which can refer to a merited as well as an unmerited bad reputation or even mean simply 'wickedness'. Nor does Rousseau insist that his situation is entirely the fault of a corrupt society, which one might have expected him to do. On the contrary, he says that he was 'overcome by [his] own heart alone'. Despots, demagogues and sages were defeated by Life. In his case it was his own heart, his 'glowing', poetic, passionate temperament which encompassed his downfall.

He points out 'the great bards of old' – chained to the car who

> 'inly quelled
>
> 'The passions which they sung, as by their strain
>   May well be known: their living melody
> Tempers its own contagion to the vein
>
>   'Of those who are infected with it – I
> Have suffered what I wrote, or viler pain! –
>
>   'And so my words were seeds of misery
> Even as the deeds of others.'   (274–81)

Lines 278–9 originally read 'Of those who hear . . . and so miserable they / Have suffered what they paint, or viler pain!'[26] A likely meaning is that the bards had to suffer both the pain of suppressing passions which they wished to indulge but did not, and, as if that were not pain enough, the 'viler pain' of having imputed to them the acting out of these passions. In changing the wording, Shelley introduced an entirely new thought, setting up a contrast between those bards who 'inly quelled' their passions and Rousseau, who did not. In so doing, he also gave a different twist to 'or viler pain!' Rousseau experienced and suffered what, as a confessional writer, he wrote about: the results of not 'inly quelling' his passions and not sublimating suppressed desires in fiction. In addition he suffered the 'viler pain' not of calumny but of infamy. A further possibility is opened up: that he has also suffered 'viler pain' than he ever wrote about, in other words that confessions were incomplete and his self-exculpations from accusations of being poxed were disingenuous. But the envious malignity of the world would also have played a part in the 'strange distortion'; it could be true, for instance, that Rousseau had suffered in some way from the results of 'impure coition' but that he was not 'rotten with the pox' or 'worn out with debaucheries'. Both lust and envy, then, would have contributed to the 'disguise'. This links the figure of Rousseau not only with Pier de Vigne but also with the diseases associated with Lechery and Envy, two of the Deadly Sins which follow the chariot of Lucifera, Worldly Pride, in *The Faerie Queene* (I, iv, xvi-xxxvi). These diseases are, respectively, syphilis and leprosy, in *The Triumph* blended into one, as in the case of elephantiasis. But what proportion is due to envy and what to lust is one of the poem's 'sequence of carefully constructed uncertainties' (Cronin's phrase).

The 'disguise', therefore, includes truth and falsehood, public self-incriminations and suppressions. It has stained even the spirit within, though the spirit 'disdains' the disguise. Rousseau, in short, feels both guilty and not guilty. His words have been 'seeds of misery' because, unlike the melody of the bards of old which has the kind of control that comes from self-discipline, and adjusts its influence to the nature of the individual reader, Rousseau's writing can infect even untroubled minds with its own unrest, an infection the more insidious because the sources of its power remain partly concealed.

Possibly, too, his words have been 'seeds of misery' because his bad reputation disheartens young revolutionaries who, looking to him as a mentor, discover the truth about his life. Shelley could have had in mind Godwin's early warning to him against publishing spiritual autobiography. It was fitting, Godwin wrote, that certain individuals should record 'all the successive turns and revolutions' of their minds; but to publish one's errors (Godwin was thinking chiefly of intellectual errors) diminished usefulness to mankind, for one lost authority thereby. 'Such a man was Rousseau; but not such a man was Bacon, or Milton.'[27] (Shelley's career can be regarded as an attempt to square Godwin's precept with his own impulses towards self-revelation.)

The 'seeds of misery' are also related to the 'world of agony', which Rousseau admits to having created; this is not merely his personal hell but the 'age of despair' following the French Revolution. Some illumination as to how these two are connected is supplied by the stanzas on Rousseau in Byron's *Childe Harold*, Canto III. Justification for following the risky procedure of using Byron to interpret Shelley is that this canto was written very much under Shelley's influence as a result of the two poets' exploration of the landscape of Rousseau's Clarens in 1816, shortly after the episode of the lady with nipples like eyes.

Byron accuses Rousseau of inciting the oppressed to 'too much wrath'; he and his compeers had overthrown good along with ill, 'leaving but ruins':

> . . . he was phrensied by disease or woe,
> To that worst pitch of all, which wears a reasoning show.
>
> For then he was inspired, and from him came,
> As from the Pythian mystic cave of yore,
> Those oracles which set the world in flame,
> Nor ceased to burn till kingdoms were no more.
>
> (III, lxxx 8–9, lxxxi 1–4)

One notices the similarity of this portrait of Rousseau to that of the errant youth in *Prometheus Unbound*, priest of a dark Apollo, who drinks deep of the maddening oracular vapour and lifts up the contagious voice. Byron's Rousseau has been inspired by 'disease or woe'. (Mania was still thought of as caused by 'vapours' ascending to the brain.) What disease or woe Rousseau was suffering from Byron does not specify; indeed he asks 'Who may know?'[28]

This passage sheds some light on why in *The Triumph of Life* Christ and Socrates are contrasted with Rousseau. Their criticism of society had its sources in service to an impersonal truth, not in a personal grievance against a corrupt society which has provided a passionate heart with opportunities for self-degradation. When someone has declared war on prejudice because of the suffering – woe, disease, or both – resulting from lack of control over his passions, 'the mutiny within', his revolutionary creed will be vitiated by the desire for revenge, which will infect others. (One remembers Godwin's warning 'Shelley, you are preparing a scene of blood!')[29]

The figure of Rousseau we interpret as simultaneously an imaginative reworking of the historical Rousseau and a projection of Shelley's worst fears of what he might prove to be in the fullness of time. The image of the spirit immured in the body of a tree was one which Shelley used elsewhere to describe himself. In 'With a Guitar, To Jane', also written in 1822, Shelley adopts the persona of Ariel: 'And now, alas! the poor sprite is / Imprisoned for some fault of his / In a body like a grave' (37–9). Shakespeare's Ariel was imprisoned in a cloven pine. A sprite would regard any body as a 'grave', and the wistful playfulness of the poem allows the reader to entertain the idea that Ariel, by having to take a mortal form, has been punished for some spritish offence. But the body like a grave also contains the grim and specific reference to Shelley's own mass of infirmities, which, it would seem, have their origin in 'some fault of his'.

The foregoing argument supplies, perhaps, one answer to the question 'Why are politics linked so strongly to lust? Why Rousseau?' We now turn to the Shape all light.

Most critics have puzzled over why the Shape should resemble other figures such as Asia, the Witch of Atlas and Intellectual Beauty (which would make her good) while offering a cup which apparently produces a bad effect on Rousseau, and have variously proposed either that she is definitely good but that Rousseau does not drink her cup out of disobedience or timidity, or that he drinks, is awakened to political consciousness and is then defeated by the enmity of the world towards all reformers. Alternatively, she is definitely bad, 'a type of Rahab, the New Testament Great Whore embodied in the natural world which is a snare for the visionary'.[30]

To resolve this, Reiman proposed that she was good inasmuch as she is a visitant from the Eternal, deceitful when she descends to the sublunary world. More recently, Richard Cronin and Lloyd Abbey have laid stress on the deliberate ambiguity of presentation throughout the poem. Cronin writes that the Shape is one of the 'sequence of carefully constructed uncertainties'; she 'flickers between being an ideal beauty and a Circean temptress'.[31] These interpretations strike us as far more promising, indeed only narrowly to miss the mark. The key to the meaning of the Shape seems to us to lie far back in Shelley's career, with 'Passion':

> Prime source of all that's lovely, good, and great,
> Debasing man below the meanest brute . . .
> Why art thou thus, O Passion?

The Shape all light is a representation of Love, with the sexual element predominating. In fact she could be called Passion, and the matching Shape in the chariot Passion's hideous simulacrum. It is not that in the sublunary world Passion is invariably a cheat, but she possesses a dual character, and her effect on any particular individual is unpredictable. In 1811 Shelley had a ready answer to the problem of Passion's different effects: Custom's chains. In 1822 he was not so sure; the fault might lie with the individual or in the very unfairness of things.

That the Shape bears a strong resemblance to the visionary Being of *Epipsychidion* has often been noted; this is another pointer to the relationship between Rousseau and the writer of *The Triumph of Life*. The chief differences between them can be accounted for by the fact that Shelley drew his symbolic landscape from both the Clarens of *Julie* and Les Charmettes of the *Confessions*. In *Epipsychidion* Shelley encounters the Being in 'the clear golden prime of my youth's dawn', that is to say, at the beginning of adolescence. Words like 'clear', 'golden', and 'dawn' are especially significant, since they recur in his description of the Shape, where they are associated, as in *Epipsychidion*, with passion. In *The Triumph* Rousseau says 'I found myself asleep', 'in the April prime'. (It was in spring that Shelley first encountered Intellectual Beauty.) As Rousseau wakes he finds that he is under a mountain 'which from unknown time / Had yawned into a cavern high and deep' (312–13). From the cavern flows 'a gentle rivulet', the sound of which makes those who hear forget 'All pleasure and all pain, all hate and love, / Which they had known before that hour of rest' (318–20).

Rousseau traces his growth from before birth to the adult state in terms of the advancing day. He distinguishes three stages of his life: a prenatal existence, the nature of which is completely unknown; birth, represented by the mouth of the cavern, which contains a well, the source of life; and an 'hour of rest' – the sleep of infancy and childhood. Wordsworth had said that our birth is but a sleep and a forgetting. Childhood is a prolongation of that sleep, in the course of which all prenatal memories are gradually expunged; it is a half-light state before 'youth's dawn', puberty. The moment that Rousseau found himself asleep in April, then, is the transitional point between boyhood and youth, represented as the moment when awareness that one is asleep is the immediate signal that one is about to awake. Thereafter, the advancing of the day is an advancing in sexual maturity:

> . . . I arose, and for a space
> The scene of woods and waters seemed to keep
>
> 'Though it was now broad day, a gentle trace
>   Of light diviner than the common Sun
> Sheds on the common Earth. . .   (332–9)

With the statement 'it was now broad day', though 'a gentle trace' of diviner light still lingered – one learns that he has reached the fullness of his youthful prime. The stream of time, which has blotted out the memory of his earlier existence, now creates in him a confusion of senses 'all the place / Was filled with mazy sounds woven into one / Oblivious melody, confusing sense' (339–41). It is this state of bewilderment which heralds the appearance of the Shape:

> 'And as I looked, the bright omnipresence
>   Of morning through the orient cavern flowed,
> And the sun's image radiantly intense
>
> 'Burned on the waters of the well that glowed
>   Like gold, and threaded all the forest maze
> With winding paths of emerald fire – there stood

> 'Amid the sun, as he amid the blaze
>   Of his own glory, on the vibrating
> Floor of the fountain, paved with flashing rays

> 'A Shape all light. . .   (343–52)

Rousseau does not directly see the sun. The cavern goes right through the mountain like a sloping tunnel, its axis and the downard tilt of its slope running from east to west.[33] Between the east and west exits of the tunnel is a well, the source of the rivulet flowing out of the cavern. The sun's rays shine through the eastern exit, burn on the waters of the well within the cavern, and light up the green spaces between the trees which then resemble a heavenly jewel. The stars, and any other sources of faint light, would be shielded from the sun's rays by the dark band of the mountain, and therefore still be just visible. Accordingly, the Shape can be associated with both the radiantly intense image of the sun reflected in the well and with these alternative sources of light, all of which contribute their brightness to her. This is of great significance in the symbolism of the poem. Shelley's draft cancellations – 'a hue of unremembered sunrise', 'sweet evening beams' – do not make his intentions clear as to the exact source of the 'gentle trace', but there seems little doubt that he meant it to include the stars – the Wordsworthian echoes support this reading, and the idea of dawn as the moment of equilibrium between the sun and the Morning Star is found elsewhere in Shelley's poetry.[34] This 'gentle trace' presided over the child's 'hour of rest', and may stem from memories of a divine pre-existence, if such it had been.

The sun is a complex image within *The Triumph of Life*, but there can be no doubt that at this point it represents sexual passion. The first rays of the sun turn the waters of Rousseau's cavern to gold. The time of day (early morning) and the season (spring) suggest that this is a first awareness of sexual desire. The well 'that glowed / Like gold', together with the imagery of mountain and dawn, recalls the 'wells' which in *Epipsychidion* symbolise Shelley's hoped-for union with Emily. These, 'the fountains of our deepest life', Shelley anticipates, 'shall be / Confused in Passion's golden purity, / As mountain-springs under the morning sun' (*Epips.*, 570–2).

But the light emanating from the Shape has a more complex meaning and a more specific origin. In lines 411–23, she is associated with Lucifer, the Morning Star, the planet Venus, symbol in Shelley 'of love, or liberty, or wisdom, or beauty, or some other expression of that Intellectual Beauty, which was to Shelley's mind the central power of the world'.[35] These two sources of light, the Sun, symbolising 'Passion's golden purity', and the Morning Star, symbolising the ideal passions of the mind, contain the essential elements of Shelley's definition of Love as a 'universal thirst for a communion not merely of the senses, but of our whole nature; intellectual, imaginative and sensitive' (*Prose*, p. 220). It is from the sun, however, that the Shape derives a 'fierce splendour' (359). This makes her, as Butter points out, not only beautiful but dangerous. She can be Pandemos or Urania, depending upon the experience and wisdom of the person to whom she offers her cup. She is accompanied by another ambiguous figure – Iris, the rainbow, who can be either a 'painted veil', an image of deceit, or a pledge of Eternity's love for the productions of Time.

The Shape descends from the cavern and moves along the stream, becoming as she does so increasingly a part of the material world. Her feet, with 'palms so tender',[36] that 'their tread broke not the mirror of its billow' are reminiscent of the 'soft and busy feet' of Desolation. She

> Glided along the river and did bend her
>
> Head under the dark boughs, till like a willow
>   Her fair hair swept the bosom of the stream
> That whispered with delight to be their pillow. –   (363–6)

Shelley's draft shows that he intended the boughs to be thought of as belonging to willows in bud.[37] The fair hair and the dark boughs mingle, producing the visual effect that the willows have suddenly burst into leaf, and supplying an emblem of the perfect union of earth and sky. (The intertwining of leaves and light is similarly used elsewhere.)[38] Boughs and hair together sweep the stream, which is delighted to be the nuptial couch, a sense reinforced, perhaps fortuitously, by 'pillow'.[39] This perfect harmony is precarious. It corresponds to the passage in *Epipsychidion* where the speaker fails to see the Being because she is 'robed in such exceeding glory', but finds her in objects of nature and poetry and in dream 'whose tremulous floor / Paved her light steps' (190–216).

One of the effects of passion is to overrule and obscure the rational part of the mind, which is what happens to Rousseau as the Shape glides towards him. The movement of her feet seems 'to blot / The thoughts of him who gazed on them'. The gazer's mind seems 'strewn beneath / Her feet like embers'. She 'Trampled its sparks into the dust of death, / As Day upon the threshold of the east / Treads out the lamps of night' (382–90). There is no certainty that she is clearing Rousseau's mind that it may receive revolutionary ideas. She *may* be doing so, but the stress falls on the sexual dazzlement and confusion of the youth. One notes, too, that the 'gentle trace' is now by implication eclipsed.

Rousseau addresses her 'as one between desire and shame / Suspended', an apt description of an adolescent taken unawares by the sexual impulse. 'Desire' and 'shame' correspond to the unruly horse and the modest horse of Plato's Phaedrus, 'shame' meaning modesty here. (Given the type of poem *The Triumph* is, 'shame' also looks forward to the disgrace and self-reproach which will overtake the unwitting Rousseau.) 'Suspended' indicates that this is the moment of balance, Libra in the zodiacal system.

Rousseau asks the Shape to 'Show whence I came, and where I am, and why.' He is now thirsting for an experience which will satisfy his whole nature – sensual, imaginative and intellectual – believing that this will reveal to him the secret of existence. The Shape's only answer is to bid him 'Arise and quench thy thirst', as she holds out 'a crystal glass / Mantling with bright Nepenthe' (358–9):

> 'And as a shut lily, stricken by the wand
>   Of dewy morning's vital alchemy,
>
> 'I rose; and bending at her sweet command
>   Touched with faint lips the cup she raised,
> And suddenly my brain became as sand
>
> 'Where the first wave had more than half erased
>   The track of deer on desert Labrador,
> Whilst the empty wolf, from which they fled amazed
>
> 'Leaves his stamp visibly upon the shore
>   Until the second bursts – so on my sight
> Burst a new Vision never seen before;
>
> 'And the fair Shape waned in the coming light   (401–12)

The 'new Vision' is that of the Chariot of Life.

A cup is a frequent symbol in Shelley for sexual experience, as in *Queen Mab* or *Prometheus Unbound*.[40] The Nepenthe it contains might be synonymous with Love as in *Prometheus Unbound* (III, iv, 163), and it *mantles* like the 'cup of joy' in *Queen Mab*. Love in turn is the same as the panacea, and thus Nepenthe is like the 'strange panacea in a crystal bowl' which the Witch of Atlas offers the elect, and which gives them 'some control / Mightier than life (*Witch*, lxix). But 'nepenthe' also suggests the Circean Nepenthes which turns men into beasts. It is a painkiller which, like opium, can either put to sleep or rouse to a state of high excitement.[41] That Rousseau touched the cup with his lips indicates that he was given the taste for sexual experience to the exclusion of all the other pleasures which form part of 'that profound and complicated sentiment which we call love', and that this extinguished modesty in him. Whether this was due to a defect in Rousseau himself or to the amorality of the Shape who has not proportioned her draught to the strength of the individual who tastes, is unexplained because inexplicable. Events are recorded and the mind creates causal relationships between them. As there are suggestions of Pope's 'A little knowledge is a dangerous thing / Drink deep or taste not', the reader is probably intended to understand that, had Rousseau drunk deep, he might have proved one of the Witch of Atlas' elect. But Rousseau is never given the choice between merely touching the cup and drinking deep. Events occur too quickly for him to make a rational decision.

Rousseau calls himself a 'shut lily', an image of youthful innocence helplessly giving way to a natural instinct, and a precisely beautiful metaphorical description of tumescence.[42] 'Stricken' both suggests the sudden touch of a magic wand and anticipates the disease that will strike Rousseau. The brilliant figure of the waves erasing first the track of deer and then the prints of the wolf is Shelley's final version of Sagittarius pursuing Capricorn. The 'empty wolf' recalls Satan's entry into Milton's Garden of Eden (*P.L.*, IV, 183–7), which will expel Adam and Eve from their bower of bliss. 'Empty' calls up other images of raging sexual appetite, such as 'foodless toads' and 'hyaena lust', and the deer ('some timid animals' in Shelley's draft) evoke the shy yet ardent 'timid lovers' of *The Witch of Atlas*. ('Timid' in Shelley, as often in Latin, is not used pejoratively and recalls Rousseau's insistence that he had been as 'timid as a virgin'.) In *Epipsychidion* these animals correspond to the gentle passions which accompany the Narrator into the forest. There is nothing in itself horrific about likening the mind to sand. (Compare 'the light sand that paves it, consciousness' in *The Sensitive Plant*, I, 105.) It is the barren landscape in which the sand is set and especially what is imprinted on it that are so dreadful. The entire passage corresponds to the flight 'towards the lodestar of my one desire' in *Epipsychidion*. In that poem it was suggested that the Being's withdrawal resulted from the very fierceness of the passion with which she was sought. In *The Triumph* the Shape wanes upon the near-erasure – they never quite vanish – of the traces of 'gentle passions'.

The Shape is eclipsed by the glare of the Chariot of Life, yet does not withdraw altogether. In *Epipsychidion* the narrator in despair hears a voice saying that the phantom which he seeks is beside him, and stumbles in weakness and haste in the forest of life. Similarly, in *The Triumph of Life*, the waning of the Shape causes Rousseau to leave his paradise and rush into the wilderness. The Shape keeps 'its obscure tenour' beside Rousseau's path, and now appears like the Morning Star, unseen during daylight, yet ever present, 'forever sought, forever lost'. Its tendency now is to restrain Rousseau from plunging into the kind of evil which, in Bloom's interpretation, she set up as a snare for the visionary. (This, we think, suggests that Bloom is in the last analysis wrong.) But Rousseau ignores her guiding presence and commits himself to 'that path where flowers never grew' (65) – the thorny wilderness in *Epipsychidion*. The images are of disjunction. Instead of the perfect mingling of flesh and spirit, briefly apprehended as truth, which Shelley insists is what we all desire most, Rousseau (and his condition is representative of an entire Western tradition in its treatment of sexuality), is now polarised between an elusive, disembodied beauty and predatory sensualism.

> me sweetest flowers delayed not long,
> Me not the shadow nor the solitude,

> 'Me not that falling stream's Lethean song,
>   Me, not the phantom of that early form
> Which moved upon its motion, – but among

> 'The thickest billows of the living storm
>   I plunged, and bared my bosom to the clime
> Of that cold light, whose airs too soon deform.   (461–8)

The 'airs' are like the 'killing air' of *Epipsychidion*, and 'too soon' contains the idea of premature ruin.[43]

This passage corresponds, as Reiman demonstrated, to the section in *Julie* where Saint-Preux, exiled from Julie and his Eden in Clarens, plunges into the excesses of Parisian life – '*le torrent*'. The word 'plunge' is used elsewhere in Shelley to describe the sexual degradation of the victim of a vicious society, which either condones catamitism, as in decadent Rome, or forces 'almost every youth of England' to endure intercourse with a diseased prostitute.[44] It seems to us likely that Shelley intended the reader to pick up a very specific allusion here. ('Thickest billows' suggests a particularly gross experience.)

The Parisian section in *Julie* includes one of the classic analyses of how a modest young man may so far forget himself as to visit a brothel while continuing to cherish the ideals of virtuous love. Saint-Preux, lured to a brothel in all innocence, congratulates himself upon his immunity to gross pleasure once he realises his predicament; he is fortified by his superior morality and thoughts of Julie. Shocked at daring to think of her in such a place, he 'veils' her image. This is his undoing. His guiding star absent, he allows himself to get drunk and on regaining consciousness finds himself in the arms of a 'creature'.[45] (The similarity to the episode in *Zastrozzi* where Verezzi, his Julia absent, succumbs to Matilda in a swoon, suggests that Shelley knew of the *Julie* episode long before he read the book entire.) What is psychologically so acute about Rousseau's treatment of the scene is that the reader can penetrate beyond Saint-Preux' self-excuses and see that it is the very image of the idealised absent beloved which initially provokes his lust and then, when dispelled, allows him to abandon self-control.[46] The deformation of Rousseau in *The Triumph of Life*, then, while not confined to his sexual behaviour, is inextricably bound up with it. He is not a libertine but someone who loathes libertinism, a man of the most exquisitely organised sensibility, whose very capacities for the highest idealism and the most refined pleasure encompass his degradation; an object fit to prompt the Spectator's despairing thought 'why God made irreconcilable / Good and the means of good' (230–1).

Rousseau joins the dance but this is not the end of his experience. And this leads us to consideration of whether the poem is 'optimistic' or 'pessimistic'. On the one hand critics like Butter believe that 'It offers no hope of an improvement in the human condition on the earth. Life is shown as almost inevitably corrupting; the only way to escape the contagion is, like Christ and

Socrates, voluntarily to accept death.' Others have seen the fragment as a prelude to a probable 'Triumph of Love'. It has been pointed out that many of the features of this dance of death contain the potential for renewal – there is a flower-strewn path to which some dancers may find their way; the charioteer's eyes may be unbandaged; from the old root a sapling may spring. Bacon, typifying the fusion of poetry and science, is neither martyr nor captive.[47]

We are inclined towards optimistic readings for the reasons that follow. Rousseau detaches himself from the dance. He is no longer the thrall of lust. Immediately after his plunge into the 'living storm', before the chariot has reached the opposite side of the valley, he observes 'a wonder worthy of the rhyme' of Dante who returned from his wanderings through Hell and Heaven with the story of 'How all things are transfigured, except Love' (476): he sees the grove grow dense with dim, misshapen forms which throng around all conditions of men.

He makes a hideous discovery which has for him an authenticity equivalent to Dante's experience of hell. He becomes 'aware' that the shadows belong to the dancers themselves. Their youth and beauty fall from them like masks, leaving 'the action and the shape without the grace'. Out of these beautiful masks the chariot 'creates' hideousness – the grotesque phantoms which swarm around the varieties of human tyranny, and which are, in fact, projections of the inward natures of the wicked. The phantoms are made out of the degradation of youth and beauty by sensualism: the examples culminate in those forms which

> like discoloured flakes of snow
> On fairest bosoms and the sunniest hair
> Fell, and were melted by the youthful glow
>
> Which they extinguished; for like tears they were
> A veil to those from whose faint lids they rained
> In drops of sorrow.   (509–14)

The 'discoloured flakes' combine the ideas of coldness and impurity; the suggestion is that they melt into tears, leaving a residue behind to obscure the rapturous gleams of youthful instinct. For Matthews these lines evoked specifically 'the tainted conventions of chastity', predicated upon an institutionalised prostitute class.[48] Certainly the general effect is to make Rousseau's 'becoming aware' culminate in the discovery that tyrants are the products and perpetuators of a society based on an ethic of sexual exploitation. To interpret society is, of course, not enough; the thing is to reform it, and Rousseau has been unable to do this. Nevertheless, his 'awareness' counts for something; he becomes a blind seer who can diagnose evil. Therein lie the seeds of spiritual gain for others, and possibly his own eventual redemption by Time.

Other indications of an optimistic conception lie in the numerous hints that Love is unconquerable. Rousseau would seem to offer the Spectator three choices. He can follow the 'thirst of knowledge' and thus risk repeating Rousseau's history, though Rousseau does imply that the Spectator might in the end achieve a greater understanding of the secret of existence than he has done. (This may be ironic, however.)[49] He can commit suicide. Rousseau, inasmuch as he seems to be Despair personified, is luring the Spectator towards this with an implicit reminder that 'The lenger life, I wote the greater sin, / The greater sin, the greater punishment' (*F.Q.*, I, ix, 43). Or, remembering that Una saved the Elfin Knight, the Spectator might escape to a retreat, a green isle or Earthly Paradise where he may ward off the poisonous arrow of the world's scorn (something that Shelley always required of the women he loved) and recover health of body and mind, with the prospect of returning strengthened to the world, a Prospero rather than an Ariel. Rousseau, like Dante's Virgil, might have been replaced by a guide of a different kind: instead of the decayed old man, a fair womanly form like Dante's Matilda, tutelary guardian of the Earthly Paradise, an apotheosis of Jane Williams.

There is a model for such a creation of hope out of the wreckage in 'Lines Written among the Euganean Hills'. Had Shelley drowned leaving the poem unfinished at the lines 'Tis a bitter woe / That love or reason cannot change / The despot's rage, the slave's revenge' (234-6), his overall intentions would be as much a matter for debate as those that inspired *The Triumph of Life*.[50] Since he did finish it, one knows that the mood of despair is lived through; the poet experiences a glorious vision of noon, and ends facing the Evening Star. His pain returns, yet his interlude on the hill, a 'green isle' in the sea of misery, has brought him a respite and kindled hopes of finding a refuge from 'passion, pain and guilt' and of the world growing young again.

The poet's stance is very similar in *The Triumph*. Both poems begin with sunrise and unhappiness; both place the poet on a green hill overlooking a plain which is compared to the sea or is the sea itself. There are therefore grounds for conjecturing that *The Triumph* would have continued to develop a similar structure to 'The Euganean Hills' and finished at dusk with the Poet ending his day in the smile of the planet Venus. Dante's assertion that 'all things are transfigured except love' is another pointer, as is the reference to Venus' light being like a jonquil, or

> the soft note in which his dear lament
> The Brescian shepherd breathes, or the caress
> That turned his weary slumber to content.　　　　(421-3)

Reiman felt that these lines tempered Rousseau's assertion that the world was a living hell.[51] There is a particular felicity in the fact that the shepherd is Brescian, and offers comfort to a syphilitic, for the former is an exorcism of a compound ghost of two characters in *Syphilis*, one a shepherd, the other a Brescian, the two young men in Fracastor's poem who caught the disease through pride rather than wickedness. Weary of pasturing his sheep in the heat of the Dog Star, Syphilus impiously complained against the Sun God and was punished. 'He first knew sleepless nights, whilst his limbs were wracked with pain.'[52] Rousseau's shepherd also sings 'I am weary of pasturing my sheep' ('Stanco di pascolar le pecorelle', the Brescian national air which Mary identified with the 'dear lament'). But his tiredness is met with a caress; he fulfils the angel's command to Adam 'Be strong, live happy and love.'

The last words of the poem may be referring back to the shepherd. They are 'Happy those for whom the fold / Of . . .' To Reiman the word 'fold' recalled yet another name for the planet Venus – the shepherd's Folding Star.[53] 'Fold' also suggests a safe enclosure, a magic circle. This star might herald the point where the cycle of regeneration is about to begin by entering the Ram, 'the true talisman of Oromazes'. (Vestigial allusions to Newton's Zodiac are scattered throughout *The Triumph*. Water lilies: the lotus, the Shape herself: Virgo, the Lion, the scales and the predatory hunt – all are present.)

The direction of our argument should be clear: that in identifying himself with a morally flawed poet (Rousseau) rather than an unflawed one (Keats) Shelley had found a way of admitting a measure of guilt without public self-incrimination. Thornton Hunt was surely wrong in supposing that Shelley would have spoken more plainly but for his 'idealism'. The example of Rousseau was a sufficient warning against self-revelation of anything discreditable in the life of one claiming to be a 'director of literature and morality'.

So ends our investigation. It is unsatisfactory to be thus inconclusive, as there are consequences for the portrait of Shelley the man which depend on whether or not one considers that he believed himself to have been at some time metaphorically or literally infected with venereal disease. That one or other was the case it seems difficult to deny. If the former, he allowed a metaphor to engage with his life to a degree greater than anyone has yet ventured to suggest; like his Hamlet he confused his mental with his physical life to the extent that hideous imaginings seemed to externalise themselves as actual disease, an example of Susan Sontag's argument that for the Romantics hidden passions came to be considered as the source of illness.[54] If the latter, then the reverse process operated: a threat of bodily disease was transmuted into a psychological malady. But we are very far from regarding this book as closing the subject; evidence may yet come to light which could sway the balance of probability one way or another. One area, for instance, not explored by us, is the possibility that Thornton Hunt recorded the source of his 'accidental' discovery. Knowledge of this could reveal either a flaw in his reasoning or give support to the authenticity of his claim.

Shelley's horror of impurity, often regarded as typical of unhealthy nineteenth-century attitudes towards sexuality, does not seem quite so easy to patronise in the summer of 1985 when predictions are being made that AIDS could prove to be the most virulent epidemic disease since the Black Death,[55] and directives against casual sexual intercourse with anyone from London give a contemporary slant to the image of the city as a contaminant. One is entitled to hope that by the time this book is published fears may have proved vastly exaggerated, and partly to have been generated by newspaper sensationalism; in the meantime, while doctors work to produce a vaccine, writers advise society that promiscuity at a time like this is highly irresponsible, something which Shelley would not have gainsaid, believing as he did that a regard for chastity, a word to which he gave his own gloss, was always a good habit to cultivate.[56] It is also at a time like this that one understands better the pressures culminating in Victorian revulsion against Regency license, of which Shelley was rightly seen by Jeaffreson to have been in a sense a forerunner. The younger generation, though, unlike Shelley, turned away 'from the groves of enlightenment and gracious living to the prison of narrow conventionality and repression' and created a society in which the figure of E. B. Impey, weighed down with infirmities and losing his mind at the end, confessing to Charles MacFarlane that his had been a 'misled, idling, vacant, wasting existence', stood as the embodiment of Shelley's Time, the repentant libertine, looking back and shuddering at his younger years.[57] But then Shelley's real fight was with *l'infâme*, a belief system which saw disease as necessary, a scourge to goad mankind into righteousness, a merited chastisement which might be tempered, but never abolished.[58]

Notes

Where not specified, the place of publication is London.

Preface

1. J. C. Shairp, *Aspects of Poetry* (Oxford U.P., 1881), p. 180.
2. *The Collected Works of Walter Bagehot*, ed. Norman St John-Stevas (8 vols., 1965–74), I, p. 475.
3. The *Shelley Concordance* gives over 135 occurrences of *poison, venom, pollute* and their cognates. (However these can be more than matched by entries for *light*.)
4. Matthews, 'Volcano's Voice', p. 192.
5. Massey, p. 2.

1. The antient infirmity

1. Wolfe, II, p. 156.
2. A lecture course and a series of tours each cost twenty guineas; though presumably Shelley's abortive training cost him nothing, thanks to his habit of not paying for services in advance, eventually the question of payment would have arisen. Information from Dr Irvine Loudon; *Letters*, I, p. 121: 'I am now as poor as a rat . . . I still remain firm in my resolve to study . . . you will see that I shall.'
3. *Letters*, I, p. 144.
4. James Gillman, *The Life of Samuel Taylor Coleridge* (1838), p. 23.
5. Medwin, p. 136.
6. *Prose*, p. 350.
7. Medwin, p. 235.
8. *Mary Shelley's Journal*, p. 27, 167n; *Letters*, II, pp. 433–4; Medwin, p. 192; T. Hunt, p. 187. See also *Rossetti Papers*, p. 240.
9. See e.g. White (still the standard biography), I, pp. 468, 543; and Wolfe, I, p. 335.
10. *Rossetti Papers*, p. 502.
11. Rossetti, *Diary*, p. 26.
12. Trelawny, p. 181.
13. *Rossetti Papers*, p. 235.
14. ibid., pp. 375–6; Norman, p. 223; Rossetti, I, pp. clxxviii–clxxix.
15. Norman, p. 170. An outside possibility is that the accidental discovery was made in some way through the marriage of Thornton's brother to Jane Williams' daughter, a marriage opposed by Hogg and Jane on health grounds among others. According to Trelawny, the brother 'was a bad lot, who infected his wife with venereal complaints more than once' (Rossetti, *Diary*, p. 145); Winifred Scott, *Jefferson Hogg* (1951), p. 240.
16. Dowden, I, p. 76.
17. John Cordy Jeaffreson, *The Real Shelley* (2 vols., 1885), pp. 260–1.
18. He speculated that Shelley had a 'romance' with a Miss Burton at Oxford. White showed that Miss Burton was an elderly blue stocking; G. M. Matthews, in a conversation with Derek Guiton, pointed out that the 'favourite' in the book of

reminiscences on which Peck based his inference was a pear tree, not a woman.

19. Richard Holmes, ed., *Shelley on Love*, p. 205.
20. Cameron, pp. 56–7.
21. *Letters*, II, p. 317. See also Pope, 'To Ld. Hervey & Lady Mary Wortley', 'Poor Sapho you grow grey, / And sweet Adonis – you have lost a tooth.'
22. *Last Man*, pp. 179, 196, 289.
23. White, II, p. 564. Leigh Hunt's delicate position vis-à-vis Sir Percy – he received a pension from him – made it difficult for him to be frank.
24. Wolfe, I, p. 335.
25. ibid., p. ix.
26. Quoted in Norman, p. 96.
27. Wolfe, I, pp. 150–3.
28. *Claire*, p. 54.
29. Wolfe, II, p. 38.
30. ibid., pp. 6, 7; this is obviously the incident alluded to by William Bengo Collyer in his review of *Queen Mab*; 'Yes, we ourselves have heard him [Shelley's atheistic 'wretched friend and co-adjutor'] avow, to the disgust of a large assembly – that the only thing worth living for, is the sensual enjoyment in which man participates with brute!' Quoted in *Shelley, Crit. Her.* p. 92.
31. Today Cranbourne Alley is a malodorous passage without *ton* or bonnet-shops.
32. Cary, I, p. 206. See Byron: 'I cannot view my *Paradise* / Without a wish to *enter there*' and marginalium, quoted by McGann, 'Child Harold's Monitor' in D. H. Reiman, M. C. Jaye and B. T. Bennett, eds., *The Evidence of the Imagination* (New York U.P., 1978), p. 287.
33. Quoted by E. J. Lovell Jr in *Captain Medwin* (1963), pp. 101–2.
34. ibid.; Trelawny, pp. 86–7.
35. Wolfe, I, pp. 24, 147–8; Jeaffreson shrewdly guessed that Shelley's account of meeting his tutor was a 'smoking'. See *The Real Shelley* (note 17) I, p. 169; Wolfe, I, p. 70.
36. Wolfe, I, pp. 139–40, 160, 133–4.
37. Clough's *Epilogue to Dipsychus* dramatises this generation gap.
38. *The Novels of Thomas Love Peacock*, ed. David Garnett (1948), pp. 653, 578; Marilyn Butler was the first to point out this change; the above interpretation, however, is ours.
39. Buchanan, p. 108.
40. Wolfe, II, p. 314.
41. See William B. Ober M.D., '*Boswell's Clap*' *and other Essays* (Southern Illinois U.P., 1979). Very likely Byron's kidney problems in 1812 had something to do with his previous contractions of gonorrhoea.
42. See Morton, *Gonorrhoea*, pp. 1–5; Bell, II, p. 234; Astruc (1770), Chapters I–IV. Gum elastic bougies are still used for strictures. See Catterall, p. 35.
43. See Morton, *V.D.*: Schofield; Willcox; 'Venereal Diseases' in *Encycl. Brit.* (1973); Catterall, pp. 87–132, 149–66; Willcox, *Progress in Venereology* (1953), p. 126.
44. *MPJ*, XII (1804), 414.
45. ibid., p. 505.
46. Quoted in Roger L. Williams, *The Horror of Life* (Chicago and London, 1980), p. 13.
47. *F. Q.*, I, Canto iv, xxvi, line 8.
48. Trelawny, p. 87.

49. *LBLJ*, I, 158; II, 46; VI, 14.
50. *Boswell's London Journal*, ed. Frederick A. Pottle (Yale and London, 1950), pp. 155–6, 198.
51. Professor Hufeland of Jena U., *A Treatise on the Art of Prolonging Life*, quoted in *MPJ*, I (1799), 262; Lawrence, p. 56. The 'pox joke' could take the form of the tortuous pun, a specimen of which has been preserved in Coleridge's marginal note on 'Small Wit' in Robert Southey and S. T. Coleridge, *Omniana*, ed. Robert Gittings (1969), p. 71 n.

> Two nobles in *Madrid* were straddling side by side
> Both shamefully diseased; espying whom, I cried –
> What *figures* these men make! The wight, that Euclid cons,
> Sees plainly that they are – Parallel o'*pippy* Dons!

'Spanish Pip' was one of the Jacobean names for syphilis; see *OED*, 'pip'.
52. Gronow, pp. 114–15.
53. Crabbe, *The Village*, II, lines 52–4.
54. 'London' in *Songs of Experience* and *Auguries of Innocence*.
55. Cooper, p. 476.
56. Quoted in Robert Gittings, *John Keats* (1968), p. 237; *London Guide*, pp. 121–2; *Claire*, p. 139.
57. Hutchinson, p. 808; note to *Peter Bell the Third*, Hutchinson, p. 351 n.; *Prose*, p. 223; Bod. MS Shelley adds. e. 11, p. 73; L. Hunt, p. 213.
58. Wolfe, II, p. 313; T. Hunt, p. 193.
59. Especially after essays such as Edward Bostetter's 'Shelley and the Mutinous Flesh' in *Texas Studies in Literature and Language*, I (1959), and the work of Cameron and Brown.
60. For some posthumous diagnoses, see L. J. Moorman, *Tuberculosis and Genius* (Chicago, 1940), pp. 192–234; A. A. Moll, 'Shelley the Invalid', *New York Medical Journal*, CX (1919), 940–1; H. St J. Vertue, 'The Tragedy of Shelley', *Guy's Hospital Reports*, XCV (1946), 65. Many early twentieth-century posthumous diagnoses of syphilis in famous men (e.g. Beethoven, Manet, Nietzsche) have recently been shown to be dubious.
61. *Zoonomia*, IV, p. 107; Astruc (1770), p. 212.
62. Brown, pp. 210–11; this conjecture was arrived at independently by Derek Guiton in his doctoral thesis, 'Shelley's Interest in Medicine' (U. of Sheffield, 1979), using slightly different reasoning.

2. From natural magic to natural science: Eton 1804–10

1. James Lind, 'Copy of a letter to the late Thomas Pennant Esq. of Downing on Typhus Fevers' (Windsor, 1803); Letter to Dr Batty, *MPJ*, XIII (January–June, 1805), 574–5. The latter has not hitherto been noted.
2. See *Q.M.*, Notes, Hutchinson, p. 834, citing Sir George Mackenzie's *Travels in Iceland*, 1811; *DNB*; W. G. Bebbington, 'A Friend of Shelley: Dr James Lind', *Notes and Queries*, new series VII (1960), 83–93; Desmond King-Hele, 'Shelley and Dr Lind', *KSMB*, XVIII (1967), 1–6; W. J. Hooker, 'Sir Joseph Banks' lost Iceland diary', quoted in *Journal of a Tour in Iceland in the Summer of 1809* (2 vols. 1813), II, pp. 116–17; Wolfe, I, p. 93.
3. Grabo quotes Cavallo extensively but seems not to have used this correspondence (BL MSS adds. 22897–8).

4. See A. M. D. Hughes, *The Nascent Mind of Shelley* (1947), pp. 26–9; Mr Patrick Strong, Keeper of College Library and collections, Eton College, Windsor (private communication); Desmond King-Hele, 'Erasmus Darwin's Influence on Shelley's Early Poems', *KSMB*, XVI (1965), 26–8; Wolfe, I, p. 33; Medwin, p. 37; *Letters*, I, p. 303. Donald Reiman has drawn our attention to Lind's correspondence with Benjamin Franklin.

5. Trelawny, p. 51.

6. *DNB*; Lind to Sherwill, 31 October 1810, in *S. & C.*, II, p. 636.

7. Cartwright, pp. 49–67.

8. ibid., pp. 54, 68; H. W. Piper, *The Active Universe* (1962), pp. 25–8.

9. 'Sketch of the Life and Doctrines of the late Dr John Brown of Edinburgh', *EMSJ*, III (1807), 499–502; 'An Account of the Chief Peculiarities of the Brunonian System', *MPJ*, I (1799), 125–6; ibid., X (1804), 181–2.

10. Cartwright, pp. 83, 103–12, 121.

11. BL MS adds. 22898, fols. 43, 47, 67, 69, 9; Cavallo, pp. 150–3; *Letters of Erasmus Darwin*, ed. D. King-Hele (Cambridge U.P., 1981), p. ix, 192.

12. Beddoes, *Notice of Some Observations made at the Pneumatic Institution* (1799), p. 6.

13. *Encycl. Brit.* (1911), article on 'Venereal Diseases'; *Reece*, VII (1822), 253; Trotter, pp. 44–5; Owsei Temkin, 'Therapeutic Trends and the Treatment of Syphilis before 1900', *Bulletin of the History of Medicine* (1955), 309–16; Beddoes, *Communications respecting the external and internal use of Nitrous Acid* (1800), p. vii; 'Sketch of the Progress of Medicine', *MPJ*, XXVI (1811), 27–8 (presumably by William Royston).

14. See letter from the Surgeon to the Society for the Relief of the Ruptured Poor in *Reece*, I (1816), 124.

15. See William Blair, *Essays on the Venereal Disease* (1798), pp. 13, 21n., 33, 46; *MPJ* (1812), 318. Blair was a surgeon of the London Lock Hospital and a critic of Beddoes. Doctors·used both nitric and what they called nitrous or 'fuming nitric acid'. See Davy, III, pp. 5–25, for a contemporary discussion on the difficulties of defining nitrous acid.

16. *Some Letters upon the Application of the Nitric Acid to Medicine from the Bombay Courier* (Bombay, 1797), p. 32. The letters are unsigned, but are known to be Scott's.

17. The attitude of the medical profession towards syphilis ranged from the indulgent ('the fruit of an unguarded moment') to the censorious. Parr's *London Medical Dictionary* hoped that its information as to how the 'fatal effects of a momentary deviation from the path of virtue' might be obviated would not hold out 'encouragement to vice' (entry 'Gonorrhoea'). The venereologist Swediaur reproached prejudiced doctors for behaving like instruments of the vengeance of God, deliberately allowing their patients to suffer, but added that this was not generally the case in London and Paris. Swediaur, *Comp. Treat.*, I, p. 108. Smollett's *Roderick Random* (1748) exhibits a similar matter-of-fact attitude.

18. Beddoes, *Reports principally Concerning the Nitrous Acid in the Venereal Disease* (Bristol, 179 7), p. 100; *A Collection of Testimonies Respecting the Treatment of the V — D — by Nitrous Acid* (1799); Robert Thornton, *The Philosophy of Medicine* (1796), II, p. 29.

19. See Nicholson, V, entry 'Nitric Acid'; Murray, I, p. 237; 'Anti-Syphilitic properties of Nitric Acid' in *Reece*, II (1817), 746.

20. BL MS adds. 22898, fol. 65.
21. *Letters*, I, p. 319.
22. Mary Shelley, *Frankenstein* (1818), ed. Peter Fairclough (Harmondsworth, 1963), p. 308; Walker contains a strikingly similar idea (p. 139).
23. For a pioneering essay on the subject, see Elizabeth Ebeling, 'A Probable Paracelsian Element in Shelley', *Studies in Philology*, XXXII (1935), 508–25; see E. J. Holmyard, *Alchemy* (Harmondsworth, 1957), p. 170; Swediaur, *Comp. Treat.*, II, p. 37, which cites the *Magna Chirurgia*; Hayter, pp. 22, 29.
24. See *The Archidoxes of Magic*, tr. Turner (1655), reprint (London and New York, Askin, 1976); Cameron, *Young Shelley*, p. 320.
25. See for instance Bell, I, pp. 23–8; Abraham Tucker, quoted in Male, p. 184; Allen G. Debus, *The Chemical Philosophy* (New York, 1977), II, pp. 547–53.
26. See M. S. Staum, *Cabanis* (Princeton, 1980); H. W. Piper, *The Active Universe* (1962), p. 1. Isaac Newton himself tried to accommodate Renaissance natural magic to rationalist natural science and made many alchemical experiments.
27. Royston, 'Hints for a Medical Topography of Great Britain', *MPJ*, XXI (January–June 1809), 3.
28. Medwin, pp. 49–50.
29. *Letters*, I, pp. 302–3.
30. For *Sadak the Wanderer*, see *The Complete Poetical Works of Percy Bysshe Shelley*, ed. Neville Rogers (5 vols. projected, Oxford U.P., 1972–   ), I, p. 20; Trelawny, p. 130.
31. Wolfe, I, p. 24.
32. Wolfe, I, p. 197; Rossetti, I, p. xlivn.
33. See, for instance, Wolfe, II, p. 336n.; *Letters*, I, p. 572, clearly describing the effects of laudanum; ibid., II, pp. 313–14.
34. Trelawny, p. 51; Thomas J. Pettigrew, 'Alexander Philip Wilson Philip', *Medical Portrait Gallery: Biographical Memoirs of Famous Physicians and Surgeons* (4 vols. in 2, 1840), III, p. 3 (of the Philip memoir); Hunter, p. 534.
35. Wolfe, I, pp. 35–6.
36. White, I, pp. 542, 742; Wolfe, II, p. 314.
37. Hutchinson, pp. 156–7.
38. *Zoonomia*, II, p. 273; Hunter, pp. 559, 524; Woodville, II, p. 385; *LBLJ*, I, 158. For a general view of opium, see Hayter.
39. The blisters on Shelley's face and hands following the 'blowing up' episode would have disguised any syphilitic rashes, real or supposed.
40. William Cowper to the Rev. John Newton, 27 November 1784; Brown, pp. 210–11 and n.
41. Thomas Beddoes, *Hygeia, or Essays Moral and Medical on the Causes Affecting the Personal State of our Middling and Affluent Classes* (Bristol, 1802), I, p. 76.
42. *Gentleman's Magazine*, LXVII (1798), 95, 282–6, 383–4.
43. Garnett's version (*Prose*, p. 359) is not reliable.
44. *Letters*, I, p. 11.
45. ibid., p. 12.
46. *Letters*, I, pp. 412, 414; Partridge, *A Dictionary of Slang and Unconventional English*, 3rd edn (1949), p. 421.
47. *Zastrozzi*, pp. 91–100. The Gregg/Archive and the 1955 Golden Cockerel edition both used an 1810 text and remarked on the missing Chapter VII. But the 1977 Arno Press facsimile, which also used an 1810 text, 'omitted' Chapter IX. This

shows that the 'omissions' were deliberate. It must have been at Shelley's request that some copies 'omitted' Chapter VII – the ones destined for his intimates – and that others 'omitted' the irrelevant Chapter IX as a blind. He made a similar special request with the *Margaret Nicholson* volume (*Letters*, I, p. 23).

48. *London Guide*, pp. 121–33 remarks on the wholesome and well-educated appearance of Regency prostitutes, contrasting them with those of thirty years earlier; Ronald Pearsall, *The Worm in the Bud* (Harmondsworth, 1969), pp. 326–30; L. Hunt, pp. 183–4.

49. White, I, p. 562; *St Irvyne*, pp. 116, 134, 202; *The Monk*, ed. Howard Anderson (Oxford, 1973), pp. 433, 441.

50. *Esdaile*, p. 306.

51. Buxton Forman, III, pp. 158–71.

52. Medwin, p. 58–9; *The Edinburgh Review*, XXV (1808), 240, gives her poems as a new publication in its July to October list; *Letters*, I, p. 129. 'Cold are the Blasts' (*Esdaile*, p. 129), which refers to Penmanmawr in Denbighshire where Felicia lived and Medwin visited, may date from this experience.

53. *Letters*, I, p. 4; Wolfe, I, p. 27.

54. Medwin, p. 39.

55. *Letters*, I, p. 348.

56. *S. & C.*, II, p. 526. 'I am afraid Mr Shelley won't ask us to Field Place this Summer—'

57. *Letters*, I, pp. 7–8.

58. Medwin, p. 68; *LBLJ*, see Chapter 1, n. 49; Hunter, p. 24; Astruc (1770), pp. 3, 23–6; Swediaur, *Comp. Treat.*, II, pp. 55, 58; advertisement in *Jackson's Oxford Journal* (1 May 1811); Parr, entry 'Gonorrhoea'.

59. *Letters*, II, p. 438.

60. *S. & C.*, II, pp. 482–92; Wolfe, II, p. 153.

3. Arsenic and aquafortis: Oxford 1810–11

1. E.g. White, I, pp. 107, 595–6.

2. MWS, 'Note on *Queen Mab*', Hutchinson, p. 836.

3. Wolfe, I, pp. 87–8.

4. See Browning's 'notorious gaffe', *Pippa Passes*, Epilogue, 96.

5. Wolfe, I, pp. 214, 235.

6. *Letters*, I, pp. 86–7.

7. *Prose*, p. 346.

8. *Sharpe*, I, p. 442.

9. ibid., I, p. 445.

10. ibid.

11. Cary, II, p. 155; I, p. 42; Anon., *The Lyre of Lord Byron*, *c*. 1840, p. 5.

12. J. G. Lockhart, *Reginald Dalton* (3 vols., Edinburgh, 1823), II, pp. 51–2. See also White, I, p. 596.

13. Thomas Moore's poetry, mild stuff to modern tastes, was severely censured for immorality. See *The Edinburgh Review*, VIII (1806), 456–65. See Cameron, p. 223; Brown, p. 248; Shelley read the poem to Lydia in *Kisses, being an English Translation or the Basia of Joannes Secundus Nicolaius* (1803), tr. J. Nott, and in Good's *Lucretius*, for he used both to compose Francis' song.

14. Hogg's italics, reproduced by Medwin, but not by Wolfe.

15. *Letters*, I, p. 23.
16. *Crit. Her.*, pp. 49, 53; White, I, pp. 589–90.
17. *Sharpe*, II, p. 204.
18. Hutten, p. 10; Paracelsus, I, p. 269; Chambers, entry 'Arsenic'.
19. W. Buchan, *Observations concerning the Prevention and Cure of the Venereal Disease . . .* with *Supplement* by Dr Buchan Jnr, 3rd edn (1803), pp. lv–lvi.
20. See Sir William Jones Memorial Number, *British Bulletin of the School of Oriental and African Studies*, 1946; Garland Cannon, *Oriental Jones* (1964); *University College Record* (1954–5), 81. For an Indian assessment, see S. N. Mukerjee, *Sir William Jones* (Cambridge, 1968). *Letters*, I, pp. 343–4, 373. Impey senior, a member of the Sussex gentry, had an observatory at Uckfield to which he invited Cavallo to observe the comet of 1807 (BL MS adds. 22898, fol. 83). In writing to the son, Sharpe was making free with Shelley's good name in the Shelley family's own heartland.
21. W. R. Dawson, ed., *The Banks Letters: a Calendar of the Manuscript Correspondence* (1958), pp. 55, 275, 479–80, 541–3, 705.
22. Wolfe, I, p. 76. Southey's notes to *Thalaba* contain a citation of Jones and those to *The Curse of Kehama* fifteen.
23. Jones, IV, pp. 367–9.
24. In Oxford after around 1807 there was a notable publicist for arsenic as a treatment in chronic rheumatism, which was one of the 'ailments' that could follow either venereal disease. This was a Dr Jenkinson, who used Fowler's solution, a development of the 'tasteless ague drop'. See John Jenkinson and Edward Hardman, *Facts determining the Efficacy of Fowler's Mineral solution in Chronic Rheumatism* (Manchester, 1805); *MPJ*, XVIII (1807), 252; XIX (1808), 477; *Pharmacopeia Londiniensis* (1809), p. 113.
25. Wolfe, I, p. 58; II, p. 38. Chapters 3–8 of Hogg's 1858 *Life* repeat his 1832 articles; Rossetti, I, p. xliv.
26. See James Evier, *A History of Pharmacy* (1937), p. 131.
27. George Nesse Hill, 'Observations on the Use of Arsenic', *EMSJ*, VI, 55–6.
28. For 'Actual Cautery' in syphilis, see Fracastor, p. 115; Astruc (1770), p. 274.
29. Grabo, p. 193; 'Diana's Trees' uses silver and mercury. The seven-shilling piece or third-guinea of Geolge III's reign is listed as a gold coin in Seaby's catalogue.
30. For a specimen of Medwin's handwriting, see Medwin, facsimile plate facing p. 504. Volume II of Medwin's 1847 *Life* contains an errata slip, which suggests that some sort of proof-checking took place. For a comparable case in Newby's publishing, see editorial notes to the Penguin English Library edition of Anne Brontë's *The Tenant of Wildfell Hall*.
31. Wolfe, I, p. 58; Cartwright, p. 42; its use as a euphoric was not reported until 1817. See Polidori, 18 June 1816.
32. Cavallo, *An Essay on the Medicinal properties of Factitious Airs* (1798), p. 139. He mentions the inhalation of ether and cicuta vapour from a teapot (p. 110).
33. E.g. John Wesley, *Primitive Physic*, 26th edn (Dublin, 1809), believed that electricity could cure leprosy, spasms and rheumatism: 'Certainly it comes the nearest to an universal medicine, of any yet known in the world' (p. 131); Hunter, pp. 370, 168; Swediaur, *Pract. Obs.*, p. 145; Morton, *Gonorrhoea*, p. 21. See Murray, II, pp. 58–9, 457–8, for a description of the application of electricity.
34. 'Obstructions' could mean both tumours and 'inspissation' or blockage of body fluids. See Astruc (1770), p. 2; Walker, pp. 367–8.

35. Wolfe, I, p. 23.
36. De Quincey, 'The Pleasures of Opium' in *Confessions of an English Opium-Eater*, p. 177 (Dent edn).
37. Wolfe, I, p. 47; Merle, p. 703; Medwin, p. 286. See *OED*, 'Constitutional'.
38. Wolfe, I, pp. 54–5, 59.
39. See John Wesley, note 33 above, pp. xi–xii; Parr, I, p. 713; Astruc (1770), pp. 49, 419; Wolfe, II, p. 83.
40. Untreated syphilis declines in infectivity after disappearance of the highly infectious rash of the secondary stage and, on average, ceases to be transmissible by body fluids within two years, though this period of infectivity may be as little as one year and as much as five. What the infectivity period would have been for syphilis arrested at the primary stage by nineteenth-century methods of treatment we have been unable to determine. Schofield, pp. 121–2; Morton, *V.D.*, p. 85; Willcox, pp. 145–7.
41. Brown, p. 210.

4. The mill-wheel's sound

1. *Nightmare Abbey* in *Three Novels by Thomas Love Peacock* (1940), p. 121.
2. G. M. Matthews, *Shelley, Selected Poems and Prose* (New York, 1964), p. 97.
3. See *Norton*, p. 389.
4. See Holmes, p. 483, and his later formulation in *Footsteps* (1985), pp. 170–77. Other theories are that she was Shelley's premature child by Claire (Claire Tomalin) or a foundling adopted from a hospital to comfort Mary (White).
5. Dowden, II, pp. 251–3. Claire's testimony was ignored by White, for whom the non-existence of the Neapolitan lady was a necessary plank in his adoption theory. Elena was also baptised, which could have been a requirement made by the family with whom Shelley left her.
6. Hutchinson, p. 431.
7. *Esdaile*, p. 295.
8. The text of 'Summer' is taken from Mary's fair copy book transcript as printed in Massey, p. 62, and 'Winter' from Buxton Forman's transcript of the draft in *B.H. I.* (Buxton Forman, I, pp. 121–5). See Massey, pp. 63–4 for a description of the manuscript and printed variants.
9. *Last Man*. pp. 224–5; for Chalvey well and Shelley, see Olwen Hedley, *Round and about Windsor* (1952), p. 166.
10. Holmes, pp. 295–6.
11. *Prose*, pp. 193–4.
12. Maxwell Fraser, *The History of Slough* (Slough Corporation, 1973), pp. 70–3; William Coles Finch, *Windmills and Watermills* (1933), p. 185; the mill was moved to a site in Kent in 1848. Both the mill and inn were burnt down, in 1882 and 1887 respectively. See also *Slough Express*, 27 August 1965, p. 32.
13. Wolfe, I, pp. 79–80.
14. The figure of a dead or dying beloved in a wintry landscape figures in *The Cold Earth Slept Below*. Dated November 1815, it is perhaps another attempt to utilise the dream, with its hedge and path. A good case could be made out to show that the poem is addressed to Claire. Medwin's suggestion – repeated as fact by several biographers – that it is misdated by a year and refers to Harriet's suicide, has nothing to recommend it except the tender-heartedness

of those who would claim that her death prompted not just remorse but a renewal of love.

15. Medwin, pp. 80–2; 89–90; 'Sydney' in *Bentley's Miscellany*, IX (1841), 168–9.
16. Medwin, p. 47.
17. *Letters*, I, p. 41.
18. Jones, X, pp. 331, 339.
19. *Esdaile*, pp. 75–80.
20. *Letters*, I, pp. 323, 282; James H. Lawrence, *The Empire of the Nairs* (1811), reprint (4 vols. in 1, New York, Scholars' Facsimiles and Reprints, 1976). See II, pp. 1–5; IV, pp. 254–6; Robert Southey, *Letters from England by M. Alvarez Espriella* (3 vols., 1808), I, p. 61; Medwin, p. 190.
21. *S. & C.*, IV, p. 1045.
22. *Alastor*, lines 280–4.
23. *Esdaile*, p. 275; *Prose*, p. 223.
24. *Hutchinson*, p. 807.
25. *Letters*, I, p. 323.
26. James Lawrence, as in note 20 above, II, pp. 13–15; Trotter, pp. 44–5.
27. *Prose*, p. 266.
28. *Letters*, I, p. 383.
29. Wolfe, I, p. 28; ibid., II, p. 157.
30. *Letters*, I, pp. 27, 35; Hutchinson, p. 808.
31. *Letters*, I, pp. 31–2; Shelley alludes to God 'whose mercy is great'. If those are Shelley's words and not Hogg's interpolation, this must be a bitter allusion to II Samuel, 24.14–15. For his sin in numbering the people, David was offered as punishment famine, flight or pestilence. He left the choice to God 'for his mercies are great'. Whereupon the Lord 'sent a pestilence upon Israel'.
32. *Letters*, I, pp. 33–4, 35, 37.
33. See Daniel Paterson, *A New and Accurate Description of All the Direct and Principal Cross Roads in England and Wales and Part of Scotland* (various dates).
34. *Letters*, pp. 39, 42, 45.
35. *Nightmare Abbey*, p. 115.
36. ibid., p. 194.
37. MWS, *Letters*, I, 17 January 1817, p. 27.
38. *Prose*, pp. 233–4.
39. ibid., p. 235; 'To the Lord Chancellor', p. 45.
40. Wolfe, II, pp. 312–13.
41. *Troilus and Cressida*, I, ii, 137; Eldon's 'leaden cowl' may ultimately derive from the lead-sheathed cap of a windmill.
42. *Charles the First*, scene v. In Fletcher's *The Maid in the Mill* the virtuous Florimel, as a strategem for saving her honour, sings a wanton song which employs the usual sexual imagery drawn from mills and milling, but also has a pining turtledove (V, ii). This was a possible inspiration for 'A Widow Bird'. The Shelleys had a complete Beaumont and Fletcher. Mary recorded Shelley's reading of it, but did not always specify titles, e.g. *Mary Shelley's Journal*, entries for 1819 of 20 August, 17 September and 10 October.
43. *The Tempest*, I, ii, 281.

5. Love and vegetables 1811–13

1. Holmes, pp. 64n., 637.

2. Rossetti, I, p. xlvi. Hogg himself is unlikely to have been a stranger to brothels. His *Life* is full of hints at amorous entanglements. His *Memoirs of Prince Alexy Haimatoff* contains passages which read like disguised accounts of visits to high-class 'houses'. One of Peacock's letters to him has the postscript: 'Hor. Sat. 2.31'. The editor of *S. & C.*, VI (p. 552), identified this as Cato's ironic congratulation to a young man seen leaving a brothel.

3. Medwin, p. 136. Medwin is especially unreliable on dates and is often out by several years.

4. *MPJ*, XXII (1809), 412; Morton, *Gonorrhoea*, pp. 15–17.

5. Wolfe, II, p. 6; Hugh J. Luke, Jr, 'Sir William Lawrence, Physician to Shelley and Mary', *Papers on English Language and Literature*, I (1965), 141–52.

6. Private communication with Dr Irvine Loudon.

7. George MacIlwain, *Memoirs of John Abernethy, F.R.S.* (2 vols., 1853), I, p. 254; II, pp. 51, 92; see also Male.

8. Abernethy (1809), pp. 17–18.

9. See *Letters*, I, p. 429, where Shelley expresses pleasure upon hearing of the 'innocent symptoms of diseased action' which Hogg had detailed.

10. E.g. *Letters*, I, pp. 119, 232, 259.

11. Trotter, p. 313. For syphilis and other diseases of the generative organs being misdiagnosed as 'hypochondriasis' or 'a violent nervous affection', see *MPJ*, XXVII (January–June 1812), 144–5. Baudelaire and De Maupassant were both told that their tertiary syphilis was 'nervous'. For 'nervous' stomach trouble as a frequent symptom of latent syphilis, see Griffith Evans, *Latent Syphilis* (Bristol and London, 1937), p. 94.

12. Trotter, p. 341.

13. *Esdaile*, p. 212; ibid., p. 156.

14. *Letters*, I, p. 348.

15. The innocent Eton boys, Gray anticipates, will soon be torn by the 'fury Passions', ending with 'keen Remorse with blood defiled, / And moody Madness laughing wild / Amid severest woe'. These in turn will be followed by diseases: 'This racks the joints, this fires the veins, / That every labouring sinew strains, / Those in the deeper vitals rage.'

16. Polidori, 30 May 1816.

17. See *Letters*, I, p. 135: Shelley was impressed by the argument that the woman's reputation suffered disproportionately from an irregular union; if he had died young, Harriet, as his mistress, would have been in a very precarious position both socially and financially.

18. Hutchinson, p. 857.

19. Swediaur, *Comp. Treat.*, II, p. 281.

20. ibid., II, pp. 158, 249.

21. See D. Fischer-Dieskau, *Schubert: A Biographical Study of his Songs* (1976), pp. 166–73, 193.

22. *Esdaile*, p. 217.

23. *Letters*, II, p. 185; *Letters of John Keats*, ed. Robert Gittings (Oxford, 1970), pp. 396–7; Richard Reece's popular *Medical Guide* (1824) voiced a commonplace in stating 'An attachment to a beloved object has been known to cure the most obstinate disorders which resisted every other remedy', p. 128.

24. *Zoonomia*, II, pp. 682–90; *Letters*, I, p. 129.

25. *Wolfe*, I, p. 197.

26. Hunter, p. 12.
27. Nicholson, article 'Philosophy, Moral', section 32; *S. & C.*, II, p. 709.
28. *Trans. LMCS*, IV (1813), 1–16.
29. Merle, p. 707. Merle received this letter six months after his last interview with Shelley at Field Place in May 1811. His reply to Shelley shows that he did not realise that the latter was married.
30. *Letters*, I, p. 184. The bay laurel is not poisonous; *Letters*, II, p. 433.
31. *Botanic Garden*, II, note on *Prunus laurocerasus*, p. 92.
32. *Zoonomia*, II, p. 682; Trotter, p. 142.
33. *Letters*, I, pp. 232, 240–1, 246, 252, 274. The Shelleys could have been practising artificial birth control; Shelley wrote in a notebook fragment of 1819 that 'any student of anatomy' was well informed about safe and aesthetically acceptable methods. He had of course been a student of anatomy in 1811. Pierpont MS MA 488, pp. 18–20, quoted in P. M. S. Dawson, *The Unacknowledged Legislator* (Oxford U.P., 1980), p. 49, and here by permission of the Pierpont Morgan Library.
34. Abernethy (1809), p. 67; Wolfe, II, p. 89.
35. *Letters*, I, pp. 305, 318, 319.
36. White's doubt (I, p. 648) as to whether Shelley ordered Celsus the physician or the Platonist is easily resolved since the latter's works are extant only in Origen's replies to them, something Shelley could have learnt from the introduction to Good, *Lucretius*.
37. *Letters*, I, pp. 342–5; *Prose*, pp. 81, 86n., 90n., 94n., 95n. The midwifery section of Nicholson contains a detailed description of how to apply ice in severe uterine haemorrhages.
38. J. F. Newton, *The Return to Nature: or, A Defence of the Vegetable Regimen* (1811), pp. 130–2. Newton cites Hunter as the authority on venereal disease.
39. See *Reece*, III (1818), 788, for an appreciation of Lambe which includes the tribute 'The doctor is an able anatomist and chemist.'
40. Wolfe, II, pp. 86–7.
41. ibid., pp. 89–91, 329–30; see Luke, note 5 above.
42. *Prose*, p. 86.
43. ibid., pp. 85, 86, 88.
44. T. Hunt, p. 185.
45. Wolfe, II, p. 61.
46. ibid., II, p. 32.
47. *OED* citation; Astruc (1770), p. 47.
48. Wolfe, I, p. 87; II, p. 31; Newton, *The Return of Nature* in *The Pamphleteer*, XX (1822), 116; *Zoonomia*, II, p. 274; Fracastor, p. 209; Astruc (1770), p. 70.
49. Woodville, I, pp. 7–8; II, p. 9; Swediaur, *Comp. Treat.*, I, pp. 207, 358; Parr, II, p. 649; *Pharmacopeia Londiniensis* (1809), p. 41; *Edinburgh New Dispensatory* (Edinburgh, 1786), p. 248.
50. Medwin, p. 20.
51. His thesis, *De Erysipelate et Hydrocele quae in Rio de Janeiro populariter endemica appelantur* (Edinburgh, 1815), gives his middle name as Bernardino, not, *pace* Peacock, Baptista. We have found the thesis to be a work of social medicine, with much emphasis on diet and the effect of climate. He seems, however, to have been no proselytiser for vegetarianism. See Wolfe, II, pp. 334–5.
52. Cameron, *Young Shelley*, p. 277; Holmes, p. 220; for dating see *S. & C.*, IV, p. 266.
53. Wolfe, II, pp. 107, 132–3.

6. Elephantiasis

1. Holmes, p. 218; Norman, p. 208; Grabo, *Shelley's Eccentricities* (U. of New Mexico, 1950), p. 45; Wolfe, II, p. 326.
2. White, I, pp. 312–16.
3. Wolfe, II, p. 47.
4. Matthew Arnold, 'Shelley' in *Essays in Criticism, Second Series* (1956 reprint), p. 147; Christopher Ricks, 'Shelley: the raging calm', *Sunday Times*, 28 July 1974, p. 36.
5. The novels of Crébillon *fils* epitomised this style, of which there are traces in Hogg's *Memoirs of Prince Alexy Haimatoff*. It reaches its nadir in Harris' *Covent Garden Ladies' Lists* of the 1780s and 1790s.
6. Shelley wrote from Edinburgh 'Mr Peacock is on a visit with us this winter', *S. & C.*, III, p. 260. Hogg printed 'Mr Peacock' as 'A new acquaintance' (Wolfe, II, p. 118). We are grateful to Nicholas Joukovsky for pointing this out.
7. Bateman, pp. 305–7; *Pears' Medical Encyclopaedia* (1963 edn), p. 164.
8. See Joseph Adams, *Observations on Morbid Poisons* (1807), pp. 289–90, for an exposition. For an example of confusion between the two diseases, see *EMSJ*, VI (1810), 161.
9. Good, *Lucretius*, II, pp. 582–4. See Chapter 3, note 13.
10. Bateman, pp. 293–8; Astruc described syphilis as 'an Iliad of a disease'.
11. Celsus, *De Medicina*, III, 25.
12. *Zoonomia*, II, p. 274. Shelley would also have read about the elephantiasis of the Icelanders in Sir George Stewart Mackenzie, *Travels in the Island of Iceland* (1811), p. 408, which in turn would have referred him to a book on leprosy in Madeira.
13. Jones, IV, pp. 367–79; see, for instance p. 219: 'Seek not to remove the veil spread over the secret of your existence'; also pp. 365, 408–11. Nizami's fable of Jesus and the pariah dog contains the later Shelleyan idea that Christ was a poet.
14. Hutten, p. 7; Astruc, I (1754), pp. 70–1; William Beckett, *Philosophical Transactions of the Royal Society*, XXXI, 55–6. See also *Biblical Dictionary*, 'Leprosy': [It] was probably much the same with the elephantiasis, or leprosy of the Arabs, Egyptians, &c . . . At present it is scarce known in Europe, unless we suppose the venereal disease to be a kind of it' (II, pp. 102–3).
15. See *Antony and Cleopatra*, III, x, 11; Donne, *Elegy IV*, lines 60–1. See also *Timon of Athens*, IV, i, 21–32.
16. See *Encycl. Brit.* (1973), entry 'Syphilis'.
17. Notes on *Queen Mab*, Hutchinson, p. 828; Cameron, *Young Shelley*, p. 390, showed that Shelley's note refers to Rees' edition of *Chamber's Cyclopaedia*.
18. For Swediaur's reputation, see Hirsch, *Biographisches Lexicon der hervorragenden Ärzte aller Zeiten and Völker*, V (Berlin, 1934), pp. 178–9; *Dictionnaire encyclopédique des sciences médicales*, series 3, VII (Paris, 1879), pp. 585–6; *LMR*, I (1814), 136. Kurt Sprengel of Hale was another Continental doctor who believed in the combination theory. Swediaur (*Comp. Treat.*, I, p. 71) expressed indebtedness to him for the idea.
19. H. H. Southey, *Quaestio Medico-historica de Ortu et Progressu Syphilidis* (Edinburgh, 1806). See advertisements in endmatter of Adams, note 8 above for evidence of the availability of Swediaur's *Traité Complet*.
20. See 'Leprosy' in the *Encycl. Brit.* (1911 and 1973); Bateman, pp. 299–303, mentions that certain authorities held that 'white leprosy' or the *Leuce* of the Greeks

was also a modification of elephantiasis. For 'the sibbens', see Willcox, pp. 127–9.

21. Bateman, p. 298; Cabanis, IV, p. 56; *Trans. LMCS*, II (1811), 428.

22. William Lawrence and H. H. Southey, 'Two Cases of the True Elephantiasis or Lepra Arabum', *Trans. LMCS*, VI (1815), 210–17.

23. See Lucretius, *On the Nature of the Universe*, tr. R. E. Latham (Harmondsworth, 1951), pp. 250–1.

24. Enormously swollen calves used as an identifying mark of the loose woman can be found in Blake (see for instance the Wyf of Bath in his design of the Canterbury Pilgrims) and Richard Dadd's *The Fairy Feller's Masterstroke*.

25. *Letters*, I, p. 126.

26. Medwin, p. 44.

27. *Quarterly Review*, V (1811), 40–60.

28. Hutchinson, pp. 270–1; e.g. Bod. MS Shelley adds. e. 18, p. 160 rev.

29. *Prose*, p. 269.

30. *MPJ*, XXII (1809), 412; Morton, *Gonorrhoea*, pp. 15–17; *Lex. Bal.*, 'Job's Dock' and 'Job's Ward'. The 'logue' possibly suggested the image of the leper's rags in *Charles the First*; *British Journal of Venereal Disease*, XVII, 4.

31. Astruc (1754), pp. 28–9.

32. Quoted in F. Buret, *Syphilis in Ancient and Prehistoric Times* (2 vols., Philadelphia and London, 1891 and 1895), I, p. 106.

33. F. R. Packard, *Gui Patin* (Oxford, 1924), pp. 151–2.

34. *Monthly Magazine*, XXXIV (August 1812), 43. He knew of Taylor for in 1817 he sent him a copy of *Putting Reform to the Vote* (*Letters*, I, p. 533).

35. Astruc, I (1754), p. 82.

36. H. M. Richmond, *KSJ*, XI (1962), 65–71.

37. Pope, 'The Second Satire of Dr. John Donne, Dean of St. Paul's Versifyed', line 47. See Patrick Strong, 'Pope, pageantry and Shelley's *Triumph of Life*', *KSJ*, XXI–XXII (1972–3), 145–59, for Shelley and Pope's *Epilogue to the Satires*.

38. Rocco was crushed to a *mummy* by the church on the twenty-seventh of December. A mummy is a shapeless mass; it is also the body of a dead Egyptian king.

39. *Letters*, I, pp. 383–4.

40. Dowden, I, p. 373.

41. Cowper, *The Task*, III, 108–20. Both Cowper and Shelley had a friend named John Newton, though at this crisis of his life Shelley's John Newton did not play the part of rescuer. By March 1814 he and Shelley were thoroughly estranged. This estrangement may perhaps have originated in Shelley's indecorous behaviour at a Christmas party given at Newton's house.

42. *Letters*, I, p. 401.

43. *Last Man*, p. 162. It rises 'an hour before noon'.

7. Pale pain, my shadow 1814–22

1. Medwin, p. 136; *Alastor*, line 615. *History of a Six Weeks Tour* (1817) stated that one object of the 1814 journey was to find a warm climate suited to Shelley's health (pp. 46–7).

2. Hogg did relieve Shelley with small sums in the winter of 1814–15. See *S. & C.*, III, p. 425.

3. *Mary Shelley's Journal* (28 February, 14 March 1815), pp. 39, 40.

4. *Mary Shelley's Journal* (November 24), p. 27.
5. For information about Pemberton, see *DNB*; *Reece*, I (1816), 80. See also Christopher Pemberton, *A Practical Treatise on Various Diseases of the Abdominal Viscera* (1807), p. 20; *Letters* I, p. 407.
6. Wolfe, II, p. 38.
7. *Letters*, I, p. 426; Chambers, 'Water'; Cartwright, pp. 4–5; Hutchinson, p. 31; MWS, *Letters*, I, p. 222.
8. *Letters*, I, p. 429; Hutchinson, p. 528; White, I, pp. 414, 698. Mary remembered the date incorrectly as July.
9. Dowden, I, pp. 528–30.
10. Wolfe, II, p. 340.
11. *Letters*, I, p. 429.
12. Good, III, p. 297.
13. Pearson, p. 79; Swediaur, *Comp. Treat.*, II, pp. 86, 93; Parr, II, p. 99.
14. Wolfe, II, p. 89.
15. See *OED*; Rousseau, *Confessions*, Garnier edn, p. 374; Wolfe, II, p. 17.
16. See Yeats' story of Wilde's last visit to a prostitute in *Autobiographies* (1956), pp. 327–8.
17. See *Letters*, II, p. 363, for a (non-bawdy) complex wordplay involving mutton, carnal desire and the two senses of spirits.
18. Lambe's vegetarianism was flexible enough to allow meat to debilitated patients. See *Reece*, III (1818), 788.
19. Swediaur, *Comp. Treat.*, II, pp. 24, 29–30, 34, 218; ibid., *Pract. Obs.*, p. 240; Hunter, p. 27; Good, III, p. 271; Astruc (1754), part I, vol. III, pp. 310–11; ibid. (1770), p. 235; Schofield (p. 95) says of lung gummas that they are 'usually mild with some cough and possibly a little loss of weight . . . the lesions do respond to treatment'.
20. White, I, pp. 468, 473; *Mary Shelley's Journal* (26, 27 October), p. 67.
21. T. Hunt, p. 186.
22. Wolfe, I, p. 335.
23. Robert Browning to Edward Dowden in T. J. Wise, *A Shelley Library*, p. 7; White, I, pp. 344–5.
24. *Mary Shelley's Journal*, p. 6 (8 August 1814; Shelley's entry).
25. *Letters*, I, pp. 543, 556; MWS, *Letters*, I, pp. 41, 57.
26. Wolfe, II, p. 349; Peacock, *Works*, ed. H. F. B. Brett-Smith and C. E. Jones (10 vols., 1924–34), VIII, p. 200.
27. T. Hunt, pp. 187–8.
28. *Letters*, I, p. 573; Hutchinson, p. 270; Murray MS quoted Holmes, p. 513.
29. Holmes, p. 407.
30. 'Shelley has ophthalmia again.' *Mary Shelley's Journal* (23 January 1817), p. 91. Hutchinson, p. 157; Medwin, p. 192; *Letters*, II, pp. 253, 254, 259.
31. *DNB*; Swediaur, *Pract. Obs.*, p. 223; Cooper, p. 522; Abernethy (1809), pp. 193–8.
32. *Letters*, II, p. 153; see Webb, *Violet*, pp. 79–87, for a discussion of the dating and a different interpretation.
33. *Last Man*, p. 310.
34. *Letters*, II, p. 94.
35. Swediaur, *Pract. Obs.*, pp. 170–1; Pearson, p. xxxiv; Good, III, p. 403; Hunter, pp. 452, 454; William Lawrence, *A Treatise on Venereal Diseases of the Eye* (1830), p. 55.
36. Hutchinson, p. 677; *Letters*, II, p. 180.

37. Harold Avery, 'John Bell's Last Tour', *Medical History*, VIII (1964), 69–77.
38. MWS, *Letters*, I, pp. 101–2.
39. Hutchinson, p. 636.
40. Swediaur, *Comp. Treat.*, II, p. 249; T. M. Madden, *The spas of Belgium, Germany, Switzerland, France and Italy* (1867), pp. 358–66; *Letters*, II, p. 90.
41. *Mary Shelley's Journal*, 17 July 1818, p. 102; ibid, 22, 25 May, 10, 11 June 1820, pp. 133, 134; MWS, *Letters*, I, pp. 119, 136; 'Baths' in a list of household expenses at the back of vol. II of Mary's MS journal could refer either to the Naples or the Bagni di Lucca period. *Letters*, II, pp. 202, 237.
42. Cullen maintained that riding cured gleets by 'exciting an inflammation of the parts' (quoted approvingly by Swediaur, *Pract. Obs.*, pp. 63, 167). Good recommends carriage exercise and riding in the sections on hepatitis and nephritis.
43. *Letters*, II, pp. 25. 76, 288.
44. Hutchinson, p. 570; MacFarlane, p. 6; *Letters*, II, pp. 76, 82.
45. Pemberton, note 3 above, pp. 38–45; private communication with Dr Irvine Loudon. For issue-making see Benjamin Bell, *A System of Surgery*, 6th edn (7 vols., 1796), pp. 378–82.
46. *Edinburgh New Dispensatory* (Edinburgh, 1803), p. 208; William Cullen, *Lectures on the Materia Medica* (2 vols., 1773), II, p. 190; Woodville, I, p. 9; James Rennie, *A New Supplement to the Pharmacopoeias of London Edinburgh Dublin* (1826), p. 83. For examples of prescriptions using balsam of copaiba for gleets, see Astruc (1770), pp. 66, 69; *Encycl. Brit.* (1911), 'Copaiba'; *The Lancet*, II (1824), 428.
47. Carmichael, p. 52.
48. MacFarlane, p. 8; MWS, *Letters*, I, p. 89.
49. Cooper, p. 717; *Essays, Letters from Abroad, Translations and Fragments, By Percy Bysshe Shelley*, ed. Mrs Shelley (2 vols., 1840), II, p. 194.
50. William was prescribed gamboge, aloes, wormwood and scammony, according to prescriptions signed by Bell and headed τεχνου (of the child) in the back of vol. II of Mary's journal. The first is especially strong. The diuretic prescription is headed εαυτου (of himself), but the opiate is unassigned. All prescriptions are in Bell's hand.
51. *Biographie Universelle* (Paris, 1843), IV, p. 58; Vaccà's first published work was a critique of Benjamin Bell's surgery. See *Claire*, pp. 464–6.
52. Hutchinson, p. 635; see also MWS, *Letters*, I, p. 136; ibid., p. 168; *Letters*, II, pp. 229, 242, 249, 254, 332, 336; Rossetti, *Diary*, p. 177; *Rossetti Papers*, p. 580.
53. *Claire*, p. 466. Stocking follows White in this. See White, I, p. 707 for a somewhat supercilious attitude towards Shelley's doctors. He considers them, Vaccà apart, to have been insufficiently aware of Shelley's 'neurasthenia'.
54. Trelawny, p. 51.
55. See Abernethy, 'On Diseases Resembling Syphilis' in *Surgical Observations* (1804), for an instance of his recommendation of regimen, exercise and country air instead of medicine. Andrea Vaccà Berlinghieri, *Traité des maladies vénériennes* (Paris, 1800), pp. 38, 43; Blair, *Essay on the Venereal Disease and its treatment*, 3rd edn (1808), p. 13; see Parr, I, p. 306 for pain and kidney stones.
56. MWS, *Letters*, I, p. 175.
57. *Trans. LMCS*, VIII (1817), 173–200; *Reece*, II (1817), 550; Charles Bell (the distinguished neurosurgeon brother of John Bell), 'Of the Nitro-Muriatic Bath in Cutaneous Diseases which resemble Syphilis' in *Surgical Observations* (1821); Medwin, p. 269.

58. Parr, I, pp. 157, 162; *MPJ*, XXXVIII (1817), 221.
59. Medwin, pp. 269–70. Southey's *Don Espriella's Letters* (vol. II, p. 327–39), read by Shelley in 1811, has a detailed (and contemptuous) description of the magnetic method of dissolving the stone. The practitioner imagined him/herself laying elongated spiritual fingers on the affected part.
60. T. Hunt, p. 191; Trelawny, pp. 51–2.
61. Medwin, p. 435; Gronow, p. 118. He wrote that he met Shelley at Genoa. This must have been a mistake for Lerici.
62. *Letters*, II, pp. 433, 435–6; Wolfe, II, p. 336; see for instance Trelawny, pp. 106–7, 140–8, 189; Rossetti, *Diary*, p. 177.
63. Norman pp. 133–8; White, II, plate facing p. 400, pp. 521–2.
64. For a description of the onset of neurosyphilis, see Schofield, p. 110. Maupassant was plagued with eye trouble, neuralgia, abnormal sensitivity to cold, gastric troubles and insomnia for eleven years before being overtaken by *tabes dorsalis*. See Dr Charles Ladame, *Le Calvaire Pathologique de Maupassant*, appendix in Pierre Borel, *Le Vrai Maupassant* (Geneva, 1951), pp. 127–49. For myopia, see Medwin, p. 233, but Trelawny contradicted this (Rossetti, *Diary*, p. 262).
65. Trelawny, p. 158; MWS, *Letters*, I, p. 248; *Letters*, II, p. 445 and note.
66. *Letters*, II, p. 47.
67. W. B. Yeats, quoted from *The Circus Animals' Desertion*, III, in *Collected Poems* (1958), p. 392.

8. The myth of syphilis

1. Lawrence, pp. 54, 55, 57, 58.
2. Lawrence could not have known the Shelley passage as it was not published until 1930.
3. See Eatough. For a bibliography, see Fracastor, pp. 233–8.
4. Fracastor, pp. 148–51.
5. Coleridge, *Anima Poetae* (1895), pp. 262–3, speaks of the 'elegancies and manly politure' of Fracastor, in the same breath as Petrarch in an entry of 1808. See Coleridge, *Notebooks*, I, *1794–1804*, ed. Kathleen Coburn (1957), entry 161a and corresponding notes.
6. Wordsworth said he gave Coleridge the idea of shooting the albatross. Perhaps Coleridge adopted the suggestion because he saw possibilities of combining the motif with Fracastor's allegory.
7. White, I, p. 76. William Roscoe, whose *Life of Lorenzo de Medici* Shelley read in 1816, has an extended reference to Fracastor in his *The Life of Leo X*.
8. Good, II, p. 583; Good alleges that Fracastor imitated Lucretius' description of the plague of Athens.
9. Fracastor, II, lines 388–408, pp. 126–9.
10. See for instance the commentaries of Matthew Henry (1708–10) and Thomas Scott (1788–92).
11. Cameron (*Esdaile*, pp. 285–6) believes that the *Soliloquy* was written before *Queen Mab* was started in the summer of 1812. On the other hand, it is the last poem in the notebook as prepared for publication and could have been the latest to be written. It might have been a discarded portion of *Queen Mab*.
12. *Esdaile*, p. 286.
13. Shelley uses 'remit' in the sense of 'hand back' in his prose. See e.g. *Letters*, II, p. 211.

14. See *Paradise Lost*, ed. Alistair Fowler (1971), notes on pp. 175–6, 254, 525.
15. See *Fracastoro's 'Syphilus'* (note 3 above), pp. 22, 164; Swediaur (I, p. 103) cites Cornelius de Pauw. Brown (pp. 13–14 and note) conjectured that Shelley, like Byron, might have known something of De Pauw.
16. For instance *Candide*, chapter 4 and Bryan Edwards *Civil and Commercial History of the British West Indies*, 2 vol. abridgement (1794), pp. 31–2 and note.
17. Brown (pp. 76–7) has some acute observations on Shelley's sensitivity to latent sexual meanings in dead metaphors.
18. *R. & H.*, line 1293; 'Ode to Liberty', lines 222–3; Edward Meyerstein, *A Life of Thomas Chatterton* (1930), p. 441: 'Mr Cross says [Chatterton] had the foul disease and had calomel and vitriol of Cross for that purpose.'
19. *Dictionary of Scientific Biography* (New York, 1972), vol. V, pp. 106–7.
20. See *OED*, Plague sb. 3a.
21. *Sickness*, IV, line 1403; see Carlos Baker, *Shelley's Major Poetry* (Princeton U. P., 1948), pp. 24, 26n.
22. Earl Wasserman, *Shelley, a Critical Reading* (Baltimore, The Johns Hopkins U. P., 1971), pp. 269–75. We find the examples he gives unconvincing. See William Empson, *Milton's God*, revised edn (1965), p. 286.
23. The lines were added to the Bodleian draft in a hand that looks like Mary's. If they were her contribution, this would indicate that she partook of this habit as well.
24. *Prose*, p. 222; G. M. Matthews, 'Whose Little Footsteps?' in Reiman, Jaye and Bennett, eds., *The Evidence of the Imagination* (New York U.P., 1978), pp. 254–61.
25. Wolfe, I, p. 194; Southey, Coleridge and Wordsworth all wore their hair long during their revolutionary period.
26. An unequivocal example is *Julian and Maddalo*, line 425.
27. William Fergusson, 'Observation on the Venereal Disease in Portugal as affecting the constitution of the British soldiery and natives', *Trans. LMCS*, IV (1813), 1–16; Good, III, p. 399; Swediaur's name for the Black Lion was 'cancer gangrene of the penis' (*Comp. Treat.*, II, p. 421).
28. Butter, pp. 3–4.
29. See 'On Life', *Prose*, pp. 172–5.
30. Hutchinson, p. 479.
31. *Prose*, pp. 173–4.
32. T. S. Eliot, 'Ben Jonson' in *The Sacred Wood* (1920), p. 115.
33. Dante, Epistol. xiii to Can Grande. Ross Woodman, *The Apocalyptic Vision in the Poetry of Shelley* (U. of Toronto P., 1964), pp. 159–60, Stuart Curran, in *Shelley's Annus Mirabilis* (San Marino, 1975) and Timothy Webb in *The Violet in the Crucible* have illuminatingly developed the portrait of a 'Renaissance' Shelley.
34. Cabanis, III, pp. 265–8 (our translation).
35. See Edward Sackville West, *A Flame of Sunlight: The Life and Work of Thomas De Quincey*, 2nd edn (1974), pp. 9–13; Leslie A. Marchand, *Byron, a Biography* (1957), I, pp. 57–8.

9. Nightshade, well, forest

1. A detailed examination of Shelley's self-reflexive imagery is to be found in Keach, pp. 79–117.
2. Matthews, 'Volcano's Voice', pp. 191–3.

3. *Prose*, p. 295.
4. See 'Lines: Far, far away' and *Epips.*, lines 412, 463.
5. Shelley would have encountered the concept of homeopathy in both Pliny's *Natural History* and Milton's preface to *Samson Agonistes*.
6. Benjamin Walker, *Encyclopaedia of Metaphysical Medicine* (1978), entry 'Homeopathy'; Walter Pagel, *Paracelsus* (Basel, 1958), pp. 146–7.
7. Good, III, p. 404; Pearson, p. 79; Swediaur, *Comp. Treat.*, II, p. 378; ibid, *Pract. Obs.*, pp. 258–9; Parr, I, p. 100; *LMR*, XI (1819), 211; Gataker (1757), pp. 26–7. Parr considered it to be a vegetable antisyphilitic surpassed in effectiveness only by sarsaparilla and mezereon.
8. 'A nightshade' was seventeenth-century slang for a prostitute, as in Beaumont and Fletcher's *The Coxcomb* (II, ii, 36), a play on the subject of wife-sharing. Shelley is not likely to have known it before he met Peacock, however.
9. *Esdaile*, pp. 180–1; Hutchinson, p. xxv; *Letters*, II, p. 361. Hogg had not told him the plant's name.
10. Nicholson, V, entry 'Pharmacy'; the hidden name was pointed out to Derek Guiton by G. M. Matthews.
11. Neville Rogers' reading, later adopted by *S. & C.*, is undoubtedly the correct one.
12. *Letters*, II, p. 403; *Prose*, pp. 171–5.
13. *Esdaile*, 'A Winter's Day'.
14. Byron referred to his 'carnal knowledge' of Claire as 'commerce'; see *LBLJ*, VI, p. 76; Cary, I, p. 51.
15. *Prose*, pp. 304, 305.
16. *L. & C.*, lines 1123–5. It figures as one of the most useful plants in the ancient herbals; its juice was applied to scabs, leprosy and other skin complaints while leaves and stalks were applied to cancers and gangrene. See Pliny, *Natural History*, xxiii, sec. 21; Dioscorides, iv, sec. 182; Fracastor, II, line 155.
17. Paracelsus, II, pp. 132–3.
18. Thompson, p. 123.
19. *Letters*, II, pp. 262–3.
20. Norton, p. 372; such criticism does not give full weight to the 'sensations' which are 'as a thirst' and the bodily 'frame' on which the divine music of love is played in *On Love*. See for instance White, II, 259–63; Glenn O'Malley, *Shelley and Synaesthesia* (Evanston Ill., Northwestern U.P., 1964).
21. Cameron, pp. 284–6; Brown, p. 66.
22. *Letters*, II, 363.
23. See the quotation from the *Vita Nuova* in the Advertisement to *Epipsychidion*, Hutchinson, p. 411.
24. See Parks C. Hunter, Jr, 'Textual Differences in the Drafts of Shelley's *Una Favola*', *Studies in Romanticism*, VI (1966), 58–64.
25. William James, *The Varieties of Religious Experience* (1902), pp. 380–1.
26. See Chambers, entry 'Venereal', which cites Sydenham for the view that venereal disease is spread by the breath; cf. *London Guide* on streetwalkers: 'Their breath is contamination, their touch is infection' (p. 129), and the description of the witch Lorrinite in *The Curse of Kehama*, a passage which Shelley frequently repeated, according to Medwin (p. 44). Lorrinite resigns her body to the Demons of the air, from whom she draws the power to inflict by means of a look 'All plagues which on mortality can light . . . Diseases loathsome and incurable' (XI, 3–6). The mithridatic 'poison-damsel' of folklore has often been interpreted as a

woman infected with venereal disease (*Folklore*, XXXVIII (1927), 328), though there is no evidence that Shelley knew of this.

27. Nahum Tate, *Syphilis or a Poetical History of the French Disease* (1686). See for instance his rendering of I, lines 360–4.
28. Darwin, *Temple of Nature* (1803), pp. 158–9 and note.
29. Eatough, p. 57.
30. *Letters*, II, p. 81.
31. Bod. MS Shelley adds. e. 8, p. 107.
32. ibid., p. 106. Shelley had difficulty with this part of the poem; the page ends with the word 'chaos' in large letters.
33. Brown, p. 210; William Empson, *Seven Types of Ambiguity*, 2nd edn (1953), pp. 160–1; Matthews, 'Volcano's Voice', p. 211.
34. For instance in the poetry of Garcillaso de la Vega.
35. Cabanis observed 'On voit souvent ces malheureux [maniacs] s'arracher les testicules' (III, p. 343), one probable source for the image.
36. *Vindication*, pp. 274, 282–3.
37. Wolfe, II, pp. 326–7.
38. Medwin, pp. 48–9, 107–8, 124–5; Wolfe, II, pp. 317–20.
39. See Claude C. Brew, *Mary and Shelley in 1817* (1971), p. 47.
40. James Lawrence refers to 'Queen Anne's Liquid Spring' as one of the pleasures of Eton in 'Ode to an Eton Friend', printed in *The Etonian out of Bounds* (1828); Olwen Hedley, *Round and About Windsor* (1952), p. 166; *Last Man*, pp. 224–5; Maxwell Fraser, *The Story of Slough* (Slough Corporation, 1973), pp. 36–7. The spring, which was a medicinal one, no longer exists.
41. White, I, p. 54.
42. Harriet Grove's association with the Vision is supported by very similar imagery used by Shelley in his review of *Mandeville* when describing the similarly named Henrietta (*Prose*, p. 310). Did Godwin choose the name because of his knowledge of Shelley's life history? Harriet Shelley could then be the mortal form, 'not true', as Thornton Hunt surmised, because Shelley certainly considered that she had betrayed him to Eliza Westbrook. Alternatively, assuming that Shelley listed the 'mortal forms' in order not of chronology but of importance, Harriet Shelley could be one of the 'fair' whose beauty dies away, and Harriet Grove the one not true. Cameron argued that Harriet Shelley is also the quenched 'Planet' in line 313. To add to the confusion, Shelley's draft line originally read 'Some were true but oh, not made for me' (Bod. MS Shelley adds. e. 8, p. 108).
43. Bod. MS Shelley adds. e. 8, p. 107.
44. Hutchinson, p. 425.

10. White hair and frail form

1. Chernaik, pp. 566–7, 575.
2. See Neville Rogers, ed., *The Complete Poetical Works of Percy Bysshe Shelley*, vol. I (Oxford, 1972).
3. Holmes, p. 305.
4. Wordsworth wrote 'Lines Written in Very Early Youth' at the age of sixteen. Shelley gave the same title to an *Esdaile* poem, probably in ironic allusion. 'Early youth' then, probably means late adolescence in Shelley.
5. *Letters*, I, p. 281.

6. ibid., pp. 319, 323.
7. In 1817 the Shelleys' marriage had been considerably strengthened by Mary's support during his fight for his children; consequently Shelley's portrayal of their life together in the 'Dedication' to *Laon and Cythna* is entirely different.
8. For instance Evan K. Gibson, 'Alastor: A Reinterpretation', *PMLA*, LXII (1947), 1022–42.
9. Hutchinson, p. 30.
10. *Letters*, I, pp. 429–30; Dowden, I, p. 529.
11. Medwin, p. 24.
12. 'Cenomanus' (Fracastor's word) is rendered as 'Veronese' by both Wynne-Finch and Eatough, but the location of his origin ('where rich Ollius flows past the lush meadow-lands of Lake Sebinus') shows him to be Brescian, as the entry on Fracastor in the *Dictionary of Scientific Biography* (New York, 1972) correctly states. The Cenomani are identified with the Brescia (Brixia) area in Pliny's *Natural History*, III, 130; Good, *Lucretius*, I, p. 17 and II, p. 610.
13. Fracastor, p. 85 (I, lines 392–8).
14. ibid., p. 83 (I, lines 366–8).
15. We have failed to find a model for this line in Virgil, Lucretius, Ovid or Milton.
16. Brown, pp. 216, 219; Medwin, p. 48; Wolfe, II, p. 117.
17. *Letters*, I, p. 41.
18. See *S. & C.*, II, p. 709. For Bruno see L. S. Boas, *Harriet Shelley* (Oxford U.P., 1962), p. 178.
19. *Letters*, p. 46. See Medwin, p. 46, for legends about St Leonard's Forest, including references to a headless spectre and a serpent. A benign snake figures in *R. & H.*
20. Holmes, p. 638.
21. *Lex. Bal.*; Bryan Edwards, *Civil and Commercial History of the British West Indies* (2 vol. abridgement 1794), pp. 31–2 and note, which cites Stow on the edict governing medieval Southwark brothels.
22. Cary, I, p. 52.
23. *L. & C.*, lines 1123, 1205.
24. Locock, pp. 55–6; *S. & C.*, VI, pp. 1101–3; we have made extensive use of Massey's transcriptions of the *Prince Athanase* drafts (Massey, pp. 135–57).
25. Bod. MS Shelley e. 4, fol. 72r rev.; Massey, p. 147.
26. ibid.
27. For an informative treatment of this, see Brown, pp. 117–49.
28. *Shelley on Love*, ed. Richard Holmes (1980), p. 125.
29. ibid.; see J. E. Raven, *Plato's Thought in the Making* (Cambridge U.P., 1965), p. 117, for an account of how Plato has been misinterpreted – by others, not by Shelley – on the matter of physical love.
30. *Letters*, I, p. 35.
31. *Letters*, I, p. 403.
32. Wolfe, I, pp. 294–5.
33. Massey, p. 147.
34. *B–H*, I, Rogers, p. 222. The equation found in Shelley between leaves, hair and meteors has its origin in the Latin *coma*.
35. Martinus Rulandus, tr. A. E. Waite, *A Lexicon of Alchemy* (1964), p. 460. Rulandus is glossing Paracelsus.
36. *B–H*, I, fols. 14r, 15r, 14v; Massey, p. 294.

37. See *Adonais*, XX.
38. G. M. Matthews, 'Shelley's Lyrics' in *The Morality of Art: Essays Presented to G. Wilson Knight* (1969), reprinted in Norton, p. 683 and note.
39. Rousseau, *Confessions*, pp. 377–80; tr. Cohen, pp. 300–2.
40. *Polidori*, pp. 125–8. Neither Polidori's later version in his preface to *The Vampyre* nor Medwin's (p. 156) are as authentic.
41. E.g. Wolfe, I, p. 85.
42. Strabo's *Geography* mentions three classes of monster within the same paragraph: the *Cynocephaloi* (dog-headed), *Sternophthalmoi* (bosom-eyed) and the *Stegopodes* (web-footed) in the context of a discussion on the conscious mixture by poets of myth and fact (I.2.35, Loeb edn, p. 157). See *Witch*, line 136.
43. Rousseau, *Confessions*, p. 374; tr. Cohen, pp. 297–8.
44. Ovid, *Metamorphoses*, tr. Mary M. Innes (Harmondsworth, 1968), pp. 77–8.
45. Rieger, p. 146.
46. Carlos Baker, 'The Traditional Background of Shelley's Ivy-Symbol', *Modern Language Quarterly*, IV (1943), 205–8.
47. *Letters*, II, p. 205, n. 3.
48. In addition to the Fracastor parallel noted in Chapter 8, there are also echoes of Coleridge's *A War Eclogue* and of Voltaire's description of Chapter V of *Candide* of the 1755 Lisbon earthquake. This is accompanied by fire and is supposedly caused by an underground vein of sulphur linking the city with Lima. A sailor rushes into the ruins in search of venal sex. The preceding chapter is about Pangloss' contraction of, and treatment for, the pox, in which he argues that the disease's existence is necessary in the best of all possible worlds.
49. The original of the cup is now in the British Museum, Dept of Medieval and Later Antiquities, Cat. 1885–6–16.1, but is said to be made of olive wood. See *Rossetti Papers*, p. 432.

11. Evil, the immedicable plague

1. *Sickness*, I, line 390.
2. A. Clutton-Brock, *Shelley: The Man and the Poet*, 3rd edn (1924), pp. 210–11.
3. E.g. *L. & C.*, lines 3240–3.
4. Rieger, p. 112; Brown, p. 208. For Curran see note 44 below.
5. See T. S. Eliot's approving comment in *The Use of Poetry and the Use of Criticism* both in its original form in the 1933 edn and in the second edn (1964), pp. 144–5.
6. Quoted by Michael Tanner in review of *Mozart*, *TLS*, 7 October 1983, 1074.
7. *Vindication*, pp. 123–4.
8. MWS, *Letters*, I, p. 43; *Letters*, II, p. 115 on the fact that writing *The Cenci* 'kept up' his pain.
9. *Letters*, II, pp. 267–8.
10. Lawrence, pp. 64, 71.
11. See Webb, *Violet*, pp. 156–7, who refers the reader to Wasserman's analysis in *Shelley, a Critical Reading* (Baltimore and London, 1971).
12. William Empson, review of H. W. Piper's *The Active Universe*, *Critical Quarterly*, V (1963), 270.
13. E.g. *P.U.*, II, ii, lines 70–82; *L. & C.*, lines 2615–32.
14. *Paracelsus*, I, p. 4.
15. Erebinthus, a name found in Pliny, and suggesting 'terebinth' (turpentine) is

252 Notes to pages 184–95

another of Shelley's restful, green, pine-clad isles. In Aristophanes' *Frogs* and *Acharnians*, 'Erebinthos' means *membrum virile*; the latter instance occurs in a scene in which two girls disguised as pigs are taken to market to be sold as concubines rather than starve. We consider that this scene, as well as *The Frogs* was a source for *Swellfoot*. The island's connotations of curative sexuality are reinforced by the epithet 'bee-pasturing'. At this point, however, the wanderer in the labyrinth of Shelley's associative mental processes becomes dizzy.

16. For an excellent discussion of Shelley's imaging of mental processes in bodily terms, see Keach, pp. 42–78.
17. *Q.M.*, IV, lines 246–252; 105–7.
18. ibid., VI, lines 33–8.
19. Hutchinson, p. 272.
20. *Prose*, p. 286; *Paradise Lost*, ed. Alistair Fowler (1971), p. 254n. on IV, line 998.
21. Cameron, p. 479.
22. Helena Shire, *A Preface to Spenser* (1978), p. 127.
23. See for instance *Romeo and Juliet*, II, iv, 35; *Troilus and Cressida*, V, x, 35, 49; *Timon of Athens*, IV, iii, 152–3; *Measure for Measure*, I, i, 53, 55; *Antony and Cleopatra*, I, iv, 27.
24. *Sickness*, II, lines 575–9.
25. Zillman, p. 149n.
26. Wasserman, *P.U.*, p. 45.
27. F. A. Pottle, 'The Role of Asia in the Dramatic Action of Shelley's *Prometheus Unbound*', in Ridenour, ed., *Shelley: A Collection of Critical Essays* (Englewood Cliffs, New Jersey, 1965), p. 135.
28. Cameron, p. 516.
29. See *Biblical Dictionary*, I, 'Almond'; Trelawny, p. 180.
30. Walker, p. 47.
31. Cartwright, p. 113.
32. Davy, III, p. 329.
33. ibid. pp. 294, 290. Asia seems to have become an immaterialist under the vapour's influence. See *P.U.*, II, iv, lines 9–11.
34. Walker, p. 231.
35. Davy, III, p. 132. A note gives 'leaves, bark, and wood of trees' as examples of vegetable matter which might produce this reaction. Matthews, *Volcano's Voice*, pp. 206, 212.
36. Nicholson, III, 'Gas'.
37. Davy, III, p. 269n.
38. Dowden, II, p. 120.
39. Thompson, pp. 113–14; H. W. Parke and D. E. W. Wormell, *The Delphic Oracle* (2 vols., Oxford U.P., 1956), I, pp. 24–6.
40. See also *Hellas*, lines 586–90, where Crete and Cyprus, homes of the Minotaur and Venus respectively, are called 'mountain twins . . . that from each others' veins / Catch the volcano fire and earthquake spasm'.
41. For Thetis as a 'kind of whoredom' and other interpretations, see Zillman, p. 335.
42. Zillman, pp. 510–11; Lucan, *Pharsalia*, IX, lines 762–88. Jupiter's poisoning of Thetis is radically unlike his treatment, in myth, of Semele, whose immolation grieves him deeply.
43. C. E. Pulos, 'Shelley and Malthus', *PMLA*, LXVII (1952), 113–24; Cameron, pp. 528–9.

44. Stuart Curran, *Shelley's Annus Mirabilis* (San Marino, U. of California P., 1975) p. 128.
45. Wasserman, *P.U.*, pp. 161–2 and note.
46. Matthews, *Volcano's Voice*, p. 222; Malthus, *Second Essay on Population* (1872 edn), p. 50.
47. Lucan, *Pharsalia*, VI, lines 744–5.
48. See Jolande Jacobi, ed., *Paracelsus: Selected Writings* (1951), p. 326. 'If a man discovered or produced the "stone", it accomplished his "second birth", the birth of the pure, dross-free body.'
49. Norton, p. 187n.; see Zillman, pp. 524–5, 543–6, for a summary of comment on the location of the caves.
50. Wasserman, *P.U.*, p. 154.
51. Davy, *Elements of Chemical Philosophy*, part I, vol. I (1812), pp. 261–2.
52. Grabo, p. 190; Cavallo to Lind, 6 January 1796, BL MS adds. 22898, fol. 61; Walker, p. 247. Grabo thought the cavern was the Grotta del Cane, which has carbon dioxide fumes. Good, *Lucretius*, II, p. 536, said the Grotta emitted 'azotic vapour'; this description, misleading because 'azote' was Lavoisier's name for nitrogen, might have given Shelley license for a nitrous-fuming cave.
53. Davy, III, pp. 22–5.
54. *Botanic Garden*, II, 147–50.
55. Cronin, pp. 143, 164.
56. See Christopher Ricks, *Milton's Grand Style* (Oxford, 1963), pp. 110–17.
57. M. H. Abrams, *Natural Supernaturalism* (New York, 1971), pp. 306–7. See also *P.U.*, III, iii, lines 34–63.
58. Fracastor, pp. 78–9 (I, lines 316–18).
59. *Shelley, Crit. Her.*, p. 192.
60. *Letters*, II, p. 258.
61. See N. I. White, 'Shelley's *Swellfoot the Tyrant* in Relation to Contemporary Political Satire', *PMLA*, XXXVI (1921), 332–46. It seems to have escaped notice that the 'eleven legs' of the Gadfly refer to the eleven years up to 1820. Scandal began in 1809 when the 1806 'Delicate Investigation' into the Queen's morals became public knowledge. See G. D. Stout, *The Political History of Leigh Hunt's 'Examiner'* (St Louis, Washington U. Studies, 1949), p. 46.
62. Hutchinson, p. 394.
63. *Letters*, II, p. 177.
64. Norton, p. 210n.
65. *Letters*, II, p. 368.
66. See for instance, Cabanis, III, pp. 306–7.
67. See Parr, I, pp. 382, 597, 688; Swediaur, *Comp. Treat.*, II, p. 79.
68. 'The Boat on the Serchio', line 108; *Epips.*, line 73.
69. *Letters*, I, p. 416, written when oppressed by the 'loathsome meaning' of the 'impure' in October 1814.

12. Egyptian bondage: *Charles the First* and *The Triumph of Life*

1. This is still a controversial view, to defend which would take up too much space here. We accept many of Cameron's arguments (Cameron, pp. 261–3).
2. For dating, see Cameron, pp. 411–12 and notes.
3. See Clarendon, *Selections from the History of the Rebellion and Civil Wars* (World's

Classics, Oxford U.P., 1954), pp. 147–51. Vane played an essential part in the trial of Straf·ord by contradicting his father's testimony. (Bulstrode Whitelocke, *Memorials* (1732 edn), p. 43.)

4. Bod. MS Shelley adds. e. 7, p. 242 rev.; he correctly listed Haslerig, Hampden, Pym, and Cromwell as the four restrained from embarking for America (ibid., p. 250 rev.) but substituted young Vane for Haslerig and added Cromwell's daughter when drafting the play (ibid., adds. e. 17, p. 33). See also Buxton Forman, III, pp. 104–5.

5. 'The populace were wittily compared to Balaam's ass, whose mouth the Lord had opened.' Catherine Macauley, *History of England*, II, p. 265. The idea of the dead animal in London fields as a subject for a poem had been present in Shelley's mind from as early as 7 October 1814. See *Mary Shelley's Journal*, p. 18.

6. See R. Woodings, 'Shelley's Widow Bird', *RES*, new series XIX (1968), pp. 411–14.

7. Catherine Macauley, *History of England*, II, pp. 155–6. See IV, p. 422, where Macauley calls into question Charles' sexual purity.

8. *Letters*, II, p. 310.

9. Wolfe, II, p. 339.

10. *Apology against a Pamphlet . . . against Smectymnuus*, facsimile edn (Urbana, U. of Illinois P., 1950), p. 32.

11. *Letters*, I, p. 51; ibid., I, p. 84.

12. *Prose*, p. 67.

13. *Prose*, p. 289.

14. Reiman, pp. 60, 73–9.

15. BL MS adds. 47225, fol. 109; see *Confessions*, p. 754.

16. See *S. & C.*, III, p. 355 for documentation of Shelley's interest in Rousseau during the summer of 1814.

17. *Letters*, II, p. 361. See 'On the Genius and Character of Rousseau', *Blackwoods*, XI (February 1822), 152: 'The insanity of a man of genius, who walked about the streets of Paris in an Armenian cloak and caftan and who played cup-and-ball after having written *Emile*'.

18. Matthews, 'Triumph', pp. 107–8.

19. *Inferno*, Canto xiii; Cary's translation, used by Shelley, has informative notes.

20. *Blackwood's*, XI (February 1822), 153. It is now believed that he died of apoplexy or uraemia; see F. C. Green, *Jean-Jacques Rousseau* (Cambridge U.P., 1955), p. 358.

21. Rousseau, *Confessions*, pp. 750–1 (our translation).

22. ibid., pp. 750, 415–16, 427–32. Rousseau in his *Testament* later swore that the nephritis was not caused by venereal disease despite doctors' refusal to believe him. This was not published until 1907, however. See J.-J. Rousseau, *Oeuvres Complètes* (Paris, 1959), I, p. 1226.

23. For a study of Rousseau's reputation during the Romantic era, see Edward Duffy, *Rousseau in England* (Berkeley, U. of California P., 1979), a book to which we are much indebted, though our interpretations diverge.

24. Reiman, p. 241.

25. *Letters*, II, p. 145; for a comment see Brown, pp. 148–9.

26. See Reiman, p. 173.

27. Letters, I, p. 261.

28. For the view that Rousseau was maddened by disease, see *Blackwood's*, note 17

above, which attributed his acute sensibility 'not to a spirit of refined or superior orgnisation, but to mere physical weakness; nay more, to a distempered state of nerves, brought on by debauchery'. This number contained a review of *Epipsychidion*, so might have been sent to Shelley.

29. *Letters*, I, p. 270n.
30. For a convenient summary of the interpretations of the Shape, see Lloyd Abbey, *Destroyer and Preserver* (U. of Nebraska P., 1979), p. 165. See especially Harold Bloom, *Shelley's Mythmaking* (New Haven, 1959), p. 271; Peter Butter, 'Sun and Shape in Shelley's *The Triumph of Life*', *RES*, new series XIII (1962), 40–1; Reiman, pp. 69–73.
31. Cronin, pp. 218–19; Abbey, note 30 above. Cf. Milton, *Apology* (note 10 above), p. 33 for the idea of a cup of love offered only to the 'worthy', while the rest are 'cheated' by a sorceress with a 'thick intoxicating potion'. The passage occurs in the context of Milton's self-defence against the charge of being a bordello-haunter. Shelley ordered Milton's prose works in July 1820.
32. See Matthews, 'Triumph', pp. 108–9; Reiman, pp. 60, 73–9.
33. See F. M. Stawell, 'Shelley's *Triumph of Life*', *Essays and Studies*, V (1914), 124; Cameron, p. 449.
34. See 'The daystar shines, the daybeam dawns' in 'Death-spurning rocks!', *Esdaile*, p. 82.
35. W. B. Yeats, *Essays and Introductions* (1961), p. 46.
36. Shelley uses 'palms' probably to avoid the homophony of 'soles' and 'souls'. As precedent he had the Greek 'tarsos' which can mean either palms or soles.
37. Bod. MS Shelley adds. c. 4, fol. 39r; Reiman, pp. 60, 179. The willow buds seem to derive from a French or English landscape since the time of time of year is April. Italian willows bud in February, according to *Letters*, II, p. 78.
38. See, e.g., *P.U.*, IV, lines 271–3: 'Like swords of azure fire, or golden spears / With tyrant-quelling myrtle overtwined, / Embleming heaven and earth united now'.
39. This reading answers Matthews' objections to Reiman's retention of the ms 'their' which he wished to emend to 'its' on the ground that 'their' had no plural antecedent (G. M. Matthews, review of Reiman in *Journal of English and Germanic Philology*, 1967, p. 604). For a discussion of the arbitrariness of the billow-willow-pillow rhyme, see Keach, p. 185.
40. *P.U.*, I, lines 809–11. It also appears in a Latin fragment in Shelley's hand in the front of Claire Clairmont's first journal notebook (BL MS Ashley 394). See *Claire*, p. 60; Stocking's transcription is not entirely accurate, but the point is unaffected.
41. See *OED* entries 'Nepenthe' and 'Nepenthes'; Hayter, p. 29.
42. Cf. *Witch*, lines 105–6: 'And old Silenus, shaking a green stick / Of lilies'.
43. 'Soon' is cancelled, but adopted by Reiman on the grounds that it was preferable to Matthews' doubtful reading 'fierce' of an uncancelled word above (Bod. MS adds. c. 4, fol. 47v). See Reiman, p. 199. Examination of the ms and comparison with the 'venomed melody' passage in the *Epipsychidion* draft leads us to conclude that the uncancelled word is 'poison', which for metrical reasons resisted incorporation.
44. *Prose*, p. 223; see also the following suggestive passage from *Blackwood's*, V (April 1819), 9: 'The moment he sets his foot within the walls of a city, I am obliged to quit him . . . his earthly blood begins to ferment, – and poor, pitiful

bodily self stands forth, and with its soiled and misty mantle, covers and conceals all things . . . in despair [he] plunges into the throng and becomes as mean and as wicked as they are.'

45. Rousseau, *Julie* (Paris, 1960), pp. 275–6.

46. Rousseau, *Confessions*, tr. Cohen, p. 331, said that St Preux' lapse was based upon a disgraceful adventure of his own.

47. Butter, note 30 above, p. 40; Edmund Blunden, *Shelley* (1946), p. 294; Cameron, pp. 454–7.

48. Matthews, 'Triumph', p. 123.

49. *Triumph*, line 307. The draft cancellation is even more explicit: 'And I from thee may then the secret' (Reiman, p. 179).

50. Donald Reiman's forthcoming facsimile edition of *The Triumph of Life* (New York, Garland Press) will summarise the evidence against the belief of Matthews and others that the poem had reached an impasse.

51. Reiman, p. 69 and note. He suspected that 'Shelley refers to some specific poet, or lover or figure from folk-story from the region near Brescia'. We put forward this suggestion as near-confirmation of his suspicion.

52. Fracastor, pp. 211–12 (book III, lines 288–332).

53. Reiman, pp. 82–3. See also Cameron, p. 473.

54. See 'Byron and Shelley on the character of Hamlet', *New Monthly Magazine*, XXIX, part II (1830), 333. The same page has an example of 'infamy' used, apparently by Shelley, in the sense of 'wickedness' – 'his shock at the detected infamy of his mother'. For authenticity and possible authorship, see Reiman, p. 100, and C. E. Robinson, *Shelley and Byron* (Baltimore and London, 1976), pp. 148, 270.

55. E.g. 'Million Americans could have AIDS', *Guardian*, 31 July 1985, p. 6. But see also 'Risk factors of an AIDS epidemic' (letter from C. G. Geary of the Royal Infirmary, Manchester, in *The Times*, 14 August 1985).

56. See, e.g., Martin Amis, 'Making Sense of AIDS', *The Observer*, 23 June 1985, p. 17–18, and Christopher Hitchens discussing Larry Kramer's *The Normal Heart* (*TLS*, 12 July 1985); *Letters*, II, p. 199.

57. Muriel Jaeger, *Before Victoria*, reprint (Harmondsworth, 1967), p. 9, still a helpful introduction to the change in manners between 1787 and 1837; Mac-Farlane, pp. 177–83.

58. For an excellent summary of the history of perception of disease in Western culture, see the first chapter of Jeffrey Meyers' *Disease and the Novel, 1880–1960* (1985).

Notes on texts

Quotations from Shelley's poetry, prefaces and notes are taken from Hutchinson with the following exceptions:

The Revolt of Islam has been given Shelley's original title *Laon and Cythna* throughout; Massey has been used for constructing texts of *Prince Athanase* and 'Summer and Winter'; *The Triumph of Life* is an eclectic text, which, as a result of an examination of the Bodleian MS, takes from both G. M. Matthews, 'Shelley's *Triumph of Life*: a New Text', *Studia Neophilologica*, XXXIII (1960), 271–309, and Donald Reiman's text in Norton. For poems in the *Esdaile Notebook*, the text used is *Esdaile*, except in one case where the reading of *The Esdaile Poems*, ed. Neville Rogers (Oxford U.P., 1966), is adopted.

Other prose quotations are taken from *Prose* and from *Letters*. Extracts from Shelley's translation of the *Symposium* are taken from *Shelley on Love*, ed. Richard Holmes (1980).

The translation of *Una Favola* has been made by us from Buxton Forman's transcript of Shelley's draft.

Symbols, short titles and abbreviations

Where not specified, the place of publication is London.

[ ]	Authorial interpolation.
?	Before a word, a conjectural reading.
Abernethy	John Abernethy, *On the Constitutional Origin and Treatment of Local Diseases* ('My Book'), 1st edn (1809).
Astruc (1754)	John Astruc, *A Treatise of Venereal Diseases* (1754 edn).
Astruc (1770)	ibid., tr. and ed. Chapman (1770).
Bateman	Thomas Bateman, *A Practical Synopsis of Cutaneous Diseases*, 2nd edn (1813).
Bell	John Bell, *The Principles of Surgery* (3 vols., 1815).
B–H	The Bixby-Huntington Notebooks.
Biblical Dictionary	John Brown, *Dictionary of the Holy Bible* (2 vols., Bungay, 1824 edn).
BL	The British Library.
Botanic Garden	Erasmus Darwin, *The Botanic Garden* (2 vols. 1791).
Brown	Nathaniel Brown, *Sexuality and Feminism in Shelley* (Cambridge, Mass., Harvard U.P., 1979).
Buchanan	Robert Buchanan, *A Poet's Sketchbook* (1883).
Butter	Peter Butter, *Shelley's Idols of the Cave* (Edinburgh U.P., 1954).
Buxton Forman	*The Shelley Notebooks*, ed. H. B. Forman (3 vols., Boston, The Bibliophile Society, 1911).
Cabanis	'Rapports du physique et du moral de l'homme' in P-J-G Cabanis, *Oeuvres Complètes* (5 vols., Paris, 1823–5).
Cameron	K. N. Cameron, *Shelley, the Golden Years* (Cambridge, Mass., Harvard U.P., 1974).
Cameron, *Young Shelley*	K. N. Cameron, *The Young Shelley, Genesis of a Radical* (New York and London, 1950).
Carmichael	Richard Carmichael, *An Essay on the Venereal Diseases which have been confounded with Syphilis* (Dublin, 1814).
Cartwright	F. F. Cartwright, *English Pioneers of Anaesthesia* (Bristol and London, 1952).

Cary	H. Cary, *The Slang of Venery* (2 vols., privately printed, 1916).
Catterall	R. D. Catterall, *A Short Textbook of Venereology* 2nd edn (1974).
Cavallo	Tiberius Cavallo, *An essay on the Medicinal Properties of Factitious Airs* (1798).
Chambers	Abraham Rees, ed., *Chambers's Cyclopaedia* (1786).
Chernaik	Judith Chernaik, 'The Figure of the Poet Shelley', *English Literary History*, XXXV (1968), 566–90.
Claire	*The Journals of Claire Clairmont*, ed. Marian K. Stocking (Cambridge, Mass., Harvard U.P. 1968).
Cooper	Samuel Cooper, *A Dictionary of Practical Surgery* (1809).
Cronin	Richard Cronin, *Shelley's Poetic Thoughts* (1981).
Davy	*The Collected Works of Sir Humphry Davy* (9 vols., 1839).
DNB	*Dictionary of National Biography.*
Dowden	Edward Dowden, *The Life of Percy Bysshe Shelley* (2 vols., 1886).
Eatough	*Fracastoro's Syphilis*, tr. Geoffrey Eatough (ARCA Classical and Medieval Texts, Papers and Monographs, 12, 1984).
EMSJ	*Edinburgh Medical and Surgical Journal.*
Encycl. Brit.	*The Encyclopaedia Britannica.*
Epips.	*Epipsychidion.*
Esdaile	P. B. Shelley, *The Esdaile Notebook*, ed. K. N. Cameron (New York and London, 1964). Quoted by permission of the Carl H. Pforzheimer Library.
F.Q.	*The Faerie Queene.*
Fracastor	Girolamo Fracastor, *Syphilis, or the French Disease: A Poem in Latin Hexameters*, tr. Heneage Wynne-Finch (1935).
Good	John Mason Good, *The Study of Medicine*, ed. Samuel Cooper, 3rd edn (5 vols., 1829).
Good, *Lucretius*	Lucretius, *The Nature of Things, A Didactic Poem*, tr. John Mason Good (2 vols., 1806).
Grabo	Carl Grabo, *A Newton among Poets* (Chapel Hill, North Carolina U.P., 1930).
Gronow	*Selections from the Reminiscences of Captain Gronow*, ed. Nicholas Bentley (Folio Society, 1977).
Hayter	Alethea Hayter, *Opium and the Romantic Imagination* (1968).
Holmes	Richard Holmes, *Shelley, the Pursuit* (1974).
Hunt, L.	Leigh Hunt, *Lord Byron and Some of his Contemporaries* (1828).
Hunt, T.	Thornton Hunt, 'Shelley, by one who knew him', *The Atlantic Monthly*, XI (February 1863), 184–204.

Hunter   John Hunter, *A Treatise on the Venereal Disease*, 3rd edn (1810).

Hutchinson   *Shelley, Poetical Works*, ed. Thomas Hutchinson rev. G. M. Matthews (Oxford U.P., 1970).

Hutten   Ulrich von Hutten, *A Treatise on the Venereal Disease*, tr. Daniel Turner (1730).

Jones   *The Works of Sir William Jones*, ed. Baron Teignmouth (13 vols., 1807).

Keach   William Keach, *Shelley's Style* (London and New York, 1984).

KSJ   *Keats-Shelley Journal*.

KSMB   *Keats-Shelley Memorial Bulletin*.

Last Man   Mary Shelley, *The Last Man*, ed. Hugh J. Luke Jr (Lincoln, U. of Nebraska P., 1965).

Lawrence   D. H. Lawrence, *Selected Literary Criticism*, ed. Anthony Beal (1956).

LBLJ   Lord Byron, *Letters and Journals*, ed. Leslie Marchand (12 vols., John Murray, 1973–82).

L. & C.   *Laon and Cythna*.

Letters   *The Letters of Percy Bysshe Shelley*, ed. F. L. Jones (2 vols., Oxford U.P., 1964).

Lex. Bal.   *Lexicon Balatronicum, 1811 Dictionary of the Vulgar Tongue*, reprint (Chicago, 1971).

LMR   *London Medical Repository*.

Locock   C. D. Locock, *An Examination of the Shelley Manuscripts in the Bodleian Library* (Oxford U.P., 1903).

London Guide   Anon., *The London Guide and Strangers' Safeguard against the Cheats, Swindlers and Pickpockets that abound within the Bills of Mortality* (1818).

MacFarlane   Charles MacFarlane, *Reminiscences of a Literary Life* (1917).

Male   Roy Male Jr, 'Shelley and the Doctrine of Sympathy', *U. of Texas Studies in English*, XXIX (1950), 183–203.

Mary Shelley's Journal   *Mary Shelley's Journal*, ed. F. L. Jones (Norman, U. of Oklahoma P., 1947).

Massey   Irving Massey, *Posthumous Poems of Shelley: Mary Shelley's Fair Copy Book* (Montreal, McGill-Queen's U.P., 1969).

Matthews, 'Triumph'   G. M. Matthews, 'On Shelley's *The Triumph of Life*', *Studia Neophilologica*, XXIV (1962), 104–34.

Matthews, 'Volcano's Voice'   G. M. Matthews, 'A Volcano's Voice in Shelley', *English Literary History*, XXIV (1957), 191–228.

Medwin   *Medwin's Revised Life of Shelley*, ed. H. B. Forman (Oxford U.P., 1913).

Merle   Joseph   Gibbons   Merle,   'A   Newspaper   Editor's
                      Reminiscences', *Fraser's Magazine*, XXIII (1841), 699–710.

MLR   *Modern Language Review.*

Morton, *Gonorrhoea* R. S. Morton, *Gonorrhoea* (1977).

Morton, *V.D.*   R. S. Morton, *Venereal Diseases* (1966), reprint (Harmonds-
                      worth, 1970).

MPJ   (London) *Medical and Physical Journal.*

Murray   J. Murray, *A System of Materia Medica and Pharmacy* (2 vols.,
                      Edinburgh, 1810).

MWS, *Letters*   *The Letters of Mary Wollstonecraft Shelley*, ed. Betty T. Ben-
                      nett (3 vols. projected, Baltimore, Johns Hopkins U.P,
                      1980–   ).

Nicholson   *Nicholson's British Encyclopaedia* (6 vols., 1809).

Norman   Sylva Norman, *Flight of the Skylark: The Development of
                      Shelley's Reputation* (London and U. of Oklahoma, 1954).

Norton   *Shelley's Poetry and Prose*, ed. Donald H. Reiman and Sharon
                      B. Powers (New York, 1977).

OED   *Oxford English Dictionary.*

Paracelsus   *The Hermetic and Alchemical Writings of. . .Paracelsus*, ed.
                      A. E. Waite (2 vols., 1894).

Parr   Bartholomew Parr, *London Medical Dictionary* (2 vols., 1809).

Pearson   John Pearson, *Observations on the Effects of various Articles of
                      the Materia Medica in the Cure of Lues Venerea*, 2nd edn (1807).

P.L.   *Paradise Lost.*

PMLA   *Publications of the Modern Language Association of America.*

Polidori   *The Diary of Dr. John William Polidori*, ed. W. M. Rossetti
                      (1911).

Prose   *Shelley's Prose, or the Trumpet of a Prophecy*, ed. David Lee
                      Clark, corrected edn (Albuquerque, U. of New Mexico P.,
                      1966).

P.U.   *Prometheus Unbound.*

Q.M.   *Queen Mab.*

R. & H.   *Rosalind and Helen.*

Reece   *Reece's Gazette of Health.*

Reiman   Donald H. Reiman, *Shelley's 'The Triumph of Life': A Critical
                      Study*, Illinois Studies in Language and Literature (Urbana, U.
                      of Illinois P., 1965).

RES   *Review of English Studies.*

Rieger   James Rieger, *The Mutiny Within: The Heresies of Percy Bysshe
                      Shelley* (New York, 1967).

Rogers	Neville Rogers, *Shelley at Work* (Oxford U.P., 1956).
Rossetti	W. M. Rossetti, 'Memoir of Shelley' in *The Poetical Works of Percy Bysshe Shelley*, ed. Rossetti (2 vols., 1870).
Rossetti, *Diary*	*The Diary of W. M. Rossetti, 1870–1873*, ed. Odette Bernard (Oxford U.P., 1977).
Rossetti Papers	*Rossetti Papers: 1862–1870, a Compilation*, ed. W. M. Rossetti (London and New York, 1903).
Rousseau, *Confessions*	J.-J. Rousseau, *Les Confessions* (Paris, 1964) and *The Confessions of Jean-Jacques Rousseau*, tr. J. M. Cohen (Harmondsworth, 1953).
St Irvyne	*St Irvyne, or The Rosicrucian* (New York, Arno Press Facsimile Reprint, 1977).
S. & C.	*Shelley and His Circle, 1773–1822*, ed. K. N. Cameron and Donald H. Reiman, vols. I–VI (Cambridge, Mass., Harvard U.P. and Oxford U.P., 1961–73). Quoted by permission of the Carl H. Pforzheimer Library.
Schofield	C. B. S. Schofield, *Sexually Transmitted Diseases*, 2nd edn (Edinburgh, London and New York, 1975).
Sharpe	*Letters to and from Charles Kirkpatrick Sharpe*, ed. Alexander Allardyce (2 vols., Edinburgh and London, 1888).
Shelley, Crit. Her.	*Shelley, The Critical Heritage*, ed. James Barcus (London and Boston, Routledge and Kegan Paul, 1975).
Shelley-Rolls-Ingpen	*Verse and Prose from the Manuscripts of Percy Bysshe Shelley*, ed. Sir John C. E. Shelley-Rolls and Roger Ingpen (privately printed, 1934).
Sickness	William Thompson, *Sickness, a Poem* (1747) in *The Poetical Works of William Thompson* in *A Complete Edition of the Poets of Great Britain*, ed. R. Anderson (13 vols, 1795).
Swediaur, *Comp. Treat.*	F. X. Swediaur, *A Comprehensive Treatise on the Symptoms, Consequences, Nature and Treatment of Syphilitic Diseases* (2 vols., 1819).
Swediaur, *Pract. Obs.*	ibid., *Practical Observations on Venereal Complaints*, 3rd edn (Edinburgh, 1788).
Swediaur, *Traité*	ibid., *Traité complet sur les symptômes, les effets, la nature et le traitement des maladies syphilitiques*, 5th edn (2 vols., Paris, 1804).
Thompson	C. J. S. Thompson, *Magic and Healing* (1947).
Trans. LMCS	*Transactions of the London Medico-Chirurgical Society*.
Trelawny	E. J. Trelawny, *Records of Shelley, Byron, and the Author* (1878), ed. David Wright (Harmondsworth, 1973).
Triumph	*The Triumph of Life*.

Trotter   Thomas Trotter, *A View of the Nervous Temperament*, 3rd edn (Newcastle, 1812).

Vindication   Mary Wollstonecraft, *Vindication of the Rights of Woman* (1792), ed. Miriam Brody Kramnick (Harmondsworth, 1975).

Walker   Adam Walker, *A System of Familiar Philosophy in Twelve Lectures* (1799).

Wasserman, *P.U.*   Earl Wasserman, *Shelley's 'Prometheus Unbound': a Critical Reading* (Baltimore, Johns Hopkins U.P., 1965).

Webb, *Violet*   Timothy Webb, *The Violet in the Crucible* (Oxford U.P., 1976).

White   Newman Ivey White, *Shelley* (2 vols., 1947).

Willcox   R. R. Willcox, *A Textbook of Venereal Diseases and Treponematoses*, 2nd edn (1964).

Witch   *The Witch of Atlas.*

Wolfe   *The Life of Percy Bysshe Shelley, as comprised in 'The Life of Shelley' by Thomas Jefferson Hogg; 'The Recollections of Shelley & Byron' by Edward John Trelawny; 'Memoirs of Shelley' by Thomas Love Peacock,* ed. Humbert Wolfe (2 vols., 1933).

Woodville   William Woodville, *Medical Botany* 2nd edn (2 vols., 1810).

Zastrozzi   Eustace Chesser, *Shelley and Zastrozzi: self-revelation of a neurotic* (Gregg/Archive, 1965).

Zillman   *Shelley's 'Prometheus Unbound': A Variorum Edition,* ed. L. J. Zillman (Seattle, U. of Washington P., 1959).

Zoonomia   Erasmus Darwin, *Zoonomia: or the Laws of Organic Life* (2 vols., 1796).

Index

264